LEARNING
HOW TO READ
NEW TESTAMENT GREEK
WITH PEOPLE JUST LIKE YOU

RANDALL D. McGIRR

Context Scripture Translating, Inc.
Dallas, Texas

Learning How to Read New Testament Greek with People Just Like You. Copyright © 1992 by Randall D. McGirr. All rights reserved. No parts of this book may be reproduced in any manner whatsoever without written permission.

Printed in the United States of America.

Published by Context Scripture Translating, Inc., P.O. Box 181018, Dallas, Texas 75218.

LIBRARY OF CONGRESS CATALOG CARD NUMBER: 91-78002

INTERNATIONAL STANDARD BOOK NUMBER: 0-9631877-0-8

Contents

List of the STEPS   v
Words of Thanks   viii
Words of Introduction   3

PART I: People Just Like You

1. *Newcastle, Wyoming*   9
2. *Lincoln, Nebraska*   11
3. *Passau, Germany*   15
4. *Howenweep National Monument, Utah*   18
5. *Paradise Valley, Arizona*   22
6. *Scottsdale, Arizona*   25
7. *Phoenix, Arizona*   27

PART II: They Begin Learning How to Read New Testament Greek

8. *From Alpha to Omega*   33
9. *Universal Greek Pictures*   47
10. *Getting the Settings Right*   69
11. *Adding the Finishing Touches*   86

PART III: Their First Twenty-Five STEPS

STEPS 1-25   106
12. *Learning New Testament Greek STEP by STEP*   107

PART IV: What They're Thinking after Six Months

13.	Back to School	183
14.	Sidetracked?	186
15.	Behind the Scenes	191
16.	Lake Powell	210
17.	Books, Burros, and Balancing Rocks	218
18.	Catfish and Motivation	229

PART V: Their Next Twenty-Five STEPS

STEPS 26-50   250

PART VI: What They're Thinking after a Year

19.	The Interview	311

PART VII: Their Final Twenty-Five STEPS

STEPS 51-75   322

Vocabulary   385
Index   407

The STEPS

1. SW, ὁ-words, ὁ λόγος, Roles, ὁ, Punctuation, Word Order — 111
2. CW, Live Video, PLAN, παιδεύω — 115
3. EW, Add-a-Phrase Words with One Role; SW, Directing Role — 119
4. EW, Add-a-Phrase Words with Two Roles — 123
5. SW, ἡ-words with -ος Endings — 127
6. SW, τό-words, τό — 130
7. EW, Add-a-Phrase Words with Three Roles — 133
8. CW, εἰμί — 135
9. SW, ἡ-words, τιμή — 137
10. SW, ἡ-words, οἰκία, Accents — 139
11. SW, ἡ-words, δόξα — 143
12. SW, ὁ-words, νεανίας — 145
13. EW, Add-on Words with Three Sets of Endings μόνος, δίκαιος — 148
14. EW, Add-on Words with Two Sets of Endings, φρόνιμος — 151
15. CW, Necessary Role — 153
16. EW, This and That — 156
17. EW, Add-on Words χρυσοῦς — 158
18. CW, Active, Middle, Passive; Departed Forms — 160
19. CW, Live Video and Recorded Video — 163
20. CW, Combining Camera-Words with Add-a-Phrase Words — 166
21. CW, Bright Light, Dim Light, μή, οὐ — 168
22. CW, Flashing Light/Active — 171
23. CW, Flashing Light/Middle; Departed Forms — 173
24. CW, Future Photo — 175
25. AW, Live Video/Small All-Around Words — 177
26. SW, ὁ-Words, σωτήρ — 251
27. SW, ὁ-Words, φύλαξ, Dictionary Forms — 253

28.	SW, ἡ-Words, λαμπάς	255
29.	SW, ὁ-Words, ἀγών	258
30.	SW, τό-Words, γένος	260
31.	SW, ὁ-Words, βασιλεύς, πόλις	262
32.	AW, PARTs, Live Video/Active, Middle, Passive; Future Photo/Active	264
33.	AW, Future Photo/Middle and Passive	268
34.	CW, Current Photo	271
35.	CW, Previous Photo	274
36.	AW, Current Photo/Middle and Passive	275
37.	CW, Current Photo/Active, Current Photo/Small All-Around Words	277
38.	CW, Previous Photo/Active; AW, Current Photo	279
39.	CW, Normal Photo/Middle; AW, Normal Photo/Middle	281
40.	CW, Normal Photo/Middle/Dim and Flashing Light	283
41.	CW, Normal Photo/Bright	285
42.	AW, Normal Photo/Active	287
43.	CW, Normal Photo/Passive/Bright Light; AW, Normal Photo/Passive	289
44.	CW, Normal Photo/Passive/Dim and Flashing Light; AW, Small All-Around Words	291
45.	CW, Future Photo/Passive	293
46.	EW, Add-a-Thought Words, ὅς, ἥ, ὅ	295
47.	EW, Add-a-Thought Words, ἵνα, γάρ, καί, εἰ	298
48.	CW, ποιέω	300
49.	CW, τιμάω	303
50.	CW, δουλόω	306
51.	SW, τίς, τις	323
52.	EW, ἐμός, σός, ἡμέτερος, ὑμέτερος	325
53.	SW, ἐμαυτοῦ, σεαυτοῦ, ἑαυτοῦ	327
54.	EW, Add-On Words, ἀληθής	329
55.	New Testament Reference Books	332
56.	Traditional Grammatical Terms	335
57.	CW, Major Forms, δοξάζω	344
58.	CW, ἄγω	348
59.	CW, βλέπω	350

60.	CW, αἴρω	352
61.	CW, Normal Photo 2, Miniphoto	354
62.	AW, Add-on Words, Comparisons	358
63.	AW, Numbers	360
64.	CW, τίθημι	362
65.	CW, δίδωμι	364
66.	CW, ἵστημι	366
67.	CW, πίμπλημι	368
68.	CW, δείκνυμι, κεῖμαι, Optative	370
69.	CW, Irregular Camera-Words	373
70.	CW, οἶδα	375
71.	CW, εἰμί	377
72.	Evaluation	379
73.	Review and Preparation	381
74.	The Goal	382
75.	The Source	383

Key to Abbreviations: SW=Something-Words, CW=Camera-Words,
  EW=Extra-Information Words, AW=All-Around Words

Words of Thanks

To Mr. Carl High, who struggled for months sorting out the technical problems that are inherent in a book of this nature and size. He was much more than a technical assistant, however. He was a faithful, patient, and encouraging friend.

To Mr. Johann Gasselhuber, who spent many sleepless nights keeping the computers functioning.

To the authors, Werner Stoy and Klaus Haag, for kindly allowing me to use the Greek exercises which first appeared in their book, *Bibel-Griechisch leichtgemacht*, published in 1983 by Brunnen Verlag in Giessen, Germany.

To my wife, Diane, and my youngest son, Koleran, who typed and checked the Greek texts.

To Randy and Kirsten, who taught me, their father, the joys and benefits of self-learning.

To the many thousands of people—today and over the centuries—whose careful hands and caring hearts have insured that the marvelous words of the Teacher from Nazareth be delivered to us unscathed.

To Dean and Linda and their children; to Marian, Liz, and Eddie; to Harmon and Louise; to Jim and Barbara; and to John and Carol, who see in the writings of Jesus' disciples works of great value that are worth knowing as fully and precisely as possible. This book is the beginning of their story. May the final chapters be written in the lives of the readers.

Randall D. McGirr
1992

For
Diane

Introduction

Words of Introduction from John Frey

If you're anything like me, then you're probably kicking yourself for actually going out and buying a teach-yourself Greek book. You did it because all those books and letters in the New Testament are important to you, and you'd give a lot to be able to read them the way they were first written. But deep down, you're thinking it most likely won't work out. Greek will just be too tough to handle.

I know how you feel. In my high school days I couldn't diagram a simple sentence without breaking out in a sweat. And if my problems in English weren't enough to convince me I had no talent for languages, then my one-semester fling in Spanish class removed any doubt.

The fact is, I've never had much to do with book-learning of any kind. I grew up working as a carpenter with my dad, and when it came time to go to college I just kept working, thinking I'd put it off for a while to build up some cash reserves. Then I met Carol, we got married, Andy was born, we bought a house, and I guess you can figure out the rest.

So, you're probably asking yourself, what's a sawhorse cowboy like me doing writing the introduction to a language book? Well, don't fall over when you hear it, but it just so happens I've learned to read the New Testament in Greek.

Did that get your attention? I thought it would. Now you want to know how such a miracle came about, right? I guarantee you, it's not because there's anything special about me. It all began about eight years ago when I ran into Dean McLain. At the time, I wasn't much of a believer and certainly wasn't overly interested in the Bible. But when Dean and his family moved in next door, things began to happen.

You'll read about all that later on in the book. For now it's enough to say that Dean never once asked me if I'd like to learn to read the New Testament in Greek. He *assumed* I was going to learn it. You'd have thought it was the most natural thing in the world to do, like buying groceries or going for a jog.

I told him I could hardly read the comics; how was I supposed to learn something as complicated as Greek? He just laughed, saying my lack of education might just be the advantage I need to make a go of it. That's the sort of thing you hear a lot if you're around Dean much.

Now let me tell you something about this book. First of all, it's actually two books in one. It's full of lessons and exercises and charts and everything you'd expect to find in a language book, but it's more than that. It's also the story of real people who worked and struggled and helped each other to learn Greek.

How to Read New Testament Greek

I met these folks for the first time one evening seven years ago in the McLains' living room. There's Jim Garvey, a businessman about my age who owns a good-sized plumbing supply company; Marian Lawson, a retired school teacher who is still going strong; Liz Serringer, who back in those days was a college student; Eddie Garcia, the teen-age son of a migrant worker; Harmon Smith, a professor at Phoenix College; and of course Dean McLain, his wife, Linda, and their four children, Buddy, Peggy, Tommy, and Katy. I'm sure you'll enjoy meeting them as much as I have.

One of the real helpful things about this book is being able to switch back and forth between the language lessons and the chapters that record the conversations and experiences we all had learning Greek. We got a lot of our questions answered during those informal times. Many of the questions had nothing at all to do with Greek—questions of a more personal nature—but they were important to work through to keep us going when things got tough. The structure of the book and notes scattered throughout the text make it easy to find the places that correspond to one another. You'll catch on.

Here's an overview of how the book is set up:

Part I You meet the people you'll be learning Greek with.
Part II You sit in on the very first session, learn the Greek alphabet, and attend a tour of Universal Greek Pictures. (You'll enjoy this.)
Part III You take your first twenty-five STEPS into New Testament Greek.
Part IV You find out how everyone is doing after six months.
Part V You take the next twenty-five STEPS.
Part VI You meet with everyone after a year to evaluate progress.
Part VII You take the final twenty STEPS.

As you can see, it's not exactly the kind of setup you'd expect to find in a language textbook, and it doesn't read much like a textbook either. All those Latin words that used to drive me crazy have been replaced with the kind of words a person is used to hearing every day. That was a big help to me when I got into learning all the details. I found out all those rules and regulations weren't nearly as complicated as they were made out to be.

Now, I know you may think that the whole purpose of this book is to help you read and understand Greek. That seems logical enough, but, as Dean would say, there's only one problem with it: A book—even if it's a great one—can never accomplish a goal like that; at least not for everyone it can't. As long as people are people, they will need more than just a book to learn something. They'll also need encouragement and reminders and explanations and sometimes a good hard kick...well, you're getting the idea, right?

That's why this book wants to be a bit more than a book; it also wants to be a door to a friend or two who might be able to give you some help when you need it. Read through the information on page 129, and use the address mentioned there to drop us a line whenever things grind to a halt; they probably will. Whoever gets

Introduction

your letter may not have all the answers, but they'll probably be able to sympathize with you, and sometimes that's enough. I doubt I'd have ever gotten very far if I hadn't gotten a helping hand when I needed it the most. It also needs to be said that working through the lessons in this book is just a beginning. It's kind of like laying a foundation. When you're done you're not really done. You'll still have the job of framing up the walls and the roof, and you still have to do all the finishing work.

That may sound discouraging, but I figure it's better to know what you're facing right from the start so you don't underestimate things. Building a house is a big job—I ought to know—and I can tell you that learning Greek was more work than any house I ever built. Unless you're a whole lot faster than I am, you'll have to figure it will be a few years before you can move into that Greek New Testament and feel at home in it.

I'll leave you with a bit of advice from my dad: He said, *You don't have to be afraid of any job, if you've got the right tools to do it.* I hope you'll find a good set of tools in this book to help you lay a foundation for a house made of the only materials that will never fail: the words and thoughts of Jesus Christ.

PART I:

People Just Like You

Newcastle, Wyoming
October, 1982

"But, mother, I see no reason why you can't at least spend a month or two with the Hansens down in Phoenix. You and daddy had such big plans for the house there. I think you'd enjoy it."

Marian Lawson was inwardly amused as she sat at the breakfast table listening to her daughter, Anne. Normally she would have hated to see her upset, but she was enjoying it this time. It brought life and movement into the house and memories of serious family discussions. That's what she missed.

"Just give it a try." Anne was pleading now. "You can come back anytime you want to. Just jump in the car and in twenty ridiculous little hours you're home again."

"Just a minute there," said Marian, raising her eyebrows. "Who do you think I am? Mario Andretti? Old folks like me don't just jump into cars and gallivant across half the country."

"Oh, mom, you know what I mean. What do you say? I hate to think of you spending the winter here all alone."

"All alone! I'm surrounded by friends and neighbors. Why, the phone practically rings itself off the wall."

"I mean here, alone, in this big house. It's not as though you're deserting the place or walking out on your friends. Some of them are down in Arizona anyway, and besides, you can come back in the spring and pick up where you left off."

"Well, I'll give it some thought, but there's no more time to talk now. We've got to get you over to Rapid City. It's a good two-hour drive and we need to be there an hour before the plane takes off. I don't want my two grandchildren and their father to meet the plane and find no mommy on it."

"Oh, all right. I'll get the suitcases ready, but you can bet I'm going to bend your ear every one of those two hours to get you to say 'yes' to the Hansens."

"Oh, no, my ears are already stinging."

Marian had retired in May after thirty years as a grade school teacher. Concerned that her mother make a good adjustment in her first year away from teaching, Anne had flown down from Ottowa to spend ten days with her.

Five years earlier, Anne's father, a well-known lawyer in eastern Wyoming, had died unexpectedly at the age of fifty-nine. It had been a shock for her mother, whose life had revolved around her husband. Although Marian was a well-adjusted, lively, witty woman, Anne remembered how long it had taken for her to recover.

In the difficult months following her father's death, Anne had made many trips to Wyoming to be with her mother. She observed during these times how Marian's activity as a school teacher played a major role in helping her to get her feet back on the ground. Teaching occupied her mind and forced her to be involved in the needs and concerns of others. Now, with the school a thing of the past, Anne didn't want her mother to feel a deep sense of loss again.

The Hansens were long-time friends of the family. Years ago, thinking of the retirement years, they and the Lawsons had each built small homes in Arizona. The Hansens had offered to travel to Arizona with Marian and help her get situated in the house, but she was not sure she would be happy trying to start a new existence in Arizona, even if it was only for a few months a year. The retirement plans she had made with her husband seemed somehow unrealistic without him.

Anne, however, felt Marian should not give up the plans without at least giving them a try. She was convinced that her mother was outgoing enough to enjoy the challenge of meeting people in a new living situation, and she thought she should make the change as soon as possible. It was already late fall, school was in session, and the hard Wyoming winter was sending its first blasts of freezing wind.

The drive to Rapid City through the scenic Black Hills brought back many memories for Marian and Anne. The bends and curves of Highway 16 recalled scenes of countless roadside picnics. Side roads led them off in their thoughts to beautiful lakes and rustic pine lodges where they had spent many holidays. Higher up in the mountains the dark blue-green spruce trees were white from the first autumn snow.

Marian felt deep pleasure in the serenity of the familiar beauty. Her senses were fine-tuned to enjoy every moment with her daughter. As they drove through Keystone and turned on to the final stretch of highway leading to Rapid City, Anne began to talk about Ottowa and her girls and the plans she and her husband had made for the coming months: One of the girls would be starting school; there was shopping to do; friends from Wisconsin were coming for Thanksgiving.

Suddenly Marian felt very empty and lonely. She remembered that in a few hours she would be driving back down this road again, alone with the mountains and with her memories. The memories would still be rich, but they would not be shared; the mountains would still be beautiful, but the sight of them would make her unbearably sad. In that moment of reflection, she knew she had made her decision: She would call the Hansens as soon as she got home.

Lincoln, Nebraska
November, 1982

The four hundred foot tower of the Nebraska State Capitol loomed on his left as Harmon Smith threaded his car through the heavy, late afternoon traffic. Loosening his tie, he tried to relax. An urgent, high-pitched voice streamed out of speakers in the back. With some irritation in his movement, he flicked off the radio.

"How can people fall for that stuff?" he muttered to himself. Hoping to listen to some good music during the twenty minutes he needed to cover the distance from the university to his home, he'd tuned in the local religious station. Instead of finding music, he'd broken in on a radio preacher enthusiastically expounding a passage from Isaiah. The speaker claimed to have received a special, illuminating insight from the Lord as to the deeper meaning of the text.

Harmon was not a theologian and certainly not an expert on the Old Testament, but he figured he knew enough to recognize that the man in the radio showed little interest in *illuminating* the meaning of the passage. Instead he was turning it into a convenient launching pad for his own brand of ideas.

It was almost dark when Harmon pulled into the driveway of the two-story brick house that had been in his family for two generations. Built in the thirties and situated on a large, corner lot, it had an open porch that fully covered the two sides of the house facing the intersection. Ancient oaks in the front gave the house the look of a distinguished old gentleman.

"I'm home, Louise," he called, as he stepped into the tiny entryway in the back of the house and wrestled off his coat. Warmth contrasting sharply with the subzero temperature outside flowed from the kitchen. It was a cold autumn.

"Hi, honey. Am I glad you're home. Phil Ashworth has been trying to contact you."

"Oh?" Harmon entered the kitchen, rubbing the cold from his hands. His wife was standing at the sink slicing carrots. "And what does he want?"

"You know that Ted is speaking at a conference this weekend. Well, the man who was supposed to take his place in the pulpit this Sunday had to cancel. Said he has to be at the funeral of an aunt—in Iowa, I believe."

"Don't tell me. I'm supposed to step in, right?"

"They can't seem to find anyone else at such short notice. It's already Friday."

He tried to hold it back, but the groan came out anyway. In earlier days he'd have dropped everything for the opportunity to speak about the faith that had become such a central part of his life. During the late fifties and early sixties he'd been active as a Christian student often participating in projects considered radical at the time. For Harmon in those days, the message of Christ had been the comprehensive answer to all of life's ills. Words like *failure* and *disappointment* had ceased to be part of his vocabulary.

"But we were going to visit Harv in Ames on Sunday."

How to Read New Testament Greek

"I know. He'd be disappointed. Can we make it if we leave at noon?"

"Honey, it's a good 190 miles up there. Either we leave on Saturday or not at all."

The years following Harmon's student days had done little to dampen his enthusiasm for the faith as he became a prominent Christian spokesman in Lincoln—the conservative, midwestern home of the University of Nebraska where he was completing his tenth year as a professor of Anthropology.

For several years, however, a growing struggle with his conscience had made him increasingly reluctant to raise his voice about his faith. At first his doubts were so small he dismissed them as normal fallout in the daily proceedings of spiritual warfare. The doubts persisted, however, particularly when he could no longer ignore certain inconsistencies in his life.

Harv and Mel, the Smith's two sons, were among the first to toss wrenches into the finely tuned mechanism of Harmon's beliefs. He still remembered vividly the day when he was sitting out on the porch having a long conversation with a neighbor he'd been trying to reach for Christ. The boys—eight- and ten-years-old at the time—burst out the door fighting and calling each other the worst possible names.

It was not so much the embarrassment of such occurrences that bothered him as it was the effect they had on the validity of the message to which he was so committed. It sounded so logical and compelling when it was proclaimed from the soapbox, but it was proving difficult to translate into his own living room. And it didn't seem to be translating into society, either, at least not as Harmon had envisioned it.

Changing the world had been part of the message of the sixties, and Christian students did not hesitate to write it on their banners as they reveled in the surging spirit of their movement. Harmon, too, had committed himself to it and thrown his weight into the battle by supporting the political ambitions of an attorney who had received a great deal of exposure from both the Christian and secular media. The candidate was known as a born-again Christian who championed moral values in a quest to turn society around. Few had invested more time and energy in the campaign than Harmon. The close defeat hurt, but not nearly as much as the news of the candidate's impending divorce exactly one year later.

That was when the hot fire slowly began to fade from Harmon's convictions, and gradually he found himself sidestepping public speaking engagements. For a time he was able to maintain a degree of fervor by diverting his attention more and more to his local church. He saw in it the one place where the message of Christ was meant to find its highest realization, where brothers and sisters in Christ would love and serve one another in unity and harmony, and where the example of Christians would be salt and light for the people around them. But it turned out to be the place where his beliefs took their greatest beating.

It was one night in the fellowship hall of the church when senselessness and helplessness seemed to shake him like an earthquake. For months the members of the church had been trying to resolve the question: Should we build a new sanctuary or not? At first, conversations were subdued, thoughtful, and objective. With time, however, opinions polarized, tempers flared, and prayers turned into ammunition for one side to use against the other. *Lord, help our brothers come to their senses so they see the folly of their thinking.*

Harmon tried to be a mediating force, but it was clear to the various factions that he, too, was by no means neutral about the matter. On that night the unthinkable happened. One of the elders announced that a third of the members were in agreement they could no longer be a part of a church obviously heading in the direction this one was. In short, they were leaving. The unexpected pronouncement was followed with kindly expressions of good will, but the atmosphere was one of icy shock.

In the following days, Harmon responded with calm acceptance. He couldn't bring himself to blame anyone. In fact, no one seemed to be wrong. Everyone had a Bible and used it to support his position. That's what bothered him the most. It was as though they had all somehow been driven to a place of parting against their will.

Although he was sad and disappointed, the emotion that overpowered him—and this surprised him more than anything else—was curiosity: Not a curiosity that was nothing more than a yearning for a plausible explanation to a nagging question, but a curiosity that welled up in him, peeling off the doubt that had grown large in his life and begun to ferment into dread.

Why dread? He'd asked himself this question over and over. Why the growing darkness in his heart? *Fear* was the answer he had to hear from himself; fear that he could have been wrong all along; fear that Jesus was not who he was made out to be; fear that he, the trained anthropologist, had been captivated by a religion of his culture; fear that had he grown up among Moslems or Hindus he'd have been just as captivated by their beliefs.

For years he had suppressed the fears in a hot cauldron of conviction. He determined his faith was true because it worked, and he was the one who would demonstrate that it works. That's what he had heard from his mentors in the sixties, and he had determined that he, Harmon Smith, would be living proof of the validity of faith in Christ.

The end had come, however. The crusade was over, and Harmon knew it. But it wasn't the end he had feared and dreaded. When he gave up trying to be what he couldn't be and gave up trying to build what he couldn't build, he found he wasn't giving up Christ at all, but himself. It had been pride that had been feeding his doubt and his fear. Fear of what? *Fear that the truth might turn out to be different than he envisioned it.* It was nothing less than a fear of the truth itself!

This was the realization that finally freed him to face the fear and doubt, not arrayed in his own armor of expectations, but open and honest and vulnerable like a child. Too long he had seen himself as a guardian of the truth, corralling it, explaining it, defending it, verifying it, treating it as his very own. And in his enthusiasm he had slowly ceased to be committed to truth itself, embracing rather his own understanding of it.

That's why the Bible, too, had become a stiff, manipulated thing in his hands. Although the Bible had been his constant companion for many years, his proof text for innumerable debates, and his reference for countless talks, he was nevertheless unsure—fear played an increasing role here, too—as to what the Bible really taught.

Most of what he knew about the Bible came from teachings and writings about it, from thoughts that had already been sifted through the minds of others. He had collected an imposing library of Christian literature, but he'd had little direct experience with the Scriptures themselves.

The nagging fear that the Bible might not be the absolute revelation of God had driven him to seek the confirmation of experts and authorities, increasing in the end his dependency on the thoughts of others. Although turning to books and commentaries had seemed a logical step at the time, the many contradicting opinions of the experts—he had collected seven conflicting interpretations of the Book of Acts alone—merely added to his feelings of uncertainty.

When he decided, however, to once again become a searcher of the truth and not a possessor of it, his deepest fears were not realized. His interest in the Bible did not grow slack, and his faith did not turn cold. In fact, he found himself more motivated than ever to examine and understand the message of the Scriptures.

He also felt moved to take another difficult but needed step: It was time to quit playing the role of the influential professor and step into roles more needy of his attention, namely those of husband, father, and...child. Yes, he needed to become like a child again, clothed in curiosity and eager to learn. That's what was on his mind when Louise heard him dial the phone in the hallway.

"Hello, Phil? Louise told me---. Yes, I know. But I know a better replacement. Who? You, of course."

There was a long pause.

"I know you've never done it before. All the more reason to start now. You'll do fine."

Another pause.

"No. We'll be spending the day with Harv in Ames. He's expecting us and we're not going to change our plans. Besides---. Don't worry. You'll do fine. Make it short and sweet. You don't have to impress anyone. Believe me, Phil. You don't have to impress anyone."

Passau, Germany
July, 1983

It was at the end of the meal when Liz noticed Grossvater straighten his shoulders and heard him speak the words to her father he could no longer hold back: "*Ach, das sind viele Jahre, die ihr schon drüben seid.* You've been there so many years."

Liz's father showed no surprise. He knew the topic would be brought up. It always was. He fingered his wine glass and took another sip of the cool Veltliner. "I know," he said, "it's been over ten years. I would never have thought we'd stay so long."

"You'll be coming back, won't you?" Hans Serringer leaned forward and looked into his son's eyes, "We'd like to see you come back."

Liz was sitting next to her father. She could feel the tension between him and her grandfather. It increased with each trip back to Germany. When she was nine-years-old, her father had been offered a manager's position in a large electronics firm in Cincinatti. It had been hard for her grandparents to see them leave. They accepted it, thinking it would be for only a few years.

A decade had passed, however, and Liz's family was still in America. They had adjusted quickly to life in the suburbs of Cincinatti where Liz had attended an excellent private school. After graduation, she received a scholarship to study architecture at a large university in Arizona.

The move to America and the beginning of her studies in Arizona had been the two major events in her life. A third was of a more personal nature: Through the influence of a friend in high school and through reading the New Testament, she had committed herself to follow Jesus Christ.

Liz knew that her father and Grossvater Hans would not argue or exchange hard words. Disciplined and self-confident, the Serringer men were seldom emotional. The war years had cast their shadow over Grossvater's childhood in Bavaria, a state in Southern Germany. His father, listed as missing, never returned from the Russian front.

After the war he put off going to the university, because he had to work to support his mother and younger brother and sister. He was almost thirty years old when he was finally able to take up studies at the University of Passau. Now he was now nearing retirement from his post as director of a *Gymnasium*, a college preparatory high school in the same city.

As a child Liz remembered how Grossvater's presence had dominated family gatherings. Like a venerable professor he sat at the big oaken table in the dining room and directed conversation. He had strong opinions about everything from how to grow tomatoes to the expediencies of France's nuclear power policies or the merits of classical music. There were also times when Grossvater could be a warm and kind man, but Liz most vividly remembered his stern countenance and unbending manner.

Liz's father was much like Grossvater with the exception that it was much easier to discuss things with him. He often invited her to a favorite coffee shop where they would sometimes sit for hours and talk.

During one of their conversations, the topic of the Bible had come up. "The Bible is not necessarily history," he had said, "but neither is it simply fiction. It's kind of a mixture of both, as I see it. Take the story of Abraham, for example. It was written well after the Jews had established their theocracy to illustrate the ethical nature of the new God, the *one* God that had become the center of the religious thinking of the Israelites. It particularly shows their development away from the practice of human sacrifice, as opposed to the peoples living around them. Abraham may very well be a historical figure, and his movement from Ur through the fertile crescent may also reflect a reliable tradition known to the writers. That's why I say it's fiction *and* history."

Liz did not agree with her father's analysis and did her best to present some opposing arguments, but his explanations, carefully formulated in the language of science, and expressed with businessman-like geniality, made her objections sound superficial and childish in comparison. Although she felt frustrated because her father's views kept them from addressing the more personal aspects of the biblical message, she did not feel that he was necessarily being closed-minded. He was merely expressing the generally accepted view of the Bible as it was perceived and taught in the educational milieu in which he had grown up.

This trip to Europe had done much to help her understand her father and mother. She recognized for the first time the many influences that were so powerful in their thinking. On side trips to France and Italy, she heard views similar to those of her father's from European teen-agers and college students. Most of them were well-read, much more so than their counterparts in the United States, and the literature they were reading was mostly the kind in which Christianity is assigned a place outside the boundaries of modern science and relegated to the position of an ethical system on a par with the other religious and philosophical systems of the world.

Liz also observed a deeply entrenched Christian tradition which many Europeans seemed to accept right along with their skepticism, seeing no contradiction in the two. A law student in Munich offered this explanation: "The acceptance of a synthesis of historical philosophical developments is often the most flexible position to assume. We Europeans have learned to float in the ebb and tide of conflicting ideologies as they've sent their champions in regiments back and forth across the continent. The majority has learned the danger of taking sides too quickly and chosen rather to await the moment of greatest advantage before declaring itself. So, you see, although few would ascribe to a belief in the tenets of the Christian faith, nevertheless, even in Europe, the Christian faith still continues to be a moral heavyweight—enough, at least, that many think it wise to keep a foot in the door."

That was the kind of talk Liz often heard at home and from other relatives. She seldom knew how to respond to it.

"*Wir werden mal sehen,*" Liz heard her father saying in response to Grossvater. "We'll see, we'll see."

Liz knew they would never be returning to Germany, but not even her father could muster the courage to tell Grossvater. No one contradicted Grossvater.

Howenweep National Monument, Utah August, 1983

"Let's call it a day, Tommy. We'll get cooked if we stay out here any longer."

"OK," said the wiry nine-year-old, seemingly unbothered by the heat. He began to unscrew the fitting that secured his father's camera to a tripod.

Dean McLain slowly poured water from a clear plastic bottle onto the back of his neck, letting the water seep into his sweaty shirt. Then he took a long drink. On a ridge eighty feet above them, a man paused to train binoculars on the pair, then went on.

They were standing in the upper end of a deep gash in the desert floor near the southern part of the border between Utah and Colorado. Nestled around them were the ruins of an ancient people—the Anasazi, *the Old Ones*—who had built a wide-reaching net of villages in the high deserts of the American Southwest. In the thirteenth century they suddenly disappeared, leaving behind impressive architectural structures, which gave testimony to a culture that had ingeniously braved a hard and merciless land for over a thousand years.

Dean had set up his photographic gear near the Square Tower, one of the largest buildings in the handful of Anasazi settlements encompassed by Howenweep National Monument. Hidden from a distant observer, the tower presented visitors with a startling view when they gazed over the sides of the deep gully. Raising its angular, stony head over a stand of blue-green juniper trees, it stood forth like a sentinel out of the past, still intact and still guarding a cool spring under a ledge not far from its base.

Dean retreated to a shaded bench near the spring where he swung a backpack around one shoulder. Using the tripod as a walking stick, he started up a path that slowly wound its way out of the gulch. Tommy followed with the equipment case. When they reached the parking lot next to the monument headquarters, they stowed their gear in the back of a well-worn van and headed for a small log cabin that served as the visitors' center. As one of the most isolated national monuments in America, Howenweep did not have facilities ranking among the most modern in the National Park Service.

A tiny air conditioner was laboring in one of the two small windows when they entered. A counter divided the one-roomed cabin into a visitors' area and a small office. "Hi, Ken," said Dean, greeting the ranger they'd met earlier in the morning. "How're things going?"

"Tolerable," said the ranger, who had been writing at his desk. He leaned back in his chair. "Get all your pictures taken?"

"We're right on schedule, but we sure wish it was October around here instead of August." Dean and Tommy were standing beside the water cooler gulping down water as fast as they could refill the small paper cups.

"I know what you mean. The heat can get mean in these parts. I was watching you fellas a few hours ago, and if you don't mind my asking, there's something I can't figure out. Most folks who take pictures out here are interested in the ruins, but you fellas looked like you were shooting away from the ruins at some pretty uninteresting scenery. Are you seeing something I'm not seeing?"

An amused look swept over Dean's face. "Yes, I guess you could put it that way. But it would be more accurate to say we were photographing things that might be there."

"Huh?" said the ranger, scratching his head. "Now you've really got me confused."

"We're on a project initiated by the Anazasi Heritage Center over in Delores. It's a survey to help the archaeologists decide which new excavations to begin in the coming years."

"New excavations, eh? But why here? These digs are over sixty years old."

"I suppose the romantic picture of archaeology is one of adventurous men braving the wilds to turn up long lost cities, but that search-and-find phase of archaeology is mostly a thing of the past. Nowadays most archaeologists are busy trying to complete the many major sites which in most cases have only been partially excavated. Even at a site like Howenweep which has seen extensive archaeological activity, there's still much to be done. There are probably dozens of promising sites within a mile or two of here, and plenty of rubble to sift through around the major structures."

"No doubt about that," said Ken. "I could put you on to a few finds myself. I've tramped around this whole area. It's amazing what you can turn up with just the kick of a boot."

"I'll take all the tips I can get," said Dean. "Maybe you could give me a half-hour of your time before you open up tomorrow morning."

"Be glad to. I'll jot down a few X's on a map of the area and give you a direction or two."

Dean noticed a number of framed pictures on the ranger's desk. "Wife and children?" he asked.

"Yup. Daughter is married and lives in New Jersey, and son is in the Air Force."

"So you and your wife are alone out here?"

"Have been for about five years."

"Whew," said Dean, "you must like the solitude. Do you come from around here?"

"Nope. Grew up smack in the middle of New York City."

"New York! Who'd have guessed it. I can usually listen to a man talk and know where he comes from, but you sure fooled me. What brought you all the way out here?"

"Oh, I left New York as soon as I could hold a job, and I've spent most of my life trying to stay as far away from big cities as I can."

"Sounds like you have some bad memories."

"That would be an understatement."

"I lived for many years in a large city myself," said Dean, "and I know how ugly it can be. But I guess I was lucky enough to have a father who proved to be a good guide in that environment. He showed me how even the dirtiest and most chaotic urban centers can be as breathtaking or awesome as any wilderness area."

"Your dad must have been a magician. I've never seen a street that could match one of the canyons out here."

"It wasn't streets and buildings that formed the landscape my dad led me through. It was human hearts. They're the things that are so plentiful in big cities, and he taught me to discover the trails that lead through them. Granted, some can be as dangerous and infested as a swamp full of cottonmouths, but there are others that are as deep and beautiful as the Grand Canyon or as intricate as the spires at Bryce. In that sense a city is full of wilderness areas that have never been charted—areas with surprise canyons, unclimbed mountains, wild animals, untouched forests, beautiful sunsets, and it's all there just waiting to be discovered. It just depends on how willing a person is to risk the hazards of journeying into a person's life."

"Hmm. That's an interesting outlook you've got there," said the ranger, rubbing his chin.

"I know that big cities have a bad reputation," said Dean, "but sometimes the statistics show a different picture. There are actually metropolitan areas that have lower rates of crime than in the rural areas surrounding them."

"My wife would like to hear what you're saying. She's never been as happy living out in the country as I have."

"Don't get me wrong," said Dean, "I'm no salesman of life in the city. I enjoy the wide-open spaces as much as anyone. It's probably just the archaeologist in me saying that sometimes things appear differently if a person takes the time to probe under the surface. Take anonymity, for example. It's supposed to be one of the drawbacks of a big city. But for some people anonymity is a blessing, a kind of inner wilderness of solitude that refreshes as much as a hike in a forest. That kind of mind-your-own-business solitude can sometimes be hard to find in a small town or in a rural area."

"You're right about that," said Ken. "We live in a small settlement about five miles from here and not much happens that doesn't get known real fast. Say, where are you fellas staying tonight?"

"We're just across the way in the campground."

"How would you like to drop by later on for a little chat and some homemade pie?"

"Homemade pie? We could hardly pass up an offer like that, could we, Tommy. Sure it's not too much trouble?"

"No trouble at all, and I know my wife would enjoy the company."

After getting directions to the ranger's home, Dean and Tommy stepped out into the late afternoon heat. To the east they could see the dark contours of Sleeping

Dean McLain

Ute Mountain, slumbering sentinel of a people whose story comes as a dream from the distant past.

Paradise Valley, Arizona
January, 1984

It was 6:30 a.m. on Sunday when the bedside radio emitted a dull buzz. Jim punched the stop button. Not wanting to disturb his wife, Barbara, he slowly eased out of bed and slipped into a jogging suit. There was just enough light coming in behind the window shade to make out the contours of the room. Gathering together his reading glasses, a pair of socks, and shoes, he tip-toed toward the door.

Barbara's voice broke the stillness: "What time is it, honey? Is it late?"

"No. Go back to sleep. I'll wake you up in plenty of time."

"Jim, we don't have to be in church until nine-thirty. What are you doing up so early?"

"I didn't have time to get my Sunday school lesson planned yesterday."

"Well, try not to disturb the kids." She pulled the covers up around her neck and buried her head in the pillow.

Jim shuffled into the plush family room. He looked through the bay window and saw the craggy peaks of the Superstition Mountains mystically hovering in the distance. He felt the urge to put on his hiking boots and walk out into the desert.

A lump in his stomach, however, reminded him that he was not prepared for his Sunday school class. In his mind he could see a dozen squirming fifteen-year-olds, giggling, pulling at buttoned collars, wishing they were anywhere but seated in a circle of folding chairs. What would he do with them? He could get them to sing songs for ten minutes and talk for another ten, but the last twenty-five minutes had to be a lesson from the Bible.

He walked through the kitchen and plugged in the coffeepot before heading for his study. He sat down at his desk with a sigh. It was piled high with letters, order forms, ledgers, file folders, books, and an array of notepads, pens, and cassettes.

"How depressing," he muttered to himself. He glanced at a small calendar propped up in a corner. Taking his pencil he crossed off Saturday as though he were removing the final obstacle to the beginning of the day. In this brief moment of troubled confrontation with the untidy residue of a week's work, his concentration was broken by the sound of the TV being clicked on, followed by the shrill voices and pounding music of early morning cartoons.

"Oh, no!" he groaned. "The kids are already up." He walked out to the family room where he could see his ten-year-old son, sitting in front of the color console.

"Jimmy, what are you doing up so early? Turn that thing off and either go back to bed or get dressed and go outside!"

"Aw, dad, I wanna' watch TV."

"Not this morning. I've got work to do, and besides I don't want you to wake up your mother and sister."

"But they're already awake."

Jim Garvey

"I don't want to hear another word from you," he snapped. "Do you understand?"

Reluctantly, Jimmy turned off the TV and gave his dad the best frown he thought he could get away with.

Jim poured himself a cup of coffee before returning to his study. He felt irritated, not so much with Jimmy as with himself. It was a little ritual of discontent that he often indulged in, especially on Sundays. All week he had wanted to plan for this Sunday, but he put it off till Saturday. Then a phone call from some friends had led to a picnic, a movie, and a late night snack at a favorite eating place. "And now you're going to tell a bunch of teenagers how important it is to live according to the teaching of the Bible," Jim chided himself.

It irked him that he was so wishy-washy. It irked him that he was sitting in a soft, leather-padded swivel chair surrounded by wall-paneled comfort. It irked him that he lived his Christianity like a PR man, always putting on a good face. He grabbed his Bible from an eye-level shelf in the mahogany case above his desk. He thought of Jesus and the disciples, and laughed out loud as he compared his own life to theirs. "I'm just playing a big game," he thought. "I wonder how long I can keep it up?"

Getting sarcastic with himself was part of the ritual. He knew, though, that the ritual would soon be broken by the day's activities. Sunday school would turn out all right, the church service would be uplifting, a nice meal would follow at the home of his elderly parents, and then there would be a relaxed afternoon and evening to look forward to. It would all keep him from thinking, and it was thinking that fueled his discontent.

He stared at his Bible for a moment, then laid it aside and reached for a copy of the Sunday school literature that was used by his church. He looked at his watch. It was 7:40 a.m. In an hour they'd have to leave.

The Community Church they attended in West Phoenix was a good forty-five minute drive from their home. That was a long way, but the church had an excellent reputation, and Barbara and he had always thought it was worth the time to be in a church with a good youth program and an outstanding pastor. The Garveys had joined the fast-growing church within a few years of its inception, and as a member of the board of trustees, Jim was often consulted regarding practical business matters. In fact, he often felt that his involvement in the church was somewhat like running an extra company on the side. Business meetings, policy making sessions, budget planning, fund raising, and personnel hiring punctuated many of the church's demands on his time.

Jim's thoughts turned to the lesson. They were studying the life of David. He remembered having read the biblical accounts of David's life, but didn't quite know what he should think about them. The details in the Bible all read a bit different than the stories of David he had often heard, and it was a puzzle to him as to how a fifteen-year-old should apply aspects of David's adventures to his own life. Even the well-known story of the killing of Goliath baffled him. The Sunday school booklet made it so simple: David believed God; David was not afraid;

David accomplished the impossible with God's help. Conclusion? We should believe God; we should not be afraid; we should be able to do the impossible.

Jim found it difficult to accept that killing a giant was basically the same as conquering a big problem, which for a fifteen-year-old might mean passing a test or making the basketball team. After all, David was a tough, experienced character who asked God to destroy his enemies and obviously made no pretense about being willing to help do the job.

Letting his mind wander, Jim pictured himself marching out of the church leading a gang of macho Christian teen-agers out into the streets, ready to do battle with the Mafia bosses and drug dealers in the city. Armed with special sling-shots hurling shrapnel-spewing missiles, they take on the infidels—being careful to pray before every encounter, of course—and leave a trail of beheaded corpses to put the fear of God into any and all who chose to side with the forces of evil. "An interesting evangelistic approach," Jim thought to himself as he turned to the lesson in the Sunday school booklet.

He read through it, underlined a few of the more important points, and jotted down several questions of his own. Then he slipped the booklet into his Bible and leaned back in his chair. "So," he murmured, "the great Bible teacher is now ready to mesmerize his students with the profound results of his painstaking research."

Just then Jim's daughter, Amy, a tiny, eight-year-old flurry of blond hair and freckles burst into his study. "Daddy, daddy," she whined, "Jimmy won't leave me alone." Jim swept her into his arms and whirled her in his swivel chair. She giggled uncontrollably, and Jim laughed with her. "Young lady," he said, putting her down, "you need to get dressed. We have to leave in fifteen minutes."

Barbara was busy in the kitchen when Jim passed through heading for the bedroom.

"Jim, you haven't eaten anything yet."

"No time, honey. We've got to get going." When he walked into their spacious walk-in closet, his eyes wistfully drifted over to the corner where he kept his hiking boots and desert garb. He could feel the lump in his stomach again. Then he grabbed a shirt and tie.

Scottsdale, Arizona
March, 1984

Buddy was standing by his bike when he glimpsed Eddie in the crowd of students pouring out the front door of Chapparal High's big main building.

"Hey, Eddie," he called. "Over here."

The brown face with its handsome, angular features turned toward his voice, and Eddie made his way to where Buddy was standing.

"How about riding home together along our scenic route?" Buddy suggested.

"Sure. Why not," said Eddie, showing little enthusiasm. A few minutes later they were riding their bikes along a wide thoroughfare, leading them through patches of desert scenery still untouched by housing developments.

Buddy knew by Eddie's slow pedaling and lack of chatter that he was thinking deeply about something. As they came to the top of a small rise, Buddy spotted an outcropping of rocks that had always been a favorite place for quick afternoon picnics with his family.

He looked back over his shoulder at Eddie. "How about taking a little walk over by those rocks."

For a moment it seemed Eddie hadn't heard him, but then he glanced over at the picturesque pile of red desert rocks. "Sure," he said, "I don't need to be home for a while." They left their bikes behind a mesquite bush and slowly walked away from the road.

It was just over a year ago that Buddy had met Eddie, one of a handful of Hispanics in the high school. He lived with his parents in a small house on a large estate owned by a wealthy rancher who raised and sold Arabian horses. Eddie's father helped with the horses and was the caretaker of the estate grounds. Buddy had been in their home several times. It was small for seven people—Eddie had two older brothers, Johnny and Rafael, a younger sister, Marianna, and a younger brother, Julio.

They picked their way through patches of red hedgehog cactus. "Is anything bothering you?" asked Buddy.

For a time Eddie said nothing. He walked along, his eyes looking at ground in front of him. "It's my older brothers," he finally said. "They think I'm wasting my time in school and by going to Bible studies. They think I should find a job and concentrate more on baseball. Rafael says I could maybe play professional ball some day."

"But you've always had a job," said Buddy. "You help your father with his work, and you mow lawns on weekends."

"Sure, but that's not the kind of work my brothers are talking about. I don't earn enough to afford a car or to buy fancy clothes."

"What do your parents say?"

"They're happy I'm in school and getting good grades. That makes them proud of me. But they don't understand why I think the Bible is so important. My mother says it's the Padre's job to tell us what the Bible means. She's afraid I'm doing something I shouldn't be." Buddy liked Eddie's mother and father. They were simple, open-hearted people.

"I know I shouldn't let my brothers get under my skin. They just feel like most of their friends do. They're tired of being poor. They want to be someone. They want to be looked up to."

Buddy knew Eddie well enough to know that he was not in danger of being influenced by his brothers. Eddie was not fighting temptation. His struggle was one of concern. It was just one more sign of how far Eddie had come in a short time. He was able to see through the taunts of his brothers who had done some unwise things in the past two years. Eddie's parents had been shocked one evening by a visit from the police. Johnny and Rafael were suspected of being involved in a ring of car thieves. Nothing had ever been proven but the incident brought the fact out into the open that the two boys were running in a bad crowd.

"I know you'd like to do something to help your brothers," said Buddy. "The way I see it there are only two things you can do for them right now. The first is to keep on being a good example for them even if they don't appreciate it. Some day it may get their attention. And the second is probably the best thing we could ever do, and that's to pray for them. I know it doesn't seem like much, but prayer accomplishes things we could never do."

Eddie slowly nodded his head and sat down on a large flat rock. A few minutes passed before he spoke. "It's good to have a friend like you, Buddy."

The two of them walked back to their bicycles and continued on their way home. Just before they came to the big gates of the estate where the Garcias lived and worked, Eddie turned his bike onto a small path leading to a wire door in the high fence surrounding the grounds. He pushed his bike through and waved to Buddy as he coasted down a the narrow path to the Garcias' small stucco house. Buddy watched him until he disappeared through the front door. Even at this distance he could hear the noise being made by an old water cooler perched on the top of the house.

Buddy thought about Eddie for a few moments. He got little encouragement at home. He didn't have a nice air-conditioned room of his own. He didn't even have a desk or a place to study. And yet, he somehow managed to do his homework and read his Bible. Buddy breathed a short prayer: "Take care of him, Lord," and pointed his bicycle for home.

Phoenix, Arizona
September, 1984

Grab a shingle. Line it up. Start three nails. Drive them home. Grab a shingle. Line it up. Start three nails. Drive them home. It was the rhythm of a roofer. John Frey beat out the cadence as the merciless midday sun seemed to grind to a halt. Reclining on hot tar paper, he worked his way along a chalk mark stretched across the broad expanse of a ranch house roof. He took little notice of his frying pan surroundings. The sweltering desert metropolis of Phoenix had been his home for twenty years, and he liked it.

The steady drumming of the hammer in his hands did not keep the sun-browned twenty-eight year old from thinking about other matters. "We'll be meeting at seven o'clock this evening. When my friends hear I'm learning Greek, they'll think the sun has finally cooked my brain."

He wiped his forehead with a stained rag as his mind drifted back to pinpoint the turnabout in his life. It had begun eighteen months ago when the McLains moved into the house next door. They were the ones who had made him think about his purpose in life, about his family, and about God.

About God! That was the shocker. He'd always had questions about God, but had never taken the risk of airing them out in the open. They were kept private, tucked away under the surface.

Once he had made the effort to clear matters with his conscience by going to a church, but he couldn't stand the 'shirt-and-tie' Sundays, as he called them. It wasn't because he disliked the people in the pews. They seemed ordinary enough, even friendly, but he suspected them of putting on a show.

No one had to tell him he was speculating about things he had no way of knowing. All he really knew was that *he* was putting on a show. Bow your head. Pray. Stand up. Sing. Open the Bible. Read. Greet your neighbor. Smile. He tried but couldn't make it more than a game. He wondered why he had to be different. Why couldn't he fit in? Why did he have to be the one who was out of place?

Then his thoughts wandered to Carol, his wife, and to their little boy, Andy. He had carried few ideals into their marriage, knowing there would be problems. He was no romantic dreamer. But he had hoped they could avoid the fights and the boredom that seemed to infiltrate so many families.

The spats came, though, and the ten-hour work days, and the endless discussions about wallpaper and washing machines and broken air-conditioners. He stood by like a spectator watching it happen, fascinated by his own paralysis. Before he knew what was happening, bickering had escalated into bitterness, and the daily routine had turned to monotony.

Although he thought it a coward's way out, his only answer had been to work still longer hours, leaving home early and returning late to minimize confrontations. His favorite rationalization was that at work he could at least translate monotony into money.

"We don't live," he once told his wife in a moment of exasperation, "we exist." That's what they were doing—existing—when one Saturday afternoon the McLains and their four children moved into the house next door.

John was adjusting the sprinkling system in the front yard when they arrived in a truck and a van and began carrying their belongings into the house. The children, a boy and girl in their teens and another boy and girl not much younger, were helping their parents unload the truck which had been backed into the driveway of the Spanish style house.

He had briefly met Dean and Linda McLain several months earlier when they were looking at the house for the first time. Friendly folks, he'd thought at the time, estimating them to be in their late thirties or early forties.

It was when he and Carol and Andy dropped by to greet them and offer a hand, that the first of the many eye-openers occurred that they were to have with the McLains. Buddy, the oldest of the children, a stocky, athletic seventeen-year-old, asked Andy if he'd like to join them for a quick game of soccer on the front yard grass. Two kitchen chairs were hustled into service for goals, and soon Andy and his new friends were chasing a plastic ball around the yard. Buddy and his fifteen-year-old sister, Peggy, her long, curly, light brown hair bouncing behind her, deftly weaved little Andy into the game with their younger brother and sister, Tommy and Katy.

It had surprised him that teens like Buddy and Peggy would take such an interest in a six-year-old. And he was also surprised—and a little embarrassed—that the McLains had immediately stopped working when they showed up. They acted as though they had nothing more pressing to do than have a chat and a ball game in the front yard.

"Is there anything we can do to help?" Carol had asked Linda.

"You're already helping us do the most important thing we could possibly get done today," Linda said.

"Oh? And what's that?" Carol asked.

"Why, get to know our neighbors, of course," was Linda's reply.

The McLains just had a different way of thinking about life.

In the year that followed, John and his family were often together with their neighbors, and a surprisingly close relationship developed between them and the McLain children. Carol and he would have expected kids of their ages to be going in four different directions, but Buddy and Peggy always seemed willing to let the younger ones be a part of their activities, even when their teen-age friends came by. They'd ride bikes together, play basketball, or take a gang of neighborhood kids to the park—Andy included. Yes, it was the McLain children who had convinced them that this new family next door was managing to do more than just exist.

Many conversations with Dean had also introduced him to a new way of thinking. Instead of expressing a quick opinion about a matter, Dean often went to great lengths to describe *how* he went about coming to a particular conclusion.

"More important than knowing what a man thinks," Dean often said, "is knowing *where* a man has gotten his information, and *how* he has used that information to form his conclusions. Only valid input understood in a valid context will yield valid conclusions."

At first, John hadn't necessarily understood all the implications of everything Dean said, but one thing came through loud and clear: Dean was not interested in just passing on his own opinions. He was more concerned that a person know how to get facts and know what to do with them once he got them. It was Dean's commitment to facts that led John to develop an interest in the Greek language.

During their conversations, Dean often looked up words and passages in a copy of the New Testament written in Greek which he said was the language in which the Scriptures were first written. It may have been a small thing, but John remembered the powerful effect it had on him. It made him see the New Testament in a much different light: less like a religious book shrouded between two black covers, and more like an actual collection of historical documents written by real people.

These Greek writings represented the "original input", as Dean put it, of the words and teachings of Jesus Christ and his first followers. This original input had begun to greatly interest John. That's why he consented to come when Dean mentioned he'd agreed to help some friends learn New Testament Greek and invited Carol and him to join them.

John reached the end of a row, and lopped off the end of the last shingle to even up the edge. "It'll be interesting to see if Dean McLain can squeeze anything into the head of an ignorant nail-pounder like me," he thought to himself as he slowly rose to his feet.

It was one p.m. and the sun was becoming oppressive. It was time to quit for the day. For several months he'd been working fewer hours, usually beginning at six a.m. and calling it a day shortly after noon. It meant a cut in take-home pay, but it also meant more time for the family, for reading, and for friends. Carol had supported him in his decision to cut down on the hours he put in every week. She said she didn't mind passing up some of life's more tempting extras. "It's a small price to pay," she had remarked, "to make the transition from existing to living." It was one of the ways he and Carol had begun to rearrange their priorities after taking their first real steps of faith.

A half hour later John drove into the driveway of their North Phoenix home. Andy was kicking a ball in the front yard with a friend. Carol heard the car and went to the front window in the living room. She saw Andy pulling on his father's hand. John joined the game and she knew it would be another fifteen minutes before he made it into the house.

"My two men," she thought to herself, not wanting to take her eyes off them. Small, happy tears formed in the corner of her eyes. She couldn't help it. Her thoughts carried her back to their first years of marriage. Apart from Andy's birth there had been few high points. From the beginning things seemed to slide downhill. John's reaction had been to withdraw. She remembered how frantic she had become, thinking he was slipping away from her. Helplessness and fear had almost engulfed her. She began to lean on her friends and that had pulled her more and more away from her husband. Her friends comforted her, sympathized with her, agreed with her view of things, and gave her plenty of advice. For the most part, though, they, too, were struggling to cope with their own situations. Some had thrown themselves into a career; others were into hobbies, sports, school activities, or heavy shopping—if they had the money.

She remembered, too, the many hours she had spent with Linda McLain in the past year. In Linda she found a special kind of friend who was hard to classify. She was by no means a fiery feminist, but neither was she the ideal homemaker. In that regard, nothing stood out about the McLains: neither their car nor their house nor the clothes they wore. It's not that they were rag-tags. They weren't. Linda simply spent most of her time writing letters, studying, meeting with a variety of friends, and doing things with the kids when they were home.

Conversations with Linda often took unusual turns. She once told Carol in response to a question, "Before answering that question I'd like to think about it for a few days. I think it's an important question, and it needs a comprehensive answer." Carol figured most people would have just fired off their opinion and not be particularly concerned about whether they were being *comprehensive* or not. Linda took thoughts and words seriously, though. That's what Carol liked about her, and that's why she had agreed to join her husband at the McLains in the evening.

It seemed ludicrous to her that she should even entertain the idea of learning Greek. She'd never gone to college. She'd never even read a serious book. Linda had encouraged her to come, though, assuring her she'd not make a fool of herself. Reluctantly she had agreed, but she figured it wouldn't be long before things got over her head, and she'd have to drop out.

PART II:

They Begin Learning How to Read New Testament Greek

From Alpha to Omega

Carol was finishing the dishes from the evening meal when she heard a loud knock at the front door.

Peggy McLain stuck her head in. "Anybody home?"

"Come on in," called Carol. "I'm in the kitchen."

Slightly out of breath, Peggy walked in, wearing shorts, a tank top, and running shoes.

"Been out jogging in this heat?"

"No, just shooting some baskets with my brothers. When it's this hot, it doesn't take long to work up a sweat. Hey, can I help you finish up?"

"Thanks, but don't bother. I'm almost done. Has anyone shown up at your place yet?"

"Yeah, there's a few. Dad said they'd be starting in about ten minutes."

John came into the kitchen from the back patio, his son dancing around his legs. "You're an angel to stay with Andy," he said when he saw Peggy.

"Oh, he's no problem. Glad to do it. I hope you'll learn a lot today."

"I'm sure we will," said Carol. She dried her hands on a towel and took a notebook out of a drawer. "But I'll bet your father will think I'm a dunce."

"No, he won't, and besides, dad likes dunces."

John scooped Andy into his arms and gave him a big hug. "Have a good time with Peggy. Mommy and I will be back in a few hours."

Stepping out into the lingering evening heat, John and Carol walked leisurely to the McLains. A steamy mist was rising from the automatic sprinkling systems in the neighboring yards.

Linda met them at the door. She was a small, energetic woman who didn't seem old enough to be the mother of teen-agers. Curly wisps of brown-blond hair bounced above her eyes. "Got your thinking caps on today?" she asked.

"I wish I had one," said Carol.

"Oh, you'll do fine. Come on in. They'll be getting started soon."

"Anyone here we know?" asked John.

"You know Buddy's friend, Eddie, but the others are probably new to you."

She led them into the living room where John saw Dean talking with a young woman. Other guests were seated on the couch and on folding chairs placed around the room. Dean's face brightened when he saw them enter. "Good to see you," he said, shaking John's hand. "I'd like the two of you to meet Liz Serringer. She's a student at ASU who's decided to join us. I hope you'll have some time to chat after the meeting."

The doorbell rang. "That'll be our final guest," said Dean. "We can get started right away."

Sitting down next to his wife, John counted ten people in the room. "Typical," he thought to himself. It was another one of those things that intrigued John about the McLains. They always tried to maintain what Dean called 'family-distance' with people.

How to Read New Testament Greek

Dean came back into the room with a man about John's age. He pointed him to a chair and took one last look to see if everyone was present. "Linda and I are delighted you could all come this evening," he began. "At various times in the past few months, each of you has expressed an interest in learning New Testament Greek. I'm glad the time has come to take the first steps. Before we begin, however, we need to make some introductions. I know all of you, but most of you don't know one another. I'd like to ask each of you to briefly tell us something about yourself and why you're interested in learning New Testament Greek."

Dean put his hand on the shoulder of a tall, slightly balding man somewhat older than himself sitting next to him. "Let's begin with Harmon Smith," he said. "I think he's the right man to break the ice for us. Harmon, you've got the floor."

It was evident when Harmon began to speak that he was a man who felt at home in front of a group. "I grew up in Lincoln, Nebraska, and for almost twenty years was a history and anthropology professor at the university there. An acute bronchial condition, which dictated a change to a desert climate, brought me to this area a little over a year ago. I'm presently doing some lecturing at Phoenix Junior College down in the middle of the city. My wife, Louise, would normally be with me, but she left a few days ago to visit our two sons who live in Nebraska and Iowa.

"It was during my student days that I came to faith in Christ, and over the years I've tried to make some progress in that faith. Although I've invested considerable time in a study of the Scriptures during those years, I don't feel all that confident in my understanding of the New Testament. I'm actually more knowledgeable in what men have written about the Scriptures than in the Scriptures themselves. For some time now I've wanted to remedy that situation and that explains why I've decided to learn Greek. I wish I'd done it earlier in life, but I figure better late than never."

"It's good to have a historian with us," said Dean. "I'm sure we'll be able to use some of your insights in the days ahead." He then turned to a plump, elderly woman with sparkling eyes. "Now I'd like Mrs. Lawson to tell us about herself. She, too, is a newcomer to the area."

"Please call me Marian," she said. "I don't mind saying right off that I feel like a displaced person among so many young people. And to think you are all here to learn Greek! My stars! I don't know how Linda ever made me think I could be a part of this.

"Let's see, now, what can I say about myself? I lived most of my life in a small town in Wyoming and didn't begin to take any real steps of faith until about ten years ago when I was well over fifty years old. Five years later when my husband died unexpectedly"—the brightness left her face momentarily—"I was forced to go through some rather difficult times. Some friends and a loving daughter helped convince me I shouldn't give up all the plans my husband and I had made for our future. That's what brought me to Arizona.

"Now, what in the world ever made me think I should learn Greek? I guess it all started when I started meeting with Linda over a year ago. We met at the mall

From Alpha to Omega

in a very unusual...Oh, but that's a long story. If I get started telling that we'll never get finished. Anyway, as I'm sure all of you know, if you're around the McLains for very long you find yourself getting interested in the Bible. And you can't help noticing how they're always looking up things in those maroon Bibles they have, you know, the ones with all the funny writing in them. Even the kids do it. Well, the next thing you know, I'm asking what that funny writing is, and for the first time in my life I find out the New Testament was written in Greek. News to me! I guess I always thought it was written by a Mr. King James in England.

"If I'd have kept my mouth shut right then and there, I'd have probably managed to keep myself out of this whole thing, but nosy ol' me, I kept asking about this and that and before you know it, the whole family is convinced I want to learn Greek, and I can't convince them otherwise.

"So, there you have it. Trying to learn Greek at my age is probably as silly as starting a football team in a nursing home, but if learning Greek will help me understand the Bible better, then I'm willing to give it a try. You young folks will have to be patient with me, though."

"Don't worry about that," said Dean. "You may surprise yourself. We're glad to have you with us." He then addressed a tall, young man with dark hair and friendly eyes. "Jim, how about you being next?"

"My name is Jim Garvey," he began. "My wife, Barbara, is at home with our two children, Jimmy and Amy, who are ten and eight. I grew up in a Christian home and have my parents to thank for most of what I've learned in my life both regarding my faith and my occupation. When I was fairly young, not yet out of college, I took over the family business due to my father's bad health. It only worked out because my father proved to be a good teacher and was able to give me a lot of help in the first few years.

"Unfortunately, the growth and development of my spiritual life has never kept pace with the development of my life as a businessman. For quite some time now I've been convinced that needs to be changed. I think that learning Greek may be a good basic investment that will bring a lot of benefit in the long run. Like Marian, however, I have real doubts as to whether I can manage it. The only experience I've had with foreign languages has been a disaster."

"You're not alone in your fear of foreign languages," said Dean. "Few people have confidence when it comes to learning languages. We're going to be talking more about that at a later date, but now I'm going to ask a couple of the younger members of our group to introduce themselves." He looked over to Liz Serringer. "Ladies first, Liz."

"I'm an architect major at Arizona State University," Liz began. "I come from a German family that moved to America and settled in Ohio when I was nine years old. I haven't been a Christian for very long, but I've felt in the last year that I'd like to understand the New Testament better. It seems logical to me that learning to read them in the language in which they were originally written would be a help."

"Do you still speak German?" Dean asked.

"I wouldn't exactly call myself totally bilingual, but we continued to speak a lot of German at home after we moved to America, so I can speak it fairly well."

"That's good to know. I'm sure we'll be able to use some of your experience with languages in the coming weeks and months."

Dean then smiled at a handsome, brown-skinned young man sitting to his left. "I'm sure everyone is eager to hear something from Eddie. I've known Eddie since my son started going to Chapparal High School which is not far from here. Eddie, tell us a little about yourself."

Eddie looked like he'd rather sink into the deepest recesses of the couch, but he cleared his throat and bravely began to speak. "Like Mr. McLain said, my name is Eddie, Eddie Garcia. I met Buddy in school. We both play on the basketball team. He often invited me to his house, and I saw his family was real serious about being Christians. I mean, more Christian than what I'd ever thought a Christian was supposed to be. My family is pretty religious, but we don't talk...uh, open, and, you know, to each other about God.

"I guess I'm interested in Greek, because whenever we did some Bible study here, I noticed how Buddy and his dad sometimes looked in those red sort of books that Mrs. Lawson was talking about." He looked over to Dean. "Is that enough?"

"That was plenty," said Dean. "By the way, do you speak Spanish?"

"At home we speak the kind of Spanish my mom and dad spoke when they were growing up in Mexico."

"It must be pretty good Spanish," said Buddy, "because he sure doesn't have any problems in Spanish class."

"We're lucky to have a couple experienced linguists like Eddie and Liz with us," said Dean. "If we need any cross-cultural information, we'll be able to call on them to help us out."

Eddie gave Dean a look that said "Who? Me?" He'd never heard himself called an *experienced linguist* before.

Finally, Dean asked John and Carol to introduce themselves.

At the beginning of the introductions, John had felt his stomach tighten knowing he'd be expected to say something in front of the group, but his nervousness gradually left when he saw that Carol and he weren't the only academic amateurs. "Carol and I live next door," he said, "which made it easy to meet the McLains. I'd say it's mainly through their children that we've gotten interested in knowing the New Testament better. We've never seen kids who get along with each other like they do.

"It's not easy for either of us to believe we can learn Greek, but we're willing to give it a try, especially if it can help us be better parents."

"Thank you," said Dean. "I hope you'll all enjoy getting to know one another as much as Linda and I have enjoyed getting to know each of you. It's a great day for me when a group of Christians step out to learn Koine Greek, the everyday language spoken and written in the first century. It was not only the world's first

From Alpha to Omega

language to form on a truly grand scale a communicative bridge between dozens of major cultural areas and hundreds of subcultures, it was also the language used to record history's most unique message about history's most unique person.

"If it's true, as I'm convinced it is, that the writings reporting the teachings of Christ and his disciples are the most significant and crucial pieces of literature the world has ever known, then it only makes sense that understanding them in their purest form—the Greek of the first century—has to be considered a skill of great worth.

"Can any of you think of other reasons why learning the Scriptures in Greek would be of value?"

"As I see things," said Harmon, "there are a lot of speculations and personal opinions about the teachings of the Scriptures floating around in our culture. In fact, we're almost flooded with them. I don't know how we can be in a position to evaluate what's genuine and what's questionable without having some access to the source documents. Otherwise, our only choice is to pick and choose whom we're going to believe."

"It certainly isn't unusual for the Scriptures to be misused," said Dean. "Even in Jesus' day this was evidently an acute problem. The Old Testament Scriptures were often made unrecognizable by the amount of information added to them by religious groups such as the Pharisees. In Matthew 15 there is an account of a run-in Jesus had with some of the Pharisees about this very practice.

"Today we have problems that are somewhat similar. So much has been written *about* what the Scriptures are supposed to say that it's not unusual for people to be confused about what is actually taught in the Scriptures and what isn't. Learning Greek puts a tool in our hands that can help us cut through a lot of the informational jungle that often surrounds the Scriptures. Any other reasons?"

"I can imagine," said Liz, "that knowing Greek would help us understand the text more accurately. I know that translations can leave a lot to be desired. I've read Shakespeare in German, for example, and it's really awful. And reading Goethe in English is just as bad. The major thoughts are there, I suppose, but a lot seems to get lost in the translation."

"Like what gets lost?" asked Jim.

"Whew, that's tough to explain. Sometimes a translation of a book seems almost like a different text to me. We got into a big discussion about translations last year in a German literature class I was taking. The professor went through a whole list of things that drive translators batty—like words with double meanings and unique cultural phenomena and shades of meanings and rhetorical devices. I don't remember everything, but I do know that translating is more than a matter of substituting one word for another."

"It can get rather involved, indeed," said Dean. "Although translations are wonderful tools—and some of them can be extremely accurate, particularly if they're tailor-made for a specific target group—they can seldom be a complete replacement for the original. So, as Liz said, learning Greek could help you understand the texts of the Scriptures with greater accuracy. Any other reasons for learning Greek?"

"People who learn Greek project a strong message about their commitment to the message of Christ," said Linda. "It's a major investment of time and energy that won't go unnoticed. And that's the kind of example that is particularly important for children. They're instinctively more ready to believe a message expressed in the practice of daily living. Simply *telling* children the Scriptures are important will never impress them as much as demonstrating it through a major commitment like learning to read those Scriptures in Greek."

"I agree that it will not go unnoticed," said Dean. "If you begin to learn Greek, you will make it an option for other Christians who know you. Some will get the bug for the first time from you, and others who have already thought about learning Greek will be encouraged to get started."

As Dean was talking, the smell of coffee began to fill the room. "Should we take a break now?" asked Linda. "I made some cookies, and the coffee seems to be ready."

"Fine with me," said Dean. "Let's take fifteen minutes, and then come back ready to take our first steps in Greek."

As the others stood and stretched and headed for the kitchen, John introduced himself to Jim. "It looks like you and I have a few things in common, " he said. "Neither of us finished college and we're both in business for ourselves, although it sounds like your company makes mine look like small time peanuts."

"My business was dumped into my lap," said Jim. "There are plenty of times when I think I'd prefer my own peanuts to someone else's elephants."

John laughed. "Do you feel as strange as I do? Sitting here with a group of people who want to learn Greek?"

"I thought for sure I'd be the odd man out," said Jim. "But it looks like I'm not the only one."

"Maybe we can help each other out when the going gets tough."

"I'm all for that. From what Dean has told me, high IQ's aren't necessary, so I might have a chance."

Carol brought two mugs of coffee to her husband and Jim and then looked around for Marian Lawson. She found her in the kitchen refilling a cookie platter. "So you're Marian Lawson," she said. "Linda has told us so much about you."

"About me? Goodness. Linda's also told me a lot about you. Just think, we were almost best of friends before we even met each other." Marian burst into laughter. "But that's Linda, for you. Things start happening when she shows up."

"They sure do. It's been great having her next door."

"Let's see. If I remember right, you have a little boy."

"Yes, a six-year-old named Andy. Peggy is staying with him right now."

From Alpha to Omega

"Feel free to give me a call if you ever need anyone to watch after him. I don't live far away, and I'd be glad to do it."

"Wow! That's quite an offer."

"Don't be afraid to take me up on it. I love the little ones." They heard Dean calling everyone back to the living room. "It sounds like they're getting started again. We'll talk more afterwards." Carol gave Marian's arm a squeeze and headed back to her chair.

Dean began by handing out slips of paper. Here's a sample of printed Greek," he said. It's a familiar passage from the New Testament. Take a close look at it and tell me what you notice."

> Πᾶς οὖν ὅστις ἀκούει μου τοὺς λόγους τούτους καὶ ποιεῖ αὐτούς, ὁμοιωθήσεται ἀνδρὶ φρονίμῳ, ὅστις ᾠκοδόμησεν αὐτοῦ τὴν οἰκίαν ἐπὶ τὴν πέτραν.

Marian put on her glasses and examined the example closely. "Oh, my stars!" she said. "You mean I'm supposed to learn to read all those crazy scratchings?"

"Look a little closer," said Dean, smiling. "I think you'll find some familiar territory."

"Some of the letters are similar to ours," said John. "But others are totally different."

"There is some similarity," said Dean. "Our own alphabet was passed on to us by the Romans, but they in turn had received much of their alphabet from the Etruscans who had borrowed it from the Greeks. That means Greek is actually the basis of our own alphabet, and explains why many of the letters are similar. We're going to have to learn the letters that are different, of course. But that won't take long."

"How are the letters pronounced?" asked Eddie.

"Unfortunately, Eddie, the ancient Greeks never managed to invent the tape recorder so we can only guess as to how they pronounced their language back then. Usually, when people learn New Testament Greek today, they simply pronounce the letters as they would pronounce the English letters most closely corresponding to them."

Dean then gave Buddy some sheets of paper to pass around. "On the first two pages, you'll find a list entitled *The Greek Letters*. It contains the letters, their names, and a suggested pronunciation.

THE GREEK LETTERS

CAPITAL	SMALL	NAME	SUGGESTED PRONUNCIATION
A	α	alpha	a as father
B	β	beta	b
Γ	γ	gamma	g as in game
Δ	δ	delta	d
E	ε	epsilon	e as in get
Z	ζ	zeta	z as in zoo
H	η	eta	ey as in obey
Θ	θ	theta	th as in think
I	ι	iota	i as in fit (when short) i as in machine (when long)
K	κ	kappa	k
Λ	λ	lambda	l
M	μ	mu	m
N	ν	nu	n

Ξ	ξ	xi	x as in bo**x**
Ο	ο	omicron	o as in h**o**t
Π	π	pi	p
Ρ	ρ	rho	r
Σ	σ, ς	sigma	s (ς is only used when it's the *last* letter of a word.)
Τ	τ	tau	t
Υ	υ	upsilon	u as in L**u**ke
Φ	φ	phi	f
Χ	χ	chi	k (Or ch as in German **ach**, if you want at least one letter to sound foreign.)
Ψ	ψ	psi	ps as in li**ps**
Ω	ω	omega	o as in m**o**le

"It's important that you learn to recognize all the Greek letters well in the coming days. They are going to be your guides into the fascinating world of Greek thoughts. From now on you should spend time with them every day and get to know them like good friends.

"Take a look now at the third page. It's a list of Greek *double letters* along with suggestions for how to pronounce them.

DOUBLE CONSONANTS	PRONUNCIATION
σχ	sk as in **sk**i
γγ	ng as in ri**ng**
γκ	nk as in si**nk**
γξ	nks as in tha**nks**
γχ	nk as in si**nk**

DOUBLE VOWELS	PRONUNCIATION
αι	ai as in **ai**sle
αυ	ow as in c**ow**
οι	oi as in c**oi**n
υι	ouie as in **Louie**
ου	ou as in **Lou**
ηυ	eu as in **feu**d
ει	ei as in **ei**ght

"Now turn to the fourth page. You'll find a list of practical suggestions to help you learn the letters as quickly as possible.

1. Make some review cards. Write the Greek letters on one side of a card and the name of the letter and its pronunciation on the back. Carry them with you and practice them until they become second nature.

2. Learn the Greek alphabet by heart. This will help familiarize you with the letters, and will also come in handy later when you begin using a dictionary. (Here's a tip: The letters are easier to learn if you divide them into groups of four.)

3. Practice writing the letters until you develop your own style of writing Greek. There's no official way to write each letter. Just look at the printed form and reproduce it as simply as possible.

4. Think up various English words and try to write them using Greek letters. δαδ, for example, would be the spelling for *dad*. You will find some English words difficult to spell because the English sounds *j* and *w* are not used in Greek.

5. Here is a list of fifteen of the most common words in the New Testament with pronunciation helps underlined and the meaning of each word. Practice these words by covering the pronunciation helps with a sheet of paper. Then check yourself.

ἀλλά	**all a**board	*but*
ἄνθρωπος	**on throw poss**ible	*man*
διά	ra**dium**	*through*
ἔρχομαι	j**erk oh my**	*I'm coming*
ἔχω	**echo**	*I have*
ἡμεῖς	**hay may** see	*we*
Θεός	**thre**ad b**oss**	*God*
Ἰησοῦς	he h**ay Sioux** see	*Jesus*
κύριος	**curios**ity	*Lord*
λέγω	**Let go**	*I'm saying*
πᾶς	a**pos**trophe	*each, all*
ποιέω	**poi**son red **oak**	*I'm doing*
Χριστός	**Chris too s**low	*Christ*
ἀδελφός	a **del**ta f**loss**	*brother*
ἡμέρα	**hey** A**meri**c**a**	*day*

How to Read New Testament Greek

"These are only a few suggestions that other Greek learners have found helpful. Do whatever works for you to learn the Greek letters. A man like John who crawls around on a roof all day will need a different review system than a man who works behind a desk. Remember, the *amount* of time you spend is not as important as it is to do something in Greek *regularly,* even if it's only for fifteen or twenty minutes every other day. It's important to avoid going for longer periods of time without doing language work."

"There are so many little markings above the letters of these words," said Marian. "What do they mean?"

"They don't really mean anything. They're a rather complicated system of accents and breathing marks that the Greeks developed later on in history. In determining the meaning of a word, they make a difference in only a very few cases, and those can be easily learned."

"Will we need to buy a book or any other materials?" asked Jim.

"Yes, eventually there will be quite a few books you'll want to purchase. But for now, you won't need anything. I'll be providing you with a whole series of lessons[1] I've been developing over the years. As soon as all of you have mastered the Greek letters, you'll be receiving copies of them."

"When are we going to meet again?" asked Liz.

"That's going to be a surprise. Be sure to keep your eyes and ears open, and don't forget to read your mail. That's all I can say for now. I'll be staying in contact with each of you. As soon as I know everyone can recognize the letters well, things will begin to happen."

"Sounds mysterious," said Marian.

"The faster you learn the Greek letters, the faster the mystery will be solved." Linda came in with another pot of coffee, and the first Greek session was over.

Carol leaned back in her chair and thought back over the evening. She had mixed feelings. On the one hand, she was surprised at her own interest and happy that she was together with people who did not threaten her. On the other hand, it seemed silly for a housewife like her to be learning Greek. Added to that were those nagging feelings of inadequacy. Wouldn't she fall hopelessly behind in the coming months?

She looked at her husband who was talking with Dean and Professor Smith. She could see the interest in his eyes. She'd always thought it was a shame he'd never had the opportunity to get a college education. He had a bright mind. It warmed her to see him motivated to learn and grow.

---

[1] See Parts III, V, and VII: *The STEPS to Learning New Testament Greek*

John's decision to follow Christ, and his interest in the Scriptures had helped to renew their relationship. She knew it was important that they not fall back into their old lives. She wasn't sure if she could learn Greek herself, but she was determined to encourage John, and if that meant learning some strange looking Greek letters, then she was willing to do it.

UNIVERSAL GREEK PICTURES

At the beginning of the week, Marian, the Freys, and all the others who had begun to learn Greek with the McLains received an unusual announcement in the mail. It was printed on thin, shiny paper, the kind used for better quality advertisements:

McLain and Associates

on behalf of the world-renowned motion-picture studio

UNIVERSAL GREEK PICTURES

is proud to announce
the opening of America's first
studio of linguistic photography

You are invited to the
GRAND OPENING
***

Saturday, 9 a.m.
4810 E. Laurel Lane
Scottsdale, Arizona
***

As you tour the studios,
you will meet famous actors and actresses,
talk with legendary directors,
gaze on immense storerooms of magnificent scenery,
and stroll through the wardrobes of the stars.
You will even shoot your own scenes
with incredible cameras.
Don't miss this chance of a lifetime.

See you at the grand opening
of
UNIVERSAL GREEK PICTURES

* * *

How to Read New Testament Greek

Interest was high by the time Saturday morning came around. Marian Lawson was the first to arrive. She drove up in her red Corolla and parked in front of the McLains' house just as John and Carol stepped out their front door. John jogged to the car and opened the door for her.

"Goodness. What service!"

"Nothing but the best for early risers."

"You bet I'm early," she said, working her plump frame out of the bucket seat. "That invitation I received in the mail made me so curious I wouldn't miss today for anything."

"What do you think Dean has up his sleeve?"

"I have no idea, but I'm sure it will be an eye-opener, whatever it is."

As they stood there talking, more cars turned into the normally quiet side street and parked. Soon, Liz, Jim, and Harmon had joined the lively discussion on the front sidewalk. They were interrupted when they heard a loud voice from the direction of the McLains' house. Heads turned to see Buddy standing on the front step with Eddie.

"Ladeez and Gentlemen," he called, "the grand opening of Universal Greek Pictures is about to begin. Don't miss the introductory ceremonies."

Marian tucked her purse under her arm and headed for the house. "We're on our way," she said.

Buddy motioned for them to follow him around the corner to a narrow gate in the high board fence surrounding the backyard. Eddie waited by the open gate as everyone filed through and followed Buddy to the covered patio. A sign was mounted above the sliding glass doors:

UNIVERSAL GREEK PICTURES

Waiting under the sign until the small group had gathered around him, Buddy stepped up on a small stool. "I'd like to welcome you," he said ceremoniously, "to Universal Greek Pictures, the first Greek studio of linguistic photography in America. The proprietors of this modern facility, McLain and Associates, are proud that through their efforts Universal Greek Pictures has chosen this neighborhood for its first international location. They have arranged on the occasion of this grand opening to give you a personal tour.

"You will see how word-pictures are taken and developed; you will witness the production of breathtaking thought-pictures; you will marvel as you stroll through the elegant wardrobes and the vast warehouses of scenery; and you will see the mighty language cameras in action as they capture scene after scene of linguistic beauty, transforming them into pictures of stunning clarity.

"I'm sure you'll be surprised and pleased to hear that the director himself is present today to personally lead the tour. He is very concerned that you be given the best possible introduction to the Greek language. So without further delay, I now present to you the man who made it all possible, the man who brought Universal Greek Pictures to our area: Dino McLain!"

Pealing those last words with the intensity of a circus ringmaster, Buddy dramatically pointed to the double glass doors leading into the house. On cue, Eddie swept one of the doors open. The curtains parted and out stepped Buddy's dad wearing dark glasses, a brightly flowered shirt, and white slacks. He was greeted by a good natured "Bravo!" from Jim Garvey and loud applause from the others.

"Ladies and gentleman," Dean said, rubbing his hands together, "on behalf of my associates I want to welcome you to Universal Greek Pictures. We are pleased to have you here and look forward to introducing you to our whole spectrum of Greek language pictures. We carry everything from the most delicate portraits to great epic productions that defy the imagination. As specialists who reproduce the original pictures of the New Testament Greek language, it is our wish that when you are through with the tour you will have a complete overview of this marvelous first-century language."

Taking an OPEN FOR BUSINESS sign from Buddy, Dean hung it on a hook beside the door. "Step right in, folks," he said. "Don't be bashful. There's room for everyone."

Marian Lawson, moving with the speed of an experienced shopper, was the first through the door. As the others followed, Jim and John stopped for a moment by Dean.

"Never a dull moment at the McLains," said Jim, stepping back and eyeing the dazzling shirt.

"Yeah," said John. "I thought learning languages was supposed to be dull and drab."

"Don't get your hopes up," laughed Dean. "The day's just getting started. I may manage to put you to sleep yet."

The family room had been transformed into a splash of Greek letters and words. Colorful labels with Greek words had been attached to everything from the light switch to the round fireplace at the top of the wide steps leading into the living room. Streamers lined with Greek letters hung from the ceiling forming a wall-to-wall star. Two giant red Greek letters—*alpha* and *omega*—dominated one entire end of the room. Scattered in and around the man-sized letters were lists of dozens of Greek words, each in a different combination of colors.

Stationed around the room and interspersed with chairs and stools was an array of various-sized cardboard boxes capped by bright colored pennants embossed with golden Greek letters. The counter dividing the family room from the kitchen was arranged with an assortment of Greek books.

"My very honored guests," Dean said in a loud voice as he worked his way to the middle of the room through a tangle of chairs, boxes, and people. "Please find a place to sit and make yourselves comfortable. We'll get started as soon as possible." The festive surroundings had generated a carnival atmosphere.

"Before we begin our tour," said Dean, "it's important that we prepare each of you for the sights you will be seeing today. Therefore, we're going to spend the first few minutes doing a series of special eye exercises."

"Eye exercises?" said Marian, a note of surprise in her voice.

"Yes, madam. Eye exercises. We've found that not everyone knows how to view language pictures. Although we have hundreds of the most exquisite examples of Greek linguistic photography on display, it's not unusual for guests to come into our studios and not see a single one of our pictures. That's why we always take a few minutes to acclimate the eyes of our guests before every tour.

"Let's begin by looking at the shopping mall across the way." Dean pointed through the double doors to the large Paradise Valley Shopping Mall which was visible over the backyard fence. "There are two levels of reality that are observable. The first is the raw, external impression it makes on your eyes. You see the stucco walls, the entrances, the great bulk of the buildings, and the way it's situated in the middle of a large, asphalted lot. Were you to walk over to the mall, you could gather additional impressions of this kind through the senses of smell, touch, and hearing. They would all reveal something of the size, shape, texture, smell, and sound of the structure.

"The second observable reality, however, cannot be registered merely with the body's senses. It must be seen with the eyes of the spirit, that is with the *mind* and the *heart*. And can anyone tell me what it is the inner senses 'see' when they observe the mall?"

There was a long moment of silence.

"Words!" Dean burst out. "That's what they see. Words. The mall is literally surrounded by words. Words are holding it together, underlying its foundation, watching over it, and making possible everything that's being done over there. Take a good look. Do you see all those words?"

Marian was squinting. "I do see some signs and billboards."

"Oh, madam, those are only surface words. You have to look much deeper. Take a look at its development, for example."

"Its development?"

"Of course. The shopping mall didn't just fall out of the sky. It took many months to build it with thousands of tons of building materials, and it took many more months to outfit it with millions of consumer items. And every single one of those objects found its designated place and became part of a meaningful whole, because it was directed there by words—words in the form of blueprints, architectural plans, contracts, orders, charts, and dozens of other forms of linguistic communication.

"Words are actually responsible for that architectural marvel over there, not the objects out of which it was constructed. Without words and all the thoughts, plans, and instructions they conveyed, all those objects would still be nothing more than scattered pieces of minerals embedded in the ground somewhere. It's words that named those minerals, arranged their discovery, organized their refinement, and fit them together into the ingenious invention we call a shopping mall."

Dean paused, slightly out of breath, then lowered his voice as though about to reveal a great and cherished secret. "Boiling down the relationship between words and objects to its most compelling equation, we could put it this way: *Man spoke, and a shopping mall came into being.* Very similar statements were once recorded at the very beginning of the Old Testament where it says that God *spoke* and light and the earth and water and plants and animals and people came into being.

"Do you realize that according to this Scripture, language was never created, but that it was always a part of God's own character? God spoke and all of creation came into being. Do you know what that means?"

Marian was slowly shaking her head from side to side.

"It means that language is as eternal as God Himself. It means that language is no one's bright idea. It means that language comes to us across the barriers of created existence. When God spoke, the stage of the world sprang into being, cosmic lights went on, history's action commenced. The great producer spoke, and the stage of heaven and earth filled with actors and actresses and things and places and times and events. Great power resides in words, because words were never a part of creation. They were the means of creation. And the same is true today. Without words and the thoughts they generate, man couldn't produce even the simplest structure, much less a shopping mall." Dean was pacing back and forth, noticeably warming up to his subject.

"Just as our eyes need light to see and our ears need sounds to hear, so do our spiritual senses need the light and sound of words to function at full force. Do you realize, sir," he said, stopping in front of John, "that without words it would be impossible for man even to think? What would we do if we couldn't think? Nothing, that's what. We couldn't tell a joke, make a phone call, send a birthday card, sing a song, read a book, or even ask for the time. Without words we'd all turn into voiceless vegetables."

Dean was standing still now, eyes gazing in the distance, his arm raised like a veritable Statue of Linguistic Liberty. "Words," he continued solemnly, "like the cells of our bodies, are containers of life. They are the receptacles of all of life's meaning, the crucibles of creative energy, the vessels of man's very consciousness of himself." Each phrase was pronounced with such grave conviction that a moment of hallowed silence gripped the room.

"Words, and even more importantly the combinations of words we call sentences, may seem at first glance little more than squiggly lines on paper or fleeting wisps of sound dissipating in the air, but in reality they are intricate symbolic organisms capable of performing life's most amazing feat: They take the film of meaning and project it in spectacular and unlimited ways on the screen of human understanding. No man-made camera even comes close to accomplishing such a feat."

Dean raised his finger to make another point, but an inner voice seemed to stop him. He stepped back. "I'm sorry," he said, "I seem to have gotten a bit carried away. That happens to us directors in language studios sometimes, particularly when we talk about the importance of words. I do hope, though, that my explanation helps you understand why Universal Greek Pictures is so unique, and why our pictures of words and thoughts must be viewed with our inner eyes, the eyes of the mind and the heart.

"Let's give those eyes a brief workout now. Please look at the shopping mall once again. From a distance you wouldn't necessarily know that the mass of buildings you are looking at is a shopping mall. If I call it a university, does that change the picture of the buildings in your mind any?"

Everyone was staring at the mall in the distance. "Yes," said Marian, "that changes the picture."

"What do you see now?"

"The people there are no longer shoppers but students, and the inside is full of classrooms instead of shops. The whole atmosphere is different."

"What happens to the picture in your mind if I call all those buildings a hospital?"

"The people change again. Now they're patients and visitors and doctors. And inside the buildings there are long corridors and waiting areas and operating rooms."

Dean's eyes filled with wonder. "Isn't it amazing how one little word can manhandle such a mass of buildings. Give it a try again. Look at those buildings, and first think of them as a shopping mall, then think of them as a university, and finally think of them as a hospital. Observe how they change. First, mall; then university; then hospital."

"Even my sense of smell is affected," said Carol. "The word *hospital* puts the antiseptic right in my nose."

"You're experiencing the magical power of words. They are able to take meaning and actually project such a realistic picture of it on your mind that you sometimes think you're part of the picture itself. Words can make your mouth water or your stomach turn; they can make you laugh uncontrollably or cause your hair to stand on end with terror. Pictures of meaning are what language is all about, and that's what you must remember if you really want to understand the true nature of Universal Greek Pictures. It's a giant film studio in which the Greek words of the New Testament are used to help people who speak English reproduce the pictures of meaning that those words originally produced in the minds of the people who first read or heard them.

"The Greek words used in the New Testament once exploded with meaning in the minds of the original readers in the same way that words like *shopping mall, hospital,* and *university* explode with meaning when we hear them. One major task of Universal Greek Pictures is to help our customers discover the pictures of meaning hidden within those Greek words."

At this point, Buddy moved an easel with several large sheets of poster board to the center of the room. "Ladies and gentlemen," said Dean, "it's now time for us to begin our official tour through Universal Greek Pictures." Eddie placed a colorful placard on the easel.

McLain and Associates
presents

UNIVERSAL GREEK PICTURES

Now casting, filming, directing, and producing
the writings of the Greek New Testament

THE GREATEST SHOWS ON EARTH!

Universal Greek Pictures
is proud to make available to the general public
the original linguistic components
used by the men who produced and directed
the New Testament writings.

From the smallest letters
to the most epic literary masterworks.
Nothing is missing.

"Universal Greek Pictures," said Dean, "specializes in the kinds of pictures that are projected on the mind by New Testament Greek words. We have several departments in which our work is carried out." Buddy put another large sheet on the easel.

How to Read New Testament Greek

> **DEPARTMENTS**
>
> I. **Word-Pictures:** Combining letters into words.
>
> II. **Thought-Pictures:** Combining words into sentences.
>
> III. **Literature-Pictures:** Combining sentences into books, letters, reports, and other literary units.
>
> IV. **Translating**: Transferring word-pictures, thought-pictures, and literature-pictures from one language to another.

"The first three departments are dedicated to the three most significant kinds of pictures that the Greek language produces: *word-, thought-,* and *literature-pictures.* The fourth department specializes in transferring Greek language pictures into English language pictures. Today we'll be touring the first two departments: the department of Greek word-pictures, and the department of Greek thought-pictures. The other two departments will have to wait for another time."

Dean walked over to a box labeled γράμματα *(letters).* "You just happen to be sitting in the middle of the department of word-pictures where the most elementary task at Universal Greek Pictures is performed: Greek letters are used to create Greek words." He took three cards out of the box. On one a large red omega (ω) was visible, on the second a blue sigma (ς), and on the third a green phi (φ).

"Standing alone," he said, holding up the cards, "letters have no real power to make pictures. It's only when they are put together in those little combinations we call words that they spring to life. Take these three little letters, for instance. By themselves they have little meaning. With a little teamwork, however, they form the word φώς which means *light.*"

Dean rummaged around in the box searching for more letters. "Here's a rho (ρ)," he said, "and an omicron (ο) and an epsilon (ε). With the help of (φ) and (ω) they can form the word φορέω which means *carry.* The two words together—φώς and φορέω—are the basis of our English word *phosphorus* which literally means a substance that *carries light.*"

"Letters," he said, tossing the cards back into the box, "are the raw material for all the pictures we produce at Universal Greek Pictures. They are like the brushes and paint of an artist. Without them there would be no tools of the trade. Letters are the building blocks of language: the remarkable little symbols that make words possible. Once you've mastered their use, you can use them to form genuine Greek word-pictures. In fact, I just happen to have some beauties right here."

He picked up a small box beside the γράμματα box. "Everyone is invited to take a Greek word-picture home today." Dean held out the box to Eddie who reached in and pulled out the word τό ὄρος *(the mountain)*.

"Would you look at that. This young man just got himself the picture of an entire mountain." Dean went from person to person, letting each choose a word. "Don't lose these valuable word-pictures, ladies and gentlemen. Take them home and put them in a safe place. They are heirlooms of ancient Greece, chosen by Jesus and his disciples to communicate their incomparable message to the world. There are thousands of picture-producing words in this section of Universal Greek Pictures. From here the words are channeled into our next department where they learn to work together with other words to form sentences—the linguistic power packs that make the pictures of whole thoughts possible."

"Why is the picture of a word different from the picture of a thought?" asked Jim.

"A very good question, sir. Take the word *university*, for instance. Although it portrays a very sophisticated picture in our minds, it doesn't say anything. It doesn't ask a question or give an instruction or make a statement. If I were to walk up to you and say *university*, you'd think I was crazy. But if I tell you, *Universities educate qualified, high-school graduates*, you'd understand a statement of fact. Or if I ask you, *Are you going to register at the university this year?*, you know you're being asked a question. And if I tell you *Stay away from the university*, you know that I'm giving you a warning.

"In all of these examples, a *message* or a *complete thought* is portrayed on the screen of your mind. The word *university* is only part of the scenery. It has to work together with other words to form a sentence, because only sentences can portray the picture of a complete thought. That's why fitting words together into sentences is one of our major concerns here at Universal Greek Pictures.

"In order to help customers make whole scenes of thought out of word pictures, the department of thought-pictures provides customers with a complete selection of the three kinds of words that make thought-pictures possible. And you'll be happy to hear that each one of these three kinds of words comes with a complete set of---"

"Just a minute," Jim broke in. "You say there are only *three* kinds of words?"

"Yes, sir. Three kinds of words work together to make sentences. In fact, to my knowledge, there are only three kinds of words that have ever been discovered in any language."

"Only three kinds of words?" murmured Jim, a touch of disbelief in his voice. "I'd swear my English teacher came up with hundreds of different kinds, and she gave them all names I could never keep straight."

"I suspect she was emphasizing some of the finer points, sir," said Dean. "That's not hard to do when you're dealing with words. Each one tends to have its own little idiosyncrasies. In that sense, words are a lot like people. Sometimes it's hard to tie them down. I know a father, for example, who has fourteen children, and he never can seem to keep their names and birthdays straight. He'll tell you, however, that he has only two kinds of children: Some are boys and some are girls. We mean something similar when we say there are only three kinds of words. We mean there are only three general categories of words or only three major functions that words can perform in a thought."

"Major functions?"

"Let me explain it this way, sir. Do you happen to be a photographer?"

"Of sorts."

"Think about the last time you took a picture of your wife. What did you need to take the picture?"

"Well, I guess I needed a camera."

"And...?"

"And? I...uh...needed my wife."

"Right," said Dean. "To take a picture you need a camera and something or someone to take a picture of. Nothing complicated about that. The same thing is true of the picture of a thought. In order to get a picture of a thought you've got to have words that are being photographed and other words that do the photographing."

"You're going to have to run that by again," said Marian, "very slowly."

"Yes, ma'am," said Dean. "Customer service is uppermost in our thoughts. Take the thought, *Joe hit Bill*, for example. *Joe* and *Bill* are the words that are being photographed. They're the words that are playing the roles in the picture. *Hit* is the camera-word shooting the action. Watch what happens when we change the camera-word: *Joe **ignored** Bill*, *Joe **congratulated** Bill*, *Joe **helped** Bill*, *Joe **arrested** Bill*. Notice how the picture changes even though *Joe* and *Bill*, the words that are being photographed, stay the same. Isn't it amazing? It's just like having a slide projector in your head. Obviously, the camera-words are the big bosses in the world of thoughts."

"What about the third kind of word?" asked Liz. "You've used only two kinds in your examples."

"Thank you for reminding me. The third kind of word—the kind we like to call the *extra-information word*—is not always necessary to make a picture of a thought, but it's the kind of word that fills in the picture with all the color and flavor it often needs, to make it as precise as possible.

"Let's take our original thought, *Joe hit Bill*, and toss in a few extra-information words just to see what happens: **Big, mean, 300-pound Joe ferociously hit the unwary Bill with a baseball bat.** Do all those extra-info words spice up the original picture of the thought for anyone?"

"Too much, if you ask me," said Marian, turning up her nose. "If he'd pelted him with a pillow, it would've been a much nicer thought."

"Wonderful," said Dean. "You're getting the idea. With extra-information words you can take a thought and change it around just to your liking. You can use them to dress up the words that are having their picture taken or to adjust the angle of the camera-words; whatever you like. They're marvelous little things."

Dean began to look through the remaining sheets of poster board. "Let's take a moment to summarize what we've said about the pictures of thoughts." He found the one he was looking for, and placed it on the easel.

SENTENCES PORTRAY THE PICTURES OF COMPLETE THOUGHTS

Sentences consist of
SOMETHING-WORDS which are photographed,
CAMERA-WORDS which do the photographing,
and ***EXTRA-INFORMATION WORDS*** which are in
charge of all alterations and adjustments.

"You notice that here at Universal Greek Pictures we like to call the words that have their picture taken, *something-words*. That may not sound very elegant, but we use it because it's the one description that fits so well. *Something-words* are simply any kind of a word that can be considered to be *something*. They include people, places, things, concepts, names, characteristics, and anything real or imagined that has ever been labeled with a word.

"Just think for a moment how important something-words are. Any word that is in any way a something—even if it's nothing more than a figment of the imagination—belongs here. Without something-words, Greek wouldn't amount to much. It would be like a house without walls or a tree without a trunk or a banquet without food. Without something-words, the camera-words would have nothing to photograph. Greek would be like a black hole of nothingness.

"Universal Greek Pictures, however, is well-stocked with something-words." Dean pointed to a sign hanging over the fireplace.

How to Read New Testament Greek

> **If it's something,
> and it's got a name,
> you'll find it here.**

"Yes, sir," he said. "That's our promise to our customers. Anyone or anything that was ever part of a Greek thought-picture in the New Testament you can find right here."

While Dean was talking, Peggy and Linda had begun passing around several plates of homemade cookies. "Ahh," said Jim. "Cookie is one of my favorite something-words."

"I could also be interested in the something-word *coffee*," murmured John.

"Our cafeteria will soon be turning out all the coffee you can drink," said Dean, "along with a tasty lunch courtesy of Universal Greek Pictures."

"Long live UGP," said Jim, a plate of cookies in his lap.

"While you're enjoying your refreshments, ladies and gentlemen," said Dean, "please turn your attention to the boxes situated around you. Each one is a reservoir for certain kinds of something-words." He took a card out of a large blue box sitting next to Liz, labeled τά μεγάλα *(large objects)*. "Here's an example of a good, solid something word: ἡ πέτρα *(rock)*." Then out of a λαός *(people)* box, he produced the card ἡ μήτηρ *(mother)*. "Isn't that a beautiful word? What would we all do without it?"

Walking around the room, plucking words from various boxes, Dean expounded about the special qualities of each word. Out of a ζῷον *(animals)* box came ὁ ἄρκος *(bear)*, out of a χρόνος *(time)* box ἡ ἡμέρα *(day)*, out of a χαρακτήρ *(characteristic)* box ἡ αὐτάρκεια *(contentment)*, and out of a πραγματεῖαι *(activities)* box came ἡ πεῖρα *(experiment)*.

"Aren't these something-words wonderful? And isn't it amazing that they don't have to be things that are visible to the natural eye? In the world of thoughts even vivid pictures of the invisible are possible. Things like *love* and *kindness* and *dependability* take shape. And objects in the physical world take on new images. A man is more than a creature with arms and legs, for example. He becomes a *father* or an *artist* or a *gardener*, each word adding a deeper layer of meaning to the picture."

"What are those little letters in front of the words?" asked Marian.

"A very good observation, madam. Those tell us whether the words are masculine (ὁ), feminine (ἡ), or neuter (τό)—distinctions we don't make in English, but which are made in many other languages in the world."

"What good are they if we don't need them in English?"

"I wish I could say they serve an important function. In some ways the masculine, feminine, neuter division of something-words is helpful, particularly in determining how words in a thought are related to one another—we'll be talking about that later—but in other ways the division is neither necessary nor logical. After all, how can an *oven* (ὁ κλίβανος) be masculine or a *rock* (ἡ πέτρα) be feminine or a *child* (τό τέκνον) be neuter? We just have to remember that in every language there are ways of speaking and writing that are not necessarily logical. Why do we write English words like *thought, tough, bough, hiccough*, and *dough* with the letters *ough*? We don't even pronounce any two of them the same. There's nothing very logical about that, but we continue teaching it to our children anyway."

"You're right there," said Marian. "I always felt like a criminal making little children put in *gh's* all over the place for no reason at all."

"Do those little words indicate only masculine, feminine, and neuter," asked Carol, "or do they also have a meaning?"

"They also mean *the*," said Dean.

"You mean there are three *the's* in Greek?" said Marian.

"Why, madam, there are not only three the's in Greek, but I am delighted to be able to announce that there are, to my knowledge, seventeen different ways to say *the* in Greek."

"What!" said Marian, looking shocked. She shook her head, muttering something about needing two months just to learn how to say *the*.

"I can see you're overwhelmed by this piece of good news," said Dean. "All these years you've had to say the same old boring *the* in English and now Universal Greek Pictures offers you the chance of a lifetime: seventeen glorious ways to add life to the drab and dreary word *the*."

Marian gave him her best 'you've-gotta'-be-crazy' look.

"Since we're in the business of making pictures of Greek thoughts," said Dean, stepping back to the middle of the room, "we need plenty of words to do the acting for us, and that's the main job of something-words, the stars in the cinematic world of thoughts. They're the ones who stand in the spotlights and let camera-words take their pictures. Therefore, like all good actors and actresses, something-words have to be able to switch roles."

"What exactly do you mean by roles?" asked John.

"In our *Joe hit Harry* thought, *Joe* and *Harry* are the something-words doing the acting and each is playing a different role. Joe is the hitter and poor Harry is taking the beating. We know these are the roles they are playing because of certain clues provided in the English sentence. The main clue is the *placement* of the words. Joe is the hitter because he comes first, before the camera-word *hit*. To switch roles, all Joe and Harry have to do is change places in the sentence. In that case *Harry hits Joe*. Then it's Harry who does the hitting, and it's poor Joe who takes the punches. It's as simple as that, because in English roles are usually determined by their *location* in a sentence."

"In Greek, however, the location of a word in a sentence is less important. Greek something-words usually change their roles by changing their *endings*. In

How to Read New Testament Greek

English we automatically zero in on *where* each word is in the sentence. In Greek we have to learn to zero in on the *endings* of each word. To show you how something-words change roles by changing their endings, I've invited one of our star something-words to join us today to demonstrate how a real pro changes roles."

At Dean's bidding, Buddy and Eddie quickly moved a small table into the center of the room and placed a puppet theater on it that had a miniature stage and a red velvet curtain. When the theater was in position and Buddy had taken a seat behind it, Dean turned to the audience. "Ladies and gentlemen, it gives me great pleasure to present one of my favorite something-words."

The curtain parted, revealing the word ὁ ὀφθαλμός *(the eye)* written in bold black letters on a large card propped up in the middle of the stage.

```
PRESENTING
ὁ ὀφθαλμός
```

"'Οφθαλμός is particularly concerned about how people *see* things, and that's why he's agreed to join us today to demonstrate the four major roles that Greek something-words play in the picture of a thought." The curtain closed.

"First, ὀφθαλμός is going to give us a brief preview of all his possible roles." Dean looked over the top of the theater. "Are you ready back there?"

"Ready," came Buddy's muffled voice from behind the stage. The curtain parted, revealing a chart:

```
PRESENTING
ὁ ὀφθαλμός
in all his major roles
```

	Singular	Plural
Necessary role	ὀφθαλμός	ὀφθαλμοί
General supporting role	ὀφθαλμοῦ	ὀφθαλμῶν
Directing role	ὀφθαλμῳ	ὀφωαλμοῖς
Accomplishing role	ὀφθαλμόν	ὀφθαλμούς

"Please notice," said Dean, "that there are four possible roles: the *necessary* role, the *general supporting* role, the *directing* role, and the *accomplishing* role.

We will demonstrate in just a moment the meaning behind each role. For now, it's important to notice that ὀφθαλμός changes from role to role by changing his *endings*. And notice, too, that each role can be played in either singular or plural."

"'Οφθαλμός is now going to leave us for a moment to prepare to demonstrate each of the roles, beginning with the *necessary* role which in some ways is the most important of them all. It is the only role that is absolutely necessary in every picture of a complete thought. As with all the roles, it is recognizable by the ending of the word. In the case of ὀφθαλμός, the endings are -ος in singular and -οι in plural."

Buddy nodded to Dean when he was ready. "I now present ὀφθαλμός in the necessary role in Luke 2:30," said Dean. The curtain slid aside revealing the following sentence:

> εἶδον οἱ ὀφθαλμοί μου τὸ σωτήριόν σου·
> saw (the) eyes   my (the) salvation   his
>
> My *eyes* saw his salvation.

"Check that ending, ladies and gentlemen. Do you see that οι? Isn't it glorious. A necessary-role ending of superb quality. No question which word is in the necessary role in this thought. Let's give ὀφθαλμός a hand for this marvelous performance." Dean clapped his hands enthusiastically. Two or three joined in. The others couldn't quite bring themselves to applaud a word written on a piece of paper.

"Goodness," said Marian, "those words are certainly all mixed up. And why are there so many *the's* thrown in?"

"As I said, madam, word order is not so important in Greek. The endings are important. That's why we often have to shift the words around when we translate, as we did in this example."

"And what about the *the's?*"

"Ah, yes, the *the's*. Well, the ancient Greeks just liked to sprinkle a lot of *the's* into their language. Sometimes they have the same meaning as ours, and sometimes you just have to ignore them."

"I don't think I quite understand what the necessary role really is," said Carol. "Could you explain that a bit more?"

"Of course. Every picture of a message has to have at least one something-word in the necessary role, otherwise you just can't put a thought together that says anything. If you try to make a thought-picture without a something-word in the necessary role, it's like trying to take a photo in the dark. You just won't get a picture. Take the phrase ...*slammed on the brakes*, for example. There's no something-word in the necessary role and therefore the words do not convey a message. Can you imagine walking up to someone and saying, *Slammed on the brakes*? They'd think you'd gone wacko. If you let a something-word play the necessary role, however, a complete thought springs to life: ***The driver slammed on the brakes.*** Now the words convey a message. In English the something-word in the necessary role usually takes its place in front of the camera-word and gets things started. In Greek, however, it's the ending of the word that tells us which word belongs in that leading position in English.

"Now observe how ὀφθαλμός does a quick change and steps into another role—the *general supporting* role—in a scene from I Corinthians 15:52. In this role ὀφθαλμός steps into the background to help out another something-word. Watch how he does it." Dean removed the Luke passage and underneath it was the new verse:

πάντες δὲ ἀλλαγησόμεθα ἐν ἀτόμῳ ἐν ῥιπῇ
all   and   be changed   in moment   in twinkling

ὀφθαλμοῦ...
of-eye

...and we will all be changed,
in a moment, in the
twinkling *of an eye*...

"Do you see that οῦ ending? It indicates that ὀφθαλμός is now in a general supporting role, that it is now helping another something-word, ῥιπῇ *(twinkling)* in this case. It helps answer the question *what kind of twinkling?* The answer? The twinkling *of an eye,* of course.

"A something-word in the general supporting role is usually translated into English with an *of*-phrase or by using an *'s* on the end of the word. Thus, we have the *twinkling of an eye,* or an *eye's twinkling*. Other examples of this in English are: the barking *of a dog*, or a *dog's* barking, and the shirt *of a soldier*, or the *soldier's* shirt. In English the clues that identify the general supportive role are an *'s* or an *of* phrase directly following a something-word. In the case of a Greek word like ὀφθαλμοῦ, however, it's the -ου or -ῶν ending.

"Now let's ask ὀφθαλμός to do another quick change and demonstrate from Acts 28:27 the next role for us: the *directing role*. In this role a something-word teams up with a camera-word to produce some fancy filming." The curtain opened, revealing the next card:

> μήποτε   ἴδωσιν   τοῖς ὀφθαλμοῖς
> otherwise they-would-see   the with-eyes
>
> ...otherwise they would see
> with (their) eyes...

"Do you see that οἷς ending? It signals that ὀφθαλμοῖς is now giving the camera-word ἴδωσιν some extra directives. It helps answer the question *how will they see?* The answer? *With their eyes,* of course.

"In English we usually translate a Greek word playing this role with phrases beginning with *in, to, with, for,* or *by.* Other examples of this role in English are: *He hit the ball **with a bat**, He went there **by foot**, He rode **to the game**,* and *They worked **with tools**.* Notice that each time the question *how?* or *where?* is being answered. This is typical of the something-words playing the directive role. They like to tell the camera-word *how* or *where* to do what it's doing.

"And now the picture of a thought from John 9:14 will demonstrate the final role played by a something-word: the *accomplishing* role. In this role a something-word *completes* or *accomplishes* the action of the camera-word. Watch how ὀφθαλμός does it." Dean uncovered the final card:

> ανέῳξεν   αὐτοῦ   τοὺς   ὀφθαλμούς
> he-opened   his   the   eyes
>
> ...he opened *his* *eyes.*

"Do you see the -ούς ending? It indicates that ὀφθαλμούς is now playing the accomplishing role and is completing the action of the camera word ανέῳξεν *(he opened)*. It completes the action by answering the question: *What did he open?* The answer? *His eyes,* of course.

"In English we usually translate a Greek word playing this role by simply placing it after the camera-word. Other examples of this role in English are: *He opened the **door**,* and *He opened the **letter**.* It tells what the camera-word completes or accomplishes, and that's why we call it the accomplishing role.

How to Read New Testament Greek

"And now, ladies and gentlemen, ὀφθαλμός is returning to give us an overview of all his roles."

PRESENTING
ὁ ὀφθαλμός
in all his major roles

	Singular	Plural
Necessary role	ὀφθαλμός eye	ὀφθαλμοί eyes
General supporting role	ὀφθαλμοῦ eye's	ὀφθαλμῶν eyes'
Directing role	ὀφθαλμῷ with an eye	ὀφθαλμοῖς with eyes
Accomplishing role	ὀφθαλμόν eye	ὀφθαλμούς eyes

"A big thanks to ὀφθαλμός for this impressive demonstration of role playing. Now, let's do a quick review of all the roles. Something-words can play any of four different roles in a thought. The first is the *necessary role*. It always has to be there. *The man is sleeping.* Try to make a thought-picture without a something-word playing the necessary role and it's like taking a picture in the dark. You just won't get a clear picture. *...is sleeping,* for example, is not a complete thought.

"A something-word in the *general supporting role* adds information to another something word. *The man's hat is red.* The word *man's* is supporting the word *hat* by answering the questions *whose?* or *which?* or *what kind?*

"A something-word in the *directing role* gives instructions to a camera word by telling it *how* or *where* to do something. *She's digging **with her hands**.*

"And finally, a something-word in the *accomplishing role* completes the action of a camera word. *He saw the **truck**.* It answers the questions *what?* or *who?* he saw. It's important to remember, of course, that the *endings* of the words are the keys to recognizing which role a something-word is playing in a thought.

"As a grand finale, Universal Greek Pictures is now going to present a sentence in which all four roles are being played by something-words." The curtains parted once more.

> οἱ ἀπόστολοι   τοῖς   ἀνθρώποις
> The apostles   to-the   to-men
>
> τὸ εὐαγγέλιον   τοῦ   κηρίου   ἔλεγον.
> the good-message of-the   of-Lord   were-telling
>
> The apostles were telling the good news
> of the Lord to the men.

"The -οι ending tells us ἀπόστολοι is playing the necessary role and that it is plural. By adding it to the camera word ἔλεγον, we get the basic framework of the thought: *The apostles were telling...*

"The -οις ending tells us ἀνθρώποις is in the directing role and is therefore directing the camera-word as to how, where, to whom, or when it is to do what it does. In this case it is telling *the good news **to the men***.

"The -ον ending tells us that εὐαγγέλιον is playing the accomplishing role and is therefore telling us *what* the camera-word is accomplishing. It is *telling **the good news***.

"The -οῦ ending tells us that κηρίου is playing the general supporting role and is therefore adding extra information to another word, in this case εὐαγγέλιον, and should be translated with an *'s* or with an *of*: the **Lord's** good news or the good news **of the Lord**.

"Thus our final translation presents us with the complete thought picture in which all the something-words are playing their unique parts. *The **apostles*** (necessary role) *were telling the **good news*** (accomplishing role) *of the **Lord*** (general supporting role) *to the **men*** (directing role).

"Presto! Just imagine, ladies and gentlemen. You've not even been in the studios of Universal Greek Pictures for two whole hours and you've already translated your first Greek sentence. That's a sensation and each of you will receive a special gift copy of this sentence at the end of the tour, compliments of Universal Greek Pictures."

"I hope it'll fit into my car," drawled Jim.

"As you have seen, ladies and gentlemen, there are eight different endings for each something-word, because each of the four role endings has a singular form and a plural form. Do you know that the English word *eye* can only be written in four different ways: *eye, eye's, eyes'* and *eyes*. That means ὀφθαλμός, the Greek word for eye, gives you twice the selection of forms. That's what I call getting your money's worth! But when it comes to variety, you haven't seen anything yet. You may think that Greek something-words all change their endings in the *same* way, but let me hasten to tell you that most Greek something-words are more creative than that. Take a look at the versatile endings of these choice words." The curtain opened, revealing three different words.

ἡ οἰκία
house

	Singular	Plural
Necessary role	οἰκία	οἰκίαι
General supporting role	οἰκίας	οἰκιῶν
Directing role	οἰκίᾳ	οἰκίαις
Accomplishing role	οἰκίαν	οἰκίας

ὁ σωτήρ
savior

	Singular	Plural
Necessary role	σωτήρ	σωτῆρες
General supporting role	σωτῆρος	σωτήρων
Directing role	σωτῆρι	σωτῆρσιν
Accomplishing role	σωτῆρα	σωτῆρας

τὸ ἔργον
work

	Singular	Plural
Necessary role	ἔργον	ἔργα
General supporting role	ἔργου	ἔργων
Directing role	ἔργῳ	ἔργοις
Accomplishing role	ἔργον	ἔργα

"Tell me what you see."

"The pattern of endings seems to be different for each word," said Jim.

"Does every Greek word have a different set of endings?" asked Eddie, who was carefully examining each word.

"Unfortunately, no, Eddie," said Dean. "I reckon there are about twenty different possibilities, and each Greek something-word follows one of those patterns." Eddie breathed out a low whistle.

"I know that sounds a bit complicated," said Dean, "but you have to look at the positive side of it. It's a great opportunity to increase your powers of recognition."

Marian grumbled something about not even being able to remember her own telephone number.

"Why are there so many different endings?" asked Jim. "Couldn't they agree on a standard form?"

"Well," said Dean, "I suppose if languages were put together by planning committees, they'd probably come out more logical. Most languages, however, are the result of hundreds of years of development in which dozens of different linguistic traditions and dialects compete with one another in the shaping of the new language. It often happens that differences are left unresolved, and two or more linguistic forms simply learn to tolerate one another in the same language. The different endings in the Greek language are, to some degree, the result of linguistic tugs-of-war that were never resolved."

Buddy and Eddie carried the small table and puppet theater to the side of the room.

"Ladies and gentlemen," said Dean, "that concludes our tour of the something-words. We could spend days here, but we must move on. Let's take fifteen minutes for coffee and then continue our tour with a visit to the most dynamic department in Universal Greek Pictures: the department of camera-words. There you will see sights that defy the imagination: real functioning time machines, for example, that can whisk you into the past or future at the mention of a single syllable. So don't go away. We're just getting started."

Jim turned to John as they stood and stretched. "I'm not sure, but I think I almost understood most of that. How about you?"

"It's a whole new world for me," said John. I'm sure I'll need to hear it a few more times before it sinks in."

"Well," said Marian, overhearing them. "I'll need more than just a few more times." She patted her hairdo and took a deep breath.

Getting the Settings Right

Harmon, a tall glass of iced tea in his hand, joined Jim and John, who were looking at the decorations that had transformed the McLains' house into Universal Greek Pictures. "Did you expect anything like this, today?" he asked.

"What a surprise," said John. "I could never have imagined anything like this. I'm sure getting a different view of language from the one I had before."

Outside, Linda was talking to Carol on the patio. "I hope my husband hasn't been taking things too fast."

"It's been a lot and I'm probably not understanding everything, but I have to admit I'm actually enjoying it. Thanks for insisting that I come."

Liz had joined Eddie and Buddy who were seated together at a small breakfast table. "Who did all the work turning the house into a language studio?" she asked.

"It was a family project," said Buddy. "And Eddie came by last Sunday to help me make some of the props."

"What do you think of the presentation so far, Eddie?" Liz wondered how a teenage boy would react to a Saturday spent learning Greek.

"It's been great," he said. "I'll probably need ten years to learn Greek, but I guess it's worth it if it helps me understand the Bible better."

"What do your parents think about your learning Greek?"

"They don't understand why I want to, but they're not against it. They're just happy that I'm staying in school. All my brothers quit when they were about my age."

"And what do you think about school?" Her fascination for the small-framed boy was growing.

"It's okay, I suppose," he said. "But I didn't like it for a long time. Before I met Buddy, I just sat in class and waited for the bell to ring."

After coffee cups had been filled for the second or third time, Buddy announced that the tour was ready to resume and asked everyone to follow him to the next session. Leading the way into the living room, he called everyone's attention to a sign on the wall:

ATTENTION!
You are entering a zone of restricted noise.
Filming may be in progress.

Dean was in the living room standing in front of a makeshift curtain. He waited until they were all seated.

"In our introduction," he began, "you learned that at Universal Greek Pictures we are in the business of using words to produce pictures of meaning. To create these pictures, however, we need no film, cameras, or projectors. We have something that works much better and is not nearly as limited: *words*, plenty of flexible, reliable, learnable, creative, dynamic *words*.

"All by itself a word is capable of projecting a picture of incredible complexity. We saw a demonstration of that with words like *university* and *hospital*. But that is only the beginning of the power of words to produce pictures. We also saw that when words are combined with other words, they can actually portray a complete thought that makes a statement or asks a question or gives a command or warning. Does anyone remember how words manage such a phenomenal trick?"

"There are certain kinds of words—you called them something-words—that play the roles in each scene," said Liz. "Other kinds of words—the camera-words—take the pictures, and still other kinds of words add any extra information."

"Very good, young lady, and how far did we get in analyzing this fascinating process?"

"We saw how a Greek word can play four different roles by changing endings."

"Excellent," said Dean. "Does anyone remember the names we gave the four roles?"

"The first one was the necessary role," said John. "Then there was the director and the completer or something like that."

"Close, very close. Anyone remember those last three roles?"

"One was the supporting role or the general supporting role," said Jim.

"Directing and accomplishing were the other two," said Liz.

"Now we've got them all," said Dean. "*Necessary, general supporting, directing*, and *accomplishing*: the four roles that are played by something-words, the stars at Universal Greek Pictures.

"Remarkable though they are, something-words cannot hold a candle—or should I say spotlight?—to the incredible words you are about to meet now: the words that are among the most powerful and versatile linguistic photographic instruments the world has ever seen: the fabulous *Greek camera-word*.

"If we think of something-words as the skin, muscles, and bones of the pictures of thoughts, then camera-words form the nerve center that injects life into a thought and gives it movement, feeling, and expression. Imagine, if you can, a world with nothing but something-words. It would be as if everything and everyone had turned to stone with stillness and motionlessness draping every object like a shroud. The earth would be frozen in time like a huge, drab museum. But let a few camera-words snap their shutters, and the earth begins to spin, plants take root and grow, people sing and dance, and birds fly. Like the strings on a marionette, camera-words make something-words spring to life,

Getting the Settings Right

making it possible for us to exist in a moving and living world, projecting one creative scene after the other.

"I know you are all anxious to see one of these technological wonders in action, so without further delay, I now unveil Universal Greek Pictures' most prized possession: a genuine, functioning model of a camera-word." Dean drew open the curtain.

What appeared was a contraption worthy of Gyro Gearloose. Great quantities of glue and construction paper had transformed a large cardboard box into an oversized camera mounted on a tripod of old broomsticks. The word παιδεύω, written in large letters on a card, was sticking out of a slot on the top of the cardboard camera, and four rows of buttons were visible on the side. Beside the first row was the letter *P*, above the second, the letter *L*, above the third, the letter *A*, and above the fourth, the letter *N*.

PICTURE ⇒	Live Video	Recorded Video	Normal Photo	Future Photo	Current Photo	Previous Photo
	○	○	○	○	○	○

LIGHT	**A**CTION	**N**ECESSARY ROLE	
○ Bright	○ Active	○ I	○ we
○ Dim	○ Middle	○ you	○ all of you
○ Flashing	○ Passive	○ he, she, it	○ they

How to Read New Testament Greek

"Isn't it beautiful, ladies and gentlemen?" Dean slowly circled the camera, a look of pride and admiration in his eyes.

"As you can see," he said, pointing to the rows of buttons, "a rather involved series of adjustments has to be made before a picture can be taken. Learning the meaning of each of these buttons is the whole key to the skillful operation of a Greek camera-word. Before taking a picture of a thought, a camera-word must be loaded with four different kinds of information. That's why you see four rows of buttons on the camera. Each row corresponds to one of the four areas of input. And each button corresponds to the informational options in each area."

"Oh, oh," said Marian. "Now you're starting to hit us with computer talk. That's one generation gap I haven't managed to cross yet."

"Sorry, madam," said Dean. "I'll try to put it another way. Think of the recipes you use when you're cooking. For the sake of illustration let's say they all require one of four different kinds of ingredients: *liquids, grains, fruits or vegetables,* and *spices.* Under the *liquid* heading the options are *oil, water, milk, juice,* and *cream;* under *grains: whole-wheat flour, rolled oats* and *rye;* under *fruits and vegetables: bananas, potatoes, onions, oranges,* and *radishes;* and under *spices: salt, pepper, paprika, garlic,* and *cloves.* These roughly correspond to the four areas of information that our camera word needs. Are you following me?"

"Keep it up," said Marian. "You're talking my language now."

"Preparing a recipe, then, is just a matter of choosing the necessary options—in the right amounts, of course—from each of the four areas of ingredients. It works the same way when it comes to putting together a 'recipe' for the picture of a thought. Certain ingredients simply have to be in the camera-word, or it won't turn out right."

"Let me see if I've got this right," said Marian. "We only have to learn four headings and a handful of options under each one of them. Is that correct?"

"Well...uh...that will certainly be a good beginning."

"Aha, there must be a catch somewhere. It's not going to be that easy."

"No, not quite that easy. But, madam, is that all you have to know about cooking to be a good cook? Just the names of a few ingredients?"

"No, actually not. You've got to know more than that."

"What, for example?"

"Hmmm, let me see now...there's the whole matter of measuring and temperatures and baking times, and---"

"See," said Dean. "It's not any different when it comes to being a skillful user of Greek camera-words. If cooking can get rather involved—and I assume you're telling me it can—then it should be no surprise that it requires a certain level of skill and knowledge to understand the works of a precision instrument like a Greek camera-word. To help us better understand how a Greek camera-word functions, I've invited παιδεύω, one of the most experienced and communicative camera-words at Universal Greek Pictures, to join us today.

Getting the Settings Right

"παιδεύω has many meanings: *to educate, to teach, to train, to discipline, to bring up children, to instruct, to correct, to guide;* all of them are related in one way or another to the task of helping someone to learn. That's why I asked παιδεύω to help us today.

"When παιδεύω heard he would be in charge of the presentation, he began to work overtime preparing a complete overview of all the different kinds of pictures he is capable of producing, and I can tell you it was quite a workout. He pushed every combination of buttons possible and had the resulting thought pictures recorded on an ingenious chart that I now have the pleasure of presenting to you. So, without further delay, on behalf of παιδεύω and Universal Greek Pictures, I now present to you the breath-taking panorama of a full-fledged Greek camera-word in action."

To Dean's right stood a tall book case. On its upper edge a six-foot wide roll of paper had been attached in venetian blind style. Dean reached up and untied a ribbon holding the roll together. The paper neatly unraveled to reveal a chart closely resembling the side of the camera with the buttons.

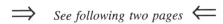

"Goodness," said Marian. "Do you mean to tell me that all those words are actually only *one* word?"

"Yes, madam, isn't it marvelous! You have one of the wonders of the linguistic world in front of your eyes. Just look at all those ingenious endings."

"There seem to be a lot more changes than just the endings," John said, gazing intently at the chart.

"Yes indeed." said Dean. "An experienced camera-word like παιδεύω has no trouble making changes at both ends. Why, we even have some camera-words that change in the middle."

"Oh, my stars," said Marian.

"Do all the Greek camera-words change in the same way?" asked John.

"Greek camera-words just happen to be every bit as resourceful as their counterparts over in the department of something-words. Some of them take great pleasure in developing their own way of doing things. Although the forms of παιδεύω are representative of many Greek camera-words, there are others that follow different kinds of patterns."

"I could have guessed as much," said Marian.

"Madam," said Dean, "I can see you are once again amazed and overwhelmed by the astounding intricacies of the Greek language."

"I'm what?"

P_{ICTURE} ⇒ ⇒ ⇒			VIDEO	
L_{IGHT}	A_{CTION}	N_{EC.ROLE}	Live	Recorded
B R I G H T	Active	I — we you — all of you he,she,it — they	παιδεύ-ω -ω -ομεν -εις -ετε -ει -ουσιν	ἐπαίδευ-ον -ον -ομεν -ες -ετε -εν -ον
	Middle	I — we you — all of you he,she,it — they	παιδεύ-ομαι -ομαι -όμεθα -ῃ -εσθε -εται -ονται	ἐπαιδευ-όμην -όμην -όμεθα -ου -εσθε -ετο -οντο
	Passive	I — we you — all of you he,she,it — they	παιδεύ-ομαι -ομαι -όμεθα -ῃ -εσθε -εται -ονται	ἐπαιδευ-όμην -όμην -όμεθα -ου -εσθε -ετο -οντο
D I M	Active	I — we you — all of you he,she,it — they	παιδεύ-ω -ω -ωμεν -ῃς -ητε -ῃ -ωσιν	
	Middle	I — we you — all of you he,she,it — they	παιδεύ-ωμαι -ωμαι -ώμεθα -ῃ -ησθε -ηται -ωνται	
	Passive	I — we you — all of you he,she,it — they	παιδεύ-ωμαι -ωμαι -ώμεθα -ῃ -ησθε -ηται -ωνται	
F L A S H I N G	Active	you — all of you he,she — they	παίδευ-ε -ε -ετε -έτω -έτωσαν	
	Middle	you — all of you he,she — they	παιδεύ-ου -ου -εσθε -έσθω -έσθωσαν	
	Passive	you — all of you he,she — they	παιδεύ-ου -ου -εσθε -έσθω -έσθωσαν	

Getting the Settings Right

PHOTOGRAPHS				
Normal 1	Normal 2	Future	Current	Previous
ἐπαίδευ-σα -σα -σαμεν -σας -σατε -σεν -σαν	ἔλαβ-ον -ον -ομεν -ες -ετε -εν -ον	παιδεύ-σω -σω -σομεν -σεις -σετε -σει -σουσιν	πεπαίδευ-κα -κα -καμεν -κας -κατε -κεν -κασιν	ἐπεπαιδεί-κειν -κειν -κειμεν -κεις -κειτε -κει κεισαν
παιδεύ-ομαι -ομαι -όμεθα -ῃ -εσθε -εται -ονται	ἐλαβ-όμην -όμην -όμεθα -ου -εσθε -ετο -οντο	παιδεύ-σομαι -σομαι-σόμεθα -σῃ -σεσθε -σεται -σονται	πεπαίδευ-μαι -μαι -μεθα -σαι -σθε -ται -νται	ἐπεπαιδεύ-μην -μην -μεθα -σο -σθε -το -ντο
ἐπαιδεύ-θην -θην -θημεν -θης -θητε -θη -θησαν		παιδευθή-σομαι -σομαι-σόμεθα -σῃ -σεσθε -σεται -σονται	πεπαίδευ-μαι -μαι -μεθα -σαι -σθε -ται -νται	ἐπεπαιδεύ-μην -μην -μεθα -σο -σθε -το -ντο
παιδεύ-σω -σω -σωμεν -σῃς -σητε -σῃ -σωσιν	λάβ-ω -ω -ωμεν -ῃς -ητε -ῃ -ωσιν		πεπαιδεύ-κω -κω -κωμεν -κῃς -κητε -κῃ -κωσιν	
παιδεύ-σωμαι -σωμαι -σώμεθα -σῃ -σησθε -σηται -σωνται	λάβ-ωμαι -ωμαι -ώμεθα -ῃ -ησθε -ηται -ωνται			
παιδευ-θῶ -θῶ -θῶμεν -θῇς -θῆτε -θῇ -θῶσιν				
παίδευ-σον -σον -σατε -σάτω -σάτωσαν	λάβ-ε -ε -ετε -έτω -έτωσαν			
παίδευ-σαι -σαι -σασθε -σάσθω-σάσθωσαν	λαβ-οῦ -οῦ -εσθε -έσθω-έσθωσαν			
παιδεύ-θητι -θητι -θητε -θήτω -θήτωσαν				

75

How to Read New Testament Greek

"You will be even more impressed, however, as we learn how παιδεύω performs his amazing photographic feats. As you can see, the buttons are conveniently ordered according to the letters *PLAN*, reminding us that every Greek camera-word produces thought-pictures according to a four-fold *PLAN*. Each one of the letters *P, L, A,* and *N* represents one of the four settings. In order to understand a Greek camera-word and see the picture it wants us to see, we need to make sure we know each of these four settings well.

"The first is *P* and it stands for *Picture*. Along the top row you can see that παιδεύω can take six different kinds of pictures. Two of them are videos and four are various kinds of photos. Can someone tell me the difference between videos and photos?"

"I'd say that videos are actually motion pictures that record the movement of objects," said John, "whereas photos are still-shots. They're pictures of...a...well, part of a---"

"I know," said Dean. "It's hard to put into words. Maybe we could say that a video captures a certain scene over a period of time, and a snapshot captures only a certain moment or a certain aspect of a scene."

"Under the video heading are two options: *Live* and *Recorded*. What is the major difference between live and recorded videos?"

"Live video means what you are viewing is taking place right now in the present," said Liz, "and a recorded video has to be of something that has already taken place. It has to be in the past."

"Right you are, young lady," said Dean. "First of all, let's watch παιδεύω in a *live video* picture." He pressed several buttons and extracted a card from a slot in the front of the camera.

Live Video

"Do you see that picture moving in the here and now?" He pushed some more buttons. "And now here's a *recorded video*."

Recorded Video

Getting the Settings Right

"Notice how you still have movement, but that it's moved into the past? Switch back and forth between the two a couple times and see how the picture changes: παιδεύω *(I am training)*, ἐπαίδευον *(I was training)*, παιδεύω *(I am training)*, ἐπαίδευον *(I was training)*. Notice how the Greek camera-word changes to produce the change in the picture. In English we use helping words like *is* and *was* to change the settings on our camera-words. In Greek, however, the camera-word changes either its *beginning* or its *ending* or sometimes even its *middle* to change pictures."

"Its middle?" said Marian. "But that would make it a totally different word."

"Greek camera words are so flexible that sometimes they do seem to contort themselves into completely new shapes.

"Now, take a look at the first of the photographs." Dean pulled another card out of the camera.

Normal Photo

"This is a ***normal photo***. You notice there is no movement. Now take a look at the ***future photo*** which is a photo of the future."

Future Photo

"Incredible, isn't it? You just add that little σ to the -ω ending and it whisks you right into the future. The third kind of photo is almost as amazing.

Current Photo

77

How to Read New Testament Greek

"This photo, the *current photo,* is an ingenious combination of both the past and the present. That's why we call it the *current* photo. Although it's a picture of something taken in the past, it's still an up-to-date picture of what or whom was being photographed. It's actually two English thoughts in one."

"Maybe that's why it looks like they tried to start the word twice," said Eddie. "because it's actually two words in one."

"Hey, you may be right, young man. I never thought of that." Dean scribbled something in a notebook. "I'll pass that observation on to our office of research and development so they can build it into our instructional audio-visuals. They're always looking for good ideas to help people remember things." Dean then produced another card from the camera.

> ἐπεπαιδεύκειν
> I had trained

Previous Photo

"We call the final kind of photograph the *previous photo*, because it's a photo taken previously to another photo. Do you see how the *had* accomplishes that task? Now let your eyes move back and forth from one snapshot to the other and see how the picture changes: ἐπαίδευσα *(I trained),* παιδεύσω *(I will train),* πεπαίδευκα *(I have trained* or *I am trained),* ἐπεπαιδεύκειν *(I had trained).* Now go back to the chart and try going back and forth between the *videos* and the *photos* and observe what happens to the pictures." Dean ran his finger along the top line of the chart.

"Are these the only kinds of pictures that can be taken?" asked Harmon.

"These are the six major kinds," said Dean. "But when you get to know Greek camera-words better—and I hope you will—you will discover they are capable of making some very interesting and flexible adjustments. Now let's try out the next row of buttons and find out what happens. *L* stands for light. As you know, all cameras need a certain amount of light to function well. The first pictures we looked at were all taken in *bright light* which, in the world of thought-pictures, signals *reality* or *matter-of-factness*.

"The picture of a thought taken in *dim light*, however, takes a step back from reality to the place where everything still hangs in the balance. It portrays that which *should* or *shouldn't* be; that which is *contemplated* or *sought after*; that which is *potential* or *probable*—everything that's not yet entered the light of reality. Therefore, it can have several English translations." Dean pulled a card from the slot.

> παιδεύῃς
> (so) you'd be training

Video Live in Dim Light

Getting the Settings Right

"The word *so* is used in the English translation to show you that camera words in the *dim light* are often used following words like *if, don't, won't, so that, in order to,* and *should.* A normal photo in dim light looks like this:

παιδεύσῃς
(so) you'd train

Normal Photo in Dim Light

"It's pretty obvious that dim light puts us into a hypothetical world where there is no past or present. The picture that is hoped or wished or planned, however, has the characteristics of either a video or a photo, depending on the choice of picture."

Dean punched more buttons and extracted another card. "The excitement level starts to rise when we push the button for a *flashing light*.

παίδευε
train (be training)

Video Live in Flashing Light

"The *flashing light* says it's time to move from theory to practice; it signals that you've entered the world of commands. When παιδεύω takes a picture with a *flashing light*, he puts on a uniform and starts giving orders. The command in *live video* assumes a continuous action. It's similar to when the coach says 'keep on moving'. Now, let's look at a *normal photo* taken in flashing light:

παίδευσον
start training

Normal Photo in Flashing Light

"The command issued as a *normal photo* is very similar, but is usually used in situations where a one-time action is commanded, or where only part of a process is meant. Take a moment, now, to compare all the pictures we've examined. Let your eyes first go along the top row of the chart and observe how the picture changes as you move across. (Note: To do this exercise, refer to the *Camera-word* section of

How to Read New Testament Greek

the UNIVERSAL GREEK PICTURES WORD CHART) Then move down the columns and review once more what happens when we change the light from *bright* to *dim* and then to *flashing*." All eyes were focused on the chart.

"This may be a dumb question," said John, "but does English work in the same way? I mean, I've never thought of language in this way, making pictures and all that."

"In English we also have camera-words, sir. They just produce their pictures with a different system. They need plenty of attachments or *helping words* as they are often called—all those *will's* and *would's* and *am's* and *have's* and *been's*. The list seems to go on and on. Greek camera-words have all the attachments built-in, so to speak. That's one of the major differences between Greek and English.

"I see that παιδεύω is now ready to demonstrate the two remaining built-in attachments that complete the **PLAN** of a Greek camera-word. *A* stands for *action* and *N* stands for the *necessary role*, and these two functions of a camera-word are closely related. To understand how these settings work, it will help if you remember our discussion about the four roles played by something-words. We learned that there was one role that always had to be in the picture of a thought. We called it the *necessary role*. In the thought *I am training the children, I* is the something-word in the necessary role. *I* has to be in the thought or it wouldn't be a complete thought that conveys a message. *...am training the children* simply portrays no clear message.

"In an English thought, the something-words in the necessary role almost always have to be specifically spelled out. In a Greek thought, however, the something-word in the necessary role is *included* in the meaning of the camera-word and doesn't always have to be specified."

"I think I hear you," said Jim, "but I'm going to need that one more time."

Dean pointed to the first box of information under the letter *N*.

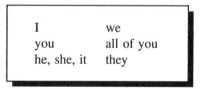

"One of these little something-words is always tucked away in every Greek camera-word. Can you guess how we know which one?"

"Undoubtedly by the ending," said Jim.

"Absolutely right. And you can see that our chart has included all the endings. Using them is easy. All you have to do is replace one ending with another. Let's try each ending in the first box under *Live Video* and see what happens.

Getting the Settings Right

παιδεύω	I am training
παιδεύεις	You are training
παιδεύει	He is training She is training It is training
παιδεύομεν	We are training
παιδεύετε	All of you are training
παιδεύουσιν	They are training

"Do you see how each new ending puts a new something-word in the necessary role?"

"Aren't there any words that mean *I* or *you* or *he* in Greek?" asked John.

"Yes, there are, but they are usually only used for emphasis or clarity. It's when they're not there, however, that you may get confused and find yourself looking for a mysteriously missing word. All you have to remember is that every Greek camera-word has a something-word in the necessary role packed inside it. That's why one of your first tasks in understanding a Greek thought is to examine the ending of each camera-word and figure out if it means *I, you, he, she, it, we, all of you,* or *they*."

"And what's the *A* button for?" asked Jim.

"Ah, yes," said Dean. "We certainly don't want to forget part of the PLAN. *A* stands for ***Action*** and the options under it are a set of directions that determine the action of the something-word in the necessary role. There are three possibilities: *active, passive,* and *middle*."

"Let's first look at the ***active*** setting." Dean selected the *active* button and took a card out of the slot on the top of the camera.

παιδεύω
I am training

"*I* is *active*, *I* is performing the task of the camera-word. Watch what happens, however, when we switch to *passive*.

> παιδεύομαι
> I am being trained

"Now *I* is the one being trained. The action of the camera-word is happening to the word in the necessary role. *I* is passively involved, and that's why we call it passive. Now take a look at the *middle* setting.

> παιδεύομαι
> I am training myself

I is both performing and receiving the action of the camera-word. Therefore *I* is *both* actively and passively involved in the action of the camera-word."

"Just a minute," said Marian. "The ending didn't change. In fact, nothing changed. Only the meaning."

"That does happen sometimes, madam. This is just one case in which the middle and passive forms are the same. Not all the forms in Greek are necessarily different. There are a few exceptions."

"Well, thank heavens for that, but how do you know which is which?"

"The same way you know which meaning is meant when you confront a word like *trunk* in English. Just put it in a sentence and the context tells you if it's a *tree trunk*, a *car trunk*, or a *trunk in the attic*.

"Now that you understand how all the buttons work, you can look at any of the examples of παιδεύω on the chart and see the wide range of pictures that it can produce. You will soon discover for yourself the clever and sometimes subtle ways in which παιδεύω changes his form to make a completely new picture. The word *PLAN* helps you remember that there are four important pieces of information in every camera-word. When translating a Greek sentence, the first thing you need to do is locate the main camera-word and make sure you know all four parts of the *PLAN*.

"The letters *P, L, A,* and *N* help you remember what those four parts are: *PICTURE* with *live video, recorded video, normal photo, future photo, current photo,* and *previous photo*; *LIGHT* with *bright, dim,* and *flashing*; *ACTION* with *active, passive,* and *middle*; and *NECESSARY ROLE* with *I, we, you, all of you, he, she, it,* and *they*. Camera-words are the chief directors in the studios of

Getting the Settings Right

Universal Greek Pictures. If you know their *PLAN*, then you're on your way to understanding the thoughts they portray.

"Ladies and gentlemen, that completes our demonstration of the camera-words at Universal Greek Pictures. The final part of our tour will begin this afternoon. I invite you to join me now in the cafeteria for lunch, compliments of Universal Greek Pictures." Enthusiastic applause greeted Dean's invitation.

Buddy and Eddie led the way into the kitchen where Linda and Peggy had been busy arranging platters with sandwiches, plates of nachos, and salad bowls. "Fill your plates and find a place to sit," said Dean. "Our efficient waitresses will soon be standing by to fill any wish you might have."

"That last presentation was very interesting," said John, sitting down next to Dean at the oak table in the corner of the kitchen. "I'd never realized that words do so many things. The explanation that we add attachments to camera-words in English, whereas Greek has everything built-in was particularly interesting. Does that mean the end result is the same then?"

"What do you mean?" asked Dean.

"Does it mean that both languages can express exactly the same meanings but just do it in different ways?"

"That's a tough question to answer."

"Why is that?"

"The problem stems partially from the word *meaning* itself. It's doubtful that even people who speak the same language understand the same words in the same way."

"Really?"

"Let me try to illustrate what I mean. Take a simple word like *moon*, for example. A child undoubtedly understands the word in a much more superficial way than, say, a scientist who understands the intricate movements of the solar system and automatically integrates the moon into complicated contexts that are fully unknown to a child. In certain contexts, however, a child and a scientist may understand very nearly the same thing when they hear the word *moon*.

"The idea of meaning simply has many different aspects to it. We could put it this way: Words have levels of meaning or *domains* of meaning, as linguists like to say."

"It sounds like you're saying that meaning is a pretty relative concept," said Jim, who had been listening from the other side of the table.

"If *relative* is supposed to mean wishy-washy or lacking any standards of measurement, then it is certainly *not* that. All languages operate according to very detailed laws to which the whole idea of meaning is bound. But on the other hand, words and the thoughts expressed by them cannot be neatly tied down like a mathematical equation. Words and the meanings they express are as multifaceted and dynamic as the people who utter them.

"It's important for us to realize that learning the meaning of a new word in a language is only partially a matter of learning a definition for that word. It is also

83

a matter of getting to know that word in a variety of contexts, and it's a matter of gaining some experience with the word, of living with it for a while and learning its special personality.

"The word *moon*, to go back to that example, is an old friend for most of us, and for that reason it can convey many intricate meanings. For example, in describing the relationship I have with my wife, I once told a friend that *she's the sun in our marriage, and I'm the moon*."

"You should have been a song writer," said Jim.

"It was a bit mushy, all right, but the statement delivers a lot of meaning. First of all the use of the word moon injects a romantic element into the thought, and secondly, it projects a picture of give-and-take. Both of these meanings, however, can only be perceived by someone who has had some experience with the word *moon*. The romantic notion of the moon is imbedded in English music and literature, and the give-and-take motif is based on the general knowledge that the moon is merely a reflector of light that actually comes from the sun. My poetic statement wouldn't have much meaning for someone who is not acquainted with these literary and scientific aspects of the moon."

"In other words," said John, "to really understand the Greek words, we need to do more than just find an English word to replace them."

"Exactly," said Dean. "We need to get away from the idea of 'learning vocabulary'. It's better to think of meeting words and getting to know them. Each word has its own depth and its own layers of meaning. We need to sink our teeth into them to get all the flavors."

"Speaking of sinking teeth into things," said Jim, giving Buddy a nudge with his arm. "I think we need another plate of sandwiches. Eddie and Buddy totally decimated the last one."

"Peggy!" Buddy hollered. "Form a sandwich brigade fast. We're about to go under."

"By the way," said Jim, "are we on a tight schedule today, or do we have some time to blow?"

"No pressure," replied Dean. "If you feel like relaxing or going for a walk, it's fine with me. I'd rather have the customers wide awake than dozing while I'm presenting the products."

"You've still got those horseshoe pits along your back fence, don't you? Anyone for playing a game?"

"Now you're talking," said John. "What do you say, Dean? Jim and I will take on Harmon and you."

"And the winners have to play Eddie and me," said Buddy.

"Fine with me," said Dean. "Let the tournament of the century commence."

"But not until we've finished off a few more sandwiches," said Jim."

Adding the Finishing Touches

While the men were playing horseshoes, the women went for a short walk in the intense afternoon heat. When they returned, everyone retreated to the air-conditioned comfort of Universal Greek Pictures. Armed with glasses of iced tea, they gathered in the living room for the remainder of the tour.

Dean began by unfurling a sign above the picture window:

> **WARDROBE   SCENERY   ALTERATIONS**

Below the window were three large baskets, each covered with a white cloth.

"I would now like to welcome you," said Dean, "to the most colorful and many-faceted section of Universal Greek Pictures. We call the hardworking words in this department ***extra-information words***. They are responsible for the spice and the variety of the Greek language. When our something-words need sprucing up, or when our camera-words need to sharpen their focus, this is where we send them.

"Without the kind of words found in this department, our pictures would be intolerably boring and lackluster. Just think, there would be no such things as *green* ties, *striped* shirts, *tweed* skirts, or *fuzzy* boots. Everyone in our pictures would have to be dressed alike. And because it would be impossible to run *fast* or to shop *leisurely* or to page *slowly* through a magazine, all movements would be dreadfully monotonous. Without these words we couldn't take a photo of anyone talking *with a friend* or walking *through a field of corn* or standing *on a mountain* or swimming *in a lake*. Life without the words in this department would be lonely and limited."

Dean removed the cloths covering the baskets. "We like to keep our extra-information words clean and fresh. You never know when you might need one at a moment's notice to add that something extra to the picture of a newly constructed thought."

The first basket was labeled *ADD-ON WORDS*, the second *ADD-ON PHRASES*, and the third *ADD-ON THOUGHTS*. "As you can see, there are three ways in which our extra-information words perform their duties: first, as *add-on words* that are attached individually to other words; secondly, as *add-on phrases* that also add their information to other words; and finally, as *add-on thoughts* that are not only grafted on to other words, but also onto whole thoughts."

Puzzled looks showed up around the room.

"We've arranged for a series of demonstrations," said Dean, "that will hopefully make all of this clear for you. I've asked the something-word ὁ ἄνθρωπος *(man)* to be in charge of these demonstrations today. He'll be showing us how our extra-information words can really change a man.

"By way of introduction and for the sake of a brief review, ἄνθρωπος will

Adding the Finishing Touches

begin by showing us how he plays the four roles. His performance should remind you of ὀφθαλμός, who plays the four roles with the same endings." Dean produced a large flip-chart from behind the bookshelves and turned to the first page.

PRESENTING
ὁ ἄνθρωπος
in all his major roles

	Singular	Plural
Necessary role	ἄνθρωπος	ἄνθρωποι
General supporting role	ἀνθρώπου	ἀνθρώπων
Directing role	ἀνθρώπῳ	ἀνθρώποις
Accomplishing role	ἄνθρωπον	ἀνθρώπους

"Take a good look at the endings just to orient yourself. Now, we'll let ἄνθρωπος team up with παιδεύω and τέκνον *(child)* and a few other words to form four thoughts in which ἄνθρωπος plays all four roles." Dean turned the page.

Necessary role:
ὁ ἄνθρωπος παιδεύει τὰ τέκνα.
The **man** is training the children.
General supporting role:
ὁ φίλος τοῦ ανθρωποῦ παιδεύει τὰ τέκνα.
The **man's** friend is training the children.
Directing role:
ὁ φίλος ἄγει τὰ τέκνα τῷ ἀνθρώπῳ.
The friend is leading the children **to the man**.
Accomplishing role:
ὁ φίλος παιδεύει τὸν ἄνθρωπον.
The friend is training the **man**.

How to Read New Testament Greek

"Although ἄνθρωπος has done a good job playing his roles in these thoughts, you notice that we really don't know too much about him: We don't know anything about his character or his looks or his age or any of the kinds of information that extra-information words specialize in providing."

Dean rummaged around in the basket of *add-on words*. "I know there must be a good add-on word here somewhere. Ah, here we are. Just the one I was looking for." He held up a card.

καλός, ή, όν
good, useful

"I told you καλός was a *good* add-on word. Now watch what happens when καλός adds his information to ἄνθρωπος." He turned to a new page.

ὁ καλὸς ἄνθρωπος, *the good man*
Playing all his major roles

Necessary role:
ὁ καλὸς ἄνθρωπος παιδεύει τὰ τέκνα.
The **good man** is training the children.
General supporting role:
ὁ φίλος τοῦ καλοῦ ἀνθρώπου παιδεύει τὰ τέκνα.
The **good man's** friend is training the children.
Directing role:
ὁ φίλος ἄγει τὰ τέκνα τῷ καλῷ ἀνθρώπῳ.
The friend is leading the children **to the good man**.
Accomplishing role:
ὁ φίλος παιδεύει τὸν καλὸν ἄνθρωπον.
The friend is training the **good man**.

"Can someone tell me what's taking place here?"

"When the ending of ἄνθρωπος changes," said John, "the ending of καλός also changes."

Adding the Finishing Touches

"Exactly," said Dean, "and if you look closely you'll see that καλός changes its endings in such a way that they *correspond* to the endings of ἄνθρωπος. Add-on words are the real quick change artists in Universal Greek Pictures' cast of words. Regardless of what role the something-word is playing, an add-on word has a wardrobe to match."

Dean turned to the chart. "Here's a complete portrait of καλός with all of its endings."

ROLE	TYPE	singular	plural
Necessary General supporting Directing Accomplishing	ὁ- words	καλός καλοῦ καλῷ καλόν	καλοί καλῶν καλοῖς καλούς
Necessary General supporting Directing Accomplishing	ἡ- words	καλή καλῆς καλῇ καλήν	καλαί καλῶν καλαῖς καλάς
Necessary General supporting Directing Accomplishing	τό- words	καλόν καλοῦ καλῷ καλόν	καλά καλῶν καλοῖς καλά

"So many endings!" said Marian.

"Yes, madam, you certainly get your money's worth with a good add-on word."

"Why are there so many?"

"If you remember," said Dean, "there are three kinds of something-words: ὁ-words, ἡ-words, and τό-words. They all have different endings, and καλός has to be able to match all of them. For an ὁ-word, καλός is an ὁ-word; for an ἡ-word, καλός becomes καλή, an ἡ-word; for a τό-word, καλός becomes καλόν, a τό-word."

"The first card of καλός I showed you had καλός written in the way you find it in a dictionary. If you remember, it indicated the three different ways in which κάλος changes its endings." Dean held up the card once again.

καλός, ή, όν
good, useful

"The endings ός, ή, and όν simply indicate the pattern of endings used by καλός. The ός is the ὁ-word ending (or the *masculine* ending); the ή is the ἡ-word ending (or the *feminine* ending); and the όν is the τό-word ending (or the *neuter* ending)."

"Why is that necessary to know?" asked Jim. "They all change the same way, don't they?"

"By no means!" said Dean. "Our add-on words would never dream of being so dry and dull. Some of them have developed their own particular way of doing things. That's why the dictionary gives you the extra clues. There are other add-on words that change their endings differently than καλός." Marian looked at Jim and rolled her eyes.

"All this is to show you how καλός adds his information to a something-word. What do you suppose happens when he adds his information to a camera-word?"

"Oh, no," said Marian. "More endings!"

"Not ending*s*, madam," said Dean, "but *ending*. That's right, only one more ending."

"You mean there's no chart with rows and rows of forms?"

"Nope, only one more ending, and that does the job." Dean found a place in the flip-chart. "Look at how καλός adds information to παιδεύω."

> παιδεύει καλῶς τὰ τέκνα.
> He is training the children **well**.

"That little ending -ως tells us that καλός is now adding information to the camera-word in the thought."

"And that's really the only ending? Even when παιδεύω changes endings?"

"Yes, madam, παιδεύω can change as much as it wants to. Καλῶς stays the same."

Dean then moved the basket of *add-on phrases* to the center of the room. "Sometimes an add-on word just isn't big enough to fill the information needs of a something-word or a camera-word. That's when *add-on phrases* come in handy. They are so flexible that they can add their information to either a something-word or a camera-word. They're not particular at all."

Dean pulled a handful of cards out of the basket and shuffled through them. "The add-on phrases are always introduced by add-a-phrase words like διά which means *through*, μετά which means *with*, ἀπό which means *from*, ἐν which means *in*, or εἰς which means *into*." He tossed the cards back into the basket.

"There's so many of them that you can always find one to add that something extra you need." He turned to a new page. "Here's a few examples of how they work."

Adding the Finishing Touches

> Ὁ ἄνθρωπος ἐν τοῦ οἴκου παιδεύει τὰ τέκνα.
> The man **in the house** is training the children.
>
> Τὰ τέκνα παιδεύονται μετὰ καλῶν λόγων.
> The children are being trained **with good words**.

"Please notice that the first phrase ἐν τοῦ οἴκου adds information to the something-word ἄνθρωπος, and the second phrase μετὰ καλῶν λόγων adds information to the camera-word παιδεύονται."

"How can you tell if a phrase is adding information to a something-word or to a camera-word?" asked Jim.

"You can probably answer that question yourself, because English phrases just happen to work much the same way as Greek phrases. If I were to say, for example, *The man **with a limp** walked by the house*, then you know automatically that the phrase *with a limp* is describing the something-word *man* and not the camera-word *walked*. It describes what kind of man walked by the house, namely *a man **with a limp**.*"

"But if I say, *The man walked by the house **with a limp***, then you know that *with a limp* is describing the camera-word *walked*. It describes *how* the man walked by the house. He walked by *with a limp*."

"That's pretty obvious," said John.

"Why is it obvious?"

"It just sounds right, I guess."

"Why does it sound right?"

"Oh, boy," said Marian, "an interrogation."

"It sounds right," said Dean with a smile, "because of the position of the phrase in the sentence, and because of the meaning of the phrase in relationship to the other words. Those are two components of what we call context. Listen to the two thoughts once more. *The man **with a limp** came in the door*, and *The man came in the door **with a limp**.*"

"Putting the phrase right after *man* made it describe *man*, whereas moving the phrase to the end of the thought associated it with the camera-word *came*. Theoretically, in the last example, the phrase could add information to the something-word *door*. In other words, *The man came in the door **which had a limp***. We automatically omit this possibility, however, simply because of the meaning of the word limp. Only living creatures limp, not inanimate things like doors.

"Yes, add-on phrases are wonderful little things, but when it comes to adding information to a word, not even add-on phrases can match the power of the words in our third basket: the *add-on thoughts*."

Dean took several cards out of the basket of *add-on thoughts*. "It is actually possible to add a whole thought to a something-word, to a camera-word, or to another thought. The handy little words that make it possible are *add-a-thought words*. Take a look at these examples."

> ...τὸ δόμα τὸ δεχόμεθα ἀπ' αὐτοῦ
> ...the gift which we're receiving from him
>
> ...οἵ ἄνθρωποι οἵ πιστεύουσιν εἰς τὸν κύριον
> ...the men who are believing in the Lord

"Can anyone discover the *add-a-thought words*?"

"Are they the τὸ in the first example and the οἵ in the second?" said Liz.

"Right. τὸ means *which* and it hooks the thought *which we are receiving from him* onto the word *gift*. And οἵ means *who* and hooks the thought *who are believing in the Lord* onto the word *men*. Isn't it amazing how such little words can hang so much additional meaning onto a something-word? In a sense they are actually replacement words for the something-words to which they attach themselves. In English they are mainly the words *who, whose, whom, which,* and *that*, and, as in Greek, all you have to do is hook one of them on a something-word and you can hang as big a thought on it as you want.

"Here's an example of what I mean." Dean fished a small card out of the basket and held it up.

> He's the man *whose* car rolled into the lake last week while he was riding on the roller coaster.

"Do you see all that information after the word *whose*? Why, the possibilities are unlimited. Add-on words and add-on phrases just can't provide the volume of information that is possible with an add-on thought, and it's the little *add-a-thought words* like *who* and *which* that make it possible."

Adding the Finishing Touches

Dean turned to a new page on the flip-chart. "Here's an overview of one kind of Greek *add-a-thought words* that makes add-on thoughts possible."

ROLE	TYPE	singular		plural	
Necessary General supporting Directing Accomplishing	ὁ- words	ὅς οὗ ᾧ ὅν		οἱ ὧν οἷς οὕς	who whose to whom whom
Necessary General supporting Directing Accomplishing	ἡ- words	ἥ ἧς ᾗ ἥν		αἱ ὧν αἷς ἅς	who whose to whom whom
Necessary General supporting Directing Accomplishing	τό- words	ὅ οὗ ᾧ ὅ		ἅ ὧν οἷς ἅ	which whose to which which

"I think there's a conspiracy afoot," said Marian. "A small handful of English words is constantly being replaced by a whole chart full of Greek words."

"It's perfectly logical, madam," said Dean. "Since Greek something-words can play four different roles and come in three different types—ὁ *masculine*, ἡ *feminine*, and τό *neuter*—then Greek add-a-thought words that add extra information to them, also have to be able to play any of the four roles and conform to any of the three types.

"For now it's enough to remember that there are three different ways to add information on to a something-word: with an *add-on word* like καλός, with an *add-on phrase* introduced by an *add-a-phrase word* like ἐν *(in)*, or with an *add-on thought* introduced by an *add-a-thought word* like ὅς *(who)*.

"There's one more kind of *add-a-thought word*. It is used to add one or more thoughts to another thought." He turned to the next page. "Here's a good example.

> οἱ ἄνθρωποι παιδεύουσιν τὰ τέκνα αὐτῶν,
> The men are training their children,
>
> ἵνα δουλεύσωσιν ἀλλήλοις.
> **so that** they will serve one another.

"See how that little word ἵνα *(so that)* is used to tack an extra thought onto the first thought, *The men are training their children*? It's not adding extra information to any *one* of the words in the thought but to the *whole* thought. It's explaining *why* the men are training their children. They're training them *so that* they'll serve one another."

He took a handful of cards out of the basket. "Why, there are dozens of these powerful little add-a-thought words. γάρ, for example, which means *because*, or ἐάν which means *if*, or ἀλλά which means *but*. All of them can be used to add a thought anywhere you'd like to have it."

"No charts?" asked Marian.

"No charts, madam. These add-a-thought words don't have to change like the add-on words, because they don't have to match the role of a something-word. They add their extra information to a thought, and there are no ὁ-, ἡ-, or τό- thoughts."

"Thank heavens for that!"

Dean returned the basket of add-on thoughts to its place. "It's easy to remember the extra-information words. There are **add-on words** like *big* and *quickly*; there are **add-on phrases** like *in the bucket* and *over the hill*; and there are **add-on thoughts** like *...which is the best thing you could ever do*, and *...because he's such a nice guy*. That's it: only three kinds of extra-information words, but they are so flexible that you can use them to alter the picture of a thought in any way you choose. You can do it ever so slightly, for example, with the delicate brush stroke of an add-on word like *gently* or powerfully with the broad sweep of a mighty add-on thought like *which causes the earth to shake and high mountains to tremble in a cataclysm of chaos*. And with that final display of linguistic fireworks, ladies and gentlemen, our demonstrations in the department of extra-information words are complete, and we are now nearing the end of our tour. As a special conclusion, we've saved one of the most spectacular words at Universal Greek Pictures for our last presentation. But before we reveal this interesting and unusual specimen, we're going to let you stretch your legs and make a quick trip to the cafeteria. Please be back in exactly fifteen minutes. You won't want to miss the grand finale."

Adding the Finishing Touches

As the others made their way to the kitchen, Harmon stayed behind to chat with Dean. "I was wondering when you'd get around to mentioning the—how did you put it?—unusual specimen."

"I figured you'd know what I was talking about," said Dean.

"Yes, it's omission up to this point has been rather conspicuous. I'm curious to know what you're going to call it and how you're going to fit it into the whole scheme of things."

"What name would you give it that would best describe its functions for the people who are here?"

"Hmm. Good question. I'm afraid not many of us college professors are used to approaching terminology in that way. In fact, we kind of like to use technical terms no one understands. Makes us look good, you know."

"I know what you mean," laughed Dean. "I'll be interested to know what you think about my choice of terminology."

"Up to now, it's been a real eye-opener—which is not to say that I don't have a lot of questions—but you can bet that when you start talking about the 'unusual specimen', I'll have my ears open."

The fifteen-minute break had stretched into twenty minutes by the time Buddy managed to coax the more talkative participants back into the living room for the final session. Dean, standing next to the flip-chart which he had covered with a white cloth, waited until everyone was seated.

"Ladies and gentlemen," he said. "Today, you have seen a sample of the major components of the Greek language. First you were introduced to the something-words like ὁ ὀφθαλμός *(the eye)*, which play any one of four different roles in the picture of a message: *the necessary role, the general supporting role, the directing role,* and *the accomplishing role.*

"Then you observed the picture-taking power of camera-words like παιδεύων with their four different adjustments: *Picture, Light, Action,* and *Necessary role.*"

"Finally you met the *extra-information words*: special *add-on words, add-on phrases,* and *add-on thoughts* that add extra information to something-words, camera-words, and even to whole thoughts.

"Marvelous words, all of them. But as wonderful as they are, you'll be surprised to hear that Universal Greek Pictures has saved it's most special word for the very last; a word that defies the imagination; a word that can surpass the picture-making power of any word in any language in the world; a word that knows no equal. I now have the great pleasure of introducing you to the real star of our cast of words, the word that can do more than all the others, the word that can do it all: the mighty **all-around word**." Dean swept away the cloth covering the flip-chart.

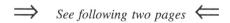

PICTURE ⇒ ⇒ ⇒			VIDEO
ACTION	ROLE	TYPE	Live
ACTIVE	Necessary General supporting Directing Accomplishing	ὁ	παιδεύ-ων -ων -οντες -οντος -όντων -οντι -ουσιν -οντα -οντας
	Necessary General supporting Directing Accomplishing	ἡ	παιδεύ-ουσα -ουσα -ουσαι -ούσης -ουσῶν -ούσῃ -ούσαις -ουσαν -ούσας
	Necessary General supporting Directing Accomplishing	τό	παιδεῦ-ον -ον -οντα -οντος -οντων -οντι -ουσιν -ον -οντα
MIDDLE	Necessary General supporting Directing Accomplishing	ὁ	παιδευόμεν-ος -ος -οι -ου -ων -ῳ -οις -ον -ους
	Necessary General supporting Directing Accomplishing	ἡ	παιδευομέν-η -η -αι -ης -ων -ῃ -αις -ην -ας
	Necessary General supporting Directing Accomplishing	τό	παιδευόμεν-ον -ον -α -ου -ων -ῳ -οις -ον -α
PASSIVE	Necessary General supporting Directing Accomplishing	ὁ	παιδευόμεν-ος -ος -οι -ου -ων -ῳ -οις -ον -ους
	Necessary General supporting Directing Accomplishing	ἡ	παιδευομέν-η -η -αι -ης -ων -ῃ -αις -ην -ας
	Necessary General supporting Directing Accomplishing	τό	παιδευόμεν-ον -ον -α -ου -ων -ῳ -οις -ον -α

PHOTOGRAPH			
Normal 1	Normal 2	Future	Current
παιδεύ-σας -σας -σαντες -σαντος -σάντων -σαντι -σασιν -σαντα -σαντας	βαλ-ών -ών -όντες -όντος -όντων -όντι -ούσιν -όντα -όντας	παιδεύ-σων -σων -σοντες -σοντος -σόντων -σοντι -σουσιν -σοντα -σοντας	πεπαιδευ-κώς -κώς -κότες -κότος -κότων -κότι -κόσιν -κότα -κότας
παιδεύ-σασα -σασα -σασαι -σάσης -σασών -σάση -σάσαις -σασαν -σάσας	βαλ-ούσα -ούσα -ούσαι -ούσης -ουσών -ούση -ούσαις -ούσαν -ούσας	παιδεύ-σουσα -σουσα -σουσαι -σούσης -σουσών -σούση -σούσαις -σουσαν -σούσας	πεπαιδευ-κυῖα -κυῖα -κυῖαι -κυίας -κυιών -κυίᾳ -κυίαις -κυῖαν -κυίας
παιδεύ-σαν -σαν -σαντα -σαντος -σάντων -σαντι -σασιν -σαν -σαντα	βαλ-όν -όν -όντα -όντος -όντων -όντι -ούσιν -όν -όντα	παιδεύ-σον -σον -σοντα -σοντος -σοντων -σοντι -σουσιν -σον -σοντα	πεπαιδευ-κός -κός -κότα -κότος -κότων -κότι -κόσιν -κός -κότα
παιδευσάμεν-ος -ος -οι -ου -ων -ῳ -οις -ον -ους	βαλόμεν-ος -ος -οι -ου -ων -ῳ -οις -ον -ους	παιδευσόμεν-ος -ος -οι -ου -ων -ῳ -οις -ον -ους	πεπαιδευμέν-ος -ος -οι -ου -ων -ῳ -οις -ον -ους
παιδευσαμέν-η -η -αι -ης -ων -ῃ -αις -ην -ας	βαλομέν-η -η -αι -ης -ων -ῃ -αις -ην -ας	παιδευσομέν-η -η -αι -ης -ων -ῃ -αις -ην -ας	πεπαιδευμέν-η -η -αι -ης -ων -ῃ -αις -ην -ας
παιδευσάμεν-ον -ον -α -ου -ων -ῳ -οις -ον -α	βαλόμεν-ον -ον -α -ου -ων -ῳ -οις -ον -α	παιδευσόμεν-ον -ον -α -ου -ων -ῳ -οις -ον -α	πεπαιδευμέν-ον -ον -α -ου -ων -ῳ -οις -ον -α
παιδευ-θείς -θείς -θέντες -θέντος -θέντων -θέντι -θεῖσιν -θέντα -θέντας	γραφ-είς -είς -έντες -έντος -έντων -έντι -εῖσιν -έντα -έντας	παιδευθησόμεν-ος -ος -οι -ου -ων -ῳ -οις -ον -ους	πεπαιδευμέν-ος -ος -οι -ου -ων -ῳ -οις -ον -ους
παιδευ-θεῖσα -θεῖσα -θεῖσαι -θείσης -θεισών -θείσῃ -θείσαις -θεῖσαν -θείσας	γραφ-εῖσα -εῖσα -εῖσαι -είσης -εισών -είσῃ -είσαις -εῖσαν -είσας	παιδευθησομέν-η -η -αι -ης -ων -ῃ -αις -ην -ας	πεπαιδευμέν-η -η -αι -ης -ων -ῃ -αις -ην -ας
παιδευ-θέν -θέν -θέντα -θέντος -θέντων -θέντι -θεῖσιν -θέν -θέντα	γραφ-έν -έν -έντα -έντος -έντων -έντι -εῖσιν -έν -έντα	παιδευθησόμεν-ον -ον -α -ου -ων -ῳ -οις -ον -α	πεπαιδευμέν-ον -ον -α -ου -ων -ῳ -οις -ον -α

"Oh, no," said Marian. "The chart to end all charts."

"Don't worry, madam," said Dean. "If you look closely you'll see there's nothing on this chart that you haven't already seen today. It's just that you haven't seen them in this combination. The all-around word is remarkable, not because it is another kind of word, but because it is actually a *combination* of all the other three major kinds of words: the *something-word*, the *camera-word*, and the *extra-information word*."

"All three?" said John.

"I know it sounds incredible, but the all-around word has some tricks up its sleeve that allow it to bounce back and forth from one department of Universal Greek Pictures to another. Once you know the tricks, the answer becomes clear. First, let's ask the question: *How can an all-around word be part camera-word*?

"Do you remember the letters *P, L, A,* and *N—Picture, Light, Action, Necessary role*—which clue us in to the information in a camera-word? Look at the chart of all-around words. Do you see how the all-around word borrowed the *P* and the *A* (*Picture* and *Action*) parts of a camera-word and made them its own?

"Secondly, how can an all-around word be part something-word? Do you remember the four roles—*necessary, general supporting, directing, accomplishing*—played by something-words? Look at the chart again. Do you see how the all-around word has borrowed the *role* part of a something-word and called it its own?

"Finally, how can an all-around word be part extra-information word? Do you remember the three *types*—ὁ, ἡ, and τό—of add-on words and how they can match the endings of any of the three types of something-words? Well, look at the chart once more.

"Do you see how an all-around word has ὁ-endings, ἡ-endings, and τό-endings just like an add-on word? With all of these borrowed parts, an all-around word is equipped to do almost any job that a something-word or a camera-word or an extra-information word can do.

"Do you remember the something-word ὀφθαλμός?" Dean turned to another page. "This will refresh your memory."

ὁ ὀφθαλμός in all his major roles

	Singular	Plural
Necessary role	ὀφθαλμός eye	ὀφθαλμοί eyes
General supporting role	ὀφθαλμοῦ eye's	ὀφθαλμῶν eyes'
Directing role	ὀφθαλμῷ with an eye	ὀφθαλμοῖς with eyes
Accomplishing role	ὀφθαλμόν eye	ὀφθαλμούς eyes

Adding the Finishing Touches

"An all-around word can do all that and more too. Here's παιδεύων in action."

παιδεύων in all his major roles

	Singular	Plural
Necessary role	παιδεύων	παιδεύοντες
	the one (masc.) who is training	those who are training
General supporting role	παιδεύοντος	παιδευόντων
	of the one who is training	of those who are training
Directing role	παιδεύοντι	παιδεύουσι(ν)
	with the one who is training	with those who are training
Accomplishing role	παιδεύοντα	παιδεύοντας
	the one who is training	those who are training

παιδεύουσα in all her major roles

	Singular	Plural
Necessary role	παιδεύουσα	παιδεύουσαι
	the one (fem.) who is training	those who are training
General supporting role	παιδευούσης	παιδευουσῶν
	of the one who is training	of those who are training
Directing role	παιδευούσῃ	παιδευούσαις
	with the one who is training	with those who are training
Accomplishing role	παιδεύουσαν	παιδευούσας
	the one who is training	those who are training

How to Read New Testament Greek

παιδεῦον in all its major roles		
	Singular	Plural
Necessary role	παιδεῦον	παιδεύοντα
	the one (neut.) who is training	those who are training
General supporting role	παιδεύοντος	παιδευόντων
	of the one who is training	of those who are training
Directing role	παιδεύοντι	παιδεύουσι(ν)
	with the one who is training	with those who are training
Accomplishing role	παιδεῦον	παιδεύοντα
	the one who is training	those who are training

"First of all, notice how we need all three kinds of English words—something-word, camera-word, and extra-info word—to even translate a Greek all-around word: *the one* (something-word) *who* (add-a-thought word) *is training* (camera-word phrase). And secondly, notice how an all-around word is capable of portraying masculine, feminine, and neuter subjects. The all-around word can step into the role of a something-word and fill it to overflowing.

"But that's not all. The all-around word can take over the job of an *extra-information word* just as effectively."

Dean found another page on the flip-chart. "Do you remember the add-on word καλός?"

ROLE	TYPE		
		singular	plural
Necessary	ὁ- words	καλός	καλοί
General supporting		καλοῦ	καλῶν
Directing		καλῷ	καλοῖς
Accomplishing		καλόν	καλούς
Necessary	ἡ- words	καλή	καλαί
General supporting		καλῆς	καλῶν
Directing		καλῇ	καλαῖς
Accomplishing		καλήν	καλάς

Adding the Finishing Touches

Necessary General supporting Directing Accomplishing	τό- words	καλόν καλοῦ καλῷ καλόν	καλά καλῶν καλοῖς καλά

"An all-around word has no trouble managing that. Here's παιδεύων with just a few of its possibilities"

ROLE	TYPE		
		singular	plural
Necessary General supporting Directing Accomplishing	ὁ- words	παιδεύων παιδεύοντος παιδεύοντι παιδεύοντα	παιδεύοντες παιδευόντων παιδεύουσι(ν) παιδεύοντας
Necessary General supporting Directing Accomplishing	ἡ- words	παιδεύουσα παιδευούσης παιδεούσῃ παιδεύουσαν	παιδεύουσαι παιδευουσῶν παιδευούσαις παιδευούσας
Necessary General supporting Directing Accomplishing	τό- words	παιδεῦον παιδεύοντος παιδεύοντι παιδεῦον	παιδεύοντα παιδευόντων παιδεύουσι(ν) παιδεύοντα

"And just think, παιδεύων can do this in its *normal photo, future photo,* or *current photo* forms; and it can do all of them in *active, medium,* or *passive,* of course, for a grand total of two hundred and eighty-eight different forms. Now that's what I call flexible!"

"Two hundred and eighty-eight!" said Marian, staring at the ceiling. "Someone please hold my chair. I'm going to keel over."

"Yes, ladies and gentlemen, the all-around word with its incredible array of attachments is the supreme linguistic tool. It can out per*form* any something-word or any add-on word. But that's not all. In many instances it can also step in for a camera-word. In this function, however, the all-around word is limited to a

How to Read New Testament Greek

unique teamwork with camera-words like εἰμί *(am)*. The result is very similar to the way in which English helping words like *am, is* and *was* team up with *-ing* words to form camera-word phrases such as *am running, is running* and *was running*. There just doesn't seem to be anything an all-around word can't do.

Dean took a deep breath. "Ladies and gentlemen, with this presentation of the Greek all-around word, our tour of the first two departments of Universal Greek Pictures is now completed. There are two more fascinating departments—the *department of literature-pictures* and the *department of translating*—but one day is simply not enough time to make it from one end of Universal Greek Pictures to the other. We will inform you when a tour of the final two departments will be offered. To help you remember everything you've seen today, we want to present each of you with an exclusive copy of the UNIVERSAL GREEK PICTURES WORD CHART which gives you a complete overview of Greek *camera-words, something-words, extra-information words*, and *all-around words*. It will not only help you review what you have seen, but also will be of considerable help to you as you continue your study of the Greek language.

"In addition we also want you to have a copy of our STEPS TO LEARNING NEW TESTAMENT GREEK, a step by step series of lessons designed to help you enter the world of Greek thoughts. The STEPS will fill in all the details that were impossible to pass on to you today, and they will help you see for yourself the incredible pictures of words and thoughts and literature that were created in the writings of the New Testament." While Dean was talking, Buddy laid out copies of the chart and the STEPS on the coffee table.

"I'm also pleased to inform you that our service personnel will always be ready and willing to help you with any questions or problems you might have. Don't hesitate to give us a call at any time. We have an exclusive twenty-four hour line open for our best customers. And now, on behalf of the entire staff at Universal Greek Pictures, I want to thank you for coming, and to show our appreciation we'd like to invite you to join us for a barbecue dinner on our VIP patio."

Dean's invitation drew a burst of applause from the hungry listeners. They had already detected the aroma of hamburgers being grilled.

"Well, my friend," Harmon said to Dean as the others were collecting their copies of the chart and the STEPS. "You actually did it. You managed to push us headfirst into the muddy waters of grammar and make us like it. I had to see it to believe it."

"I'm glad to hear you thought it worked. I wasn't sure if I'd tried to accomplish too much today or not. I wanted to present a complete overview of the Greek language, but I also wanted to see if I could give everyone a new view of language itself by presenting it as something far more important and basic to life than it's usually thought to be. Do you think we made some ground in those two directions?"

"It was a lot at one time," said Harmon, "but I assume you don't expect us to remember all the details at one outing anyway. So I'd say you came close to reaching both goals. That's not bad for one day's work. Look, your charts and lessons are going like hotcakes. You must have convinced some of us that the Greek language is worth learning.

"And, by the way," Harmon put his hand on Dean's shoulder as they headed for the patio, "calling the 'unusual specimen' an *all-around word* was a stroke of genius."

PART III:

Their First Twenty-Five Steps

Contents

1. SW, ὁ-words, ὁ λόγος, Roles, ὁ, Punctuation, Word Order — 111
2. CW, Live Video, PLAN, παιδεύω — 115
3. EW, Add-a-Phrase Words with One Role; SW, Directing Role — 119
4. EW, Add-a-Phrase Words with Two Roles — 123
5. SW, ἡ-words with -ος Endings — 127
6. SW, τό-words, τό — 130
7. EW, Add-a-Phrase Words with Three Roles — 133
8. CW, εἰμί — 135
9. SW, ἡ-words, τιμή — 137
10. SW, ἡ-words, οἰκία, Accents — 139
11. SW, ἡ-words, δόξα — 143
12. SW, ὁ-words, μαθητής, νεανίας — 145
13. EW, Add-on Words with Three Sets of Endings μόνος, δίκαιος — 148
14. EW, Add-on Words with Two Sets of Endings, φρόνιμος — 151
15. SW, Necessary Role — 153
16. EW, This and That — 156
17. EW, Add-on Words χρυσοῦς — 158
18. CW, Active, Middle, Passive; Departed Forms — 160
19. CW, Live Video and Recorded Video — 163
20. CW, Combining Camera-Words with Add-a-Phrase Words — 166
21. CW, Bright Light, Dim Light, μή, οὐ — 168
22. CW, Flashing Light/Active — 171
23. CW, Flashing Light/Middle; Departed Forms — 173
24. CW, Future Photo — 175
25. AW, Live Video/Small All-Around Words — 177

Key to Abbreviations: SW=Something-Words, CW=Camera-Words,
EW=Extra-Information Words, AW=All-Around Words

Learning New Testament Greek STEP by STEP [1]

Learning a language, like climbing a mountain, is best accomplished STEP by STEP. Each of the following STEPS deals with one of the three kinds of words that make the pictures of Greek thoughts possible: *something-words, camera-words*, and *extra-information words*.

Something-words are the stars who play the roles in the world of thought-pictures. They're called something-words simply because they refer to anything real or imagined that's ever had a label put on it. *John, chimney, running, beauty, you, heat,* and *New York* are all examples of something-words.

There are four possible roles that something-words can play in a thought: the *necessary role*, the *general supporting role*, the *directing role*, and the *accomplishing role*.

All these something-words, however, would just stand around and get in each other's way if a **camera-word** didn't come along with a *PLAN* to get them organized and then take their picture. The word *PLAN* reminds us of the four important tasks a camera-word has to do when it makes a picture of a thought: 1. It determines the kind of *Picture* the thought will be (*live video, recorded video, normal photo, future photo, current photo, previous photo*); 2. It determines the kind of *Light* in which the picture will be seen (*bright, dim, flashing*); 3. It determines the kind of *Action* the word in the necessary role will take (*active, middle, passive*); 4. It determines which something-word will play the *Necessary* role (*I, you, he, she, it, we, all of you, they*). *Ran, hold, sing, wanted, clobber,* and *think* are all examples of camera-words.

The **extra-information words** add all the trimmings to the picture of a thought (*add-on words, add-on phrases, add-on thoughts*). *He ran quickly* is an example of an add-on word. *He ran with a limp* is an add-on phrase. *He ran while he was reading* is an add-on thought.

The **all-around word** is a fourth kind of word which is actually a combination of all the other three. In the picture of a Greek thought, an all-around word can step in for any of the other three kinds of words. Some English words ending with *-ing—running,* for example—can almost match the flexibility of a Greek all-around word: *Running is healthy* (something-word), *He is running* (camera-word), *Running water is convenient* (add-on word).

That's all there is to learn: three kinds of words and an all-around word. There's nothing complicated about that! They're words, however, that come in plenty of different sizes and shapes. It's the job of the STEPS to help you recognize them and understand how they work.

---

[1] This STEP and all those that follow are similar to the STEPS Dean McLain gave the visitors after the tour through Universal Greek Pictures.

How to Read New Testament Greek

No grand strategy or special system underlies the arrangement of the STEPS. The words of a language are never learned in a set sequence anyway. Have you ever heard a two-year-old ask, *Hey, daddy, which new word comes next?* It just happens to be a big, jumbled, linguistic world out there, and most kids learn as they go along, picking and choosing what they need at the spur of the moment.

The STEPS use only Greek words from the New Testament, so when you finish the STEPS and begin to read and translate in your New Testament, you'll already recognize many words.

How to use the STEPS:

Each STEP is liberally sprinkled with exercises, vocabulary, explanations, warnings, reviews, suggestions, and study tips. Plus—and this is important—each piece of new information is tied into your UNIVERSAL GREEK PICTURES WORD CHART to keep you well-oriented: The letters and numbers which run vertically and horizontally through the middle of the WORD CHART form a grid much like those used to locate places on a map. Important words and topics in the STEPS are tagged with the *letter and number coordinates* of their position on the WORD CHART so you can locate them quickly.

At the end of each STEP, you'll find an additional store-house of valuable information under the subtitle **Any questions?** There you will find answers to the questions most often asked by *people just like you,* who have previously worked through the STEPS.

There is no particular study tempo that is necessarily better than any other. Take a third of a STEP a day or three STEPS a day or whatever seems right for you. It's important, however, that you keep a regular pace, whether it be two hours a day, seven days a week, or thirty minutes a day every Monday, Wednesday, and Friday. Don't quit learning for any prolonged period of time or you'll end up having to recapture ground that once was yours.

Here are a few final tips before you start:

1. Find a good place to study where you can keep your materials ready to go. If you have to spend fifteen minutes looking for your book and another ten scrounging about for a pencil, you'll soon be spinning your wheels.

2. When you have questions, do your best to find the answers yourself. Don't give up too quickly. All the answers are not provided for you in the exercises. That is intentional; you shouldn't be tempted to think that if you fill in all the blanks correctly, then you'll know Greek. You won't. To learn Greek, you'll have to get in the ring and wrestle with the language.

What do you do, however, when your best efforts are to no avail, and you need answers? At those times do not hesitate to get some help. If you're fortunate

Introduction to the STEPS

enough to have a friend who knows Greek, give him a call. If not—which is more likely—don't hesitate to direct your questions to the following address:

>Universal Greek Pictures
>513 E. Florence Blvd., C-10
>Casa Grande, AZ 85222

Your letter will find its way into the hands of the McLains or one of their friends. I guarantee, you'll get personal treatment. Don't think that your questions have to be sophisticated, complicated, or profound to get a hearing. Remember, the only dumb question is the one that's not asked. Before writing, however, please read the information on page 129.

3. Before beginning the STEPS, make sure you have completely read the three chapters reporting the tour through Universal Greek Pictures from page 47 to page 103. In fact, reading it twice would be a good idea.

4. Make sure the UNIVERSAL GREEK PICTURES WORD CHART is handy so you can refer to it often. It is the map for every STEP you take. Some people hang it on the wall, others cover it with plastic and lay it out on their desk top, and still others fold it in such a way that the various sections are easily accessible. Each STEP is keyed both to the Word Chart (The number and letter coordinates help you find the right place) and to the pages where the subject matter is discussed during the tour of Universal Greek Pictures.

Now, a word about expectations:

What will you be able to do after you've finished the STEPS? Will you be able to read the Greek New Testament fluently?

Nope, not by a long shot.

Will you be able to do serious study in a Scriptural text?

Sorry, not that either.

How about look up a word or two?

Well, maybe, but don't count on it doing you much good.

"Hey," I can hear you saying. "What in the world *will* I be able to do then?"

It may not sound grand or glorious, but you will have carefully, STEP by STEP, climbed into the high foothills of the Greek mountains. You will have exercised your linguistic muscles, and they will be sore, but they will also be strong and ready to discover the beauty in the higher ridges beyond. That is much to have accomplished.

In other words, finishing the STEPS is *only the beginning*. After the STEPS, a steeper and more difficult path will be waiting for you, but the STEPS will have prepared you for the challenge. And up on those high ridges, you will find friends waiting for you, *people just like you,* who are catching their breath to climb to the next plateau to discover the riches in the mountains of God's Word.

STEP 1

SOMETHING-WORDS		
ROLE	sing.	pl.
	ὁ λόγ-ος	
Necessary	-ος	-οι
General supporting	-ου	-ων
Directing	-ῳ	-οις
Accomplishing	-ον	-ους
See pages 60-65, Word Chart K-1		

What you need to know:
Greek something-words can play four different roles in a sentence:

    Necessary role: ***John** is singing.*
    Gen. supporting role: ***John's** brother is singing.*
    Directing role: *He is singing **to John**.*
    Accomplishing role: *He likes **John**.*

In English we recognize words in the *necessary* role and the *accomplishing* role by their position in the sentence. The word in the necessary role occupies the place *in front of* the camera-word: *John is singing.* The word in the accomplishing role comes *after* the camera word: *He likes John.* A Greek word in the *general supporting* role is usually translated into English by a word ending with an -'s or by a phrase introduced by *of*: *John's brother is singing,* or *The brother of John is singing.* A Greek word in the *directing* role is usually translated into English by phrases beginning with the words *to, with, by, through,* or *at*.

Don't miss it!
Greek words switch roles by changing their *endings*. Here's an example of λόγος playing all four roles:
    Necessary role: ὁ λόγος φονούσει, *The **word** will shine.*
    Gen. supporting role: ...φόβος τῶν λόγων, *... a fear **of the words**.*
    Directing role: ἐλάλει τοῖς λογοῖς, *He spoke **with words**.*
    Accomplishing role: ἀκούω τοὺς λόγους, *I'm hearing the **words**.*

Strange but true:
Some camera-words such as πιστεύω and δουλεύω are *not* completed by a word playing the accomplishing role as is normally the case, but by a word in the directing role. πιστεύω τῷ λόγῳ, for example, means *I am believing **the word*** and not(!) *I am believing **with the word***.

Don't miss it!
ὁ is the word *the* that is used with all ὁ-words. That's why they are called ὁ-words. When ὁ-words change their endings, the ὁ also changes to match the endings:

ὁ *(the)*
in all its roles

	Singular	Plural
Necessary role	ὁ	οἱ
General supporting role	τοῦ	τῶν
Directing role	τῷ	τοῖς
Accomplishing role	τόν	τούς

Word Chart N-15

Give it a try:
Look at the endings and identify the roles these words are playing: ἄρτῳ, λόγος, κόσμου, θρόνον; φίλοι, καρπῶν, νόμοις, ξένους, θρόνου, ὄχλοις, φόβον, ἀγροί, ἀδελφῶν, κληρονόμος, χρόνῳ, ἄρτος, κόσμῳ, ξένοις, χρόνον, θρόνων, διαλογισμοῦ, χόρτον, συνεργοί.

Now put the right form of ὁ in front of the above words. For example: τῷ in front of ἄρτῳ and τοῦ in front of κόσμου. Now translate the above words with their form of ὁ. (You'll find a list of new words at the end of the STEP.)

Translate in this way: ὁ λόγος, *the word*; τοῦ χρόνου, *of the time* or *the time's*; τῷ κόσμῳ, *to the world* or *with the world*, τὸν λόγον, *the word*.

Don't miss it!
Many ὁ-words end with -ος and change their endings in the same way as λόγος. All the ὁ-words in this STEP are examples of these kinds of ὁ-words.

STEP 1

Don't forget!
ὁ-words are only one kind of something-word. There are also ἡ-words and τό-words. You will be meeting them soon in subsequent STEPS.

Don't miss it!
All ὁ-, ἡ-, and τό-words have two parts: a *stem* and an *ending*. To find the stem, simply drop off the ending: λόγ-ος, θρόν-ος, etc.

Don't miss it!
When you translate a sentence, always find the camera-word and translate it first. The camera words in the following sentences are ἀκούω *(I'm hearing* or *I hear)*, δουλεύω *(I'm serving* or *I serve)*, παιδεύω *(I'm training* or *I train)*, βλέπω *(I'm seeing* or *I see)*, φεύγω *(I'm going* or *I go)*, ἔχω *(I have)*, and πιστεύω *(I'm believing* or *I believe)*.

After locating the camera-word and translating it, determine which roles the something-words are playing in the sentence, and determine whether they are singular or plural.

Now, you're the translator:
1. Ἀκούω τὸν λόγον. 2. βλέπω τὸν ἀδελφόν. 3. τὸν ὄχλον βλέπω. 4. τὸν υἱὸν παιδεύω 5. γράφω τῷ κληρονόμῳ. 6. ἔχω τοὺς ὀφθαλμούς. 7. βλέπω τὸν θρόνον. 8. λέγω λόγον τοῦ νόμου. 9. ἀκούω λόγους τοῦ ξένου. 10. γράφω τῷ υἱῷ τοῦ γεωργοῦ. 11. χρόνον ἔχω. 12. τοῖς λόγοις τῶν φίλων πιστεύω. 13. βλέπω ναὸν τῶν ξένων. 14. ἔχω φόβον. 15. πιστεύω τῷ φίλῳ καὶ ἀδελφῷ. 16. φεύγω τὸν καιρὸν τοῦ πειρασμοῦ. 17. τοὺς καρποὺς τῶν ἀγρῶν βλέπω, καὶ τὸν ἄρτον τοῦ ἀγροῦ ἔχω. 18. πιστεύω τῷ λόγῳ τοῦ φίλου· φεύγω δὲ τὸν πειρασμὸν καὶ τὸν δεσμὸν τοῦ ἐχθροῦ. 19. δουλεύω τῷ νόμῳ τοῦ οὐρανοῦ. 20. Τοὺς λόγους τῶν ἁμαρτωλῶν φεύγω· ἀκούω δὲ τοὺς λόγους τοῦ θεοῦ.

Don't miss it!
Punctuation is somewhat different in Greek. The period (.) and comma (,) are the same as in English. The sign (;) is the Greek question mark, and the sign (·) is the Greek colon or semicolon.

Any questions?
Q: Doesn't the order of the words matter at all in Greek? Some of these sentences are backwards!
A: They only seem backwards, because you're used to thinking thoughts in a certain order. The *placement* of words in a sentence is an important determiner of meaning in the English language. In Greek, however, *word endings* play the key role.

113

How to Read New Testament Greek

A Greek speaker contemplating an English sentence for the first time would most likely say, *Hey, there are no endings. What a mish-mash. How are you supposed to figure out who is doing what?* In order to understand English, he would have to learn to recognize the clues provided by *word placement*. The English speaker learning Greek, however, has to learn to recognize the clues provided by *word endings*. Each system has its own logic and its own understanding of what is backwards and what is forwards.

This is not to say that word order in Greek is totally free. It isn't. We'll be learning in subsequent STEPS that Greek words often follow certain rules when they team up with other words.

New words:

ἀγρός, ὁ	field	λαός, ὁ	people
ἀδελφός, ὁ	brother	λέγω	say
ἀκούω	hear	λόγος, ὁ	word
ἁμαρτωλός, ὁ	sinner	ναός, ὁ	temple
ἀμνός, ὁ	lamb	νόμος, ὁ	law
ἀριθμός, ὁ	number	νυμφίος, ὁ	groom
ἄρτος, ὁ	bread	ξένος, ὁ	stranger
βλέπω	see	οὐρανός, ὁ	heaven
γεωργός, ὁ	farmer	ὀφθαλμός, ὁ	eye
γράφω	write	ὄχλος, ὁ	crowd
δέ	but, and	παιδεύω	train
δεσμός, ὁ	chains	πειρασμός, ὁ	temptation
διαλογισμός, ὁ	thought, consideration	πιστεύω	believe
		ποταμός, ὁ	river
δουλεύω	serve	σταυρός	cross
ἐχθρός, ὁ	enemy	συνεργός, ὁ	fellow worker
ἔχω	have	φεύγω	flee
θεός, ὁ	God	φίλος, ὁ	friend
θρόνος, ὁ	throne	φόβος, ὁ	fear
καί	and, also	χόρτος, ὁ	grass
καιρός, ὁ	time	Χριστός, ὁ	Christ, anointed one
καρπός, ὁ	fruit		
κληρονόμος, ὁ	heir	χρόνος, ὁ	time
κόσμος, ὁ	world		

STEP 2

CAMERA-WORDS			
PICTURE ⇒⇒⇒			VIDEO
L_{IGHT}	A_{CTION}	N_{EC. ROLE}	LIVE
B R I G H T	A C T I V E	I we you all of you he, she, it they	παιδεύ-ω I am training -ω -ομεν -εις -ετε -ει -ουσιν See pages 76, 81 Word Chart C-2

What you need to know:

The *live video* form of a Greek camera-word produces two varieties of thoughts. The first corresponds to its name: *live video*. It portrays *live action* in the here and now.

Οἱ γεωργοὶ φυτεύουσιν τοὺς ἀργούς.
The farmers *are planting* the fields.

The second portrays *regular or habitual action*. It shows action that takes place *regularly*. In this sense the above sentence is translated:

The farmers *plant* the fields.

The context of the thought determines which meaning is preferred. If, for example, the question is asked, *What are the farmers doing right now?*, then the first meaning is the intended one. *They are planting the fields.* That's what they're doing *right now*. If, however, the question is asked, *What do the farmers do in the spring?*, then the second meaning is the intended one. They *plant* the fields. That's what they *regularly* do in the spring.

How to Read New Testament Greek

Don't forget!
When translating a sentence, first find the camera-word, then determine its PLAN (Picture, Light, Action, Necessary role), and then translate the camera-word with the word in the necessary role.

For example, in the sentence on the previous page φυτεύουσιν is the camera-word and its PLAN is **P** = *live video*, **L** = *bright*, **A** = *active*, **N** = *they*. Therefore, we begin our translation with *They are planting* or *They plant*.

γεωργοί is the word in the necessary role (the -ος ending tells us that) which means we can substitute it for *they*. The result is *The farmers are planting* or *The farmers plant*.

Don't forget!
If a sentence has no particular word in the necessary role, then you have to use the *I, you, he, she, it, we, all of you,* or *they* which is tucked away in the camera-word itself. If γεωργοί were not in the above sentence, then we would have translated: *They are planting* or *They plant*. (The -ουσιν ending, of course, tells us that *they* is the word in the necessary role.)

Give it a try:
Which word in the necessary role—*I, you, he, she, it, we, all of you, they*—is indicated by the endings of the following camera-words: πιστεύεις, ἀκούομεν, παιδεύετε, βλέπουσιν, γράφω, ἔχει, δουλεύουσιν, λέγει, φεύγομεν, βλέπεις

Don't miss it!
There is no word for *a* in Greek. There are times when you'll have to add it to your translations.

Don't forget!
The role a word plays in a sentence in English is often determined by its *position* in the sentence. *Ted hit John*, for example, is considerably different than *John hit Ted*. In Greek, however, word *endings* are more important in determining roles. That's why word order is much more flexible in Greek.

Give it a try:
Fill in the right endings, either singular or plural:
ὁ φίλος φυτεύ____, ὁ ἄνθρωπος πιστεύ____, οἱ φίλοι γράφ____, ὁ θεὸς βασιλεύ____, οἱ γεωργοὶ οὐ νηστεύ____, ἀπόστολοι πιστεύ____, ξέν__ δουλεύουσιν, ἐχθρ____ οὐκ ἀκούει, διάκον____ δουλεύει, Φαρισαῖ__ λατρεύουσιν

Now you're the translator:
1. Ὁ φίλος τῷ λόγῳ τοῦ ξένου πιστεύει. 2. πρὸ τοῦ ναοῦ τὸν ὄχλον βλέπετε. 3. ἀκούεις τοὺς λόγους τοῦ ἀποστόλου. 4. οἱ διάκονοι τοῖς

πρεσβυτέροις ζήλῳ δουλεύουσιν. 5. τῷ ἁμαρτωλῷ τὸν λόγον τοῦ νόμου λέγει. 6. εἰς τὸν υἱὸν τοῦ θεοῦ πιστεύουσιν. 7. οἱ ἄνθρωποι τοῦ κόσμου τοὺς λόγους τοῦ ἀποστόλου ἀκούουσιν. 8. οἱ γεωργοὶ τοὺς ἀγροὺς φυτεύουσιν. 9. ἀσπασμὸν τοῖς φίλοις γράφομεν. 10. οἱ ʼΡωμαῖοι ἐν τῷ κόσμῳ κυριεύουσιν. 11. οἱ Φαρισαῖοι ζήλῳ νηστεύουσιν καὶ φόβῳ λατρεύουσιν τῷ θεῷ. 12. ὁ κύριος τὸν διάκονον τοῦ πρεσβυτέρου θεραπεύει. 13. μνημονεύετε τοὺς λόγους τοῦ υἱοῦ τοῦ θεοῦ. 14. ἐν τοῖς οὐρανοῖς καὶ ἐν τῷ κόσμῳ ὁ Χριστὸς βασιλεύει. 15. Οἱ φίλοι τοῖς λόγοις τῶν ξένων οὐ πιστεύουσιν· ἀκούουσιν δὲ τὸν λόγον τοῦ θεοῦ. 16. ἄνθρωποι τῷ διαβόλῳ οὐκέτι δουλεύουσιν, ἀλλὰ τῷ Χριστῷ. 17. πιστεύεις εἰς τὸν Χριστὸν ἢ τῷ διαβόλῳ ἔτι λατρεύεις. 18. ἐν Χριστῷ ἤδη τὸν πλοῦτον τοῦ οὐρανοῦ ἔχομεν· τῷ γὰρ λόγῳ τοῦ θεοῦ πιστεύομεν.

Study tip!

Use those unexpected bits of spare time during the day to learn Greek. Write information you need to learn or review on index cards and carry them with you. Put English clues on one side and the Greek on the other. You can review by going from Greek to English or from English to Greek. You can get a lot of information on one card; the alphabet, the endings of ὁ, ἡ, and τό, and ten new words will all fit on one side of a card.

Always keep a few cards with you. Keep them above the visor in the car; put them in your billfold or purse; stash them under your baseball cap; tape a few close to you-know-what in the bathroom; keep them handy in the kitchen or in the workshop.

Do anything you can to treat Greek like the language it is. Make it a natural part of your life. Get it out of the books and into the mainstream of your thoughts.

New words:

ἀλλά	but, rather	κυριεύω	lord over, rule
ἀσπασμός, ὁ	greeting	λατρεύω	serve
βασιλεύω	rule	μνημονεύω	remember
βουλεύω	advise	νηστεύω	fast
γάρ	because	οὐ/οὐκ/οὐχ	not
ἔτι	yet	οὐκέτι	no longer
εἰρηνεύω	make peace	Ῥωμαῖος, ὁ	Roman
ἤ	or	Σαδδουκαῖοι, οἱ	Sadducees
ἤδη	already	Φαρισαῖος, οἱ	Pharisees
θεραπεύω	heal	φυτεύω	plant

Don't miss it!

Like the words in all languages, Greek words have many meanings and many shades of meaning. *Webster's II New Riverside University Dictionary*, for example, lists thirty-one different meanings for the English word *cover*. Many Greek words have the same rich diversity of meaning.

Since the vocabulary lists at the end of each STEP usually introduce you to only one or two meanings of a Greek word, you should view each meaning as nothing more than a 'first impression' of the real character of each word. Later on, after you've finished the STEPS, you will delve deeper and deeper into the personality of the words you have met. In the STEPS, you are only making their acquaintance.

STEP 3

ADD-A-PHRASE WORDS

ROLE ⇒	GENERAL SUPP.	DIR.	ACCOMPL.
ἀντί (ἀντ',ἀνθ')	in place of, for		See page 91 W Chart N-19
ἀπό	from, away from		
ἐκ (ἐξ)	out of		
πρό	before		
ἐν		in, with	
σύν		with	
εἰς			into, in

What you need to know:

Add-a-phrase words like ἀπό (from) and ἐν (in) begin useful little phrases of extra information such as *from the town* and *in the house*. They add extra information to camera-words: *John **ran** from the town*, or to something-words: *The **man** in the house followed him.*

Strange but true:

All add-a-phrase words insist that any ὁ-, ἡ-, or τό-words in their phrases play particular roles. Some are so strict that they only tolerate *one* role. The add-a-phrase words discussed in this STEP are of that kind. Some allow two roles (STEP 5), and a select few allow as many as three (STEP 8).

Give it a try:

Translate the following phrases and be sure to notice if the something-word is singular, ἄρτου, for example, or plural ἄρτων: ἀντὶ τοῦ ἄρτου, ἀπὸ τοῦ χρόνου, ἀντὶ δεσμίου, ἐξ ὄχλου, ἐκ τοῦ ποταμοῦ, πρὸ τοῦ θρόνου, σὺν σίτῳ, ἐν τῷ κόσμῳ, σὺν ἀδελφοῖς, εἰς ναόν, ἐν τῷ κραβάττῳ, ἀντὶ νόμου, ἀπ' ἀγροῦ, ἀντ' ἀδελφοῦ, πρὸ τοῦ χιλιάρχου, ἐκ τοῦ ἀριθμοῦ, ἐν τοῖς

How to Read New Testament Greek

καρποῖς, ἐκ τοῦ πολέμου, πρὸ τοῦ λαοῦ, σὺν τοῖς συνδούλοις, ἀπὸ τῶν χοίρων.

Translate as meaningfully as possible: ἀντὶ ξένων, ἀπὸ ξένων, πρὸ ξένων

Add the right endings (both singular and plural) and then translate: ἀντί - ἀριθμός, εἰς - πειρασμός, ἀπό - ὁ οἶκος, ἐκ - ἄνθρωποι, σύν - οἱ δοῦλοι, πρό - θάνατος

Now you're the translator:
1. Βλέπω ἄνθρωπον. 2. τὸν ζῆλον τῶν δούλων καὶ τοῦ γεωργοῦ βλέπω. 3. τῷ διακόνῳ τοῦ κυρίου γράφω. 4. ἔχω τὸν πλοῦτον τοῦ λόγου τοῦ θεοῦ. 5. βλέπω τὸν ἄγγελον πρὸ τοῦ οἴκου τοῦ διδασκάλου. 6. ἐκ τοῦ φόβου τοῦ θανάτου τὸν δοῦλον ἀπολύω. 7. τὸν ἄρτον καὶ τὸν οἶνον ἐν τῷ οἴκῳ ἔχω. 8. ἀπολύω τὸν ἄνθρωπον ἀπὸ τοῦ δεσμοῦ τοῦ ἐχθροῦ. 9. σὺν ζήλῳ τῷ ἀδελφῷ τοῦ γεωργοῦ δουλεύω. 10. τὸν δοῦλον ἐν τῷ ἀγρῷ τοῦ φίλου βλέπω. 11. πιστεύω εἰς τὸν κύριον. 12. πρὸ τοῦ θρόνου τοῦ θεοῦ ἐν τοῖς οὐρανοῖς βλέπω τοὺς ἀγγέλους. 13. δουλεύω τῷ υἱῷ τοῦ θεοῦ ἀντὶ τοῦ διαβόλου. 14. ἀπὸ τοῦ πειρασμοῦ τοῦ διαβόλου φεύγω. 15. λέγω τοὺς λόγους τοῦ κυρίου πρὸ τῶν ἀνθρώπων.

Don't forget!
Some camera-words, such as δουλεύω in sentence 13, complete their meaning by teaming up with a word in the directing role instead of a word in the accomplishing role, which you would normally expect. That's why δουλεύω τῷ υἱῷ means *I am serving the son* and not *I am serving with the son*.

Don't miss it!
In the following sentences you will run into some more words in the *directing* role. Words in the directing role usually add additional information to the camera-word by answering one of the following three questions:
  1. How? They show in what way something is done and can often best be translated with phrases such as *with a broom* or *with his hands*.
  2. Where? They indicate where something is taking place and are often translated with phrases such as *at the shore* or *in the city*.
  3. When? They describe when something was done, and are often translated with phrases such as *in the evening* or *at daybreak*.

Now you're the translator:
1. Τοῖς ὀφθαλμοῖς τὸν θρόνον τοῦ κυρίου βλέπω. 2. ζήλῳ δουλεύω τῷ Χριστῷ. 3. ἀκούω φόβῳ τὸν ἀριθμὸν τῶν ἐχθρῶν. 4. φεύγω ἀπὸ τοῦ διαβόλου καιρῷ τοῦ πειρασμοῦ. 5. χρόνῳ τοῦ θερισμοῦ τῷ γεωργῷ δουλεύω. 6. βλέπω τῳ ναῷ τοὺς διακόνους.

STEP 3

Any questions?

Q: I'm not real sure about some of the translations I'm coming up with. Does it help me to translate without really knowing if I'm on the right track or not?

A: Sure. At the beginning the struggle to find the answers is more important than the answers themselves. You have to get used to working your own way step by step through a linguistic world that is new and strange to you. Which one of the above sentences were you unsure of?

Q: Number 5 gave me some problems.

A: I assume you had no problem finding and translating the camera-word δουλεύω which means *I am serving* or *I serve*. The two words in the directing role, χρόνῳ and γεωργῷ, are probably the ones that confused you.

Q: Those are the ones, all right.

A: You learned in this STEP that δουλεύω completes its action with a word in the directing role instead of a word in the accomplishing role. That means either χρόνῳ or γεωργῷ is like a word in the accomplishing role. Let's see what happens if we let χρόνῳ play the accomplishing role and γεωργῷ the directing role:

*I am serving the **time** of harvest with the farmer.*

As you can see, this translation is meaningless. How can someone serve a time of harvest? Let's try it again and put γεωργῷ in the accomplishing role and χρόνῳ in the directing role:

*I serve the **farmer** at the time of harvest.*

Now the meaning has become clear. Try to think of the words in each sentence as though they were pieces of a puzzle. There are enough clues in the STEPS to solve each puzzle, but you've got to figure out how to recognize the clues and where to find the right parts. That's the real goal of these exercises; not just to get the answers right.

New words:

ἄγγελος, ὁ	messenger	ἐκ (ἐξ)	gen: out of
ἄνθρωπος, ὁ	man	ζῆλος, ὁ	zealot
ἀπό (ἀπ'/ἀφ')	gen: from, away from	θάνατος, ὁ	death
ἀπολύω	set free	θερισμός, ὁ	harvest
ἀπόστολος, ὁ	envoy	κλῆρος, ὁ	lot, share
ἀντί (ἀντ'/ἀνθ')	gen: in place of	κράβαττος, ὁ	bed
δέσμιος, ὁ	prisoner	κύριος, ὁ	lord
διάβολος, ὁ	devil	οἶκος, ὁ	house
διάκονος, ὁ	servant	οἶνος, ὁ	wine
διδάσκαλος, ὁ	teacher	παράκλητος, ὁ	lawyer, helper
δοῦλος, ὁ	slave	πλοῦτος, ὁ	plenty
εἰς	acc: in, into	πόλεμος, ὁ	conflict, quarrel
ἐν	dir: in	πρεσβύτερος, ὁ	older man

πρό	gen: before
πῶλος, ὁ	horse
σῖτος, ὁ	grain
σύν	dir: with
σύνδουλος, ὁ	fellow slave
χιλίαρχος, ὁ	leader of 1000 men
χοῖρος, ὁ	pig

STEP 4

ADD-A-PHRASE WORDS			
ROLE ⇒	GENERAL SUPP.	DIR.	ACCOMPL.
διά (δι')	through		because of
κατά (κατ', καθ')	against, down upon		according to, along
μετά (μετ', μεθ')	with		after
περί	concerning		around
ὑπέρ	for, on behalf of		above, over, more than
ὑπό (ὑπ', ὑφ')	from		under
πρός		near, at	toward, to

See page 91, Word Chart N-20

Don't forget!
Add-a-phrase words add short phrases of information to both something-words (The **man** *with a hat*) and camera-words (He **walks** *with a limp*). Greek add-a-phrase words function much like English add-a-phrase words, with one rather unusual exception: Greek add-a-phrase words are finicky about the roles played by the something-words in their phrases.

In STEP 3 you met add-a-phrase words that only associate with something-words playing one role. Those listed below, however, are willing to associate with those playing two roles. But watch what happens when there is a role change:

διά (δι')
    gen. supporting role: *through*
    accomplishing role: *because of*

κατά (κατ', καθ')
    gen. supporting role: *against, down upon*
    accomplishing role: *according to, along*

μετά (μετ', μεθ')
    gen. supporting role: *with*
    accomplishing role: *after*

περί
    gen. supporting role: *concerning*
    accomplishing role: *around*

ὑπέρ
    gen. supporting role: *for, in behalf of*
    accomplishing role: *above, over, more than*

ὑπό
    gen. supporting role: *from*
    accomplishing role: *under*

πρός
    directing role: *near, at*
    accomplishing role: *toward, to*

Don't miss it!

When translating these phrase-words, you have to notice which role the something-word in the phrase is playing. περί τοῦ κόσμου, for example, means *concerning the world*, whereas περί τὸν κόσμον means *around the world*.

Don't miss it!

The alternate spellings in parenthesis are the form of the word when followed by a word beginning with a vowel.

Give it a try:

Translate the following phrases: διὰ τὸν ἄρτον, διὰ τοῦ ἄρτου, μετὰ τοῦ χρόνου, μετὰ τὸν χρόνον, ὑπὲρ τοὺς οἴκους, ὑπὲρ τῶν οἴκων, περὶ τοῦ κόσμου, περὶ τὸν κόσμον, κατὰ τοῦ οὐρανοῦ, κατὰ τὸν νόμον, πρὸς τῷ ἀγρῷ, πρὸς τὸν ἀγρόν.

Now give these a try: διὰ λόγου, μετ' ἀνθρώπων, περὶ τοῦ διαβόλου, περὶ τὸν θρόνον, μετὰ τοὺς λόγους, ὑπὲρ ναόν, ὑπὸ τὸν θρόνον, πρὸς τῷ λαῷ, δι' ἀγγέλων, κατὰ θρόνου, ὑπὲρ τῶν γεωργῶν, ὑφ' ἁμαρτωλοῦ, πρὸς πλοῦτον, διὰ τοὺς κληρονόμους, πρὸς τῷ ποταμῷ, ὑπ' ἐχθροῦ, ὑπὲρ ἀμνοῦ, περὶ τὸν κόσμον, μετὰ τὸν φόβον, διὰ πειρασμοῦ, πρὸς τοῖς δεσμοῖς, ὑπ' ὀφθαλμῶν, ὑπὲρ ἀριθμόν, περὶ τοῦ σταυροῦ, μετὰ θεοῦ, κατὰ τοὺς ἀποστόλους, διὰ τοὺς ἀδελφούς

STEP 4

Now you're the translator:
1. Ὁ κύριος τὸν δοῦλον τοῦ στρατηγοῦ διὰ τοῦ λόγου θεραπεύει. 2. οὐ δουλεύετε τῷ θεῷ διὰ τὸν μισθόν. 3. ἐχ τοῦ φόβου πρὸς τὸν κύριον φεύγομεν. 4. οἱ ἀδελφοὶ τῷ χρόνῳ τοῦ πειρασμοῦ μετὰ τοῦ Χριστοῦ μένουσιν. 5. ὁ δοῦλος οὐκ ἐστίν ὑπὲρ τὸν κύριον, ἀλλὰ ὑπὸ τὸν κύριον. 6. διὰ τοῦ ἐπαίνου τῷ θεῷ λατρεύεις. 7. ἀκούει τοὺς λόγους περὶ τοῦ σταυροῦ τοῦ Ἰησοῦ.

Any Questions?
Q: How can I possibly remember the meanings of these words? I have enough trouble recognizing and learning normal words without the added complication of having the meaning change when the form changes.
A: If you ever find the complete answer to that question, let me know. I'm a bit shaky on it myself. Since this feature of Greek is so unusual for English speakers, it's important for now, at the outset when the whole mountain of Greek is still in front of you, to simply *realize* that there are different possibilities of meaning depending on the role a word is playing in a phrase. Here are a few other ideas that may prove helpful:

1. Learning does not usually follow the pattern of *read, memorize, remember.* A few lucky souls may seem to learn in this way, but for the great majority learning looks more like this: *read, read again, scratch head, sort out, try to remember, forget, reread, practice, get tired, forget again, read again, etc.*

Looks grim, right? Wrong. It's actually a quite natural and effective way to learn. Most learning takes place in this bumbling sort of way. Just observe a small child learning to walk. He struggles and falls and rolls and totters and makes a total mess of the thing for months. Then, one day, he gets the hang of it and he's off and running.

If it's that way with small children who are the champions of learning, then we shouldn't be surprised if we have to go through similar ups and downs to learn something new. All any of us can do when it comes to learning a language is to keep doing the work necessary to make the miracle of understanding possible. If we keep on, understanding will grow in us.

2. Memory can be improved by taking advantage of the laws of association. I remember the first six phrase-words above by relating each word to the words of this sentence:

<u>Dealing</u> <u>cards</u>, I <u>met a</u> <u>pair of</u> <u>uppity</u> <u>U-boats</u>.
διά   κατά   μετά περί   ὑπέρ   ὑπό

And I remember the meaning of each word by forming the following pictures:
διά - I see myself <u>dealing</u> the cards *through a beacon* and then I know the two
  meanings: *through* and *because*.
κατά - I see the <u>cards</u> falling *down* and *along* the floor. Hence: *down* and *along*.
μετά - I see myself <u>meeting</u> <u>a</u> *witch actor*. Hence: *with* and *after*.

περί - I see a <u>pear</u> dressed like a boxer standing in a ring ready to fight *a bout,* and *a round* is about to begin. Hence: *about* and *around.*
ὑπέρ - I see that the U-boat is so <u>uppity</u>, because it is wearing *foreign overalls.* Hence: *for* and *over.*
ὑπό - I see the <u>U-boat</u> coming up *from under* the sea. Hence: *from* and *under.*

These pictures are all pretty ridiculous, of course, but that's what makes them work. In fact, they're almost impossible to forget. They've rattled around in my head for years now. Most so-called memory experts do nothing more than learn to make quick associations such as these.

New words:

ἀνά	acc: among, between	κατά	gen: down from, against
		(κατ'/καθ')	acc: along, according to
διά (δι')	gen: through	μένω	stay
	acc: because of	μετά	gen: with
εἰσίν	they are	(μετ'/μεθ')	acc: after
ἐνιαυτός, ὁ	year	μισθός, ὁ	salary
ἔπαινος, ὁ	praise	περί	gen: concerning
ἐπίσκοπος, ὁ	overseer		acc: around
ἐστίν	he is, she is, it is	πρός	gen: near, at
			acc: toward, to
ἥλιος, ὁ	sun	στρατηγός, ὁ	chief, magistrate
ἦν	he was, she was, it was	ὑπέρ	gen: for, in behalf of
			acc: above, more than
Ἰησοῦς	Jesus	ὑπό	gen: from
κόπος, ὁ	trouble, toil		acc: under

STEP 5

SOMETHING-WORDS		
ROLE	sing.	pl.
	ἡ παρθένος	
Necessary	-ος	-οι
General supporting	-ου	-ων
Directing	-ῳ	-οις
Accomplishing	-ον	-ους
See pages 65-67, Word Chart L-1		

What you need to know:

Most Greek words with an -ος ending are ὁ-words and ὁ, of course, is the word for *the* that accompanies them (ὁ λόγος, τοῦ λόγου, τῷ λόγῳ, etc.). There are a few ἡ-words, however, which also have an -ος ending just like λόγος. That can be a bit confusing. They look like ὁ-words but are actually ἡ-words, and therefore their *the* is ἡ and not ὁ.

This is how ἡ changes roles:

ἡ in all its roles		
	Singular	Plural
Necessary role	ἡ	αἱ
General supporting role	τῆς	τῶν
Directing role	τῇ	ταῖς
Accomplishing role	τήν	τάς

Word Chart N-16

How to Read New Testament Greek

Give it a try:
What roles are being played by the following forms of ἡ?
τῇ, τῶν, τάς, ἡ, ταῖς, τήν, αἱ, τῆς; τάς, τῆς, τῇ, τήν, ἡ, αἱ, ταῖς, τῶν; τῆς, ταῖς, τάς

Add the correct form of *the* to the following words:
βίβλου, ἐρήμῳ, ὁδός, παρθένον, ῥάβδοι, ἀμπέλους, νήσοις, βίβλοι, νόσων, ἀβύσσου, ὁδόν, ῥάβδῳ, παρθένος, νόσοι, ἀμπέλων, νήσους, παρθένου

Add the correct forms of ὁδός, βίβλος, νόσος, and νῆσος to the following forms of *the*: τῆς, τῶν, τάς, ἡ, τῇ, αἱ, τήν, ταῖς

Translate these phrases:
ἀντὶ τῆς βίβλου, τῇ παρθένῳ, ὑπὸ τὴν ἄμπελον, μετὰ τῆς ῥάβδου, κατὰ τὴν ὁδόν, ὑπὲρ τὰς ἀμπέλους, αἱ βίβλοι, ἐκ τῶν βίβλων, περὶ τὴν ἔρημον, περὶ τῆς παρθένου, πρὸς ταῖς ὁδοῖς, πρὸ τῆς ἀβύσσου, εἰς τὴν ἔρημον

Now you're the translator:
1. Οἱ γεωργοὶ τῆς νήσου τοὺς καρποὺς ἐν τοῖς οἴκοις ἔχουσιν. 2. ἐπὶ ταῖς νήσοις οἴκους βλέπετε. 3. Φαρισαῖος ἐν τῇ ἐρήμῳ ἐστὶν καὶ νηστεύει 4. παρθένοι πρὸς τῷ ποταμῷ εἰσιν. 5. οἱ ἀμνοὶ ἐπὶ τοῖς ἀγροῖς τῆς νήσου εἰσίν. 6. τῷ καιρῷ τοῦ θερισμοῦ τοὺς καρποὺς τῶν ἀμπέλων ἔχομεν. 7. ἡ παρθένος Μαριὰμ τὸν λόγον τοῦ ἀγγέλου ἀκούει καὶ τῷ θεῷ ὑπακούει. 8. ὁ κύριος Ἰησοῦς ἐν τῷ πειρασμῷ τοῦ διαβόλου ἐν τῇ ἐρήμῳ ἦν. 9. ὁ κύριος τὸν δοῦλον τοῦ στρατηγοῦ ἀπὸ τῆς νόσου θεραπεύει. 10. ἐν τῇ βίβλῳ ἔχομεν τὸν λόγον τοῦ υἱοῦ τοῦ θεοῦ· διὸ εἰς Ἰησοῦν πιστεύομεν. 11. ὑπακούομεν τῷ λόγῳ τῆς βίβλου τοῦ θεοῦ. 12. τὸν Ἰησοῦν οὐκέτι βλέπομεν ἐπὶ τῷ σταυρῷ, ἀλλ᾽ ἐπὶ τῷ θρόνῳ. 13. Ὁ Χριστὸς ὁ ἄρτος ἐξ οὐρανοῦ ὑπὲρ τῶν ἀνθρώπων ἐν τῷ κόσμῳ ἐστίν. 14. Ἰησοῦς Χριστὸς ἡ ἄμπελος ἡ ἀληθινή ἐστιν καὶ ἡ ὁδὸς πρὸς τὸν θεόν. 15. ἀπολύει ἀνθρώπους ἐκ τῆς ἀβύσσου τοῦ πειρασμοῦ διὰ τοῦ διαβόλου.

Study tip!
You know how it is with traffic jams: The flow of cars grinds to a halt, and drivers brace themselves for the worst, not knowing if the snail's pace on the pavement will last for a minute or an hour or half a day. Language learners will also experience times when the flow of progress grinds to a halt. What do you do when this happens to you?

Keep moving as best you can, even if it means inching along. Given enough time and patience, many hold-ups will unravel themselves. Let's say you're working through the exercises in a STEP and run into a word or a phrase or a sentence that stumps you. How can you find the answers? Here's how you can keep moving:

1. Reread the STEP—all of it—and do the rest of the exercises.

STEP 5

2. Do a quick review of the previous STEPS.

3. Reread those pages of the tour through Universal Greek Pictures that deal with the subject area of your question.

4. Check the Word Chart or the comprehensive vocabulary list in the back of the book.

5. Find related topics in the index.

6. If, after trying all of the above suggestions, you can't come up with a solution, record your question on a list with other questions you have and move on to the next STEP. It's very possible that with time your question will work itself out.

Unfortunately, not all hold-ups will sort themselves out. Some may turn into major affairs that just don't go away. In these cases, there's only one way to get traffic moving again: call out the language police to solve the problem.

If the day comes when you have a number of questions collecting cobwebs on your list, and you've exhausted all your possibilities to find answers, here's what you should do:

1. Describe your questions on a sheet of paper as precisely as possible, including page numbers wherever applicable.

2. Then send the questions to the following address:

Universal Greek Pictures
513 E. Florence Blvd., C-10
Casa Grande, Az 85222

Your questions will be analyzed in the laboratories of Universal Greek Pictures and the results—hopefully along with usable answers—will be returned to you as soon as possible. Don't hesitate to write. Sending your questions will not only break up your log jams, but help us to improve future editions of *Learning How to Read New Testament Greek with People Just Like You*.

New words:

ἄβυσσος, ἡ	abyss, underworld	κωλύω	hinder
Αἴγυπτος, ἡ	Egypt	μεταξύ	between
ἀληθινή	true	νόσος, ἡ	disease
ἄμπελος, ἡ	grapevine	νῆσος, ἡ	island
βίβλος, ἡ	book	ὁδός, ἡ	way
διό	therefore	παρθένος, ἡ	virgin
ἐλπίζω	expect	ῥαβδος, ἡ	staff
ἐπί	on, because of	ὑπακούω	listen to, obey
ἔρημος, ἡ	desert	ὑποκάτω	under

STEP 6

SOMETHING-WORDS		
ROLE	sing.	pl.
	τό ἔργ-ον	
Necessary	-ov	-α
General supporting	-ου	-ων
Directing	-ῳ	-οις
Accomplishing	-ov	-α
See pages 65-67, Word Chart M-1		

What you need to know:
τό is the word for *the* that accompanies all τό-words. Here's how τό changes its roles:

τό in all its roles		
	Singular	Plural
Necessary role	τό	τά
General supporting role	τοῦ	τῶν
Directing role	τῷ	τοῖς
Accomplishing role	τό	τά
Word Chart N-17		

Don't miss it!
τό-words have identical endings in the *necessary* and the *accomplishing* roles.

Give it a try:
What roles are the following words playing?
δένδρον (2x), τέκνου, ἔργων, δείπνῳ, πλοῖα (2x), δώροις, ἀρνίον, σημείου, δαιμονίοις, εἴδωλα, εὐαγγελίῳ, ἱματίων, δάκρυα, μύρον, ὅρια, πετεινόν, ταλάντου, σπλάγχνα

STEP 6

Complete the following endings:
Gen. supp. sg. δενδρ__, Nec. pl. ζῷ__, Dir. pl. ἀρνι__, Acc. pl. ποτηρι__, Nec. sg. ἐργ__, Gen. supp. pl. σημει__, Dir. sg. εἰδωλ__, Nec. pl. προβατ__, Acc. sg. δειπν__, Acc. pl. δαιμονι__

Add the correct form of τό to the following words:
τῷ προβάτ__, τὸ εὐαγγέλι__, τοῦ μυστηρί__, τὰ δαιμόνι__, τοῖς δώρ__, τῶν σαββάτ__.

Now you're the translator:
1. Τοὺς καρποὺς τῶν ἀγρῶν καὶ τῶν δένδρων καὶ τῶν ἀμπέλων ἔχετε. 2. οἱ ἄνθρωποι τοῦ κόσμου τοῖς εἰδώλοις καὶ τοῖς δαιμονίοις λατρεύουσιν. 3. ὁ Σαδδουκαῖος τὰ τέκνα παιδεύει· τοὺς δὲ υἱοὺς κωλύει ἐπὶ τῇ ὁδῷ πρὸς τὸν Ἰησοῦν. 4. οἱ οὐρανοὶ καὶ ὁ κόσμος ἔργα τοῦ θεοῦ εἰσιν· τῷ δὲ μαρτυρίῳ τῶν ἔργων τοῦ θεοῦ οἱ ἄνθρωποι οὐ πιστεύουσιν. 5. οἱ πρεσβύτεροι διδάσκαλοι τοῦ εὐαγγελίου εἰσίν. 6. ὁ λόγος τοῦ σταυροῦ τοῖς ἀνθρώποις ἐν τῷ κόσμῳ σκάνδαλόν ἐστιν. 7. ἐν τῷ δείπνῳ τοῦ κυρίου τὸ ποτήριον καὶ τὸν ἄρτον ἔχομεν. 8. τὸ εὐαγγέλιον τοῦ Ἰησοῦ δῶρον τοῦ θεοῦ ὑπὲρ τῶν ἀνθρώπων ἐστίν. 9. οἱ ἀπόστολοι τὸ μυστήριον τοῦ θανάτου τοῦ Ἰησοῦ ἐπὶ τῷ σταυρῷ λέγουσιν τοῖς λαοῖς. 10. Τὰ πρόβατα καὶ τὰ ἀρνία ἐπὶ τοῖς ἀγροῖς τῶν γεωργῶν ἦν. 11. τὰ τέκνα τοῦ φίλου ἐν τῷ οἴκῳ μένουσιν. 12. τὰ ἱμάτια ἐν τῷ οἴκῳ ἐπὶ τῇ νήσῳ ἦν. 13. τὰ τέκνα ὑπακούουσιν τῷ λόγῳ τῶν πρεσβυτέρων. 14. πρὸ τοῦ θρόνου τοῦ θεοῦ τὰ ζῷα ἐστιν. 15. μνημονεύομεν τοὺς λόγους τοῦ κυρίου· ἀληθινὰ γὰρ τὰ μαρτύρια τοῦ κυρίου ἐστίν.

Don't miss it!
The word in the necessary role and the endings of the camera-word always correspond to one another. If one is singular, the other is singular. If one is plural, the other is plural. To see an example of this, compare sentence five with sentence six:
  5. Οἱ πρεσβύτεροι......εἰσίν. The older men...(they) are
  6. ὁ λόγος............ἐστιν. The word.........(it) is
There is one exception to this rule: Sometimes camera-words treat certain plural τό-words as a mass or a unit of things. δένδρα (trees), for example, is considered singular because the trees are seen as a forest. It's only when a plural τό-word seems to refer to individual objects that the camera-word goes along with it and tacks on its own plural ending. (τὰ τέκνα...μένουσιν in sentence 11 is an example of this.)

Any questions?
Q: If the necessary and accomplishing role endings are the same for τό-words, aren't there times when they can be mixed up?
A: I suppose a mix-up is possible, but the context usually points a sure finger to

which role is meant. For example, if τέκνον and δένδρον are together in a sentence with a camera-word that means *to cut,* then it's clear that the tree is not cutting down the child, but the other way around.

Q: What's that little 'ι' underneath some of the letters like in the word τῇ?
A: The letter 'ι' is often written below the letters α, η, and ω. It's usually called the *iota subscript.* It is not pronounced. It's particularly a typical sign of the endings of singular something-words in the *directing role* and the endings of camera-words with *you* in the necessary role.

New words:

σπλάγχνα, τά	intestines(heart, compassion)	μύρον, τό	ointment
ἀρνίον, τό	lamb	μυστήριον, τό	secret
δαιμόνιον, τό	demon	ὅριον, τό	border
δάκρυον, τό	tears, weeping	πετεινόν, τό	bird
δένδρον, τό	tree	πλοῖον, τό	ship
δεῖπνον, τό	meal	ποτήριον, τό	cup
δῶρον, τό	gift	πρόβατον, τό	sheep
εἴδωλον, τό	idol	σάββατον, τό	Sabbath
ἔργον, τό	work	σημεῖον, τό	sign
εὐαγγέλιον, τό	good news	σκάνδαλον, τό	trap
ζῷον, τό	animal	τάλαντον, τό	a talent (60 to 80 pounds)
ἱμάτιον, τό	garment, cloak	τέκνον, τό	child
μαρτύριον, τό	witness		

STEP 7

ADD-A-PHRASE WORDS

ROLE ⇒	GENERAL SUPP.	DIR.	ACCOMPL.
ἐπί (ἐπ',ἐφ')	on, at, by	on, at, by	on, at, by
ἐπί (ἐπ',ἐφ')	at time of, because of	for, in addition to	to, up to, towards
παρά (παρ')	from	by, near, beside	along, at the edge

See page 91, Word Chart N-21

What you need to know:
Some add-a-phrase words (STEP 3) allow something-words to play only one role in their phrases. Others (STEP 4) allow something-words to play two roles. ἐπί and παρά are add-a-phrase words that allow something-words to play *three* roles in their phrases. As with the add-a-phrase words in STEP 4, a role change also means a change in meaning.

ἐπί, however, is somewhat of an exception to this rule. It not only has special meanings for each role, but the meanings *on, at,* and *by* are actually possible when a something-word in the phrase plays any of the three roles. That explains why ἐπί has been included in the Word Chart twice. It just happens to be one of those words that has many possible meanings.

Don't miss it!
ἐπί and παρά are shortened when they are placed before words starting with a vowel (α, ι, ε, ο, υ).

Give it a try:
What are the possible translations for these phrases?
ἐπὶ τοῦ ἐχθροῦ, ἐπὶ τῷ ἐχθρῷ, ἐπὶ τὸν ἐχθρόν, παρὰ τὴν ὁδόν, παρὰ τῇ ὁδῷ, παρὰ τῆς ὁδοῦ

Translate these phrases: ἐπὶ τοῦ δένδρου, παρὰ τὸν νόμον, παρὰ τῷ εἰδώλῳ, ἐπὶ τὸ ἀρνίον, ἐπὶ τῷ δώρῳ, παρὰ τοῦ τέκνου, παρὰ τῷ δένδρῳ, ἐπὶ σκάνδαλον, παρὰ τὸ πλοῖον, ἐπὶ μαρτυρίῳ, παρὰ τοὺς ἁμαρτωλούς

Now you're the translator:
1. Τοὺς οἴκους ἐπὶ τῶν νήσων βλέπετε. 2. παρὰ τῷ ποταμῷ ἄμπελοι καὶ

How to Read New Testament Greek

δένδρα εἰσίν. 3. φεύγετε ἀπὸ τῶν ἐχθρῶν ἐπὶ τὴν νῆσον. 4. αἱ βίβλοι δῶρον παρὰ τοῦ ἐπισκόπου ὑπὲρ τῶν διδασκάλων εἰσίν. 5. οἱ δοῦλοι ἐπὶ τοῖς πλοίοις τῶν ‛Ρωμαίων εἰσίν. 6. μεταξὺ τῶν δένδρων ἐπὶ τοῖς ἀγροῖς παρὰ τὸν ποταμὸν οἱ γεωργοὶ τὰς ἀμπέλους φυτεύουσιν. 7. ὁ ὄχλος ἐπὶ τὸν λόγον τοῦ ξένου πιστεύει. 8. τὰ δίκτυα ἐν τοῖς πλοίοις ἦν. 9. ἔλαιον καὶ οἶνον ἐν τῷ οἴκῳ ἔχετε. 10. ἀργύριον καὶ χρυσίον οὐκ ἔχομεν· τὸν δὲ λόγον τοῦ κυρίου ἐν τῷ βιβλίῳ ἔχομεν. 11. βλέπεις τὸν Χριστὸν ἐπὶ τῷ ξύλῳ τοῦ σταυροῦ. 12. οἱ ἀπόστολοι τὸ πρόσωπον τοῦ κυρίου βλέπουσιν.

Any questions?
Q: If a word like ἐπί has so many meanings, doesn't that make it sort of wishy-washy or inaccurate or hard to pin down?
A: We also have words like ἐπί in English. The word *at* is a good example. Look at it's many meanings:

He's *at* the table.	Meaning: *sitting up to*
He's coming *at* 5 o'clock.	Meaning: *on or near time of*
He threw it *at* me.	Meaning: *towards*
He's *at* the picnic.	Meaning: *attending*
He's *at* peace.	Meaning: *in state of*
They're selling *at* fifty cents apiece.	Meaning: *for price of*
He laughed *at* a joke.	Meaning: *because of*
He walks *at* his own pace.	Meaning: *according to*

As you can see, *at* is neither wishy-washy nor inaccurate just because it projects so many meanings. In fact, *at* is a favorite English word for precisely pinpointing times, places, speeds, prices, conditions, and you name it. Precisely the flexibility of words like *at* and ἐπί makes them capable of extreme accuracy. They're like adjustable wrenches which can be made to fit nuts and bolts of all sizes perfectly.

New words:

ἀργύριον, τό	silver, money	ξύλον, τό	wood
βιβλίον, τό	book	παρά	gen: from
δίκτυον, τό	net		dir: by, next to
ἐγώ	I		acc: along, past
ἔλαιον, τό	oil	πρόσωπον, τό	face
ἐπί	gen: on, with, at	σύ	you
	dir: on, because of	χρυσίον, τό	gold
	acc: on, over, up to		
θύρα, ἡ	door		

STEP 8

CAMERA-WORDS				
PICTURE ⇒⇒⇒				VIDEO
LIGHT	ACTION	NEC. ROLE		LIVE
B R I G H T	A C T I V E	I we you all of you he, she, it they		εἰμί *I am* εἰμί ἐσμέν εἶ ἐστέ ἐστίν εἰσίν

Also see STEP 71

What you need to know:

The various forms of the word *be* (am, are, is) are the most used camera-words in the English language. The same is true of εἰμί, its Greek counterpart. εἰμί has several features that distinguish it from other Greek camera-words: First of all, its endings do not closely follow the pattern of any other camera-word.

Secondly, the something-words that complete εἰμί are in the *necessary role* and not in the *accomplishing* role as would be expected. ὁ γεωργός ἀκούει ἄνθρωπον, for example, means *The farmer is hearing a man*. ἄνθρωπον is in the accomplishing role (-ον ending). Therefore, it is completing the action of ἀκούω.

In the sentence ὁ γεωργός ἐστιν ἄνθρωπος, *the farmer is a man*, however, you notice that ἄνθρωπος is in the necessary role (-ος ending) and not in the accomplishing role. This is a quirk of εἰμί that you need to be aware of.

Strange but true!

It was not at all unusual for Greek scribes to leave εἰμί out of sentences in which it actually belonged. They were able to do this because people who read Greek mentally put all the missing εἰμί's into each sentence right where they belonged. When translating such sentences into English, however, the correct form of *be* cannot be left out. So, when you run into sentences without a camera-word, you might just have to add a form of εἰμί before you can make sense out of them.

How to Read New Testament Greek

Give it a try:
Translate the following forms of εἰμί: ἐστίν, εἶ, εἰσίν, εἰμί, ἐσμέν, ἐστέ.

Now you're the translator:
1. Τὰ βιβλία δῶρον τοῦ πρεσβυτέρου ἦν. 2. παράκλητος τῶν δούλων εἶ. 3. διδάσκαλοι τῶν τέκνων ἐστέ. 4. οὐκέτι ἐσμὲν ὑπὸ τὸν διάβολον, ἀλλ' ὑπὸ τὸν κύριον Ἰησοῦν. 5. διὰ τὸν θάνατον τοῦ κυρίου τέκνα τοῦ θεοῦ καὶ διάκονοι τοῦ Ἰησοῦ ἐσμεν. 6. Ἰησοῦς ὁ ἄρτος τοῦ θεοῦ ὑπὲρ τῶν ἀνθρώπων τοῦ κόσμου ἐστίν. 7. σὺ εἶ ὁ χριστὸς ὁ υἱὸς τοῦ θεοῦ. 8. ἐγώ εἰμι ἡ ἄμπελος ἡ ἀληθινή. 9. ἐγώ εἰμι ἡ θύρα[1] τῶν προβάτων.

1 door

Any questions?
Q: How could people know where εἰμί belonged in a sentence if it was just left out?
A: Every language has elements that are so common they simply don't have to be spoken or written. If I look at you and say, *Go to the store*, for example, you know I'm talking directly to you. I don't have to say, *You go to the store*. Or if I say, *What a great day*, it's actually a complete thought even though I don't use a camera-word. That's because the two little words *it is* are always understood by an English speaker to be a part of such exclamations. I could have said, *What a great day it is*, but the short form did the job just as well.

Keep your eyes and ears open and you'll be surprised how often people use expressions in which certain words are simply understood. It was the same way with those who read Greek in the first century. εἰμί did not always have to be written for them to 'read' where it was supposed to be.

STEP 9

SOMETHING-WORDS		
ROLE	sing.	pl.
	ἡ τιμ-ή	
Necessary	-ή	-αί
General supporting	-ῆς	-ῶν
Directing	-ῇ	-αῖς
Accomplishing	-ήν	-άς

See pages 65-67, Word Chart N-1

What you need to know:
This STEP and the following two STEPS introduce you to three groups of ἡ-words that change their endings in very similar ways. Check your Word Chart (N-1, O-1, P-1) and compare the endings.
As you learned in STEP 1, most words that end with -ος are ὁ-words. (You met the exceptions to this rule in STEP 5.) In the same way, most words that end with -η or -α are ἡ-words.

Don't miss it!
ἡ-words like τιμή change their endings exactly like ἡ.

Give it a try:
Which roles are the following words playing?
φωναί, φωνῶν, φωνῇ, φωνή, φωνάς, φωνῆς, φωναῖς, ἀδελφή, ἀρχῇ, βουλῆς, ἐντολάς, ἀγάπην, εἰρήνη, κωμῶν, ἀκοῇ, βροντήν, νεφέλαι, πληγῆς, πόρναις, φιάλας
Which form of ἡ accompanies each of the above words?
Add the correct endings:
ἑορτ__, βουλ__, ἀγάπ__, παραβολ__, γραφ__, οἰκοδομ__.

Now you're the translator:
1. Οἱ Ἰουδαῖοι ἐν τῇ οἰκουμένῃ συναγωγὰς ἔχουσιν. 2. γράφεις τῇ ἀδελφῇ ἐν ἐπιστολῇ περὶ τῆς οἰκοδομῆς τοῦ οἴκου. 3. ὁ γεωργὸς τροφὴν ὑπὲρ ἐνιαυτοῦ ἐν τῷ οἴκῳ ἔχει. 4. μετ' ἐνιαυτὸν ἑορτὴ τῶν Ἰουδαίων ἦν. 5. τὰ πρόβατα τῆς φωνῆς τοῦ κυρίου ἀκούουσιν. 6. τὴν διδαχὴν τῶν

How to Read New Testament Greek

ἀποστόλων ἐν ταῖς γραφαῖς ἔχομεν. 7. ὁ φίλος τὸν λόγον τῆς ἀγάπης καὶ τῆς δικαιοσύνης τοῦ θεοῦ τοῖς ἀνθρώποις ἐν τῇ ἑορτῇ λέγει. 8. ἐν ὑπακοῇ καὶ ὑπομονῇ οἱ διάκονοι τῷ κυρίῳ ἀπ' ἀρχῆς δουλεύουσιν. 9. αἱ ἐλεημοσύναι τοῦ κληρονόμου σημεῖόν ἐστιν τῆς ἀγάπης. 10. ὑπακούετε τῇ βουλῇ τοῦ πρεσβυτέρου καὶ ταῖς ἐντολαῖς τοῦ κυρίου. 11. πιστεύομεν ταῖς διαθήκαις τῆς ζωῆς. 12. ὁ Ἰησοῦς διὰ τῆς νίκης ἐπὶ τοῦ σταυροῦ ἀνθρώπους ἀπολύει ἐκ τοῦ θανάτου. 13. ὁ θεὸς τὰς προσευχὰς καὶ τὰς ἐλεημοσύνας τοῦ ἐπισκόπου οἶδεν. 14. οἱ ἄνθρωποι τῶν κωμῶν τὸν λόγον τῆς ζωῆς ἐν παραβολαῖς ἀκούουσιν. 15. τῷ ἀμνῷ τοῦ θεοῦ τιμή.

Study Tip!

You can learn to recognize words and their meanings much faster if you learn the words within the context of sentences or phrases. This is the *natural* way to learn vocabulary. This is advantageous first of all because the context of a sentence often provides enough clues to define each word, and secondly, because it's within the context of a sentence or phrase that the various forms of a word are used. (If you only learn the dictionary form of a word, you may not recognize its other forms when you meet them in a written text.)

The sentences you translate in each STEP can be effectively used for this purpose. Choose a few representative sentences in which all or most of the new words for the STEP are found, and concentrate on learning these sentences. Jot the sentences down on cards for review purposes.

New words:

ἀγάπη, ἡ	love	οἰκοδομή, ἡ	building
ἀδελφή, ἡ	sister	οἰκουμένη, ἡ	construction, building
ἀκοή, ἡ	hearing, report		
ἀρχή, ἡ	beginning	ὅτι	because, that
βουλή, ἡ	advice, decision	πάλιν	again, return, furthermore
βροντή, ἡ	thunder		
γραφή, ἡ	writing	παραβολή, ἡ	parable
διαθήκη, ἡ	testament	παρεμβολή, ἡ	military camp
διδαχή, ἡ	teaching	πληγή, ἡ	wound, a blow
δικαιοσύνη, ἡ	justice	πόρνη, ἡ	prostitute
εἰρήνη, ἡ	peace	προσευχή, ἡ	prayer
ἐλεημοσύνη, ἡ	good deed, alms	συναγωγή, ἡ	assembly place
ἐπιστολή, ἡ	letter	τιμή, ἡ	honor
ἐντολή, ἡ	command	τροφή, ἡ	food
ἑορτή, ἡ	festival	ὑπακοή, ἡ	obedience
ζωή, ἡ	life	ὑπομονή, ἡ	patience
κώμη, ἡ	village	φιάλη, ἡ	bowl
νεφέλη, ἡ	cloud	φωνή, ἡ	sound, voice
νίκη, ἡ	victory	ψυχή, ἡ	life
οἶδεν	he knows		

STEP 10

SOMETHING-WORDS		
ROLE	sing.	pl.
ἡ οἰκί-α		
Necessary	-α	-αι
General supporting	-ας	-ῶν
Directing	-ᾳ	-αις
Accomplishing	-αν	-ας
See pages 65-67, Word Chart O-1		

What you need to know:
ἡ-words like οἰκία are much like τιμή, only wherever τιμή has an η, they have an α.

Strange but true:
Besides the four normal roles (*necessary, general supporting, directing, accomplishing*), there's another *role* in Greek called the *addressing role* that is rarely used. It was used often in classical Greek (before 300 B.C.), but had almost disappeared from the Greek of the first century. Every now and then it appears in the writings of the New Testament.

The *addressing role* was used to directly address a person. κύριε! *Lord!* κενὲ ἄνθρωπε! *You foolish man!*

Notice that the -ς falls away from κύριος and ἄνθρωπος, and that the ο is changed to ε. For the most part, however, the *necessary role* has taken over for the addressing role. θεός! *God!* means the same as θεέ! *God!* which is rarely used.

Give it a try:
Which roles are the following words playing?
θύρα, θύραι, θυρῶν, θύραις, θύρας(!), θύραν, θύρα; καρδίαν, ἁμαρτίαι, τῆς ἀνομίας, διακονία, διδασκαλία, τὰς ἐκκλησίας, ἀγοραῖς, ἡμερῶν, μαχαίραις, περιστεράν, πλεονεξία, ἀκαθαρσία.

How to Read New Testament Greek

Add the right endings to the following words:
ἡ ἀπιστί___, ταῖς πέτρ___, τὰς ἀγκύρ___, τῶν ὡρ___, αἱ χῆρ___, τῆς φθορ___, τὴν χώρ___, τῇ χαρ___, τῆς ἀγορ___.

Put each of the following words in the *necessary* role:
ἀλήθειαν, ἀδελφῆς, καρδίαι, ἐπιστολάς, ἐξουσίας, διδαχῇ, τροφαῖς, λατρειῶν, δουλεία, ὑπομονήν, παρρησίας, ἑορτάς.

Now you're the translator:
1. Βλέπομεν τὴν ἐκκλησίαν ἐν τῇ διακονίᾳ τῆς φιλαδελφίας. 2. λέγεις ἐν ἐξουσίᾳ τὸ μαρτύριον τῆς βασιλείας τοῦ θεοῦ. 3. ἡ φιλαδελφία καὶ ἡ εὐσέβειά εἰσιν μαρτυρίαι τῆς μετανοίας. 4. αἱ διδασκαλίαι τοῦ κυρίου ἀλήθειά εἰσιν. 5. ἡ ἀλήθεια ἐν τῇ ἐκκλησίᾳ τοῦ θεοῦ κυριεύει. 6. οἱ πρεσβύτεροι δουλεύουσιν ταῖς ἐκκλησίαις ἐν σοφίᾳ καὶ εὐσεβείᾳ. 7. ἡ ἁμαρτία ἐν ταῖς καρδίαις τῶν ἀνθρώπων τῆς ἀπιστίας βασιλεύει. 8. αἱ ἐκκλησίαι παρρησίᾳ καὶ εὐχαριστίᾳ δουλεύουσιν τῷ θεῷ ἕως τῆς παρουσίας τοῦ κυρίου Ἰησοῦ Χριστοῦ. 9. τὰ τέκνα τοῦ θεοῦ οὐκ εἰσιν ὑπὸ τὴν δουλείαν τοῦ διαβόλου καὶ ἐν τῇ σκοτίᾳ τῆς ἁμαρτίας, ἀλλ' ἐν τῇ σωτηρίᾳ τοῦ θεοῦ. 10. πιστεύομεν εἰς τὰς προφητείας τῆς ἀληθείας. 11. αἱ λατρεῖαι τῶν ἐκκλησιῶν χαρά εἰσιν. 12. ἡ εὐσέβειά ἐστιν σημεῖον τῆς μετανοίας. 13. τὰ πλοῖα τῶν Ἰουδαίων ἀγκύρας ἔχει. 14. τῷ κυρίῳ τῆς Ἰουδαίας χώρας ὑπακούεις. 15. αἱ ὧραι τῆς ἡμέρας φεύγουσιν.

Any questions:
Q: I still don't quite understand why there are so many accent marks above the letters of every word.
A: In Greek there are three markings placed over vowels to indicate which syllables are to be accented. Traditionally they have been called the acute (έ), the grave (ὲ), and the circumflex (ῶ). They show us which syllable should be stressed. Originally accents had different meanings, but today they are treated as though they were all the same. When accents are placed over double vowels, they are always placed over the *second* of the two vowels (εί). When capital letters are accented, the accent always appear to the *left* of the letter ('O).

The acute (έ) is the accent that is used the most, and it can appear over any of the last three syllables. If it's on the last syllable and is followed by another word, it changes to a grave (ὲ). The grave (ὲ) only occurs on the last syllable.
The circumflex (ῶ) occurs only over long vowels such as η or ω.

Sometimes certain words have such an attraction to others that when they appear together they actually give their accent to the other word (οὗτός ἐστιν, for example). Greek also has a *rough* breathing mark (ἁ) which is usually pronounced as an *h* (ἁ = ha), and a *smooth* breathing mark (ἀ) which is not pronounced. A word beginning with a vowel always has either a rough or a smooth breathing mark. The marks are above the *second* letter of a double vowel and to the *left* of

STEP 10

a capital letter.

Originally, such marks were only used in poetry. They do not show up in copies of the Scriptures until about the seventh century after Christ, and even then they were used sparsely.

Q: You mean that the men who wrote the Scriptures did not write with accents or the other marks?

A: That's right.

Q: What purpose do they serve then?

A: Well, there are a few instances where a breathing mark or an accent is the only difference between two words that are spelled the same but have different meanings. For our purposes, though, the markings have little meaning. They are passed on with the text mainly because the markings have traditionally been included in copies of the Greek New Testament, in Greek textbooks, and in other Greek reference books.

Q: Isn't that a lot of unnecessary work?

A: For people who are interested in the finer points of language, it probably isn't. But for others—particularly those who have to type the markings into books like this one—it definitely is.

Q: Why didn't you just forget the accent marks?

A: I seriously thought about it, but don't tell anyone.

New words:

ἄγκυρα, ἡ	anchor	μαρτυρία, ἡ	testimony
ἀκαθαρσία, ἡ	uncleanness	μάχαιρα, ἡ	sword
ἀκροβυστία, ἡ	uncircumcision	μετάνοια, ἡ	repentance
ἀλήθεια, ἡ	truth	νῦν	now
ἁμαρτία, ἡ	sin	οἰκία, ἡ	house
ἀνομία, ἡ	lawlessness	ὀψία, ἡ	evening
ἀπιστία, ἡ	unbelief	παρουσία, ἡ	coming, presence
ἀσέλγεια, ἡ	indecent conduct	παρρησία, ἡ	confidence
βασιλεία, ἡ	kingdom	Παῦλος	Paul
διακονία, ἡ	service	περιστερά, ἡ	dove
διδασκαλία, ἡ	teaching	πέτρα, ἡ	rock
δουλεία, ἡ	slavery	πλεονεξία, ἡ	greed
ἐκκλησία, ἡ	family of believers, gathering of believers	προφητεία, ἡ	prophecy
		σκοτία, ἡ	darkness
ἐξουσία, ἡ	authority	σοφία, ἡ	wisdom
ἕως	until	σωτηρία, ἡ	salvation
εὐσέβεια, ἡ	godliness	φθορά, ἡ	destruction
εὐχαριστία, ἡ	thanksgiving	φιλαδελφία, ἡ	brotherly love
ἡμέρα, ἡ	day	χαρά, ἡ	joy
Ἰουδαῖος, ὁ	Jew	χήρα, ἡ	widow
καρδία, ἡ	heart	χώρα, ἡ	region, land
λατρεία, ἡ	service	ὥρα, ἡ	hour

STEP 11

SOMETHING-WORDS		
ROLE	sing.	pl.
	ἡ δόξ-α	
Necessary	-α	-αι
General supporting	-ης	-ῶν
Directing	-ῃ	-αις
Accomplishing	-αν	-ας
See pages 65-67, Word Chart P-1		

Strange but true!
ἡ-words like δόξα have a mixture of endings. In their singular endings they have η's like τιμή (necessary and accomplishing roles) and α's like οἰκία (gen. supporting and directing roles). Compare the endings of τιμή, οἰκία, and δόξα on your Word Chart (N-1, O-1, P-1).

Give it a try:
What roles are these words playing?
γλῶσσαι, γλωσσῶν, γλώσσας(!), γλῶσσαν, γλώσσῃ, γλώσσης(!), γλώσσαις,

Now you're the translator:
1. Ἐπὶ ταῖς νήσοις ἐσμὲν καὶ βλέπομεν τὴν δόξαν τῆς θαλάσσης. 2. ἀκούεις τὴν γλῶσσαν τοῦ λαοῦ. 3. ἐπὶ τῇ τραπέζῃ τῆς οἰκίας ἄρτος καὶ οἶνος εἰσιν ὑπὲρ τοῦ γεωργοῦ. 4. τὰ πλοῖα ἐν τῇ θαλάσσῃ τῆς Γαλιλαίας ἦν. 5. ἐπὶ ταῖς πέτραις ἐν τῇ θαλάσσῃ δένδρα ἐστίν. 6. ἐπὶ τῆς τραπέζης τοῦ κυρίου τὸν ἄρτον τῆς ζωῆς καὶ τὸ ποτήριον τῆς σωτηρίας λαμβάνομεν. 7. ἕως τῆς ἡμέρας τῆς δόξης οἱ διάκονοι τοῦ Ἰησοῦ ταῖς ἐκκλησίαις δουλεύουσιν. 8. βλέπετε τοὺς ἀγγέλους ἐν τῇ δόξῃ τῆς βασιλείας τοῦ θεοῦ. 9. διὰ τῆς θύρας τῆς οἰκίας βλέπει τὰς ἐλαίας πρὸς τῇ θαλάσσῃ. 10. γλώσσῃ λόγους τῆς εὐλογίας καὶ τῆς βλασφημίας λέγετε; 11. ἡ ἀσέβεια ῥίζα τῶν μεριμνῶν καὶ τῆς ἀπωλείας ἐστίν. 12. βλέπομεν τὸν κύριον ἐν τῇ δόξῃ τῆς ἐνεργείας. 13. ἡ εὐσέβεια ῥίζα τῆς σοφίας ἐστίν· ἡ δὲ ἀδικία ἀρχὴ τῆς φθορᾶς ἐστιν. 14. φεύγετε ἐν ταῖς ὥραις τοῦ πειρασμοῦ καὶ τῆς ἀσθενείας πρὸς τὸν κύριον τῆς δόξης.

How to Read New Testament Greek

Study tip!
If you like to put information on cards for review purposes, you might consider arranging them into three piles that I like to call *catch, tame, and ride*.

The *catch* pile is for the cards with new information. These cards need to be reviewed daily or every other day. Cards stay in this pile until you 'catch' them, that is, until you're able to recognize and repeat the information on the card.

When you've caught a card, you put it in the *tame* pile which is for the cards you know, but easily forget. The cards in this pile should be reviewed once a week. Cards stay in this pile until you've tamed them, that is, until you're able to recognize and repeat the information on the card even after a week.

When you notice you've tamed a card, you put it in the *ride* pile which is for information you know well. The cards in this pile should be reviewed once a month. Cards stay in this pile until you're riding them, that is, until you're able to recognize and repeat the information on the card even after a month.

You can also start a fourth pile called the *stable* for cards you've ridden for a long time. Take them out once a year and see if you can still stay in the saddle.

New words:

ἀδικία, ἡ	injustice
ἀπώλεια, ἡ	waste, destruction
ἀσέβεια, ἡ	ungodliness
ἀσθένεια, ἡ	weakness, sickness
βλασφημία, ἡ	blasphemy
Γαλιλαία, ἡ	Galilee
γέεννα, ἡ	hell
γλῶσσα, ἡ	tongue, language
δόξα, ἡ	glory, honor
ἐλαία, ἡ	olive tree
ἐλευθερία, ἡ	freedom
ἐνέργεια, ἡ	power
εὐλογία, ἡ	blessing
θάλασσα, ἡ	sea
λαμβάνω	take, receive
μέριμνα, ἡ	worry
ῥίζα, ἡ	root
τράπεζα, ἡ	table

STEP 12

SOMETHING-WORDS		
ROLE	sing.	pl.
	ὁ μαθητής	
Necessary	-ής	-αί
General supporting	-οῦ	-ῶν
Directing	-ῇ	-αῖς
Accomplishing	-ήν	-άς
See pages 65-67, Word Chart K-3		

What you need to know:
A group of ὁ-words ending in -ς change their endings much like the ἡ-words in STEP 9. Look at your Word Chart and compare section K-3 with section N-1. The only differences are in the necessary role (sg.) and the general supporting role (sg.).

Strange but true!
νεανίας is an ὁ-word that changes roles much like μαθητής. Only where μαθητής has η in the singular endings, νεανίας has α (νεανίας, νεανιοῦ, νεανίᾳ, νεανιάν).

Give it a try:
What roles are the following words playing?
πολίτῃ, πολῖται, πολίτου, πολίταις, πολίτης, πολίτας, πολῖτα, πολιτῶν, πολίτην, ζηλωτοῦ, ὑποκριτής, βαπτιστά, νεανίαν, εὐαγγελιστάς, ἐργάτης, κλέπτου, προφῆτα, τελώνας, Ἰσραηλίταις, κριτῇ, μαθητῶν, βαπτιστήν, στρατιῶτα, ψευδοπροφῆται, Ἰωάννου, ζηλωτάς, ᾅδου, δεσπότας, ὑπηρέταις
Add the correct form of ὁ to the above words.

Add the correct endings to the following words:
a) τῷ βαπτιστ__, οἱ κριτ__, ὦ μαθητ__, τοῖς ὑποκριτ__, τοὺς τελών__, οἱ κλέπτ__.
b) ἐργάτ__, νεανί__, Ἰσραηλίτ__, τελών__, βαπτιστ__, ὑποκριτ__, κλέπτ__, ζηλωτ__.

How to Read New Testament Greek

Now you're the translator:
1. Ἐν τοῖς χρόνοις τοῦ νόμου οἱ πρεσβύτεροι κριταὶ τοῦ λαοῦ ἦσαν. 2. οἱ Φαρισαῖοι ζηλωταὶ ὑπὲρ τοῦ νόμου καὶ τοῦ σαββάτου ἦσαν. 3. οἱ στρατιῶται τῷ ἑκατοντάρχῃ ζήλῳ ὑπακούουσιν. 4. ἐν ταῖς χώραις οἱ ἐργάται τὰ δένδρα φυτεύουσιν. 5. ὁ νεανίας τὸν δοῦλον ἐκ τῆς δουλείας τῶν Ῥωμαίων ἀπολύει. 6. κωλύετε τὸ ἔργον τοῦ ψευδοπροφήτου διὰ τῆς μαρτυρίας τῆς ἀληθείας. 7. δουλεύουσιν οἱ νεανίαι τῷ εὐαγγελιστῇ σὺν ὑπακοῇ. 8. οὐ πιστεύετε τοῖς ψευδοπροφήταις ἀλλὰ δουλεύετε ἀγάπῃ τῷ υἱῷ τοῦ θεοῦ. 9. οἱ πολῖται τῆς χώρας τὴν μαρτυρίαν τῶν μαθητῶν ἀκούουσιν. 10. εἷς τῶν μαθητῶν λέγει τῷ Ἰησοῦ ὅτι ὁ ὄχλος ἄρτον οὐκ ἔχει.

Any questions?
Q: I was just wondering if it wouldn't be better to have a list of the answers to the exercises somewhere in the book. What good does it do if I come up with wrong answers?
A: The answers actually are in the book, but they have to be found or deduced from the explanations and charts. Linguists have long known that languages are best learned by intense involvement in the *usage* of the language. The most effective language courses emphasize usage.

Interestingly enough, those students who make the most progress are the ones who have the least fear of making mistakes. Mistakes seldom hamper learning. In fact, they are an integral part of the process. How often do toddlers fall down before they learn to walk? It's actually the *fear of making mistakes* that hampers learning.

It's also important to remember that mastering New Testament Greek is not a matter of learning to *speak* the language, but *knowing how to find answers in reference books*. The greater your skill in searching for information, the greater will be your confidence in the use of the language when you enter the advanced phases of Greek.

This is not to say you will not need some answers. When you have questions that just won't go away, write to the address on page 129. Easy answers, however, are not always helpful. Without struggle, learning seldom takes place.

New words:

ᾅδης, ὁ	underworld	ἦσαν	they were
βαπτιστής, ὁ	baptizer	Ἰορδάνης, ὁ	Jordan
δεσπότης, ὁ	master, owner	Ἰσραηλίτης, ὁ	Israelite
εἷς	one	Ἰωάννης, ὁ	John
ἑκατοντάρχης, ὁ	centurion	κλέπτης, ὁ	thief
ἐργάτης, ὁ	worker	κριτής, ὁ	judge
εὐαγγελιστής, ὁ	evangelist	μαθητής, ὁ	student
ζηλωτής, ὁ	zealot	νεανίας, ὁ	young man

STEP 12

οἰκοδεσπότης, ὁ	housemaster
πολίτης, ὁ	citizen
προφήτης, ὁ	prophet
στρατιώτης, ὁ	soldier
τελώνης, ὁ	tax-collector
ὑπηρέτης, ὁ	helper
ὑποκριτής, ὁ	hypocrite
ψευδοπροφήτης, ὁ	false prophet

STEP 13

ADD-ON WORDS			
ROLE	**T**YPE	singular	plural
		μόν-ος	
Necessary		-ος	-οι
General	ὁ	-ου	-ων
Supporting		-ῳ	-οις
Directing		-ον	-ους
Accomplishing			
		μόν-η	
Necessary		-η	-αι
General	ἡ	-ης	-ων
Supporting		-ῃ	-αις
Directing		-ην	-ας
Accomplishing			
		μόν-ον	
Necessary		-ον	-α
General	τό	-ου	-ων
Supporting		-ῳ	-οις
Directing		-ον	-α
Accomplishing			
See pages 86-89, Word Chart K-12			

What you need to know:

Greek add-on words that add extra information to ὁ-words, ἡ-words, and τό-words always make an effort to match endings with them. Therefore Greek add-on words have a set of ὁ-endings, a set of ἡ-endings, and a set of τό-endings.

Please note, however, that they only have *one* set of ὁ endings, *one* set of ἡ endings, and *one* set of τό endings. This means that because ὁ-, ἡ-, and τό-words often have *different* ways of changing their endings (as you have been learning), add-on words are not always able to make a perfect match.

The endings of μόνος, for example, match the endings of λόγος perfectly: μόνος λόγος, μόνου λόγου, etc. But the endings of μόνος do not match all the endings of μαθητής: μόνος μαθητής, μόνου μαθητοῦ, μόνῳ μαθητῇ, etc.

STEP 13

Strange but true:
Among the add-on words themselves, the endings sometimes follow a different pattern. You notice that between μόνος and δίκαιος, the ἡ-word endings are different. μόνος prefers η in its ἡ-word endings and δίκαιος prefers α.

Give it a try:
What roles are the following add-on words playing?
ὅλην, ὅλοι, ὅλη, ὅλου, (2x), ὅλων (3x), ὅλῃ, ὅλα (2x), ὅλῳ (2x), ὅλους, ὅλοις (2x), ὅλης, ὅλον, ὅλαι, ὅλαις, ὅλος; ὀλίγων (3x), ἀγαθοί, λευκάς, πιστῆς, πτωχά (2x), σοφοῦ, τυφλήν, ἄλλους, ἀληθινοῖς, ἐκλεκταῖς, πονηρόν, μικρῷ, ἄλλαι, μικραῖς, σοφάς, τιμίῳ ὕψιστον, ὑψηλῶν, περισσόν.

Fill in the correct forms of κάλος:
τοῦ__ ἄρτου, οἱ__ λόγοι, __ φόβῳ, __ ἀγροῖς; τὰ__ ἔργα, τὸ__δένδρον, __ δείπνων; τῇ__ οἰκίᾳ, ταῖς__ καρδίαις, __ ἑορτῆς, __ βουλή, __ζῷα, __ κόσμον, __ ἐκκλησίας (2x), ψυχήν__, __ εἴδωλα, __ ἐπιστολῆς, __ φωναῖς, τὸν __ πλοῦτον, __ διδαχή, __πλοίου, __εὐλογίας, οἱ__ ζηλωταί, τῷ __ ἐργάτῃ

Don't miss it:
When an add-on word adds extra information to a something-word, it either snuggles in between the *the* and the something-word (τῷ μόνῳ κληρονόμῳ) or it settles in *after* the word, in which case the *the* is often repeated (ὁ κόσμος ὁ ὅλος).

Strange but true:
When an add-on word is alone and preceded by a form of ὁ, ἡ, or τό, it automatically ceases being an add-on-word and turns into a something word. ὁ σοφός, for example, means *the wise one, the wise man,* or *the one who is wise.*

Now you're the translator:
1. Ἐν τοῖς μικροῖς ἀγροῖς καλοὺς καρποὺς ἔχετε. 2. δουλεύετε τῷ μόνῳ κληρονόμῳ. 3. ὁ κόσμος ὁ ὅλος τὸν λόγον τοῦ θεοῦ ἀκούει. 4. φίλοι, δουλεύετε τῷ νέῳ νόμῳ τοῦ κόσμου τοῦ νέου. 5. φίλε, τοὺς ὀλίγους λόγους τῶν φίλων ἀκούεις. 6. ὁ ἁμαρτωλὸς τοὺς ἀγαθοὺς λόγους τῶν φίλων τῶν πιστῶν φεύγει 7. οἱ πρεσβύτεροι πιστοὶ διδάσκαλοι τοῦ ἁγίου εὐαγγελίου εἰσίν. 8. ἄγγελος ἐν λευκοῖς ἱματίοις μετὰ Πέτρου ἦν. 9. ἐν τῇ ἁγίᾳ ἐκκλησίᾳ τοῦ κυρίου κοινωνίαν ἔχομεν σὺν ἀληθινοῖς ἀδελφοῖς. 10. ἄλλην παραβολὴν ἀκούετε. 11. ἔχομεν βεβαίαν ἄγκυραν τῆς ψυχῆς. 12. οἱ σοφοὶ τοῦ κόσμου οὐ δουλεύουσιν τῷ υἱῷ τοῦ θεοῦ. 13. ἡ ἐκλεκτὴ τῷ κυρίῳ τῆς δόξης δουλεύει. 14. οὐ πιστεύουσιν τῷ πονηρῷ, ἀλλὰ τῷ ἀληθινῷ καὶ δικαίῳ. 15. οἱ πτωχοὶ οὐκ ἔχουσιν ἄρτον.

How to Read New Testament Greek

Any questions?
A: Sentence 14 seems strange to me. I translated it, *They are not believing the evil but the truth and justice.* I can see how you can believe the truth, but how do you believe evil or justice?
A: This is a good example of add-on words becoming something-words (See the **Strange but true** section above). As something-words πονηρῷ, ἀληθινῷ, and δικαίῳ each have two possible meanings, because the ῷ endings can be either ὁ-word endings or τό-word endings. (The directing-role endings for both ὁ-words and τό-words are the same.)

As an ὁ-word τῷ πονηρῷ means *the one who is evil* and as a τό-word it means *that which is evil.* It's the same with ἀληθινῷ (*the one who is true* or *that which is true*) and with δικαίῳ (*the one who is just* or *that which is just*).

Thus the translation would be: *They are not believing the one who is evil but the one who is true and just.*

New words:

ἀγαθός,-ή,-όν	good	νέος,νέα,νέον	new
ἅγιος,ἁγία,ἅγιον	holy	ὀλίγος,η,-ον	few
ἀκάθαρτος,-η,-ον	unclean	ὅλος,-η,-ον	whole, all
ἄλλος,-η,-ο	another	περισσός,-ή,-όν	remarkable, abundant
ἀληθινός,-ή,-όν	true		
βέβαιος,βεβαία, βέβαιον	reliable	πιστός,-ή,-όν	faithful
		πονηρός,-ά,-όν	evil
δικαιος,δικαία, δίκαιον	just	πτωχός,-ή,-όν	poor
		σοφός,-ή,-όν	wise
ἐκλεκτός,-ή,-όν	chosen	τίμιος,τιμία, τίμιον	valuable, honorable
καλός,-ή,-όν	beautiful, good		
κοινωνία, ἡ	commonality	τυφλός,-ή,-όν	blind
λευκός,-ή,-όν	white	ὑψηλός,-ή,-όν	high, proud
μικρός,-ά,-όν	small	ὕψιστος,-η,-ον	highest
μόνος,-η,-ον	only, alone		

STEP 14

ADD-ON WORDS			
Role	**Type**	singular	plural
Necessary General Supporting Directing Accomplishing	ὁ	φρόνιμ-ος -ος -ου -ῳ -ον	-οι -ων -οις -ους
Necessary General Supporting Directing Accomplishing	ἡ	φρόνιμ-ος -ος -ου -ῳ -ον	-οι -ων -οις -ους
Necessary General Supporting Directing Accomplishing	τό	φρόνιμ-ον -ον -ου -ῳ -ον	-α -ων -οις -α

See pages 86-89, Word Chart L-12

Strange but true!

Greek add-on words like χρόνος have no ἡ-word endings. Therefore, they are only able to match the endings of ὁ-words and τό-words, but not those of ἡ-words. What happens when φρόνιμος has to team up with an ἡ-word?

In such cases φρόνιμος simply uses its ὁ-word endings. That makes for match-ups that may look like mistakes to you—αἱ φρόνιμοι ἐντολαί, for example—but they're not mistakes at all.

Give it a try:

Add the correct form of φρόνιμος:

τοῦ __ δούλου, τὸ __ ἔργον, τῇ __ διδασκαλίᾳ, οἱ __ ἐργάται, τὴν __ εὐλογίαν, τὰ __ δῶρα, τὰς __ νόσους, τῷ __ παρακλήτῳ, αἱ __ ἐντολαί, τῷ

How to Read New Testament Greek

__ ἱματίῳ, τῆς __ χώρας, τῶν __ πολιτῶν, τῇ __ ῥίζῃ, τῶν __ σημείων, __ τραπέζαις, __ καρδίᾳ, __ δίκτυα, __ ἐκκλησία

Now you're the translator:
1. Ὁ βαπτιστὴς ἐν ἐρήμῳ τόπῳ ἦν· οἱ δὲ ἄπιστοι Ἰουδαῖοι τῇ ἀληθείᾳ οὐχ ὑπακούουσιν. 2. ἡ ἄπιστος ἀδελφὴ τοῦ ἀδελφοῦ τοῦ πιστοῦ οὐκέτι ἐν τῇ ἐκκλησίᾳ ἐστίν. 3. ἐν τῇ βίβλῳ ἔχομεν τὸν ἐπουράνιον λόγον. 4. οὐ πιστεύεις τῷ πονηρῷ, ἀλλὰ τῷ ὠφελίμῳ λόγῳ τοῦ ἀποστόλου. 5. ὁ σταυρὸς τοῦ Ἰησοῦ τοῖς πιστοῖς σωτήριον σημεῖόν ἐστιν. 6. οἱ ἀπόστολοι τὸν λόγον τὸν αἰώνιον τοῖς ἀνθρώποις λέγουσιν. 7. Τὰ πλοῖα τῶν Ῥωμαίων ἀγαθά ἐστιν. 8. ἡ σοφία τῶν ἀνθρώπων ἐπίγειός ἐστιν. 9. ἀληθινὰ καὶ σοφὰ τὰ μαρτύρια τοῦ κυρίου ἐστίν. 10. ἡ διαθήκη ἡ καινὴ αἰώνιος καὶ δῶρον τοῦ θεοῦ ἐστιν.

Any questions?
Q: Is it really necessary to do *all* the exercises?
A: No, not always. The exercises are simply there to give you some experience with the new ways of doing things in Greek. If you think you've caught on after a few examples, then move on.

There's no reason why you can't move through the STEPS at a quick pace. Learning a language like the Greek of Jesus' day is considerably easier than learning to speak a modern language. You are only learning Greek to read it, not to speak it. Therefore, you only need to learn Greek to the point of *recognition*, and not to the point of being able to reproduce it, either vocally or written.

Anyone who has ever learned to speak a language will tell you how much faster one's ability to hear and understand the language progresses in comparison to one's ability to speak the language. The same is true when comparing reading skills with writing skills. Reading comprehension quickly outpaces the ability to write.

Of the four tasks of language learning—*hearing, speaking, reading* and *writing*—you only need to learn one: *reading*, and reading is mainly a matter of recognition, the easiest task for our memories. Therefore, once you've learned to recognize the particular aspect of Greek that a STEP is teaching, move on and simply make the information in the STEP a part of your review program.

New words:
ἀδύνατος,-ον	weak	ἔρημος,-ον	desert, alone
αἰώνιος,-ον	eternal	καινός,-ή,-όν	new
ἀκάθαρτος,-ον	impure	σωτήριος,-ον	saving
ἄπιστος,-ον	unfaithful	τόπος, ὁ	place
ἔνοχος,-ον	guilty	φανερός,-ά,-όν	visible, obvious
ἐπίγειος,-ον	earthly	φρόνιμος,-ον	reasonable
ἐπουράνιος,-ον	heavenly	ὠφέλιμος,-ον	useful

STEP 15

SOMETHING-WORDS

ROLE	sing.	pl.	sing.	pl.		
	ἐγώ		σύ			
Nec.	ἐγώ I	ἡμεῖς we	σύ you	ὑμεῖς-all of you	See pages 80-81 Word Chart K-7 to O-7	
Gen.sup.	ἐμοῦ my	ἡμῶν our	σοῦ yours	ὑμῶν-all of yours		
Directing	ἐμοί to me	ἡμῖν to us	σοί to you	ὑμῖν-to all of you		
Accompl.	ἐμέ me	ἡμᾶς us	σέ you	ὑμᾶς all of you		
	αὐτός		αὐτή		αὐτό	
Nec.	αὐτός he	αὐτοί they	αὐτή she	αὐταί they	αὐτό it	αὐτά they
Gen.sup.	αὐτοῦ his	αὐτῶν their	αὐτῆς her	αὐτῶν their	αὐτοῦ its	αὐτῶν their
Directing	αὐτῷ to him	αὐτοῖς to them	αὐτῇ to her	αὐταῖς to them	αὐτῷ to it	αὐτοῖς to them
Accompl.	αὐτόν him	αὐτούς them	αὐτήν her	αὐτάς them	αὐτό it	αὐτά them

What you need to know:

I, we, you, all of you, he, she, it, and *they* are the special something-words tucked away in the necessary role in every camera-word. They don't always have to stay hidden, however. They also have their own forms (ἐγώ - *I*, σύ- *you*, etc.)

Don't miss it!

I, we, you, all of you, he, she, it, and *they* are each able to play the other three roles (nec.= ἐγώ *I*, gen. supp.= ἐμοῦ *my*, dir.= ἐμοί *to me*, acc.= ἐμέ *me*, etc.).

How to Read New Testament Greek

Give it a try:
Add the correct word in the *necessary role* to the following camera-words (Example: ____ἔχετε = ὑμεῖς ἔχετε):

____ἔχετε, ____δουλεύτε, ____ἀκούει, ____φεύγει, ____εἰσίν, ____ἦν, ____ἔχομεν, ____ἀκούετε, ____λεύετε, ____ἀκούεις

Add the correct form of αὐτός (____χρονοίς = αὐτοῖς χρονοίς):

____νόμου, ____χώραις, ____δένδρα, ____ἔργον, ____μαρτυρίας, ____ἀγάπῃ, ____υἱῷ, ____μαθητῶν, ____κυρίου, ____παρουσίαν, ____τιμῆς

Now you're the translator:
1. Ἐγώ εἰμι ὁ ἄρτος ἐκ τοῦ οὐρανοῦ. 2. σὺ εἶ ὁ ἅγιος τοῦ θεοῦ. 3. ἡμεῖς ἐκ τοῦ θεοῦ ἐσμεν. 4. ὑμεῖς οὐ πιστεύετε εἰς ἐμέ. 5. πιστεύεις μοί, Πέτρε. 6. τὸν λόγον τῆς σωτηρίας λέγουσιν ὑμῖν. 7. φεύγομεν ἀφ' ὑμῶν. 8. θεραπεύει ἡμᾶς διὰ τοῦ λόγου τῆς ἐνεργείας. 9. φυτεύομεν αὐτῷ τὰς ἀμπέλους. 10. ὑπακούετε αὐτοῖς διὰ τὴν ἀγάπην.

Study tip!
Memorizing lists of vocabulary is not only boring, it is one of the most inefficient ways to learn new words. The secret to learning vocabulary is locked up in the word *context*. Words draw their meaning from the other words around them. To illustrate: Fill in the missing letters of the following word: _ _ _ *l*.

Pretty tough, eh? Could be *mill* or *pail* or *jail* or any of dozens of other words with four letters and ending with an *l*. Now let's put the word in a sentence: *How do you expect me to drive in this _ _ _ l without a hammer?*

Not much doubt about the word now, is there? Context is so powerful, it will even define foreign words for you. Let's try it with a Greek word. What do you think the Greek word δένδρον means in the following sentence?

That δένδρον has gray bark and large, beautiful leaves.

Any question as to what δένδρον means? The moral of the story is this: Learn words in the context of a sentence or at least in the context of a phrase. That's how children learn a language; that's the natural way. No one ever gives a two-year-old lists of words with definitions to learn. Context is all the definition a two-year-old needs.

Pick out a few key sentences in the **Now-you're-the-translator** section of the STEPS that contain most of the new words you want to learn and put them on cards for review. When you understand the sentence, you'll also understand every word in the sentence, and you'll understand it in the normal way a person understands words: through the context, and not because you've tacked a memorized definition on to each word.

Any questions?

Q: Why does adding a word like ἐγώ or σύ serve to emphasize these words in Greek?

A: We actually do the same thing in English. If we want to emphasize the word *I* in the sentence, *I'll do it,* then we say, *I'm the one who'll do it,* or *I'll do it myself.* In other words, we simply choose another word for *I* such as *the one* or *myself* and toss it in for emphasis.

When the Greeks spoke or wrote ἐγώ (*I*) or σύ (*you*), they, too, were repeating the words, because ἐγώ and σύ were also included as a part of the camera-word itself. (You remember that one of the words *I, you, he, she, it, we, all of you* and *they* is packed away inside each Greek camera-word, don't you? The ending of the camera-word tells you which one.) Therefore, including words like ἐγώ or σύ in a Greek sentence is an automatic repeat of those words.

STEP 16

EXTRA-INFORMATION WORDS

ROLE	sing.	pl.	sing.	pl.	sing.	pl.
	οὗτος		αὕτη		τοῦτο	
Nec.	οὗτος	οὗτοι	αὕτη	αὗται	τοῦτο	ταῦτα
GSupp	τούτου	τούτων	ταύτης	τούτων	τούτου	τούτων
Dir.	τούτῳ	τούτοις	ταύτῃ	ταύταις	τούτῳ	τούτοις
Acc.	τοῦτον	τούτους	ταύτην	ταύτας	τοῦτο	ταῦτα
	ἐκεῖν-ος		ἐκείν-η		ἐκεῖν-ο	
Nec.	-ος	-οι	-η	-αι	-ο	-α
GSupp	-ου	-ων	-ης	-ων	-ου	-ων
Dir.	-ῳ	-οις	-ῃ	-αις	-ῳ	-οις
Acc.	-ον	-ους	-ην	-ας	-ο	-α

Word Chart O-14 to O-16, P-14 to P-16

What you need to know:
The words for *this* and *that* in Greek are οὗτος and ἐκεῖνος. They change their endings in the same way as αὐτός.

Strange but true!
Only οὗτος (sing.) οὗτοι (pl.), αὕτη (sing.) and αὗται (pl.) do not begin with a τ.

Give it a try:
Which roles are the following words playing?
αὕτη, τούτου, τούτῳ, ταύτης, οὗτοι, τούτων, ταῦτα, τοῦτον, ταύταις, ταύτῃ, αὗται, τούτοις, ταύτην, ταῦτα, τούτους, ταύτας, τοῦτο

Replace the following words with the correct forms of οὗτος and ἐκεῖνος (____χρονοίς = τούτοις χρονοίς):
____νόμου, ____χώραις, ____δένδρα, ____δοῦλον, ____ἔργον,

STEP 16

_____μαρτυρίας, _____ἀγάπῃ, _____υἱῷ, _____μαθητῶν, _____κυρίου,
_____παρουσίαν, _____τιμῆς

Now you're the translator:
1. Φεύγουσιν εἰς τὴν ἑτέραν χώραν. 2. ἡ βασιλεία τῶν οὐρανῶν ὁμοία ἐστὶν δέκα παρθένοις, 3. οὗτοι οἱ ἄνθρωποι ταῖς ἁμαρτίαις νεκροὶ ἦσαν· νῦν δὲ τῷ κυρίῳ ᾽Ιησοῦ ἐν δικαιοσύνῃ καὶ ἀγάπῃ δουλεύουσιν. 4. ταῦτα γράφεις τοῖς φίλοις ἀδελφοῖς. 5. βλέπετε τὰς καινὰς οἰκίας ταύτας καὶ ἐκεῖνον τὸν ἄξιον ναόν. 6. ὁ μὲν τῶν δούλων τῷ κυρίῳ μετὰ χαρᾶς δουλεύει, ὁ δὲ ὀλίγῳ ζήλῳ. 7. οἱ μὲν τὸν λόγον τὸν σωτήριον ἀκούουσιν καὶ πιστεύουσιν, οἱ δὲ οὐκ πιστεύουσιν. 8. ὁ κύριος ἀποστέλλει τοὺς μὲν ἀποστόλους, τοὺς δὲ διδασκάλους. 9. οὗτός ἐστιν ὁ ἀγαπητὸς υἱὸς τοῦ πρεσβυτέρου τῆς ἐκκλησίας ἐκείνης. 10. Εἶπεν δὲ πρὸς αὐτοὺς τὴν παραβολὴν ταύτην.

Don't miss it:
Generally οὗτος and ἐκεῖνος team up with something-words in this order: οὗτοι οἱ ἄνθρωποι *(these men)*. If there is no *the* along for the ride, however, then οὗτος or ἐκεῖνος are placed *after* the word: ἄνθρωπος οὗτος *(this man)*.

Any questions:
Q: In sentence 5 I keep coming up with *the new houses these* and *the worthy temple that*. Hmmm...
A: You always have to ask yourself whether you should include a translation of a Greek *the*. Sometimes you should; sometimes you shouldn't. This is a case where it shouldn't be translated. *These new houses* and *that worthy temple* represent normal English translations. Don't be afraid to consult your own feeling for the English language to determine what belongs in a translation. Don't forget: When it comes to speaking the way you speak, you're the expert.

New words:

ἀγαπητός,-ή,-όν	beloved	κάτω	under
ἄνω	above	νεκρός,-ά,-όν	dead
ἄξιος, ἀξία, ἄξιον	worthy	ὁ μέν - ὁ δέ	the one -the other
ἀποστέλλω	send	ὁ δέ	but whoever
δέκα	ten	ὅδε, ἥδε, τόδε	this
εἶπεν	he said	ὅμοιος, ὁμοία, ὅμοιον	similar, same
ἕκαστος,-η,-ον	each one		
ἐκεῖνος, ἐκείνη, ἐκεῖνο	that	οὗτος, αὕτη, τοῦτο	this
ἕτερος,ἑτέρα, ἕτερον	another	τὸ πνεῦμα	spirit
		φίλος,-η,-ον	devoted

157

STEP 17

EXTRA-INFORMATION WORDS

Role	Type	singular	plural
Necessary General Supporting Directing Accomplishing	ὁ	χρυσ-οῦς -οῦς -οῦ -ῷ -οῦν	-οῖ -ῶν -οῖς -οῦς
Necessary General Supporting Directing Accomplishing	ἡ	χρυσ-ῆ -ῆ -ῆς -ῇ -ῆν	-αῖ -ῶν -αῖς -ᾶς
Necessary General Supporting Directing Accomplishing	τό	χρυσ-οῦν -οῦν -οῦ -ῷ -οῦν	-ᾶ -ῶν -οῖς -ᾶ

See pages 86-89, Word Chart M-12

Strange but true!

Greek words don't like it when certain vowels come together. When it happens, the two usually chain react to form another vowel or a double vowel, or one of the two vowels simply disappears. When ε and ο bump into each other, for example, they transform themselves into ου.

Here's a summary of how vowels change when they run into each other at the *end* of a word:

ε + ο = ου

ε + α = α (when preceded by ε, ι, or ρ) otherwise to η in all other cases.

ε + ω, ου, οι, or αι = ω, ου, οι, or αι (the ε just gets swallowed)

The plural of τό-words are the only exceptions to the rule: They always end in -α.

STEP 17

What you need to know:
The endings of add-on words like ἀργυροῦς and χρυσοῦς are the result of vowels coming together (χρυσε- + -ος = χρυσοῦς).

Give it a try:
What roles are the following words playing?
ἀργυροῦς, ἀργυρᾶ, ἀργυροῦν, ἀργυρῷ, ἀργυρᾶν, ἀργυρῶν, ἀργυραῖς, ἀργυροῦ, χρυσῆ, χρυσοῦ, χρυσᾶ, χρυσοῖ, χρυσῷ, χρυσαῖ, χρυσῆν, χρυσῶν, χρυσοῦς, χρυσῇ

Now you're the translator:
1. Τοῦ κυρίου ἡ γῆ ἐστιν. 2. ὁ Ἰησοῦς κύριος τοῦ οὐρανοῦ καὶ τῆς γῆς ἐστιν. 3. δόξα θεῷ καὶ ἐπὶ γῆς εἰρήνη. 4. τὰ χρυσᾶ καὶ ἀργυρᾶ εἴδωλα φθορὰ τῶν πολιτῶν τῆς χώρας ἦν. 5. ὁ κύριος τῶν κυρίων περὶ τῶν λαῶν σιδηρᾷ ῥάβδῳ βασιλεύει. 6. τὸ καλὸν δῶρον τῶν διδασκάλων ὑπὲρ τῆς μικρᾶς ἐκκλησίας ἀργυροῦν ποτήριον ἦν. 7. οἱ ἄνθρωποι τῆς γῆς τοῖς δαιμονίοις καὶ τοῖς εἰδώλοις τοῖς χρυσοῖς καὶ τοῖς ἀργυροῖς καὶ τοῖς χαλκοῖς λατρεύουσιν. 8. οἱ πρεσβύτεροι πρὸ τοῦ θρόνου τοῦ θεοῦ τὰ λευκὰ ἱμάτια καὶ ἐπὶ ταῖς κεφαλαῖς στεφάνους χρυσοῦς ἔχουσιν. 9. οἱ ἐχθροὶ πρὸ τοῦ οἴκου σού εἰσιν. 10. οἱ ἀδελφοί μου εἰς τὸν υἱὸν τοῦ θεοῦ πιστεύουσιν.

Any questions?
Q: Sentence one baffled me for a while, but I think I've got it: *The earth is of the Lord* or *The earth is the Lord's*. Sentence three, however, is not so clear.
A: Sentence three is tricky. I'll give you a clue. You have to add not one, but *two* forms of εἰμί. Now give it a try before reading on.
How did you do? Did you come up with two sentences joined by καί? *Glory be to God and peace (be) on earth.* The second *be* is an example of a hidden *be* in English and is, of course, not necessary to include in the English translation.

New words:
ἀργυροῦς,-ᾶ,-οῦν	silver
γῆ, γῆς, γῇ, γῆν, ἡ	earth
κεφαλή, ἡ	head
σιδηροῦς,-ᾶ,-οῦν	iron
στέφανος, ὁ	wreath, crown
συκῆ, ἡ	fig tree
χαλκοῦς,-ῆ,-οῦν	copper
χρυσοῦς,-ῆ,-οῦν	golden

STEP 18

CAMERA-WORDS			
PICTURE ⇒⇒⇒			VIDEO
LIGHT	ACTION	NEC. ROLE	LIVE
B R I G H T	M I D D L E	I we you all of you he, she, it they	παιδεύ-ομαι I am training myself -ομαι -όμεθα -ῃ -εσθε -εται -ονται See pages 81-82 Word Chart C-3

Don't forget!
Camera-words contain four kinds of information:
1. *Picture* (six possibilities: *live video, recorded video, normal photo, future photo, current photo, previous photo*),
2. *Light* (three possibilities: *bright, dim, flashing*),
3. *Action* (three possibilities: *active, middle, passive*),
4. *Necessary role* (eight possibilities: *I, we, you, all of you, he, she, it, they*).

The letters of the word PLAN—**P**icture, **L**ight, **A**ction, **N**ecessary role—highlight the four kinds of information.

Before beginning this STEP and STEPS 19-24, be sure to reread pages 71 to 83 and carefully study the camera-word section of your Word Chart.

What you need to know:
Thus far only *active* forms of camera-words have been used in the exercises. *Active* means the word in the necessary-role is the *initiator* or the *doer* of the action of the camera-word: παιδεύω τὸν τέκνον, *I am training the child.*

Passive means the word in the necessary role is the *receiver* of the action of the camera-word: παιδεύομαι ὑπο τοῦ κυρίου, *I am being trained by the Lord.*

Middle is a mixture of both active and passive meanings. The word in the necessary-role is *both doer* and *receiver* of the action of the camera-word: παιδεύομαι, *I am training myself.*

STEP 18

Don't miss it!
Both the medium and passive *live video* forms of a camera-word are the same. The context determines which translation is preferred.

Give it a try:
Translate the following forms of παιδεύομαι and remember that each has two possibilities: παιδεύομαι, παιδεύονται, παιδεύω, παιδεύεται, παιδεύουσιν, παιδεύῃ, παιδεύετε, παιδεύεται, παιδεύομεν, παιδεύεσθε, παιδευόμεθα, παιδεύονται

Strange but true:
Normally, the dictionary lists the *live video/bright/active/I* form of a camera-word. παιδεύω, for example. Some of the camera-words in your vocabulary list, however, are listed with *passive/medium* forms. Why is that?

These are words whose active forms at one time or another 'departed' and never came back. They're known as camera-words with *departed* forms. Their active meanings were adopted by their passive and medium forms. In the process the passive and medium forms also 'lost' their passive and medium meanings. All that remained were *passive* and *medium* forms with *active* meanings. ἔρχομαι, for example, means *I am coming*.

That may seem confusing, but it's just another of those quirks of the Greek language that you'll have to get used to.

Now you're the translator:
1. Οἱ νεανίαι ἐν τῷ ποταμῷ λούονται. 2. κωλύεσθε ἐν τῇ ὁδῷ τῆς ζωῆς. 3. ὁ γεωργὸς τὰς ἐλαίας φυτεύεται. 4. μετὰ τὸν κόπον τῆς ἡμέρας οἱ ἐργάται ἀπολούονται. 5. οἱ ἅγιοι ἐν τῇ ὁδῷ ὑπὸ διαβόλου κωλύονται. 6. ὁ δοῦλος θεραπεύεται ὑπὸ τοῦ κυρίου. 7. ἐκ τῶν δεσμῶν τοῦ πονηροῦ ἀπολυόμεθα ὑπὸ τοῦ υἱοῦ τοῦ θεοῦ. 8. οἱ ἄνθρωποι ἀπ᾽ Ἀδὰμ κυριεύονται ὑπὸ τοῦ θανάτου. 9. ὑπὸ τοῦ κυρίου παιδεύῃ εἰς διακονίαν ἐν τῇ ἐκκλησίᾳ αὐτοῦ. 10. δέχεσθε τοὺς φίλους εἰς τὸν οἶκον ὑμῶν. 11. ὁ φρόνιμος δοῦλος ἐν τοῖς ὀλίγοις ἀγροῖς τοῦ γεωργοῦ ἐργάζεται. 12. ὁ ἀδελφὸς ὁ ἄπιστος πορεύεται εἰς τὴν ἔρημον. 13. εἰσέρχονται εἰς τὴν οἰκίαν τοῦ Πιλάτου. 14. ἐργάζεσθε ζήλῳ καὶ μετὰ χαρᾶς. 15. οὐκ ἐργαζόμεθα ὑπὲρ τοῦ ἐχθροῦ, ἀλλὰ δουλεύομεν τῷ δικαίῳ κυρίῳ.

Any questions?
Q: Why did some words lose their active forms, and why would passive forms all of a sudden take on active meanings?
A: If you look at the active meanings of most of these words, you'll see that either a medium/passive idea is contained in the word itself, or a passive usage of the word would be meaningless. How could you express ἔρχομαι (*I am coming*)

How to Read New Testament Greek

as a passive, for example? The result—*I was being coming*—is meaningless.

Every language goes through historical changes that lead to unusual practices. We say *one **mouse** and two **mice**; Why not* one **house** and two **hice**? Or we say *we **run** to the beach to **sun** ourselves*; why don't we say *we **ran** to the beach and **san** ourselves?*

We just have to learn to live with such inconsistencies, and accept that each language, like each individual who speaks it, often has a mind of its own.

New words:

Ἀδάμ	Adam	εἰσπορεύομαι	go in
ἀπέρχομαι	leave	ἐκπορεύομαι	go away
ἀποκρίνομαι	answer	ἐξέρχομαι	go out
ἀπολούομαι	clean oneself up	ἐργάζομαι	work
ἀναλύω	untie, depart	ἔρχομαι	come
ἀπολούω	wash up	ἱλασμός, ὁ	reconciliation
βουλεύομαι	deliberate, resolve	λούομαι	wash oneself
δέχομαι	receive	λύω	free, let loose
διέρχομαι	go through	λούω	wash
εἰσέρχομαι	enter	πορεύομαι	walk, travel

STEP 19

CAMERA-WORDS			
PICTURE ⇒⇒⇒			VIDEO
LIGHT	ACTION	NEC. ROLE	RECORDED
B R I G H T	A C T I V E	I we you all of you he, she, it they	ἐπαίδευ-ον I was training -ον -ομεν -ες -ετε -εν -ον See page 76 Word Chart D-2

What you need to know:

When you view a *live* program in television, you know that what you are seeing is happening the moment you see it. The athlete you are viewing *is running* on the track as you view the program.

When you view a *recorded* program, then you know that what you are seeing is not taking place as you see it, but that it took place sometime in the past. The athlete you are viewing *was running* on the track.

A camera-word switches from *live video* to *recorded video* by adding an ε- to the beginning of the word and by attaching a new set of endings.

Don't miss it!

The recorded video form of a camera-word depicts not only the typical moving picture of a video recording, but also *repeated* or *habitual* action in the past (*He worked for years on a farm*), and *attempted* actions in the past (*He **tried** to be a farmer*).

Strange but true!

As you learned in STEP 17, two vowels that come together on the end of a word often react in unusual ways. The same is true when an ε- is added to the beginning of a camera-word. If the word begins with a vowel, then this is what usually happens:

How to Read New Testament Greek

ε + α = η   ε + αι = ῃ
ε + ο = ω   ε + οι = ῳ
ε + ε = η   ε + ει = ῃ

ω, η, and ου simply swallow the ε.

Give it a try:
What word is in the necessary role?
ἐπαίδευες, ἐπαιδεύομεν, παιδεύεις, ἐπαιδεύετε, ἐπαίδευον (2x!), παιδεύεται, παιδεύω, ἐπαίδευεν, παιδεύετε, παιδεύονται

Fill in the corresponding *recorded video* form:
παιδεύετε -   παιδεύω -
παιδεύουσιν -   παιδεύει -
παιδεύεις -   παιδεύομεν -

Translate the following words:
ἐβασίλευεν, ᾐρηνεύετε, βουλεύῃ, ἐθεράπευες, κυριεύουσιν, ἐλατρεύομεν, ἐμνημόνευον, νηστεύεις, ἐφύτευον, ἔμενες, ἠλπίζομεν, κωλύονται

Now you're the translator:
1. Οἱ ἐργάται ἐν τοῖς ἀγροῖς αὐτῶν δένδρα καὶ ἀμπέλους ἐφύτευον. 2. οἱ ἀπόστολοι εἰς τὸν Ἰησοῦν ἐπίστευον καὶ ἐδούλευον αὐτῷ ἐν ἀγάπῃ καὶ ἐν παρρησίᾳ. 3. ἐν παραβολαῖς ἔλεγεν αὐτοῖς τὸν λόγον τῆς βασιλείας τοῦ θεοῦ. 4. οὐ μόνον ἔλυεν τὸ σάββατον, ἀλλὰ καὶ ἐδούλευεν τοῖς τελώναις καὶ ἁμαρτωλοῖς καὶ ἔλεγεν τὸ εὐαγγέλιον αὐτοῖς. 5. ἐκώλυες τούς φίλους ἐν τῇ ὁδῷ εἰς τὴν ζωήν. 6. ἡ ἀλήθεια ἔλυεν ἡμᾶς ἀπὸ τῆς δουλείας τῆς ἀνομίας 7. περὶ τῆς οἰκοδομῆς τῆς ἐκκλησίας ἔγραφες. 8. τὸν κύριον τῆς δόξης ἐβλέπετε· οὐ δὲ ἐπιστεύετε εἰς αὐτόν. 9. οὐκ ἐλύομεν τὰς ἐντολάς τῶν ἀνθρώπων. 10. τῇ δικαιοσύνῃ καὶ τῇ ἀληθείᾳ ἐδουλεύετε.

Any questions?
Q: How am I supposed to remember all the exceptions to the rules?
A: You can't. Well, I mean you can't learn them *in a short period of time*. For now it's simply important that you know there *are* exceptions, and that you know something of the nature of the exceptions. Then, later on, something will click when you run into words that don't quite behave like they're supposed to, and you'll at least have an idea of what the problem could be.

When you start working in the Greek New Testament, you will be using reference books that will give you most of the information you need regarding exceptions to the rules. To use these books, however, you need to be able to recognize the kind of information they're giving you, and that is one of the main goals of the STEPS.

STEP 19

The STEPS are preparing you to travel the Greek highway by introducing you not only to the rules of the road, but also to the washouts, the potholes, and the sharp curves. At this point you can't be expected to recognize all of them, so they'll jar your linguistic bones every now and then. Eventually, however, you'll begin to see them coming and find yourself swerving just in time.

STEP 20

CAMERA-WORDS			
PICTURE ⇒⇒⇒			VIDEO
L_{IGHT}	A_{CTION}	N_{EC. ROLE}	RECORDED
B R I G H T	M I D D L E	I we you all of you he, she, it they	ἐπαιδευ-όμην I was training myself -όμην -όμεθα -ου -εσθε -ετο -οντο Word Chart D-3

What you need to know:
Sometimes add-a-phrase words (δία, κατά, μετά, etc) combine with camera-words to form new camera-words: εἰς + πορεύομαι = εἰςπορεύομαι.

Strange but true:
When a camera-word with an add-a-phrase word on the front changes to a *recorded video* form, the ε- is not attached to the front of the word, but *between* the add-a-phrase word and the camera-word. Therefore, the video-recording form of εἰσπορεύομαι is εἰσεπορευόμην.

Problems arise, of course, if the add-a-phrase word happens to end with a vowel. Then the vowel bumps into the ε-, and as you have already learned, Greek vowels won't tolerate that much closeness without a reaction.

In this case, since the ε- is so important, the vowel on the end of the phrase-word usually disappears. Therefore, when ἀπολούω changes to a recorded video (ἀπό + ἔλουν), it becomes ἀπέλουον.

Give it a try:
What are the settings of these camera-words? Live video or recorded video? Active, middle, or passive?
ἐπαιδευόμεθα, ἐπαιδεύετο, ἐπαιδεύοντο, ἐπαιδεύου, ἐπαιδεύεσθε, ἐπαιδευόμην, ἐπαίδευον, παιδεύονται, ἐπαίδευεν

STEP 20

What is the corresponding *recorded video* form for each of the following words: παιδεύω, παιδεύονται, παιδεύεις, παιδεύομαι, παιδεύουσιν, παιδεύῃ, παιδεύεται, παιδεύει, παιδευόμεθα, παιδεύεσθε

Now you're the translator:
1. Οἱ διάκονοι ἐν τῇ ὥρᾳ τῆς προσευχῆς εἰς τὴν συναγωγὴν ἐπορεύοντο.
2. ἐδέχεσθε τὸν πτωχὸν μετὰ χαρᾶς εἰς τὴν οἰκίαν ὑμῶν. 3. ἡ ἐκκλησία τὴν βουλὴν τῶν πρεσβυτέρων ἐν ὑπακοῇ ἐδέχετο. 4. ἀπεκρίνετο οὖν ὁ Ἰησοῦς καὶ ἔλεγεν τοῖς Ἰουδαίοις. 5. οἱ ἄπιστοι ἐκ τῆς ἐκκλησίας ἐξεπορεύοντο. 6. αἱ προσευχαί σου καὶ αἱ ἐλεημοσύναι σου εἰσεπορεύοντο πρὸ τοῦ θεοῦ. 7. ἀπελυόμεθα ἐκ τῶν δεσμῶν τοῦ ἐχθροῦ ὑπὸ τοῦ φίλου τοῦ πιστοῦ. 8. οὐκ ἀνελύετε τὰς ἐντολὰς τοῦ θεοῦ. 9. μετὰ τὰς ἡμέρας τῆς ἑορτῆς οἱ Γαλιλαῖοι ἐξεπορεύοντο εἰς τὰς κώμας αὐτῶν. 10. οἱ ἄνθρωποι τὴν φωνήν τοῦ κυρίου ἤκουον. 11. ἡ διδαχὴ τῆς σωτηρίας ἤρχετο πρὸς τοὺς λαοὺς τῆς οἰκουμένης. 12. ἤλπιζεν ἐπὶ τῇ σωτηρίᾳ τοῦ υἱοῦ τοῦ θεοῦ. 13. ἠργάζου ἐν ὑπομονῇ τὰ ἀγαθὰ ἔργα τοῦ κυρίου. 14. ἀπεστέλλομεν τοὺς ἀδελφοὺς πρὸς τὴν ἑορτὴν τῆς ἐκκλησίας ὑμῶν. 15. ἡ πιστὴ ἀδελφὴ εἰς τὸν οἶκον τοῦ πρεσβυτέρου εἰσήρχετο.

Study Tips!
Sometimes it can be a help to get an overview of what lies ahead before you continue on your way. The same is true of language learning. It can help to know what's coming before you get entrenched in too many details.

You can get an overview of what's ahead in the STEPS, for example, by speeding through the next ten or fifteen STEPS. As you do it, quickly underline a few important points, try an example or two, and read through the vocabulary. The helicopter view you get, may help you make more sense of the individual pieces of the linguistic puzzle you're trying to put together.

I know that the Introduction to the STEPS claims languages are best learned step by step, but that is only intended as a general guideline. Every now and then, it is also wise to lay down your backpack and run up the trail a bit to get a feel for what's coming.

STEP 21

CAMERA-WORDS			
PICTURE ⇒⇒⇒			VIDEO
LIGHT	ACTION	NEC. ROLE	LIVE
D I M	A C T I V E	I we you all of you he, she, it they	παιδεύ-ω (so) I'd be training -ω -ωμεν -ῃς -ητε -ῃ -ωσιν See page 78 Word Chart C-5
D I M	MIDDLE	PASSIVE	I we you all of you he, she, it they	παιδεύ-ωμαι (so) I'd be training myself -ωμαι -ώμεθα -ῃ -ησθε -ηται -ωνται Word Chart C-6,7

Don't forget:
The letters of the word PLAN—Picture, Light, Action, Necessary role—highlight the four kinds of information in a camera-word.

What you need to know:
Greek camera-words depict the pictures of thoughts in one of three different lights: *bright, dim,* and *flashing.* Thus far the STEPS have only used camera-words with *bright* lights in the exercises. The *bright-light* form of a camera-word depicts a picture of reality or a statement of fact: ἀκούομεν τοὺς λόγους τοῦ Παύλου, *We are hearing the words of Paul.*

The *dim-light* form of a camera-word, however, projects a picture of possibility or probability: ἦμεν ἐν Ἰερουσαλήμ ἵνα ἀκούομεν τοὺς λόγους τοῦ Παύλου, *We were in Jerusalem **in order to hear** the words of Paul.* It is a thought that is not yet reality.

STEP 21

Don't miss it:
Camera-words use the dim light:
1. in thoughts introduced by ἵνα *(in order that)*
2. in thoughts introduced by ἐάν *(if)*
3. in thoughts that express inner conviction or desire
4. in thoughts that prohibit something: μὴ ποῆτε, *Don't do it!*
5. In thoughts that ask a deliberating question:
   παιδεύωμαι, *Should I be training myself?*
   Notice that all these usages deal with thoughts that have not yet become reality or fact.

Don't miss it:
μή (not) is the word that *negates* the dim-light form of a Greek camera-word (οὐ negates bright-light forms).

Give it a try:
Determine the PLAN (**P** = video-live or video-recording, **L** = bright or dim, **A** = active, middle, or passive, **N** = *I, we, you...etc.*) of the following camera-words:
παιδεύηται, παιδεύωμεν, παιδεύω, παιδεύονται, παιδεύῃ (3x!), παιδεύωσιν, ἐπαίδευον, παιδεύῃς, παιδεύωμαι, παιδεύητε, παιδεύετε, παιδεύωνται, παιδεύησθε, παιδεύουσιν, παιδευώμεθα, παιδεύομεν

Now you're the translator:
1. Οἱ ἄνθρωποι ὀφθαλμοὺς ἔχουσιν, ἵνα βλέπωσιν τὰ ἔργα τὰ ποικίλα τοῦ θεοῦ. 2. ὁ Ἰησοῦς Χριστὸς ἦλθεν, ἵνα οἱ ἄνθρωποι σωτηρίαν ἔχωσιν. 3. ἦλθεν, ἵνα ἀπολύῃ ἡμᾶς ἀπὸ τῆς δουλείας τοῦ θανάτου καὶ ἐκ τῆς ἀνάγκης τῆς ἁμαρτίας. 4. τὰ τέκνα κελεύομεν, ἵνα μὴ δουλεύωσιν ταῖς ἐπιθυμίαις. 5. λέγετε τοῖς τέκνοις, ἵνα ἀπολούωνται. 6. ἐὰν ὁ οἰκονόμος ἔρχηται, τοὺς ἐργάτας ἀναπαύει. 7. δεχόμεθα τὸν παλαιὸν ξένον εἰς τὸν οἶκον ἡμῶν, ἵνα ἀναπαύηται. 8. ὁ κύριος ἦλθεν, ἵνα ἀπολύησθε ἐκ τῆς φθορᾶς. 9. σπουδῇ δουλεύωμεν τῷ κυρίῳ ἐν ἀληθείᾳ καὶ ἐν ταπεινοφροσύνῃ. 10. κωλύωμεν τὰ ἔργα τοῦ δόλου καὶ τῆς κακίας καὶ τῆς αἰσχύνης. 11. τῇ ἀνομίᾳ καὶ τῇ πλάνῃ μὴ δουλεύωμεν, ἀλλὰ τῷ ἁγιασμῷ. 12. ἀκούωμεν τὰς ἐπαγγελίας τῆς εὐλογίας τοῦ θεοῦ. 13. πορευώμεθα εἰς τὴν Αἴγυπτον. 14. ἐργαζώμεθα ἐν τοῖς ἀγροῖς, ἵνα ἐν τῇ ἡμέρᾳ τοῦ θερισμοῦ καρποὺς ἔχωμεν.

Any questions?
Q: Translating some of these sentences is tough. There are so many bits and pieces of information to keep in mind, and something always seems to get lost in the shuffle. How do you keep from getting frustrated?
A: Hey, not all kinds of frustration are necessarily bad. The exercises and texts are not there to be completed as though *finishing* was your major task. They're

How to Read New Testament Greek

there to make you wade around in the language.

Dive in and enjoy the water. Your goal shouldn't be to find the answers as quickly as possible and have it over with. The important thing is that you start to get a feel for the language, and that means spending time with it. Little children don't get upset because they understand so little of what is transpiring linguistically around them. They just keep plodding on from word to word, and instead of getting frustrated when they make mistakes, they giggle and laugh.

You might take a clue from the kids and try giggling when you get frustrated. Then, remind yourself that *looking up words in reference books* is going to be a big part of the game in your future career as a Greek scholar. And if that's the case, why not lower the frustration level right now by preparing yourself to be a master searcher and finder of needed information? You could begin by taking measures to make it easier to find things quickly in the materials you are now using. Here's a few ideas to get you thinking in the right direction:

1. Jot down information you often need on index cards and keep them handy when you're studying.

2. Put some tabs in your book to mark those pages you often have to locate.

3. Keep your Word Chart handy. It gives a good overview of most of the elements of New Testament Greek. If you don't want it on the wall, pack it in transparent plastic and lay it on your desk as a work mat. If you don't like that idea, fold the Word Chart in such a way that you can find the various sections in a hurry. The key is to stay oriented. Frustration sets in when you get lost.

4. Keep reviewing previous STEPS, and while you're at it, bring some creativity and humor into your work. If you're learning the word φύλαξ *(guard)*, tell yourself *fools* φύ need to be **locked** λαξ up and *guarded*. If you want to remember the word ὄνομα *(name)*, think of yourself being crowned a king with the name ῎Ονομα the Great. See yourself under a huge banner with ὄνομα written on it. The crazier the picture, the more likely you are to remember it.

5. Keep yourself organized. Messiness is the breeding ground of frustrations.

New words:

ἁγιασμός, ὁ	holiness	θυμός, ὁ	anger
αἰσχύνη, ἡ	shame	κακία, ἡ	badness
ἄν	if	κελεύω	call, order
ἀνάγκη, ἡ	necessity	οἰκονόμος, ὁ	house manager
ἀναπαύομαι	be refreshed	παλαιός,ά,όν	old
ἀναπαύομαι	rest	παύομαι	cease
ἀναπαύω	let rest	παύω	cause to stop
δόλος, ὁ	treachery	πλάνη, ἡ	error, deception
ἐάν	if, in case that	ποικίλος,η,ον	various kinds
ἐπαγγελία, ἡ	promise	σπουδή, ἡ	haste, diligence
ἐπιθυμία, ἡ	desire	ταπεινοφροσύνη, ἡ	humility

STEP 22

CAMERA-WORDS			
PICTURE ⇒⇒⇒			VIDEO
LIGHT	ACTION	NEC. ROLE	LIVE
F L A S H	A C T I V E	you all of you he, she, it they	παιδευ-ε be training, train -ε -ετε -έτω -έτωσαν See page 79 Word Chart C-8

What you need to know:
Camera-words depict the pictures of their meanings not only in *bright* light (reality) and *dim* light (possibility), but also in *flashing* light. *The flashing-light* form of a camera-word projects a *command*. παίδευε τὸν τέκνον, *Train the child.*

Don't miss it:
μή (not) negates the flashing light form of a Greek camera-word (οὐ when the light is bright).

Give it a try:

Determine the PLAN (**P** = *live video* or *recorded video*, **L** = *bright* or *dim*, **A** = active, middle, or passive, **N** = I, we, you...etc.) of the following camera-words: βασιλεύει - εἰρηνεύετε - κυριευέτω - λάτρευε - μνημονεύῃ - ἐφύτευες - νηστευέτωσαν - βουλεύεις - μένουσιν - ἠλπίζετε - κωλυέτω - ὑπήκουον - λάμβανε - λουέτωσαν - παύω - ἀναπαύετε - βουλεύονται - ἠρχόμεθα - δέχεσθε - ἀπεκρίνοντο - λῦε

Now you're the translator:
1. Πίστευε τούτῳ τῷ ὅρκῳ τοῦ νεανίσκου. 2. τὸν ἰσχυρὸν φόβον τῶν ἐχθρῶν βλέπετε. 3. Πέτρε, τῷ ἀγαπητῷ υἱῷ τοῦ θεοῦ δούλευε. 4. μένετε ὑπὸ τὴν βασιλείαν τοῦ υἱοῦ τοῦ θεοῦ. 5. λέγετε τοὺς σωτηρίους λόγους τοῦ θεοῦ τοῖς σοφοῖς καὶ τοῖς πτωχοῖς. 6. ἐπὶ τοῦ ξύλου τοῦ σταυροῦ τὸν

υἱὸν τοῦ θεοῦ βλέπετε. 7. οἱ πιστοὶ τὸν πειρασμὸν ἐκεῖνον τοῦ ἐχθροῦ φευγέτωσαν. 8. ὁ ἐπίσκοπος τῷ μὲν τῶν πιστῶν γραφέτω, τῷ δὲ ἀποστελλέτω τὸ δῶρον τῆς ἐκκλησίας. 9. μὴ δούλευε τούτῳ τῷ κόσμῳ τῷ πονηρῷ. 10. τοῖς γνωστοῖς λόγοις τῶν ὑποκριτῶν μὴ πιστεύετε. 11. μὴ βλεπέτω τὸν πειρασμὸν τοῦ κόσμου καὶ τὸν διωγμὸν τῶν ἐχθρῶν. 12. οἱ ἐκλεκτοὶ τῶν λόγων τῆς πλάνης μὴ ἀκουέτωσαν.

Any questions?
Q: The last sentence left me in a tangle.
A: What did you come up with?
Q: *Don't listen you chosen ones of deceptive words.* That can't be right.
A: A *flashing-light/they* form is usually best translated by using the helping word *should*: *They should listen* or in this case: *The chosen ones should not...*
τῶν λόγων could have thrown anyone off the track. This happens to be a case in which a word in the general supporting role is translated as though it were in the accomplishing role. ἀκούω does this often, although it also uses words in the accomplishing role to complete its action. It can't seem to make up its mind. Therefore, the translation is: *The chosen ones should not listen to deceptive words.*

In STEP 3 you were introduced to a similar situation: camera-words that complete their action with words in the directing role.

New words:

γάμος, ὁ	wedding	λίθος, ὁ	stone
γνωστός,ή,όν	known	μέσος,η,ον	in middle of
διωγμός, ὁ	persecution	νεανίσκος, ὁ	young man
ἵππος, ὁ	horse	ὅρκος, ὁ	oath
ἴσος,η,ον	same	τρόπος, ὁ	way, means
ἰσχυρός,ά,όν	strong	τύπος, ὁ	picture, model
κλάδος, ὁ	branch		

STEP 23

CAMERA-WORDS			
PICTURE ⇒⇒⇒			VIDEO
LIGHT	ACTION	NEC. ROLE	LIVE
F L A S H I N G	M I D D L E	you all of you he, she, it they	παιδεύ-ου be training yourself -ου -εσθε -έσθω -έσθωσαν Word Chart C-9

Don't forget:

Certain camera-words such as ἐργάζομαι, ἔρχομαι, and δέχομαι (STEP 18) have *medium/passive* forms with *active* meanings. The active forms and the med/passive meanings have *departed*, leaving only the medium or passive forms and the active meanings.

θεραπεύεσθε, for example, a normal camera-word without departed forms, means: *All of you should be healing yourselves* or in a passive sense: *All of you should be being healed.*

δέχεσθε, however, which has departed forms, means, *All of you should keep on receiving*, which is an active meaning.

Give it a try:

What is the PLAN of these camera-words? And how would you translate them? Example: παιδεύου, **P** = video-live, **L** = flashing, **A** = Mid/pass, **N** = you. Translation (middle): *Be training yourself*, translation (passive): *Keep on being trained* or *Let yourself keep on being trained.*

παιδευέσθω, παιδεύεσθε(!), παιδευέσθωσαν, παιδεύου, νήστευε, φυτευέσθω, ἐβασίλευεν, βουλεύου, ἠρηνεύετε, θεραπεύεσθε, κυριευέτω, ἐλατρεύομεν, κωλύονται, ὑπήκουες, λαμβάνωμεν, ἀποστέλλητε, ἐργάζου, ἤρχοντο, ἀπερχέσθωσαν, ἐπορεύοντο, ἀποκρινέσθω, ἐδέχεσθε, ἔλουον, ἀπολουέσθω, ἀναλύῃ(!), παύου, κελεύῃς, ἀναπαύεσθε, ἐβουλεύου

How to Read New Testament Greek

Now you're the translator:
1. Ἐν τοῖς ἀγροῖς τοῖς λοιποῖς τῶν γεωργῶν ἐργαζέσθωσαν. 2. τὸ τέκνον ὑπὸ τῆς παιδίσκης παιδευέσθω. 3. δέχεσθε τοὺς φίλους εἰς τὸν οἶκον ὑμῶν. 4. πορεύου πρὸς τὸν κύριον. 5. ἀπολύου ὑπὸ τοῦ κυρίου ἐκ τῆς δουλείας τῆς ἀδικίας. 6. ὁ δοῦλος ἐρχέσθω καὶ τῷ κυρίῳ δουλευέτω κατὰ τὸ μέτρον τῆς ἐνεργείας αὐτοῦ. 7. ἐν τῇ καλῇ ὁδῷ τὸ φρόνιμον τέκνον μὴ κωλυέσθω. 8. μὴ ἀποκρίνου ἐν ὀργῇ τῷ ἐχθρῷ. 9. εἰς τὴν δόξαν τοῦ κυρίου πολιτεύου. 10. μὴ βουλεύεσθε ὑπὸ τοῦ πονηροῦ.

Any questions?
Q: Aren't the translations of θεραπεύεσθε and δέχεσθε at the beginning of this step a little unusual? *Should be being healed* and *keep on receiving* sound strange to me.
A: You're absolutely right. We don't normally express ourselves quite like that. They are attempts, however, to put the *Greek live video* part of the picture into the translation. That would be missing if we were to use more normal English expressions such as *You should be healed* or *Receive*.

There are, of course, better and more natural ways to translate live video commands, but at the beginning stages of learning Greek it would not be helpful to get overly involved in principles of translating. We're going to save that for the second *with-people-just-like-you* book.

New words:

γυμνός,ή,όν	naked	λοιπός,ή,όν	remaining, from now on
θησαυρός, ὁ	treasure		
ἱκανός,ή,όν	sufficient, appropriate	μέτρον, τό	measure
		μωρός,ά,όν	foolish
καπνός, ὁ	smoke	ὀργή, ἡ	anger
κενός,ή,όν	empty, worthless	παιδίσκη, ἡ	maid, servant-girl
κοινωνός, ὁ	partner	πολιτεύομαι	live as a citizen (of a country)
κρυπτός,ή,όν	hidden		
λιμός, ὁ	hunger	Χριστιανός, ὁ	Christian

STEP 24

CAMERA-WORDS			
PICTURE ⇒⇒⇒			PHOTOGRAPH
LIGHT	ACTION	NEC. ROLE	FUTURE
B R I G H T	A C T I V E	I we you all of you he, she, it they	παιδεύ-σω I will train -σω -σομεν -σεις -σετε -σει -σουσιν See page 77 Word Chart: G-2
B R I G H T	M I D D L E	I we you all of you he, she, it they	παιδεύ-σομαι I will train myself -σομαι -σόμεθα -σῃ -σεσθε -σεται -σονται Word Chart G-3

What you need to know:

When a Greek camera-word depicting a *future* photo is translated into English, it is necessary to use the helping word *will:* παιδεύσεις, *You will train.* In Greek, however, just inserting that little letter σ between the root of the word παιδεύ- and its live video ending -εις is enough to shoot the picture into the future.

Don't miss it!

The Greek camera-word can only take a photo of the future. It has no future video as does English (*You will be training*).

What is the difference between a photo and a video picture?

A video picture depicts continuation, progress, or repetition. Examples: *He is walking, The plant is growing, He takes three pills a day.*

A photo, however, depicts an *aspect* of an action, anything from a moment in time (*He hit the nail*) to a summary of many actions (*They won the ball game*).

How to Read New Testament Greek

Give it a try:
What is the PLAN of the following camera-words?
παιδεύσω, παιδεύσετε, παιδεύσειν, παιδεύσεις, παιδεύσει, παιδεύσομεν, παιδεύσῃ παιδεύσουσιν, παιδευσόμεθα, παιδεύσεσθε

Translate these future photos:
παιδεύσω, παιδεύσομαι, παιδεύσεσθε, παιδεύσεις, παιδεύσονται, παιδεύσεται, παιδεύσετε, παιδεύσει, παιδευσόμεθα, παιδεύσουσιν

Now you're the translator:
1. ἔρχεσθε πρὸς τὸν Ἰησοῦν· ἀναπαύσει ὑμᾶς. 2. ἐν τῷ καινῷ κόσμῳ τοῦ θεοῦ σὺν Χριστῷ βασιλεύσετε. 3. οἱ στρατιῶται οἱ πιστοὶ τὸν δοῦλον ἐκ τῆς δουλείας τῶν Ῥωμαίων ἀπολύσουσιν. 4. οἱ τελῶναι καὶ οἱ ἁμαρτωλοὶ τῷ σωτηρίῳ εὐαγγελίῳ πιστεύσουσιν. 5. ὁ κύριος κατὰ τὸν αἰώνιον λόγον αὐτοῦ τοὺς πιστοὺς αὐτοῦ ἀναπαύσει. 6. ἔρχεται ὥρα καὶ νῦν ἐστιν ὅτε οἱ νεκροὶ ἀκούσουσιν τῆς φωνῆς τοῦ υἱοῦ τοῦ θεοῦ. 7. Ἐγώ εἰμι κύριος ὁ θεός σου ...
οὐ μοιχεύσεις ...οὐ φονεύσεις...

New words:
ἄνεμος, ὁ	wind	μοιχεύω	commit adultery
δεῖ	one must, it is necessary	ὅτε	when, while
		φονεύω	murder, kill
θεμέλιος, ὁ	foundation		

STEP 25

SMALL ALL-AROUND WORDS	
ACTION	LIVE VIDEO
Active	παιδεύειν
Middle	παιδεύεσθαι
Passive	παιδεύεσθαι

Word Chart C-21

What you need to know:

The small all-around word is *small* because it has very few forms compared with other Greek words, and it is *all-around* because it sometimes functions like a camera-word and other times like a something-word (It's not an add-on word, however, like its big brother, the all-around word).

In this STEP, you will meet the *live video/active* and *medium* forms of the small all-around word, and learn one way in which a small all-around word functions as a camera-word.

Don't miss it!

In some thoughts a small all-around word expresses the *purpose* or *intent* of the camera-word.

δεῖ τὰ τέκνα παιδεύειν
*It is necessary **to train** (to be training) the children.*

δεῖ ὑπό τοῦ υἱοῦ τοῦ θεοῦ παιδεύεσθαι
*It is necessary **to be trained** by the son of God.*

When translating such occurrences of the small all-around word, it is often best to use the English word *to,* which expresses purpose or intent when used with a camera-word.

Give it a try:

Translate the following small all-around words:
παύειν, λούειν, δέχεσθαι, εἰρηνεύειν, ἐργάζεσθαι, βασιλεύειν, ἀποκρίνεσθαι, ἀπέρχεσθαι, παιδεύεσθαι, κελεύειν, φυτεύεσθαι, κωλύεσθαι

How to Read New Testament Greek

Make small all-around words out of the following camera-words (A = active, M = middle):
Example: Just drop off the *live video* ending -ω, and add the correct ending of a small all-around word: -ειν. The result is παιδεύ-ειν.
βουλεύω M, ὑπακούω A, κυριεύω A, νηστεύω A, λαμβάνω M, ἀποστέλλω A, εἰρηνεύω A, φυτεύω M

Now you're the translator:
1. Κελεύεις τοὺς ἀδελφοὺς δουλεύειν τῷ υἱῷ τοῦ θεοῦ. 2. ἔχομεν ὀφθαλμοὺς τὰ καλὰ ἔργα τοῦ θεοῦ βλέπειν. 3. δεῖ τὸν πειρασμὸν τοῦ ἐχθροῦ φεύγειν. 4. ὁ νόμος τοὺς ἀνθρώπους παιδευέτω δουλεύειν τῷ ἀληθινῷ θεῷ. 5. κέλευε τὸν ἁμαρτωλὸν τοῖς λόγοις τοῦ πονηροῦ μὴ πιστεύειν. 6. δεῖ τὰ ἔργα τοῦ διαβόλου μὴ ἐργάζεσθαι. 7. οἱ εὐαγγελισταὶ πορευέσθωσαν τοῖς λαοῖς λέγειν τὸ εὐαγγέλιον. 8. οἱ πρεσβύτεροι τοὺς πιστοὺς ἀδελφοὺς ἐν τῇ ἐκκλησίᾳ ὑμῶν κελεύουσιν τὸν λόγον τῆς ἀληθείας ἐν ὑπομονῇ δέχεσθαι. 9. οἱ ἐργάται παύονται ἐν τοῖς ἀγροῖς ἐργάζεσθαι. 10. κελεύσεις τοὺς διακόνους σου κατὰ τὴν ἀλήθειαν τοῖς κριταῖς ἀποκρίνεσθαι.

Any questions?
Q: So many of the sentences still seem to be such a tangle. Will it ever be possible for me to put them together without taking hours to do it?
A: Sure, but it will take time for your eyes to be trained to see things in a different order. Over the years, you have become accustomed to ordering information in certain ways. Take the number *27*, for instance. You record it in your mind as *twenty-seven* or 20 + 7, first the *tens* and then the *ones*. In many languages, however, *seven-twenty or 7 + 20* is the pattern used, first the *ones* and then the *tens*.

The switch in the order is confusing at first. When you hear *seven-twenty,* it sounds like *seventy-two.* You can imagine the misunderstandings and mistakes that result when beginners in such a language record their first addresses and telephone numbers!

A different word order is not unique to the Greek language. Most languages have their own opinion about where words are supposed to show up in a sentence. Some even prefer that they be read from right to left, or from top to bottom.

People in different cultures do many things in a different order. Even the order in which food is served varies from culture to culture. In most parts of America, dessert is considered the perfect finishing touch to a good dinner. It's often the other way around in Austria, however, where a fancy, late-afternoon dessert is the perfect appetizer for the evening meal. Even taste buds have to have time to adjust to that kind of turnabout.

Learning a new language involves much more than just learning new words. It thrusts us into a whole new way of thinking, a whole new approach to the ordering

STEP 25

and categorizing of information. It's actually a great opportunity. Few experiences compare with language learning as a catalyst for expanding our horizons of understanding. It forces us to venture into the unknown territory of new thoughts and perspectives.

It's no wonder your mind protests when asked to give up the old familiar ways of doing things. That's only natural. Give it time and keep moving. The mind, like the body, gets cranky when it gets too comfortable. Exercise is just the thing to get the juices flowing again and bring back the joy of discovery your mind possessed when it was a child.

PART IV:

What They're Thinking after Six Months

Back to School

It was nearing 4:30 on a Wednesday afternoon when Marian put the finishing touches on a pot roast and slid it into the oven. On Wednesdays she cooked the evening meal for the McLain children to give their mother a free day for appointments. It was more than just a favor for Linda, however, it was also something she was doing for herself. The sound of children's voices in her home flooded her with memories of many happy days spent as a mother and as a grade school teacher. Although most of her friends would say she had 'made the adjustment' to living alone since her husband's death, the absence of life in the house still overpowered her at times.

She particularly enjoyed the McLain children who seemed less affected by the emotional pressures that dogged the heels of many teens and preteens she knew. In fact, she often had the distinct feeling they were the ones taking care of her instead of the other way around. A few weeks earlier Buddy and Peggy had decided they were going to help her with her Greek studies. It amused her to think of two bright-eyed teen-agers sitting her down—her, a veteran teacher—and trying to cram a new language into her head.

She remembered thinking how silly she had felt those first days and weeks struggling to learn the Greek letters and work through the lessons Dean had given her. It was new and interesting, but she couldn't escape the thought that it was an unrealistic thing for her to be doing.

Much to her own surprise, however, learning Greek had set several positive forces into motion. It had not only given her a challenging task to do at home, but—and this is what she had least expected—precisely the seeming impossibility of the undertaking injected her with an energetic outlook she hadn't had for years.

Learning Greek was a big project. It forced her to think in terms of goals that were many years ahead. And it forced her to think about learning, about growing, and about changing. In the last ten years she had quit learning and growing. Instead, she had allowed the past to catch up and overtake her, shrinking her future into a hazy, insignificant program of hobbies and activities with no greater purpose than to keep her busy or to occupy her mind.

Unwittingly her days had gradually turned into a tired shuffle of small talk, short walks, and little plans. Bigness had dropped out of her life and become the unexpected curse of growing old. She was left feeling small and empty. It was the big projects—marriage, raising a family, career, house-building—that had once fueled her emotions with the hopes, fears, joys, and sweet tingles of anticipation that assured her she was needed and involved in something important. One by one, though, the big goals had disappeared like fading rainbows.

She was grateful for the people who had helped her at the crucial crossroads. What would she have done without her daughter who had refused to let her turn inward? What would she have done without Ed and Lauren Hansen who had helped move her to Arizona and were always there when she needed them? And where would she be without Linda McLain who had challenged her to be a tool in God's hands in the coming years?

She heard a knock on the door. "It's open," she called.

Tommy and Peggy came in, talking and laughing. "τί κάνεις?" piped up Tommy when he saw Marian.

"Κάλα," she answered, surprised that she had not forgotten the how-are-you-I'm-fine routine in modern Greek that Buddy had taught her and his younger brother and sisters. "When are Buddy and Katy coming?"

Tommy unloaded a pile of books on the kitchen counter. "Buddy should be here soon. He gets out of basketball practice early today. And Katy's already here. She's playing out in the front yard."

"Mmmmm, what do I smell, Mrs. Lawson?" Peggy was hovering over the stove.

"Oh, it's just a pot roast with a few potatoes and carrots. Nothing special."

"We'll see if it's nothing special. You could turn dry oatmeal into a feast."

"Ho, ho. Compliments like that just may get you an extra piece of pie, young lady."

"There's pie, too?"

"And what's your mother doing today?"

"She said she was seeing some girls at Mesa Community College. And afterwards, I think she's visiting a woman in Tempe."

"Your mother certainly is in demand."

Marian thought about her own efforts to reach out to other people. It was a concept that was new to her. Although she'd been a faithful member of a church all her life, she had never thought of herself as having any personal spiritual responsibility toward others. It was Linda who had first gently challenged her to take a long look at her relationship to Jesus Christ by doing some serious reading in the New Testament, and then encouraged her to look outside herself to others who also had hurting hearts.

She had learned that suffering can play an important and meaningful role in life and that her own suffering could actually be a bridge to others. As time went by, she had indeed found she could empathize with those who had suffered loss or disappointment. The result was a growing list of acquaintances and neighborhood women who had begun to drop by or call her on the phone.

It was during this process of coming out of her own shell and establishing new relationships that she realized she had so little of substance to say to others. That's when she began closely observing Linda and saw the key role the Scriptures played in her relationships, both at home and with friends and neighbors. Before she knew what happened, she found herself sitting in a circle of people interested in learning New Testament Greek. How ludicrous it had seemed at the time. Greek? At her age? But the longer she stuck with it, the more she realized that the New Testament was a precision instrument, capable of performing tasks she had never dreamed possible. What could be more logical than developing the skills to use such a tool?

It embarrassed her to think that her earlier use of the Scriptures had been much like taking her new sewing machine and using it as nothing more than a paper weight. She had always prided herself on being a good seamstress, and she had one of the best performing machines on the market. It was a high tech marvel that she knew inside and out. It actually made her angry to think she had taken the time to become a meticulous and skilled operator of a sewing machine and at the same time had gone on using the New Testament like a blunt needle with a worn-out piece of thread.

It was an anger that she knew was of the good kind--the kind that had motivated her in earlier days to start new programs in the school or help her husband tackle injustices that surfaced in his work as a lawyer. And it was an anger that did something else, too: It made her think her husband would have liked to have seen her this way again, with color in her face and fight in her voice.

Buddy disturbed her thoughts as he strode into the house. "τὶ κάνεις; *How are you?*" he asked with a sparkle in his eyes.

"κάλα," she answered. "πολὶ, πολὶ κάλα. *Very, very good.*"

Sidetracked?

"Hi, honey." Linda had just taken the car keys out of her purse as Dean walked into the house. "Glad you're home on time. I need to drive over to ASU to meet with Liz."

"Liz Serringer?"

"Right. She called this morning and asked if we could get together."

"Do you know where she lives?"

"In a sorority in one of the big dorms on University Drive. I'm sure I'll have no trouble finding her." Linda gave her husband a quick kiss and stepped out of the house into the warm air.

Cruising south on 48th Street in light traffic, Linda's thoughts turned to Liz. She'd been wanting to get to know her better from the first time they'd met. Normally she would have simply called and arranged a time to meet, but for some reason she kept putting it off. Outwardly Liz appeared to be an uncomplicated young woman, but there was something about her—a kind of reservedness that Linda couldn't quite put her finger on—that seemed to hide a very private person. It made Linda think it wiser to wait for Liz to make the first move.

She was also looking forward to talking to Liz, because she had a secret she knew would surprise her. Like Liz, Linda, too, had German parents. She had even been born in Germany. After the outbreak of World War II, when she was a baby, her parents had escaped to the United States.

Passing Papago Park she left the Phoenix city limits and crossed the bridge over the dry bed of the Salt River into Tempe, the home of Arizona State University. Turning east on University Drive she quickly found a place to park not far from Liz's dorm. As she approached the front entrance, she saw Liz coming towards her wearing a brightly colored T-shirt and bermudas, the ensemble that seemed to be the universal uniform of Arizona college students.

"You made it," said Liz. "I'm so glad you could come. Let's go into the lounge to talk. It's cool in there."

Inside, they found comfortable chairs next to a window. In the distance they could see the university's football stadium wedged between two rugged desert buttes.

"I've heard that majoring in architecture is quite demanding here," said Linda. "Are you finding you're able to keep pace?"

"The first couple years were difficult. They really put pressure on the beginners to narrow down the field. It's definitely not a major for students who are here to have fun."

"Would you say there's a lot of those around?"

"Enough. ASU has a good reputation as an up-and-coming school in the academic world, but it also gets its share of party majors. I suppose most people think of it as good, clean fun, but it's not all it's made out to be. A lot of kids who are on their own for the first time show up with plenty of money in their pockets, and they sort of go crazy. Within a year or two some of them are pretty messed up. There are 70 women up on my floor, and I spend a lot of time just trying to keep some one of them from doing some really dumb things. There are girls who get so caught up in their emotions that it's almost scary."

"Sounds like you've got plenty to keep you busy. Are you able to find any time to keep up on Greek?"

"So far I've been able to do quite a lot, but Greek does have something to do with why I invited you to drop by."

"I hope your questions aren't too complicated. I'm not exactly the Greek expert in the family."

"Oh, my questions don't have anything to do directly with Greek. They're of a more personal nature. You see, I have some Christian friends who think it's a waste of time for me to be learning Greek."

"A waste of time?"

"You probably know that I've been active with one of the Christian groups on campus. Well, one of the leaders heard I was learning Greek and told me he thought I could be using my time more wisely. He said we have translations that are sufficient for Bible study, and Greek simply takes time away from other more important matters."

"What did you say to him?"

"I guess it surprised me, so I didn't say anything at all. There are things I could have said, I suppose, but I didn't know if I should or not. What would you have said to him?"

"Goodness. I'm going to have to think about that for a moment. I do think it's good that you chose not to say anything without first thinking about it. Let's see now, there's actually several rather large questions wrapped up in what you've just told me. The best thing we can do is try to sort them out and handle them one at a time.

"Let's start with the question as to whether learning Greek is a time waster or not. To be honest, I think we'd have to admit that in certain cases the leader who spoke with you could be absolutely right. If a person were to learn Greek, for example, to impress someone with his knowledge or use Greek studies as a hideaway from the demands of everyday living, then learning Greek would certainly be a waste of time. Wrong motives always lead to an abuse of time. But that's true of anything we do, not just learning Greek. Everything we do should be tied in as much as possible to a love for God and to a desire to serve our fellow man.

"It probably shouldn't surprise us, however, if learning Greek strikes a lot of people as an undertaking with little immediate practical worth. It's simply not an everyday sort of thing that people do, and therefore it can easily be thought of as unnecessary."

"Is there anything I can say?"

"Sure. You could begin by explaining that you see learning Greek as an investment in your future effectiveness in the Scriptures. That's certainly one sense in which learning Greek is a good use of time."

"Future effectiveness? What do you mean exactly?"

"Let's say that two men are visiting a third world country in which there are very bad health conditions. Both decide they want to do something for the people in that country. One man takes a first-aid course and immediately starts doing what he can. The other man, however, returns home, seemingly turning his back on the needs. He enrolls in a medical school, however, and shows up again seven years later.

"During those seven years it may seem that the man who stayed is doing a lot for the people and that the other is wasting his time. But when the second man comes back as a qualified doctor, it is possible that he will accomplish much more, medically speaking, in a very short time than the man with first-aid training could do in all of his life.

"I'm not suggesting that your leader is doing first-aid work. In fact, he's probably invested considerable time himself in various kinds of ministry preparation. I'm simply trying to illustrate that an investment in preparing for the future can be a very wise use of time, although at the moment it may seem wiser to meet needs that seem more urgent. And I would certainly put learning Greek into the category of good preparation for life. Anything that helps us sink deep roots into the teachings of Christ has the potential of making better spiritual doctors out of us in the future."

"Now, let's turn to the matter of translations for a moment. As you know yourself, it's a topic that is seldom understood. There are two extreme positions: On the one hand, there are those who are of the opinion that certain translations are extremely accurate renditions of the original and worthy of unreserved trust. On the other hand, there are those who doubt the reliability of any translation, sometimes calling the entire process of text transmission into question. I don't believe the facts would support either position.

"Translations, if they are done well—and that's a big *if* involving many factors—can substantially reproduce meaning from one language to another. However, it is also true that in the translation process a certain amount of content fall-out cannot be avoided. The amount of fall-out depends on the skill of the translator, for example, or the degree to which the translation matches the language level of the reader."

"I know how that is," said Liz. "I've done plenty of translating from English to German and the other way around, and some words and concepts are almost impossible to translate without losing a lot in the process."

"If you find it's difficult to translate between two living languages that are contemporary to one another and share many cultural parallels," said Linda, "then just imagine the translating problems that come up between languages separated by two thousand years and reflecting cultures that have much less overlap. In such a case, knowing the original languages can be a tremendous help, and it's absolutely indispensable to the person who wants access to firsthand information.

"I've also found out that people who know Greek can be of real help to those who are dependent on translations. They can help them answer many questions that are otherwise impossible to answer. For the first fifteen years of our marriage, I couldn't read Greek. You can't imagine how often I asked Dean for information from the Greek text. It was so much of a help, in fact, that I finally decided I could be of much more service to others if I knew some Greek myself."

"And you learned it?"

"Like any language, I don't think you can ever reach a point where you can say you've totally learned it, but with a house full of helpers like I've got, I could hardly avoid at least getting to a point where I can use it with some confidence. I really wish now that I had done it years earlier. I use it much more than I would have ever thought."

"So you really don't think I'm getting my priorities tangled up by learning Greek?"

"That's a question you'll have to answer for yourself, but from my point of view it would seem logical for people who consider the Scriptures to be the words of God to highly value the language in which those Scriptures were first written. Just think of the thousands of young people right here on this one campus alone who are taking Spanish, French, Japanese, German, or Russian courses, and no one seems to consider that a case of misplaced priorities. Why then would anyone, particularly a believer, think it unimportant for a young person to want to learn the language of the Scriptures? What other language could possibly have a higher priority?

"Besides, Liz, I think that if you learn Greek in a balanced, disciplined way, you will also have time to fulfill your responsibilities to your fellow Christians and to the people you associate with every day on campus. In fact, I think your involvement with Greek could possibly increase your effectiveness in serving Christ right where you are. You'll be setting a good example for others by demonstrating your commitment to the Scriptural message, and you'll be opening the door to increased understanding of that message. That has to help you grow as a follower of Christ."

"I wish the leader of our student group was here and could hear all the things you've said."

"Maybe we ought to briefly discuss how we should communicate with fellow believers who don't necessarily share our views about certain matters."

"I'm all ears."

"Much of the teaching in the Scriptures is in the form of principles, and principles by nature can be applied in various ways. It's clear, for example, that believers ought to know the Scriptures well and be obedient to them. No one would argue with that. But nowhere in the Scriptures are we told in great detail exactly *how* or *where* or *when* or in what *manner* we should learn them. Nor are we told what kind of translation or which particular reference works we should use. These are matters that are left to us, and it's not unusual for Christians to have many different convictions in applicational areas like that.

"The Scriptures teach clearly that we should not judge one another in such matters of applicational conviction. I've always found the fourteenth chapter of

Romans instructive in this regard. You might want to take a look at it later on."

"But doesn't the Bible also teach that we should be like-minded?"

"Being like-minded in the Scriptures does not mean picking out someone's opinion to be the one everyone else has to adhere to. Likemindedness in the Scriptures is more akin to *Christmindedness*. It means conforming to his mind, and it certainly means having an attitude of love and forgiveness and acceptance toward our brothers and sisters with all their various convictions. I think it's possible to have convictions of our own in applicational areas and at the same time to have a high regard for the opinions of other Christians who might think differently. We don't have to defend our own convictions as though they were the best of all possible choices.

"This kind of attitude will help you feel relaxed and at home with believers of all stripes and colors. And, let me add, it is an attitude that will keep you in good stead with your future husband and children. Even husbands and wives discover that they don't always have the same outlook about things. If they don't learn to accept one another and learn to live in the presence of a dissenting opinion, then the fabric of the marriage will begin to rip and tear."

Linda paused. "Am I still on your wave length?"

"If you only knew," said Liz. "We've only talked for a short time, but I feel better already. I'm sure I'll have a lot more questions this year."

"That means we'll be getting together again. That's great. *Und das meine ich wirklich. Du kannst mich zu jeder Zeit anrufen.*"

"Oh!" exclaimed Liz. "I had forgotten you can speak German. Dean told me that after the two of you were married, you lived in Austria for a few years."

"That's true, but did you know I could speak German before I met Dean?"

"No, I didn't realize that. Did you learn German in school?"

"My father and mother are both German. Like you, I was born in Germany."

"Why, I had no idea. In fact that... I mean, I wonder..."

"What?"

"I was just wondering if maybe we could get together for another talk, real soon."

Behind the Scenes

Louise stepped into her husband's study. He was writing at his desk, hunched over in the concentrated posture that signaled he was hurrying to capture a thought. She waited until the tense shoulders relaxed and the flurried motion of the pen ceased. "When did you say Dean was coming, honey?"

Taking off his reading glasses, Harmon leaned back in his chair. "He said he'd try to make it before six-thirty."

"That early? I hope you didn't make him feel he *had* to come at that time."

"Suggested the time himself. He must be an early riser. Besides, at that time in the morning there's not much traffic out on Central. It makes the drive down here less of a hassle."

"I'll put some coffee on for you. Shall I get some rolls in the oven?"

"Sounds great."

After three years in Phoenix, Harmon and Louise were just beginning to grow accustomed to their new surroundings. It hadn't been easy for them to leave their family home in Nebraska where Harmon had grown up. They had lived in it all their married lives and had never anticipated living anywhere else. Harmon's aged parents were still in the house. They regularly went back for visits, but Harmon's health, which had markedly improved in the dry Arizona climate, dictated that the visits be kept short.

When they first moved to Arizona, they had considered settling in one of the new housing developments so plentiful in Phoenix and its suburbs, but they couldn't imagine themselves living in a large, modern house with desert landscaping. The special charm of an older house surrounded by stately trees was too much a part of their understanding of the word home.

They finally purchased a small stucco house in one of the older sections of the city and only a short drive from the college where Harmon taught. There were no ancient oaks in front of the house, but their street was beautifully lined with matching columns of towering palm trees, and orange and lemon trees filled both the front and back yards with lush splashes of ornamental green.

When Harmon heard a car enter the driveway, he slipped the papers he was working on into a notebook and went to the front door. He found Louise already outside talking with Dean. It was still cool, but the morning air was quickly soaking in the warmth of the rising sun. The long, stately palms were casting thin, spidery shadows across the surrounding yards.

"Good morning," said Harmon. "Glad you made it." The two men shook hands.

"It doesn't take much to motivate me to come down to your little oasis here," said Dean, "especially when Louise has her oven fired up." The smell of freshly baked bread was in the air.

They went into the kitchen, and while Louise was serving coffee and hot rolls, Harmon revealed the purpose of his request for a get-together. "For quite some time now, I've been wanting to ask you a series of questions that are related to the whole process of self-learning Greek. They're questions that do some probing behind the scenes."

"Sounds intriguing."

"I've been impressed with a lot of what you're doing, and it's made me curious to know some of the reasoning behind it all. That OK with you?"

"Sure. When it comes to evaluating something, it's usually more important to analyze the *why* than the *what*. At any rate, you've got me interested. Fire away."

Harmon opened a small leather notebook. "Let's start with grammar. The way I figure it, what you've basically done with us in Greek is to take an honored and venerable grammatical system and change it from top to bottom, not only in terms of the terminology you use, but also conceptually by rearranging categories and by reworking the language charts.

"Now don't get me wrong, I think it's an excellent idea. As a teacher I've been particularly interested to watch how it's helped the others to pick up grammatical concepts quickly and without the usual confusion. First of all, I'd like to know, how you developed this system, secondly, how accurate you think it is, and thirdly, how people who use your system will be able to relate to the traditional system when they run into it in reference books?

Dean scratched his forehead. "You sure know how to get some mileage out of a question.

"It's a rather long story how I developed the approach to grammar you first heard about during the tour of Universal Greek Pictures. I'll try to give you the short version. Years ago, because I was involved in various archaeological projects around the Mediterranean Sea, I had to become at least conversational in several different languages. In my role as a language learner, I came into frequent contact with other language learners and noticed how most of them struggled with grammatical concepts. In fact, I struggled with them myself even though I'd had plenty of linguistic experience. That raised a few questions in my mind, because, theoretically at least, knowing the grammar of a language is supposed to make language learning easier and faster.

"It was also during those years that I began to notice the number of believers who at one time or another had made an effort to learn New Testament Greek and then given it up. At first I didn't think much of it, but as the years rolled by, I found I was hardly running into *anyone* who was successfully learning Greek. That's when the problem actually began to alarm me. Even many people who had taken courses at the university or graduate school level were telling me they didn't feel very competent in the Greek language and admitted to using it very little.

"How did you learn Greek?" asked Harmon.

"I was fortunate to learn it from my father. He always used it, and he made it so interesting for us kids that learning Greek was no different than learning anything else you learn when you're growing up."

"Did you figure out why people were not successfully learning Greek and why other language learners were having problems with grammar?"

"I did some research on the matter for a number of years—at first informally by doing some reading about language learning and asking questions of anyone I ran into who had tried to learn Greek, then later by collecting information in a more systematic way. I put together some questionnaires, for example, and interviewed various individuals—linguists and school teachers mainly—who I thought might have some insight into the problems people have with language learning. I concluded there were not just one or two problems, but a whole series of problems that worked together to put a lock on the door to New Testament Greek for most people."

"Got the list in your head?"

"I can probably summarize the major issues. First of all, a lot of confusion has been caused because traditionally, one grammatical system—the one developed to describe the Latin language—has been borrowed as a framework to describe the workings of many other languages including Greek and English."

"Why has that been a problem?"

"It's like buying one size uniform for all the players on a softball team. It may fit two or three of the players well, but most of the others are going to be mighty uncomfortable. Take the word *participle*, for example. In English most people think of a participle as that *-ing* word we use so often. Some might also remember there's such a thing as a *past participle*. When a certain kind of word in Greek is also called a participle, people naturally assume that it's generally the same kind of word as an English participle. As you know, it is not. There may be some overlap, but a Greek participle is much more than an English participle could ever be, both in form as well as function. Trying to press a Greek participle into the arm holes of an English participle is like trying to press a two-hundred-and-fifty-pounder into a uniform made for a ten-year-old. It can't help but confuse an English speaker and be as much of a hindrance as a help.

"Secondly, the grammatical terms themselves are a big part of the problem. Some are so strange and unusual that learning them is almost like having to learn another language itself. Most language learners find it's enough of a job to learn a new word without also having to remember that the word is a *subordinating conjunction that introduces a dependent clause*. A lot of jittery language learners get scared away by that kind of linguistic harassment."

"In other words," said Harmon, "grammar, the very tool that is supposed to help people understand a language better, becomes itself a barrier to understanding."

"Sometimes that's the case."

"You talked about a *series* of problems. What are others?"

"There are problems that are kind of psychological spin-offs of the problems I've already mentioned."

"Psychological spin-offs?"

"Yes. I've talked to many people, for instance, who were convinced that they weren't talented or gifted in languages and that no amount of effort would ever be sufficient for them to actually learn another language. They came to this conclusion because of their lack of success in languages in school or because of frustrations they had in English grammar classes.

How to Read New Testament Greek

"This is an unfortunate conclusion for people to reach, because God has made us to be linguistic creatures. We speak, because He speaks. Speaking is not essentially a matter of talent any more than walking or eating or breathing is a matter of talent. Some may be faster or slower at speaking, walking, eating, or breathing, but it's natural for humans to do any of them and do them well."

"Don't you think, though, that learning a foreign language is essentially different than learning to walk?"

"Not really. If you want, you might compare learning a foreign language to learning a movement with our feet that is 'foreign' to us—something like square dancing, for example. Some people may be convinced they could never square dance because they think of themselves as being clumsy or uncoordinated; others might try it, and then give up when they find themselves struggling with the complicated steps. The problem, however, is not that they *can't* learn to square dance, but that they just don't want to take the time to do it. They could easily learn square dancing if they simply gave their brains and muscles time to make the various steps a part of their practiced repertoire.

"It's true, of course, that there are people who have linguistic abilities that are definitely products of unusual talent, in the same way that there are gifted dancers who can do things ordinary people can't, but simply learning another language in not in this category. It's not unusual even in the so-called primitive areas of the world to find whole populations who speak a handful of languages without thinking anything about it. If learning languages were a matter of talent then only special individuals in a given population would be bi-, tri-, or quadlingual, but that's not the case.

"My experience is that even people who think they are language dunces are capable of incredible linguistic feats without being aware of it. A few weeks ago I had a chat with Kevin, a twelve-year-old boy in our neighborhood who is one of Tommy's friends. In Kevin's own words, he hates school and anything that has to do with reading or writing. I only had to mention the word *English* to hear a mournful groan.

"When I switched the subject to baseball, however, he lit up like a flood light at Yankee Stadium. I found out he could rattle off the starting nine of most of the major league teams and he knew many of the batting averages of the players, not just for this year but past years. I asked him what Mickey Mantle hit in 1956 and he knew it!

"No one can tell me that kid doesn't have the talent to learn a foreign language. Of course he could. He would have to value it as highly as he does baseball, however. It's because he loves baseball that his young mind stores up the language of that national sport like a computer. You can see with this example that the problem is basically one of *values* and not one of ability or talent.

"Aha," said Harmon. "*Values.* Now you've hit on a word we anthropologists like to throw around. Where do you think Greek is on today's Christian scale of values?"

"I couldn't give a comprehensive answer to that, but my surveys have indicated that only a certain percentage of believers even *know* the New Testament writings were written in Greek, and of those who do know, only a very small percentage indicated they'd ever entertained the idea that it would be a thing of value to learn. I surveyed one church of over 500 members, for example, and only *two* people said they'd ever taken any steps to learn Greek. Plus, virtually no believers I have ever surveyed had encouraged their children to learn Greek, even though many had encouraged them to learn other foreign languages. These observations would support the suspicion that Greek is not only rock bottom on the value scale, but it seldom even shows up on the scale.

"When you think that most Christians would claim to believe that the Scriptures are the written revelation of the living God, then this is an unexpected result indeed. Considering the importance Christians attribute to the Scriptures, you would expect that a fairly significant percentage of believers would indicate at least some degree of interest in the original language in which they were written. Do you think the results of my surveys would correspond to your own experience?"

"No doubt about that," said Harmon. "Of the hundreds of Christians I know—and most of them are in circles in which the Scriptures are certainly given more than lip service—I don't think I am aware of more than three or four laymen who know Greek, and I don't think any of them would claim to be very adept at it. Why do you think Greek is valued so little?"

"An adequate answer to that question gets rather involved. There's the factor we've already mentioned, of course: the aversion to learning languages that affects a lot of people in general. But that would only explain why a believer would tend to shy away from the task of learning Greek, or why he would doubt his own ability to be able to learn Greek. It certainly doesn't explain why he would fail to value Greek as a language to be learned."

"What would you say is the root problem?"

"I strongly suspect it has to do with the fact that the Scriptures, like the main person they reveal, have not only been the object of conflicting opinions throughout the centuries, but spiritual forces from many directions have aimed their biggest guns at them to twist or neutralize them. Tampering with the Scriptures has been a favorite tactic of a well-organized opposition. At various times over the years, the Scriptures have been altered, additions have been made to them, portions have been called into question, their contextual cohesiveness has been distorted, and their historical and literary integrity has been challenged. These frontal attacks on the Scriptures have probably caused less damage, however, than the mystical religious aura that the powerful spirit of tradition has managed to cast around them."

"Mystical religious aura?"

"Yes. It's the impression many seem to have that the Scriptures are somehow different than other pieces of literature; that they can only be understood in certain *spiritual ways* by certain kinds of *spiritual* persons."

"In a way that's true, isn't it?"

"Yes, it is, but within limits. Obviously the Scriptures are information from the Spirit of God for spiritually minded individuals who are to approach them with open and trusting hearts. But it goes too far if people treat the Scriptures as though they were *magical* writings which cannot be read as you would read normal literature. And it goes too far if people think the Scriptures can only be deciphered by certain special interpreters. It's good to respect the Scriptures, but if that respect becomes a superstitious awe that keeps people at a distance, then it's a respect that becomes itself a barrier to the Scriptures."

"What do you mean exactly?"

"I remember once talking to a student from a third-world country, for example. He said he wanted to learn New Testament Greek, but that he did not yet have the finances to travel to the United States to go to a theological seminary where he could learn it.

"I asked him why he thought he had to go to the U.S. to a special school to learn Greek. He was of the opinion that Greek was a special language—a spiritual language—that could only be learned from religious specialists.

"Just think, this was a young man who was already fluent in three languages. I asked him how long he thought he would need to become conversational in a fourth language. He estimated about six months! The man was a linguistic fireball with absolutely no fear of language learning, but he thought he had to raise thousands of dollars and travel to America before he could learn Greek.

"Now, don't get me wrong. I'm not saying it's bad for people to enroll in a school to learn Greek. The point I'm trying to make is this: It was this student's own superstitious assumptions which were keeping him from beginning to learn Greek with the same energy and creativity he would have used had he decided to learn any other language. He had put Greek up on a 'holy' pedestal and was 'honoring' it by keeping a respectable distance. I'm convinced this same kind of 'keep-your-hands-off' idea lingers in the minds of many people. The opponents of the Scriptures must think it a great ploy to have transformed the language of the original Scriptures from one that can be learned like any other, into an object of religious veneration.

"I'm forced to agree with your analysis, because it's a pretty good description of me a few years back. Are there other problems?"

"Yes. Many things about the society in which we live are so distracting that people find it difficult to develop the discipline and concentration necessary for the learning of a language. Particularly television and our hectic lifestyles are two big time eaters that can knock a prospective language learner out of the saddle. It's sad, but if an ambitious language learner in our society does manage to make it over most of the other hurdles to language learning, then the chances are he'll be waylaid by any one of the multitudes of distractions that are such a part of our culture. To learn Greek, people need time and concentration; it doesn't have to be a lot, but it does need to be regular. Consider this: If a person were to invest only

Behind the Scenes

three hours a week for two years—that's almost forty, eight-hour working days—he would be well on his way to being able to read Greek. And three hours is exactly how long a football game or a movie lasts on TV. That wouldn't be much of a weekly sacrifice to exchange for a knowledge of the New Testament in Greek, but for the contemporary man who's been weaned on the tube, he may prefer to be an expert in football rather than the New Testament. Here's where *values* really come into play at any rate."

"That's a rather imposing list of problems, and obviously you've thought a lot about them. What are your ideas about solutions?"

"It's pretty obvious that a series of problems is going to require a series of answers. Let's begin with the grammar problem. Because I'd translated quite a few archaeological works over the years, I began to look at the situation from the standpoint of a translator, and one day the rather simple thought came to me: If people are having trouble understanding the terminology of grammar, why not translate the traditional grammatical terms into understandable English? So I did exactly that and tried to apply the most basic principles of translating to grammatical terminology. I soon figured I was on to something big, because the more I got into it, the better I began to understand the rules of grammar myself."

"Do you think the terminology you've chosen for your translations is accurate?"

"Accurate?" Dean thought for a moment. "Accuracy in the field of translating is an illusive goal, because you're always shooting at a moving target."

"You mean people."

"Right. No two think exactly alike, so what is accurate for one, may not be for the other. What I hope to have accomplished is to have cleared up some of the bigger problems. Take the term *imperfect tense*, for example. Both words are normal English words, but together and in a grammatical context they are extremely confusing. To a child, *imperfect tense* sounds like a description of tents with holes in them. And it doesn't help much to tell him that the word tense denotes time or aspect, and that verbs in the imperfect tense express either a past progressive idea or a past habitual idea. Going that route just sinks a normal English speaker deeper into a linguistic hole of despair. It's a pity, because it's not actually complicated at all. It's just that the grammatical terms themselves add to the mystique of foreign languages, making them sound more imposing and exotic than they actually are.

"I chose to translate *imperfect tense* with *video recording*, because most Americans know that a video recording is a moving picture—that's the progressive part—and that has to be a picture of something taking place in the past because it's a recording—that's the tense part. That's not all the possible content of the imperfect tense, of course, but it's a good chunk of it. Learners also need to be taught the additional meaning that is not conveyed by the term *video recording*, but that's a small matter compared to what has to be done with traditional terms such as *imperfect tense* which not only make it necessary for you to add 100% new content, but also require subtracting wrong content. That's worse than a blood

197

How to Read New Testament Greek

transfusion; it's a blood *exchange*. And in the end you are still left with an unsuitable and misleading term to carry your content. The blood exchange will have to be repeated over and over again, because the term will continue to confuse.

"*Video recording*, however, is a term that will maintain most of its content for an average person. Ten years later he'll still recognize it and know what it means. Terms like *imperfect tense*, on the other hand, easily shake off any sensible meaning they ever had, sometimes within hours, and they only remain to remind the poor soul who struggled to stuff them with meaning that he really is a language dunce.

"To summarize, I'd say the terms I've chosen are not necessarily accurate in the sense that they give a 100% picture of each grammatical concept—many of them have to be filled out with additional meaning—but most of them do contain much more content than the traditional terms, and they avoid the problem of being misleading, which is unfortunately the case with some of the traditional terms. It may be that some of my choices are also misleading to some degree. I would only defend them by saying I hope they are *less* confusing than the terms they replace."

"That's explains why the people who learn Greek with you are picking up the grammar so quickly," said Harmon. "They're simply learning it with words that really mean what they say. What kind of response have you gotten from language teachers or linguists? Do they resent your taking liberties with their sacred grammatical concepts?"

"Not at all. Like yourself, most teachers who have talked with me have been very interested in the concept of putting grammatical terms into everyday language. I think most of them have struggled with the traditional terminology enough themselves and seen their students struggle with it enough, to be open to anything that might make the teaching task easier."

"I can understand that. And what about the fact that all the reference books use the traditional terminology? How will the people who learn your system be able to use those books?"

"They'll have to learn the traditional terminology, of course, but that is a small task once they really understand Greek grammar. A small chart is all it takes to relate the traditional terms to the new terms, and since many of the new terms I've chosen are very similar to the traditional terms, they should be easily recognizable. The first few letters of the roles, for example, *necessary, general supporting, directing*, and *accomplishing* correspond to their traditional counterparts: *nominative, genitive, dative*, and *accusative*. The new terms are actually helpful little stepping stones into the boggy waters of traditional grammar.

"Another thing I've tried to do is put the grammar of Greek into a total picture that hangs together. The traditional approach doesn't do this. This is one big reason why Greek learners feel they run into quicksand so quickly. Their books are sprinkled with hundreds of charts and diagrams that seem to be the parts of several different puzzles. In most traditional grammars, for example, participles are included with verbs in the charts. This is misleading, however, because participles actually function more as substantives, adverbs, and adjectives than they do as verbs. Calling the participle an *all-around* word solves the terminology problem, and giving the all-around word a special place in the grammatical overview places it much more realistically in the total picture of the Greek language.

"This is what I've really tried to do: help people put the grammatical puzzle together in their own mind. Once they have a framework that makes sense to them, they can easily fit the traditional terms into it."

"And have you found that it works?"

"I've often seen people run into a tough grammatical term and seen the new terminology help them quickly solve the problem. Let's say someone stumbles over the term *dative case*, for example. 'What in the world is that?' he exclaims.

"'Oh, that's just the directing role,'" I reply. 'You know, it tells the camera-word how it's supposed to do something.'

"'Aha,' comes the response, 'So that's what it is.'

"It really doesn't take someone long to get the traditional system figured out, assuming he's already got a good picture of Greek grammar in his head. In fact, I've seen some folks take great pleasure in whacking the traditional grammar down to size, as though they were finally getting even for wounds suffered in some past feud."

"Ha!" said Harmon. "You put the sword of plain English in the hands of the man on the street, and with it he slays the grammar dragon."

"Sure, and people find it's not all that difficult to slay, because the grammar dragon is mostly mythical anyway—made to look ferocious by dressing it up in a linguistic Halloween costume. Our goal should be to help people realize that grammar is not a dragon at all. It's not horrible but closer to holy, because it reflects the deepest spiritual roots of our being.

"*Grammar* itself is a word we would probably be better off doing away with. If you've noticed, I try to avoid it. It helps people understand the true nature of grammar to give it a name that does it justice. I prefer to call grammar the *art of taking words seriously*, and I like to divide it up into two parts: How to take the words of God seriously, and how to take the words of men seriously. Both of these tasks take us right back to the bedrock of our purpose for existence: *to love God and to love our fellow man.* How can we love God if we don't take what He says seriously, and how can we love our fellow man if we don't listen to what he's saying and take the time to communicate with him in his own language? We'd better not begin to address this topic, however, or we'll be here for a long time."

"OK," said Harmon. "I'm satisfied with where we've come to. If my lovely wife and fellow dragon-slayer will fill our coffee cups, we can get on to the next question."

"All hot and ready to pour," said Louise, who had been listening intently.

"The next question is not really my own. Let's say it's a question I run into a

How to Read New Testament Greek

lot in certain circles. I'd like to hear how you handle it."

"I'll be interested to hear how I handle it myself."

"I'll put it this way: Why do you think it's so important to encourage people to learn the Scriptures in their original language? Don't we have enough experts around to solve any problems in this regard? Why should I do work that someone else can do for me and probably do it much better?"

"You're wheeling out the heavy guns today."

"Just trying to keep things moving."

"First of all, encouraging people to learn Greek is not a spurning of experts. It's exactly the opposite. It's actually encouraging people to seek out the best possible experts in the original text of the Scriptures and encouraging them to use these experts at their highest level of competence.

"OK. Your point is well taken, but most people who ask this question are thinking more in terms of going to an expert in the same way they would go to a dentist when they have a tooth ache or to a mechanic when their car breaks down. They're going to have the expert do something for them and not to learn how to do it themselves."

"Sure, and that's understandable in a society where we've become conditioned to turn to specialists to solve our problems. So, why not do it when it comes to spiritual matters? It all seems so logical and comfortable. And it would be, if Jesus Christ had had nothing more in mind than setting up Christianity Incorporated to be headed by a board of directors, run by a crack team of managers, and concerned with the logistics of product distribution.

"The only problem is that Christ never taught that his teachings could only be understood by specialists who were in turn franchised to interpret them for needy consumers. In fact, it was the religious specialists of Jesus' day who turned their noses up at his band of disciples. For them they were a scruffy troop of fishermen and worse. Not a respectable expert in the bunch. Jesus threw open his treasures of wisdom and understanding to anyone who was willing to come and learn from him.

"Paul, too, challenged all men to become experts in Christ. His goal was *to teach and counsel everyone with all wisdom to present every man complete in Christ.* That's the way he put it in his letter to the Colossians."

"But wasn't Paul himself an expert?"

"Of course he was, and I'm not saying we don't need experts at one time or another. Obviously at the beginning of our venture of following Christ, for example, we are in need of wise people who are good examples of godly living. But this dependency stage is not meant to be permanent. Unfortunately, the impression is rather wide-spread that it's OK for Christians to settle down into the great, passive pool of disciples that tradition has chosen to call laymen, a word that has roughly come to correspond to what the medical world calls patients, or what the business world calls customers.

"This sort of 'leave-it-to-the-experts' mentality may be fine in the medical or business world, and it may make a lot of sense in the world of high technology where not everyone can be an expert in highly complicated fields, but it is difficult to find in the Scriptures as a model for discipleship or as an example of the relationship believers should have with the Lord. Can you imagine one of the disciples writing something like this: *If you ever have any problems or questions, try to find someone who will take care of them for you. After all, not everyone can be expected to have a detailed knowledge of the teachings of Christ.*

"A ridiculous thought! What they did write sounds considerably different. At the end of the fifth chapter of Hebrews, for example, there's a rather poignant passage that shreds the idea of laymanship—a passage directed to believers who thought they didn't have to become teachers themselves, who thought it was all right to drop out of God's school and enjoy a Peter Pan existence of perpetual spiritual childhood.

"The Scriptures do not present the teachings of Christ as a special discipline for certain kinds of people. Reliance on Christ's teachings is put in the same category as eating or sleeping or breathing. The words of God are the bread of life. We don't have specialists who eat or breathe or sleep for us. Neither can we expect someone else to implement Christ's teachings in our lives.

"The Scriptures present themselves as books, reports, and letters written by common men who were eye witnesses of the risen Lord—commissioned and empowered by him to pass on his teachings to the world. These men wrote in the common Greek language which was understood by many peoples of the first century Mediterranean world. The Scriptures were meant to be proclaimed, taught, learned, and used as a law of life by all followers of Christ. Faithful men were to pass them on to other faithful men. Fathers were to be the teachers of their families. Men like Timothy were exhorted to be accurate *workers in the Word who had no reason to be ashamed.* There is no indication that only certain kinds of individuals had the ability to understand and interpret the Scriptures."

"Does that necessarily mean that every believer has to learn New Testament Greek?"

"No, of course it doesn't mean that. There are other ways to ascertain source-level information without having to go directly to the linguistic sources. But going this other route does not necessarily require less serious work than it would require to obtain at least an intermediate understanding of Greek. The important point to remember is that without a thorough knowledge of the Scriptures there can be no spiritual maturity. Paul told Timothy in his second letter to him that it was the Scriptures that equip a man of God for every good work. Regardless of how a believer decides to learn the Scriptures, he is going to be faced with the problem of working through the text and determining its meaning. Greek is an excellent tool to use in the process, because it's in the context of Koine Greek that the thoughts of the original authors were first expressed. It would be foolish to not at least make it available to any man who desired to examine the Scriptures at that level, and it would be foolish to not encourage people to do it.

"Particularly today, I feel it's important to encourage believers to learn New

Testament Greek. In most circles of Christians there are so few believers who are competent in the original language of the Scriptures that it is actually crippling in terms of our credibility. We claim, on the one hand, that the Scriptures are the inspired revelation of God, but, on the other hand, seem to deny it by taking so little interest in the language in which they were written. In every field of knowledge, credibility is tied to an understanding of source information. Who wants to go to a doctor who does not understand medical source information? Who wants to fly with a pilot who is not an expert in aviation source information?

"Even many of the people we would normally think of as being experts in the Scriptures are, by their own admission, not really experts in the sense of what an expert is usually thought to be: someone who has access to and knowledge of source information. The evidence is that a large percentage of those trained for the clergy or for missions cannot read the New Testament in Greek, and of those who have learned Greek in a formal setting, many have never taken it beyond the level they attained while in school.

"I have talked with hundreds of religious professionals all over the world, and the great majority have readily admitted that their ability in Greek is either non-existent or, at the best, rusty. And with a few notable exceptions, hardly any of the people I talked to had any experience at all in teaching New Testament Greek to lay people.

"The result is that our situation is not only characterized by source-level deficiency when it comes to the man on the street, but also as regards those who are normally thought to be experts. If you compare this situation to other areas of highly specialized information—medicine, for example—you'll find that the situation is much different. Most doctors are quite knowledgeable in source level medical understanding, and there are vast armies of medical support persons such as nurses and medics who are also very knowledgeable in intricate medical matters. Even the fallout of source-level medical knowledge in the general population is quite heavy—in a relative sense, of course. There are many individuals, for example, who are expert in various areas of medical endeavor, although they are basically what we would call self-informed or self-taught. The same situation is true in areas as diverse as finances, sport, construction, mechanics, nutrition, computers, and so on. It is not difficult in any of these fields to find self-taught individuals who are absolute experts and even leaders in these fields.

"When it comes to the Scriptures, however, there is a great dearth of individuals who have taken the time to gain access to a source-level understanding."

"Why has this happened?"

"As I've said before, I can't help but conclude that there are forces at work with a vested interest that the Scriptures stay out of the hands of as many people as possible. It's a sign of the uniqueness of the Scriptures that no other body of writings in history has ever received the treatment—good or bad—which has almost been a matter of course for the Scriptures."

"You talk as though there's a conspiracy afoot," said Louise.

Behind the Scenes

"There *is* a rather powerful conspirator loose in the world, and he has a rather large following. It's probably wise to assume he's propagating plenty of conspiracies, particularly to discredit the Scriptures. The Scriptures themselves are full of warnings regarding this kind of thing. II Thessalonians and Galatians are two major examples. Obviously it's been a problem right from the beginning and all through history. Think of the Middle Ages when the Scriptures were kept in bondage by the superstitious belief that Latin was a holy language. Only a privileged few understood Latin and as a result whole populations were dependent on what a few experts told them about the Scriptures. The temptations to deceive people and misuse power were often too great. The result was an era known as the Dark Ages, and one very important reason why it was so dark is because the light of the Scriptures was kept under the basket of the Latin language.

"Think of the spiritual explosion that resulted in the sixteenth century when the Scriptures were finally translated into languages people really spoke. And that was only possible because previously men had once again begun to learn the Scriptures in the original language in which they were written.

"The forces of darkness, however, have never given up. They are with us today and they love to cast a cloak over the Scriptures. As in the first century, the sixteenth century, and all the centuries in between and afterwards, one of the best ways to assure that the light shines bright is to keep digging in the original writings and to keep consulting them as guides. It is certainly dangerous to subject them to the degree of neglect that is often given them today."

"Goodness," said Louise. "You've got me feeling a little uneasy in my skin."

"Oh, don't worry about that, honey," said Harmon. "Dean is an expert at making people feel queasy. And he always has such a happy look on his face when he's doing it."

"Has it been all that bad?"

"I'm sure I needed to hear it," said Louise. "How about some more rolls? You must be getting hungry."

Dean stood and stretched. "Better keep 'em coming. Looks like I'm going to need all the energy I can get."

"Yup," said Harmon. "The next question is in the chute. It's another question that's not my own, but one I'm sometimes confronted with: Why must we be so exact with the Scriptures? Isn't it true that most Christians know more than they actually put into practice? What good does it do to increase understanding when most people would be better off spending their time trying to apply what they already know? Then too, think of the millions who know nothing or very little. Isn't it smarter to try to use our time to get the word out the best we can, and not spend so much time going into depth?"

"I have to admit," said Dean, sitting down again, "that such arguments certainly sound logical in a certain context, but if we borrow an example from another context, then the problem with this kind of thinking becomes evident. Let's take the field of general education, for instance. Why aren't we satisfied with simple reading books? Why produce complicated editions of scientific works when a significant proportion of the world's population is still illiterate? Isn't it illogical to strive to create more and more accurate scientific or economic or medical works when so many people have only a rudimentary understanding in any of these and many other areas?

"The same argument transferred to a school sounds like this: Why teach seniors complicated principles of literary understanding when we have first graders who still can't read? I think you see how ridiculous such a line of reasoning actually is. The problem stems from failing to recognize the real nature of language and the great potential language has to disseminate its benefits."

"Huh? Wait a minute. I'm afraid you lost me with that last sentence."

"Sorry. I meant two things: First of all, the nature of language is inseparably linked to the whole matter of human growth, and in particular to spiritual growth. To say we shouldn't invest time helping Christians learn Greek, because there are so many people who know hardly anything about the Scriptures, is the same as saying we shouldn't be teaching high school seniors complicated subjects, because we still have first-graders around who can barely read.

"The fact is that *both* tasks are crucial. Language growth is necessary at *every* stage of human and spiritual development, and we shouldn't forget that it's the more advanced who always become the examples for the following generations. To recommend that those who are ahead should not advance until others have caught up would be paralyzing in any area. A doctor, for example, who strives for more understanding and accuracy, benefits all the doctors who follow him and learn from him. This is a good tie-in to the second point I wanted to make: the ability of language to disseminate benefits.

"With dissemination I mean the distribution of benefits to others. Take a mechanic, for example, who develops a more effective and accurate way of constructing a braking system. His effort at accuracy can actually benefit thousands if not millions of drivers by giving them improved braking capability. In this sense, accuracy is a close relative of both truth and love. An electrician who accurately wires a house, for example, insures that the electrical system corresponds to the laws of electrical power—which is an aspect of scientific truth—and insures that the family living in the house will be safe—which is an expression of human love and concern.

"In this same sense a Christian who takes great care to be accurate in understanding the Scriptures will be able to be a channel of wisdom and love to those who come in contact with him. We dare not be sloppy with the Scriptures. Paul told Timothy in II Timothy 2:15 to be a workman, who correctly handles the word of truth. A false word or a word out of context can send a person along a wrong path.

"In every area of life we value accuracy. Machinists measure in the most minute units, and computer specialists labor to produce perfectly accurate programs. They know the slightest mistake will simply multiply itself. As people who are convinced that the Scriptures are the concrete representation of the teachings of Christ and his disciples, is it not logical that we show a great deal of concern about their accurate handling? And should we not believe that such an attitude will also be of great benefit even to those who may know little of the information contained in the Scriptures?

"These are some of the reasons why I don't think it makes sense for us to avoid doing accurate work in the Scriptures simply because there are so many who are being sloppy with them or because there are others who are not putting them into practice.

"Now, let me say something about getting the word out to those who have never heard. This is certainly an important matter. We should be concerned about it and invest time in it. Learning the Scriptures at the source level, however, is certainly not a task that somehow gets in the way of proclaiming the message of the Scriptures. The two tasks actually reinforce one another. We are commanded both to *know* the message well and to *proclaim* the message well. These are both teachings of Christ that are by no means opposed to one another."

"Very interesting. I've just got one more question.

"Really, honey," said Louise. "Don't you think you ought to let the poor man go back to his family. After all, it is Saturday. The kids will have some plans, and you---"

"Don't worry," Dean broke in, "Buddy and Peggy have planned a day in the park for all the neighborhood kids. Really, there's no one waiting for me.

"See," said Harmon. "He's just out killing time. Next thing we know he'll be mooching lunch off us."

"Harmon Smith!"

"Just one more question, honey. That's all. We'll be done in a jiffy. This question is of a personal nature, and I'm asking it because of my own curiosity. It may sound a bit strange, but I'd like to know why you're doing what you're doing? I mean, why do you take time to deal with people at such a basic level of linguistic instruction? Some people would say it's a slow and tedious way of getting information across, and you certainly can't do it with a lot of people at one time. Why don't you just do the linguistic work for people and give them the results of your thinking?"

"As a much younger man I did a lot more teaching in the 'do-it-for-them' sense than in the 'help-them-do-it-for-themselves' sense. At the time, however, I didn't really feel it was the right thing for me to be doing. I've found it a lot easier on my conscience to concentrate on helping people do things for themselves.

"It all goes back to the degree to which we feel we should be interpreting the Scriptures for other people. In this regard, all I can say is that I have a great deal of confidence in the reliability of the Scriptures, but I don't necessarily have a lot of confidence in the reliability *of my own understanding* of those Scriptures. So I try to keep my own understanding in the background as much as possible."

"Isn't that a little unrealistic?"

"I know it's impossible when interacting with people not to pass on a lot of one's own understanding—I suppose I've done it today—but I think there is a difference if a person realizes it *is* his own understanding and is convinced that his own way of seeing things should never be elevated to the position of the Scriptures. I've tried to relieve the tension in my own mind in the following way: When teaching or counseling people, I try to represent the teachings of Christ in the original context the best way I know how. However, I also try, if possible, to encourage those same people at some point in time to look beyond my words—or those of other teachers or writers—to the statements of the original authors. And I make the effort to encourage them to move in the direction of the source as much as possible with the goal of becoming less and less dependent on the interpretations of others, including my own.

"In other words, at some time during the communication process, I try to make a conscious effort to refrain from trying to get people to see things the way I do, and to encourage them to make their own way in their search for truth and understanding. Very practically then, when I feel I've reached that point, I simply offer to help equip them to do source level study in the Scriptures, should they desire to do so.

"This seems to me to be a logical step in the process of discipleship in which the goal is to help a person come as close to Christ and his words and teachings as possible. I think the process breaks down if a disciple gets stuck at the feet of a middleman of some kind who interprets the words of Christ for him. I've seen people get attached to me in that way, and I never felt it was right. I'm not saying that middlemen are not necessary—we will always need to have people who are ready to proclaim and teach and warn and counsel using the Scriptures—but I think that playing the role of teacher in someone's life should be a temporary thing. Just like children grow up and leave home and start their own families, disciples should leave their teachers and become teachers themselves. The work of a teacher of the Scriptures should go beyond interpreting for a person. It should also include helping them to interpret for themselves.

"This further task, however, is not in itself an easy undertaking. Interpretive systems abound and they, too, can become barriers to the original sources, entangling people in webs of philosophical or traditional systems of thought. That's why I like the idea of getting to the linguistic sources with someone as quickly as I can. This level is the lowest possible common denominator in the search for objectivity in the sticky world of Scriptural interpretation. This is where all the experts, if they really are experts, have to go to justify their views, and it's at this level that a person can best obtain and evaluate factual information.

"I realize it's not realistic to think that everyone should be expected to do this, but, as I've said before, I'm convinced that a whole lot more should be doing it than is presently the case. And I certainly think that everyone should be encouraged to do it who really wants to. That's why I like to at least offer to help people read the New Testament in Greek. It's no cure-all, because, like any tool, it must be used accurately and with correct intentions, but it's an important step for anyone who wants to head in the direction of the source, and it can be a powerful tool to help a person see through the often confusing whirlwinds of cultural and traditional opinions that swirl around the Scriptures."

"Let's get back to those interpretive systems," said Harmon. "We are literally surrounded by hundreds of them. Some are so powerful we don't even recognize them, or if we are aware of them, they seem so strong that it's almost useless to try to communicate with someone who is captivated by them. Is there any way to avoid this sort of influence?"

"You're right, it's a difficult problem and seems to be part of our human condition. It is a great temptation for us to want to either add our two cents to the message of Christ or take something away from it. The Scriptures mention the problem often: Matthew, Colossians, Galatians, II Thessalonians, and Romans are just a few examples of writings in the New Testament in which the problem of faulty interpretation is treated in quite some detail.

"I have close friends within the circles of what we might call rather diverse interpretive systems, and I do not like to get into discussions with them at the interpretive level. I find the Scriptures get left behind very quickly. It's been my experience, however, that the closer we get to the text, the closer we move toward one another.

"The opposite is also true, of course. The more we add to or subtract from the message of the Scriptures, the more we create a framework of thought that moves further away from the source. More often than not, however, the practical division between two individuals with differing interpretive systems actually has very little to do with conscious interpretation at all. It's usually the case that people have only a vague idea of what the Scriptures have to say about a matter. They know what grandpa said about it, or they know that since their childhood such and such has always been the accepted practice or opinion, but they most likely do not have a conviction that is based on hard work they have done in the text themselves."

"I know what you mean," said Harmon. "It's the rare person who has really tried to think through why he believes what he believes. Blind acceptance is more often the problem than the application of some well-defined interpretive system."

"That's why you have to sound out each person to find out where they are in the menagerie of beliefs. But if a person is part of an interpretive system that at least gives lip service to the Scriptures, then regardless of whether he is informed or uninformed about a particular matter, he ought to at least have an interest in what the Scriptures might happen to express in regard to the topic at hand. I've found if I can get people interested in what's in a text of Scripture itself, then they begin to question their own views. I don't have to do it for them. I've been in some rather touchy situations before, and I've always found that by raising the source question I can often defuse things and put the monkey on someone else's back."

"How do you state the source question?"

"I often ask, *Where do the New Testament Scriptures directly address this*

matter in a relevant context? And what can be concluded from it?"
"I can imagine that gets people's attention."
"Yes, it does. Interestingly enough, few people are used to thinking in this fashion. More often than not, the question leads to an embarrassed silence by those who don't know the answer but feel in their bones that it is an important consideration; or it leads to hasty attempts to sidestep the issue by those who are less concerned about the relevance of the question. At any rate, people end up either in conflict with themselves or with the Scriptures, not with me.

"It's particularly interesting to find out who the people are who think that questions about the source are of importance. Sometimes those you think would be concerned about sources, aren't, and those you think would not be interested—perhaps because of the particular interpretive system with which they are associated—are actually interested. It certainly divides the men from the boys.

"I'd say by way of summary, that encouraging people to study the Scriptures for themselves, and offering to help them do it at the source level, if they so desire, is the best way I've found to get as much of the teachings of Christ as possible to the forefront, and as much of my own interpretation as possible, out of the picture. I know it doesn't always work, but I like to think I'm giving it my best shot. Does that answer your question?"

"Couldn't have asked for more," said Harmon. "And I'd say I've squeezed enough out of you for today." Louise gave her husband a grateful look. "Thanks for dropping by and giving us part of your Saturday."

"It was a pleasure, I assure you. Thanks for being interested."

Harmon and Louise accompanied Dean to his car and waved as he drove away.

"Well, honey," said Louise, "what did you think of your talk with Dean? Sorry I listened in most of the time, but I found it rather fascinating."

"I can't remember a time when I've had such an enlightening conversation. But I think I'd be doing Dean a disservice by simply accepting everything he says, or even worse, by being enthused by it. I can hear him saying it now: 'Don't believe *me*. Go get the facts for yourself, and then make up your own mind.' He's obviously not a man out looking for a following. And of all people, I should know the importance of firsthand information. I've made the mistake often enough of hanging my hat on someone else's view of things. Secondhand information has always gotten me into trouble. It may sound funny for someone like me to have to say it, someone who is already a grandfather—"

"But a very young grandfather," Louise broke in. "And quite a dashing one, at that."

"Yes, well...as I was saying, it's a bit strange for me at my age to say it's time to grow up, but it's true. It's time I grow up and start handling my thoughts and the Scriptures in a more responsible way. And I think learning Greek is one step in the right direction. So, it's back to the grindstone for this school kid. Just keep the coffee hot, honey."

"Yes, sir. Your favorite waitress will be at her post."

"Ah, what dedication." Harmon gave her a lingering kiss and headed for his study.

Lake Powell

John tried to take in what appeared to be a modern townhouse perched on two streamlined pontoons. "Not bad," he said, blowing out some air and thinking that his idea of a houseboat up to now had been the kind Mark Twain wrote about: a shack on a raft. This thing floating in front of him was a mini luxury liner.

He stepped on board along with Dani, a sturdy young Navaho who had been assigned to show him the boat and make sure he knew how to pilot it. John discovered a fully outfitted kitchen, a bathroom complete with shower, comfortable sleeping cabins, and a spacious dining room. "This floating villa is better equipped than my own home," he said as they stepped out on the rear deck.

"I don't doubt it," laughed Dani. "There's two little items out here your house definitely doesn't have." He pointed to two large white metal coverings mounted on each side of the boat. He tilted back one of the hoods, exposing an outboard motor.

"That's one of the two seventy horsepower engines that push this little buggy around. There's a few tricks you need to learn about them if you want to avoid hitting all those big, beautiful rocks out there."

"I'll hit 'em if anyone can."

"Don't worry. It's not as difficult to pilot as it might look. I'll take you for a spin and show you the ropes."

Dani then introduced John to the fine points of being a houseboat captain. Since it had no rudder, maneuvering the lengthy boat required more than just turning a steering wheel. The two engines were the boat's sole means of navigating. Sharp turns were accomplished by turning the steering wheel and shifting one engine into reverse while the other remained in forward. The key was knowing which engine to put into reverse.

As soon as John had the hang of it, Dani brought the houseboat back to the gangway where he showed John a small fishing boat tied to the pier. "The little boat goes with the houseboat," he said, jumping from the front platform to the pier. "Just tow it along behind you, and have a great three days. Give me a call with your CB if you have any trouble."

Earlier in the week, the Freys had received a call from Jess Magruder, a contractor in Phoenix who often passed work on to John. He told them he had a houseboat reserved at Lake Powell, but that something had come up, and he'd not be able to make it up to the lake for the weekend. He wanted to know if they would be interested in using the boat—without it costing them a cent.

John and Carol had accepted his offer immediately. It was like a dream come true for them. They had heard many friends rave about the unique beauty of Lake Powell, the huge scenic lake that sprawled across the northern border of Arizona into Utah. Now they were going to see it for themselves.

The boat slept fourteen so John had suggested they invite the Garveys and McLains and Eddie to come along. It didn't take John and Carol long to talk their

Lake Powell

friends into joining them. Like most Arizonians, they knew houseboats were difficult to rent on Lake Powell; they were not only expensive—costing up to four hundred dollars a day—but were often booked up years in advance. It was an opportunity that couldn't be passed up.

Sitting there alone in the captain's chair, John felt a shiver of fear grab his stomach. He could see himself returning with a mass of crumpled debris that was once a beautiful houseboat. But that thought was quickly wiped away when he envisioned what his wife and son would say when they saw it. He dropped the two silver levers into gear and headed for the loading dock on the other side of the marina where Carol was waiting with Andy.

The Garveys and McLains had decided to drive to the lake together, and they traversed the 300 miles between Phoenix and Monument Valley in good time. At Goulding's Trading Post they turned onto the last stretch of road, a seemingly endless washboard of shale and gravel supposedly leading to a marina somewhere in the distant wilderness.

All the travelers were in high spirits except for Barbara. She had some misgivings about the trip. Three days on a cramped houseboat with two other families was not her idea of a relaxed weekend at a lake. She consented to come, because she knew Jim's disappointment would have been great had she insisted on passing up the trip. It always seemed a pity to her that an outdoorsman like her husband had to be tied to a desk and forced to wear business suits most of his days. She was glad he could escape the city for a few days, even though she was not looking forward to it herself. The beating their Mercedes was taking dampened her enthusiasm even more. "Jim," she said, eyeing the gash in the landscape that was supposed to be a road, "the car is going to be a mess after this trip."

"Honey, this German tank can manage bumps better than a pick-up. Don't worry. We'll be there soon.

After 45 bone-jarring minutes they mounted a rise and suddenly the lake came into view. They were startled to see so much water in an area that was obviously a more fitting home for cactus, lizards, and sandstorms. They could see the marina lying alone on a bare piece of rock and shale jutting out into the water."

When they drove into the big lot next to the loading ramp, Jim saw John's van and parked next to it. Dean pulled up behind him, and everyone clambered out of the cars.

"I wonder where the Freys are?" asked Linda.

"Take a look over there," said Dean, pointing toward the loading dock about 30 yards away. There, seated in deck chairs on the roof of the houseboat enjoying a picnic supper were John, Carol, and Andy.

"Hello!" called John. "Glad to see you made it. Welcome to our humble little rowboat."

"Wow!" said Peggy. "Oh, wow."

"Man o' man," said Jim. "Long live Jess Magruder. The guy gave us a penthouse."

"Don't just stand there with your mouths open," said John. "Get your stuff on board, and let's push off. We need to find us a nice little cove before it gets dark."

The two families quickly transferred their luggage to the houseboat. Then, with Buddy and Eddie looking over his shoulder, John started the engines and backed away from the loading platform. In deep water, he opened both throttles, and the dual motors heaved them forward.

For a while the houseboat captured everyone's attention. Even Barbara was pleasantly surprised. She had dreaded cramped quarters, but this boat was roomy and well equipped.

One by one, however, eyes began to turn from the fascination of the houseboat to the panorama enfolding around them. Draped in the golden glow of the setting sun, immense sandstone walls and arches came into view as the boat made its way down the main channel. Red towers and spires seemed to spring out of the water and rear their heads to dizzying heights.

Dean and Linda were standing at the front railing with the wind in their faces. "How do you find words to describe something like this?" said Linda.

Dean's eyes were filled with wonder. "It's everything we ever heard it was."

John had begun to look for a place to stop for the night as soon as they were well away from the marina. About every eighth of a mile he saw side canyons branch off into unknown waterways.

"We should explore some of those canyons," he said to Jim. "We need to find a nice little cove or inlet big enough for our floating hotel. Why don't you take the small boat and find a good spot for us."

"I'm on my way, captain. I'll see if I can find a couple of seaworthy sailors to come along." He was joined by Tommy and Jimmy as he climbed into the little fishing boat. The outboard motor sprang to life, and they were soon swallowed up by the massive jaws of a great cut in the cliffs a few hundred yards away. After a few minutes the little boat appeared again and sought out another set of portals. That happened twice more before Jim could be seen steering the outboard back to the houseboat.

Back on board, Jim told John about an excellent place in one of the side canyons large enough for the houseboat. "There's no beach," he said, "but I think we can anchor against the canyon wall. There are plenty of places to secure the ropes."

"Sounds good," said John. Following Jim's directions he eased the houseboat into the mouth of a canyon with sheer 300 foot walls. John eyed the 20 yards of clearance on each side of the boat. "Just enough room for the houseboat," he thought, "but if it gets much smaller I'll have some trouble."

They soon came to a place where the canyon forked off in two directions, both of them ending abruptly at the foundations of a towering mesa. At the juncture of the fork they were greeted by a wide, quiet pool, emanating a special charm and beauty.

After the houseboat was securely anchored, there was just enough daylight left for a quick swim. A steaming pot of chili was waiting for the hungry swimmers when they were back on board. The children took their bowls and climbed the spiral stairway to the roof where chairs and tables had been set up. A canopy of stars slowly appeared, brightening the warm night.

The six adults settled into the comfortable deck chairs on the front platform. Cradling a cup of coffee in his hands, Jim leaned back and gazed at the stars. "I think I'll sell the company next week, buy myself a houseboat, and become a full time fisherman."

"Very tempting." commented John, listening to the water lapping at the canyon walls.

"It's hard to believe we were in the middle of a big city just this morning," said Carol.

"It is great out here," said John, "but I'd look forward to the next few days even if there were no lake and no mountains. Having us all together is the real treat. I hope no one minds, but I've brought a few of my bigger questions along, hoping we might be able to have some discussions. Would that be all right with everyone?"

"Count me in." said Jim. "My head needs fresh thoughts as much as my lungs need fresh air."

"I'm game too," said Dean. "In fact, why don't we get some of those questions out in the open right now. I don't think the kids are going to want to go to bed for another hour or two." He looked up toward the roof where the sounds of guitar music and singing were steadily increasing in volume. "What's on your mind, John?"

"One thing I've been struggling with is the whole matter of self-learning. I know we've covered the subject before, but I guess I'm having a tough time really believing that I can self-learn something as difficult as the Bible or the Greek language. I don't know if it's because I lack confidence or self-discipline or what. All I know is that when I sit down to tackle a Greek lesson or a passage in the Bible, I feel strange about it. It's as though I'm out of my class, like a fish out of water. I often think to myself: Hey, who do you think you are? Some kind of dreamer?"

Dean looked around the circle. "Anyone else have these kind of thoughts?"

"Can't say I'm exactly brimming with confidence myself" said Jim.

"Nor am I," said Carol. "I think it would be good to talk about it again."

"It's certainly an important matter," said Dean. "Obviously, if you're not convinced you're able to learn Greek, you're probably not going to give it an all-out effort. I'd begin by saying that what you're experiencing is a normal kind of reaction anyone feels who is embarking on a new and unknown challenge. Even small children—supposedly the champions of adaptability—resist change. I still remember how my mother and father had to drag me kicking and screaming to my first day of kindergarten when I was five years old. I was convinced I was not cut out for that big, scary thing called school.

"I wish I could report that I grew up after that, but the truth is, every time I changed schools in the years that followed, I was still that frightened little boy, overpowered by feelings of fear and inadequacy, and that includes shaky kneed entrances into graduate school and the worst case of butterflies you can imagine before I took on my first archaeological job.

"Fear of the unknown hampers most people, and it's a fear that usually teams up with feelings of inadequacy to give us that strange feeling of not belonging when we get into something new. One of man's worst fears is the fear of being a failure, which is why we usually prefer to stay in familiar territory."

"Isn't it possible, though," said John, "that a person can get into something that really is too much for him? I mean, if you took a first grader and put him in high school, it just wouldn't be realistic."

"You're right, there. If the demands of a task are greater than the capabilities or the maturity of the learner, then frustration and failure will be unavoidable. And that's probably the question on all of our minds right now. Is learning New Testament Greek a task out of the range of our capabilities? Is it like signing a first-grader up for high school? What do you think?"

"That's not really our situation," said Jim. "It seems to me a first grader would have problems in high school, because he's still a child—mentally and physically. He'd have problems because he's not had the years of learning that lead up to high school. It's different with us. We're not children, and we're not starting at an advanced level of Greek. We're starting at the beginning."

"Good observations," said Dean. "Instead of being first-graders headed for high-school, we're actually more like high-schoolers going back to the first grade. That's a perspective that ought to give us some confidence."

"I just wonder, though," said Jim, "if using the example of a child in school is totally applicable to our situation. For the most part, school children are told what to do, and their motivation for learning is often a product of peer pressure or the desire to make good grades or just to pass the course. We are more on our own and are forced to learn Greek while juggling a whole host of other time-consuming responsibilities."

"We're getting down to bedrock, now," said Dean. "Anyone got any words of wisdom for us?"

There was a moment of quiet. Small waves could be heard gently lapping against the pontoons.

"The only thing I can think of," said Carol. "is that it doesn't seem to me we're that much on our own. I would certainly have never started Greek on my own, and I don't think I'd get very far on my own."

"It's well worth remembering," said Dean, "that successful self-learners are by no means lone wolves who snap at anything resembling a helping hand. Self-learners are usually the first to recognize they need help and plenty of it.

"You may have all read stories about self-made, self-educated men who, when they reached the top, thumped themselves on the chest and said: 'I did it all myself'. Don't believe it.

"Henry Ford is probably one of the most famous examples of a successful self-learner. As a young man he worked for months out in a barn trying to put together an engine that would run his horseless carriage. Did he do it all alone? Not by a long shot. He had plenty of help.

"For one thing, he was a voracious reader who regularly plowed through the best scientific journals of his day. He read about the Otto gas engine—the forerunner of his own gas engine—in the magazine *The World of Science*. And he also had plenty of the right kind of contacts: individuals who were willing and able to pass on a valuable word of advice. One of them just happened to be Thomas Edison, considered by many to be one of the most creative minds of the nineteenth century.

"So much for the myth that self-learning is a one-man show. Even Henry Ford would have dried up on the vine of discouragement had he not had access to the writings and advice of knowledgeable men.

"Abraham Lincoln was another famous self-learner who also knew the value of written materials and helpful contacts. While he was still under the age of twenty-one and working for his father in the fields, he arranged for people from miles around to loan him books. Sometimes he walked the fifteen miles to Rockport, a county seat in Indiana, to borrow books from John Pitcher, the town lawyer. Without access to people who were willing to help and without books of the right kind, Lincoln may never have left the farm, much less made it to the forefront of American politics.

"Can anyone see some applications in these examples for us?"

"It's pretty obvious," said John, "that we need good information sources, but it's just as obvious that we need to be highly motivated. Henry and Abe weren't the kind of men to take no for an answer."

"They took the initiative, all right," said Dean. "That's really where the *self* in self-learning comes in, but without good input they'd have been sunk."

"Motivation and materials," said Jim. "Those seem to be the key words. Do we have 'em or don't we? And if we don't, how do we get 'em?"

"It's interesting, too," said Linda, "that much of what both of these men learned, at least initially, was done in their spare time, while they were employed."

"You did have to point that out, didn't you," said Jim. "Wipes out one of my best excuses."

"I always remind myself," said Dean, "that self-learning is one of the most effective and natural ways of learning there is. It's easy to fall in the trap of thinking that learning can only take place in a classroom. Much more learning actually takes place outside of classrooms, and what's more, we're all experts when it comes to self-learning."

"Experts?" said Carol, looking skeptical.

"Sure. In fact, why don't we make a list of all the things we've self-taught ourselves in our lives. I think you'll be surprised." Dean dug in his briefcase for paper and extra pencils.

"What if I can't think of anything?" said Carol.

"Oh, you'll think of something all right. You just have to get started. I'll give you a few ideas: Maybe you've self-taught yourself a sport or a skill of some kind. Or maybe you've acquired knowledge in some area to begin a handwork or a job or a hobby. There's also the skilled activities we often take for granted but which are also mainly self-learned—like eating or dressing ourselves. There are hundreds of possibilities. Think through your childhood and try to remember everything you learned then, and ask yourself how much of it was mainly self-learned."

Dean gave everyone a sheet of paper and while they were writing, he went up to the roof to check on the children. When he returned, he asked Jim to collect the papers and read them out loud to the group.

"Here goes," said Jim, after he received the last list. *"Tennis, taking care of a baby, cutting hair, chess, water-skiing, computing, business administration, hiking tours in Arizona, driving a car, golf, baseball, sewing, wiring, plumbing, auto mechanics, landscaping, nutrition, sewing, knitting, guitar, paper route, typing, fishing, photography, dancing, riding a horse, bike riding, investing, gardening, swimming, raising children, house painting, shopping, jogging, local geography, marriage, making friends, using coupons, mail ordering, paying taxes, balancing a checkbook, using the telephone, how to use a library, baking bread, treating various diseases, doing tax returns.* Looks like that's it."

"What do you say to that list?" said Dean.

"Whew," said John, "and there are probably a lot more things we didn't even think of."

"Sure, no one even mentioned some of the more obvious things like speaking, walking, eating, swatting flies, washing, combing your hair, planning meals, playing games—the list is almost endless. If we had to go to school to learn things like that, we'd be in trouble."

"It's very probable," said Linda, "that most of what we learn in life is learned through self-learning, or at least in informal settings—such as a father with a son or a friend with a friend."

"And when you think," said Dean, "that formal learning is most effective when the student steps into the role of a self-learner and treats his classroom time as nothing more than one of many sources of input, then you can see how important the whole concept of self-learning actually is. Now, I'd like you to make another list. This time jot down your *reasons* for self-learning many of the things you mentioned on the previous list. Ask yourself *why* you self-learned the things you wrote down."

When they were finished, they handed their lists to Jim again. "Here are reasons for self-learning," he began. *"Knew no other way to do it, wanted to save money, figured it was faster, knew someone who could help me, knew I could do it, had done something similar before, knew others who had done it on their own, just thought I'd give it a try, it interested me, never really thought about it—just did it.* That's it."

"Let me take a look at those," said Dean. "That's an interesting list."

"*Knew no other way.* That's *necessity.*
"*Wanted to save money.* That's *economy.*
"*Figured it was faster.* That's *efficiency.*
"*Knew someone who would help.* That's *teamwork.*
"*Knew I could do it.* That's *personal conviction.*
"*Had done something similar.* That's *experience.*
"*Knew others who'd done it.* That's *reliability.*
"*Thought I'd give it a try.* That's *readiness.*
"*Interested me.* That's *curiosity.*
"*Just did it.* That's *matter-of-factness.*

"What an excellent list of the characteristics and benefits of self-learning. And just think: it's your own list. That ought to give you some confidence that self-learning is an excellent way to learn Greek.

Just then Buddy and Eddie came down the steps. "Oh, dear," said Barbara when she saw them, "It's getting late. Our kids must be giving you fits by now."

"They're no trouble at all," said Buddy. "In fact, they're all asleep."

"Asleep?"

"We just laid the sleeping bags out on the roof. Peggy and Tommy are there, too. Eddie and I will join them later. It looks like it's going to be a beautiful, warm night."

Barbara looked over to Jim.

"They'll be fine up there," he said. "It's a lot better than sleeping at home in a stuffy bedroom. I may even join them. It's been a long time since I fell asleep looking at the stars."

"Sounds good to me, too," said John.

"I think we've come far enough with our conversation for tonight," said Dean. "We've seem to have reached a point where we can say that at least two topics would be worth discussing in the next day or two: *materials* and *motivation*. If everyone's agreed, I'd suggest we call it a day."

"Aye, aye, cap'n," said Jim. "It's too late for a mutiny anyway."

Books, Burros, and Balancing Rocks

Voices drifted up from below. First there were whispers, then giggling, then war whoops, followed by three loud splashes. Blinking his eyes, John pushed back the folds of his sleeping bag and raised himself on one elbow. The first rays of the sun blazed a blinding ribbon of light across red slick-rock sandstone cliffs towering in the distance. He felt the gentle motion of the boat.

Jim had been jarred out of a deep sleep, too. He scrambled to his feet and leaned over the railing. "Hey! What's going on down there?"

"Come on in," hollered Tommy. "The water's great." Tommy, Buddy, and Eddie were swimming slow circles near the boat.

John looked over to where Andy had been sleeping. He was gone. "Where is everybody?" he asked Jim.

"Looks like we're the last ones up. There's Andy with Peggy. She's getting him into his life jacket."

"I should have known." John slowly peered at the soft hues of red streaking the great sandstone bulwarks surrounding them. "There's no way we're going to keep those kids out of the water in a paradise like this."

"Yeah," said Jim, following John's gaze. "It sure beats running through the sprinkler."

By the time John and Jim made their way down the stairs, the smell of coffee was already in the air. A chorus of "good mornings" greeted them as they entered the cabin. Dean was sitting on the couch going through a pile of papers; Linda was setting the table; Barbara and Carol were working in the little kitchen.

"Busy as bees," said Jim. "If we'd have waited, I'll bet we'd have gotten breakfast in bed—I mean in the bag."

"You'd have been lucky to get anything if you'd have waited much longer," said Dean. "When those kids are through swimming, they'll be eating everything in sight."

"I don't know how they do it," said Linda. "It's chilly out there."

"You want to know what the kids are thinking right now?" said Jim. "They're thinking 'Look at all those crazy adults in there. How do they do it? All this beautiful water around, and they're all huddled inside.'"

Linda laughed. "I guess they're right. I don't think I've ever been in such a gorgeous place."

John grabbed a map from a pouch next to the steering wheel and sat down. "Going to chart our course, captain?" asked Dean.

"There's not much charting to do," said John, unfolding the map and spreading it out on the coffee table. "We either go upstream or downstream. Upstream the channel gets narrower, so I figure with our floating hotel we're better off heading downstream where we've got some elbow room."

"Any ports in that direction?"

"First civilization would be about three days away, but we'd run out of gas before we ever reached it. We can only put on about twenty more miles before we

Books, Burros, and Balancing Rocks

have to head back to the marina. There'll be more than enough to see in those twenty miles, though."

When the kids had been coaxed out of the water and breakfast was over, John ordered in the lines, started the engines, and slowly eased the houseboat into the middle of the little cove.

"Everyone keep an eye out for submerged rocks," John yelled. "We don't want to lose a propeller." He carefully maneuvered the big boat through the narrow waterway back into the main channel.

Seeing they were well away from the cliffs and in open water, John turned the captain's chair over to Buddy and Andy. "She's all yours," he said. "Keep her near the middle, veer to the right if you meet anyone, and give me a whistle if you have any problems." Andy sat in Buddy's lap grasping the steering wheel in his little hands.

John then stuck his head out the front door. "OK," he called. "The boat is in good hands. If you can tear yourselves away from the scenery, we can get started." Within a few minutes everyone was settled in the dining area.

"Our topic for today," said Dean, sitting down on a footstool at one end of the coffee table, "is *materials*. Not just any kind of materials, of course, but the kind we might call informational *input*. Now that may sound like a boring subject, but I guarantee you, when it comes to being crucial for both daily life and eternal life, there's few topics that can rival it. When Jesus said: *...everyone who hears these words of mine and puts them into practice is like a wise man who built his house on the rock*, he highlighted the double-layered foundation of a stable life: *reliable input* and *consistent application*. In fact, it's a principle that is universally valid, because both quality input and consistent application are prerequisites to understanding and success in almost all areas of life. Take computers, for example. Jim, you know your way around them. Does input play an important role with computers?"

"It sure does. Once your system's set up, input is the whole ball game. Wrong input equals wrong output. It's as simple as that. One reason computers can be so frustrating is that they faithfully reproduce your blunders. They'll even multiply them for you."

"I can verify that," said Dean. "And what about something a little less technical, like cooking, for example. Barbara, you've wowed us a few times with some of your creations. What would you say about input when it comes to cooking? Do you pay any attention to what you put into your specialties or can you change amounts and ingredients at will?"

Caught off guard by the compliment, Barbara's cheeks reddened. "I suppose there's some leeway in following a recipe," she said, "but you can't stray too far. And obviously you can't vary ingredients much. You'll never get an apple pie by using cherries."

How to Read New Testament Greek

"Hey, that's a description of the law of input/output in a nutshell: You want apple pie, you gotta' use apples. What about house building, John? Do you ever have to worry about input there?"

John thought for a moment. "Well, if I didn't follow an approved blueprint, it wouldn't take the inspectors long to drum me out of the business—not to mention the fact that without plans I'd build some rather strange looking houses."

"Once you get an eye for recognizing them," said Dean, "you'll notice that we're surrounded by countless examples of the law of input and output. You just can't sidestep them. You remember yesterday discussing how Lincoln needed the right kind of input to become a lawyer, and how he got it through books. Ford needed good input to become a mass producer of automobiles, and he got it through technical magazines and the advice of experts like Thomas Edison. There's just no denying that without good reliable input, any project is doomed to failure.

"We're also going to need good input if we're serious about learning to read the teachings of Christ in the original language in which they were written. I've compiled a list of books that in my opinion give you some of the best factual information now available in the three areas that are the most crucial: 1. The Greek texts, 2. the linguistic context of the texts, and 3. the cultural context of the texts. Plus, I've added a couple works that deal with the whole matter of translating information from one language to another. Anyone interested in seeing the list?"

"You bet," said Jim. "But first I'd like to know how you came up with a nice set of photocopies out here on in the middle of nowhere. Is there an office on this boat, too?"

"No," laughed Dean, "I just happen to keep copies of three or four pieces of particularly important information in my briefcase at all times, and this list of books just happens to be one of them. In my opinion the books on this list are among the most valuable reference works in all the world." Dean handed out the copies. The following books were on the list:

THE GREEK TEXT
Aland, K. and M. Black, C. Martini, B. Metzger, A. Wikren
    (Eds). 1983. *The Greek New Testament.* Third corrected edition.
    Stuttgart: United Bible Societies.
Aland, K. and B. Aland. 1982. *The Text of the New Testament.*
    Stuttgart: The German Bible Society.
Metzger, B. 1971. *A Textual Commentary on the Greek New Testament.*
    London and New York: United Bible Societies.
Metzger, B. 1964. *Text of the New Testament: Its Transmission, Corruption,*
    and Restoration. Oxford: The Clarendon Press.

THE LINGUISTIC CONTEXT
Bauer, W. and W. Arndt, F. Gingrich, F. Danker. 1979. *A Greek-English Lexicon of the New Testament.* Chicago and London: The University of Chicago Press.
Blass, F. and A. Debrunner. 1961. *A Greek Grammar of the New Testament and Other Early Christian Literature.* Chicago: University of Chicago Press.
Dana H. E. and J. R. Mantey. 1949. *A Manual Grammar of the Greek New Testament.* New York: The Macmillan Company.
Friberg, B. and T. Friberg (Eds). 1981. *Analytical Greek New Testament.* Grand Rapids: Baker Book House.
Han, N. 1971. *A Parsing Guide to the Greek New Testament.* Scottsdale, PA and Kitchener, ONT: Herald Press.
Louw, J. and E. Nida (Eds). 1989. *Greek-English Lexicon of the New Testament Based on Semantic Domains.* New York: United Bible Societies.
Moull C. F. D. 1960. *An Idiom Book of New Testament Greek.* 2nd Edition. Cambridge: Cambridge University Press.
Moulton and Geden. 1978. *A Concordance to the Greek New Testament.* 5th Edition. Edinburgh: T & T Clark.
Wigram, G. 1970. *The Englishman's Greek Concordance of the New Testament.* Grand Rapids: Zondervan Publishing House.

THE CULTURAL CONTEXT
Aharoni, Y. and A. Michael. 1977. *The Macmillan Bible Atlas.* New York: The Macmillan Publishing Company.
Barrett C. K. 1989. *The New Testament Background: Selected Documents.* Revised Edition. San Francisco: Harper and Row.
Bruce, F. 1980. *New Testament History.* Doubleday-Galilee Edition. New York: Doubleday and Company, Inc.
Coleman W. L. 1984. *Today's Handbook of Bible Times and Customs.* Minneapolis: Bethany House Publications.
Josephus, F. 1960. *The Complete Works of Josephus.* Grand Rapids: Kregal Publications.

TRANSLATING
Black D. A. 1988. *Linguistics for Students of New Testament Greek.* Grand Rapids: Baker Book House.
de Waard, J. and E. Nida. 1986. *From One Language to Another.* Nashville, Camden, and New York: Thomas Nelson Publishers.
Nida E. and C. R. Taber. 1969. *The Theory and Practice of Translation.* Leiden: E. J. Brill for the United Bible Societies.

How to Read New Testament Greek

After examining the list closely, John sat back in his chair, shaking his head. "Not a best seller on the list."

"I know how you feel," said Dean. "Some of these volumes look rather rugged, and unfortunately, this is one case where looks don't deceive. I've made no attempt to keep complex or scholarly books off the list. I've included the best ones I know"

"How will we ever be able to use books like these?" asked Carol.

"It will not be easy, but neither is it impossible. The best news is that some plans have already been made to give you some help. In a few months when you're all close to finishing the STEPS I gave you as an introduction to New Testament Greek, you'll be receiving invitations to visit Universal Greek Pictures once again. There are still two departments you haven't seen, and one of them is dedicated to making these books understandable. After the tour you'll know what you have to do to turn the books on the list into usable tools."

"Will it be necessary to have *all* these books right away?" asked Jim. "Or do we really only need a few of them?"

"Although it may seem like a lot of books, it's actually only part of a much longer list that has already been narrowed down about as far as it can go. There are at least thirty other books I'd also like to see each of you have."

"Thirty!" said John. "That would almost double the number of books I own."

"It may seem unreasonable, but I would highly recommend getting at least the books mentioned on the list as soon as possible. I know you'll not be able to use them for a while yet, but I think it will prove very motivating for you to have them."

"Maybe they'll do just the opposite," said Carol. "Especially when we see we can't read them."

"I don't think so," said Dean. "First of all, buying that many books represents a certain depth of commitment. It says: *Now I've done something big; I've taken the step of no return; I've signed on the dotted line; I'm taking the whole matter of learning Greek seriously.*

"Plus, I think the mere presence of these magnificent books on your shelves will stir your curiosity and spark your interest. They open the great storehouses of the language of Jesus' day; they stake out the route to the greatest of all sources; they offer insight into the profoundest of all messages. The more you realize what these books have to offer, the more you'll want to discover the treasures inside them.

"There's no denying that these books are going to cost you considerable time, sweat, and money—they are by no means cheap—but that should come as no surprise. Knowledge of every kind always has a high price tag. Think of the people who invest great amounts of time and money into pursuits that are of much less value than the goal of acquiring a source-level knowledge of the Scriptures.

"I have a friend, for instance, who is a real golf fan. He has one whole shelf full of golf books and a closet half full of golf magazines he's collected over the years, and I know he's pored over all of them. Add to the cost of this investment in literature, the time and money he's spent on his own game of golf—club dues, equipment, driving range, traveling, lessons—and you'll see that the small library of books I'm recommending to you is modest in comparison."

"Touché," said Jim. "I thought you were describing me there for a minute."

"I don't doubt, Jim, that we've all made similar investments at some time in our lives. Can anyone think of any examples?"

"My mother has a huge library of cookbooks," said Barbara. "They've come from all over the United States and many parts of the world. And it's not just a collection. She actually uses many of them."

"Aha. Now we know why you're such a great cook," said Dean.

Buddy swiveled around in the captain's chair. "Eddie and I have a friend in our class whose father is a real jazz fanatic. He has hundreds of books, LP's, CD's, and a stereo that takes up one whole wall in their house. I don't know if it's true, but we've heard he's spent over twenty thousand dollars on the stuff."

John let out a low whistle.

"That may sound extreme," said Dean, "but when you think about it, it's actually not all that unusual for people to make considerable investments to develop their knowledge in areas of special interest. I know people who have done it with cars and computers and photography, and I know one guy who's invested hundreds of dollars to educate himself in the care and keeping of exotic fish.

"Consider, too, what it costs to send kids to college. The point is this: It should not surprise us that *understanding* of any kind is not something to be had for nothing. Don't forget Henry Ford and Abe Lincoln, and what they had to go through to get the books and information they needed to obtain their goals.

"In the end, we have to ask ourselves if the goal of knowing the teachings of Christ at the source level is a goal that is worth making sacrifices for. Is it a big enough goal to take a bite out of my finances? Is it a big enough goal to take a bite out of my free time? Is it a big enough goal to keep me behind a desk for a certain number of hours a week? Is it a goal that will keep me going when I need not only a second wind, but a third and a fourth and a fifth?

"Anyone who's serious about learning to read the New Testament in Greek is going to have to dig deep in his chest of resources to do it, and obtaining the essential reference books is one of the most pressing needs. Trying to master the Greek New Testament without them would be like trying to build a house without tools."

"I have quite a few Christian books at home," said Jim, "but I don't have a single one on the list, and I thought I had some pretty good books. I don't see a single study Bible or commentary on the list, for example. Aren't they supposed to be good reference books?"

"Those kinds of books can be helpful," said Dean, "but they are excluded from this list because they are a step or two away from being firsthand information. One of our major purposes for learning Greek is to decrease our dependence on second- and thirdhand sources, and move more and more toward firsthand sources. What is the difference between a firsthand source and a secondhand source?"

"If someone tells you about something I supposedly said, that's getting the information secondhand," said John. "If you come to me and ask me what I actually said, that's getting the information firsthand."

"Which of the two is usually responsible for the most problems?" asked Dean.

"Secondhand information," said Carol. "No doubt about it."

"Why's that?"

"It doesn't take long for something to get put in a different light."

"Hey, dad," said Buddy. "It's like that game we play sometimes. You know, where a message is whispered from one person to another around a circle. Sometimes the message gets totally changed."

"I think we know instinctively," said Dean, "that secondhand information is a potential problem. If we accept it, it makes us dependent on the view of the carrier of the information.

"That's not necessarily bad, nor can it always be avoided. But people in our world who have to make important decisions are usually very careful about secondhand information.

"Doctors, for example, will not make a diagnosis without examining a patient themselves. They don't even like to accept another doctor's opinion without checking it for themselves. They know they could get themselves in trouble if they don't base their decisions on as many facts as possible.

"The whole ordering of society, in fact, depends on the use of original, first hand documents: birth certificates, insurance documents, driver's licenses, checks, receipts, passports, certifications, contracts, and literally hundreds of other original documents form the basis of what we consider to be a responsible ordering of information. Secondhand information is viewed with suspicion almost everywhere, even in our age of copy machines. Just try to go to a concert or a movie sometime with a *copy* of your ticket. You'll discover the importance people attach to even seemingly unimportant documents.

"People of all occupational persuasions value the reliability of factual, firsthand information, and they pride themselves on being competent to evaluate it. Such an ability to judge factual information wisely is usually associated with the characteristics of maturity, responsibility, and reliability.

"It is no different in the realm of the Spirit. The Scriptures also demand a high level of competence from serious followers of Christ. Paul told Timothy in his second letter to him to be a *workman who has no need to be ashamed, who accurately handles the word of truth.*

"The books I have recommended to you are not necessarily all examples of firsthand information, but most of them do move you in that direction. They are the books the commentators and the authors of study Bibles use themselves to form their opinions.

"Hey, John!" Buddy suddenly hollered. "We're coming to a wide place in the river." With Buddy and Andy at the helm, the houseboat had covered about fifteen miles, and they were now emerging from the end of a narrow, gooseneck bend.

Peering through the big front windows, they could all see that the narrow passage was opening into a broad, roomy basin.

John borrowed Jim's binoculars to survey the distant shore which he judged to be about a mile away. "I think I see a good place for us to spend the afternoon," he said to Buddy. "Do you see that bit of green just at the left of that outcropping of rock straight ahead?"

"Sure do."

"I may be wrong, but it actually looks like a patch of grass or maybe reeds. Try to find a good place to beach this buggy as near to it as you can."

"Aye, aye. Full speed ahead."

It was late in the morning and the temperature was approaching the high nineties when the front end of the pontoons came to rest on the pebbly shore.

While preparations were being made for lunch, Linda walked a short distance from the boat and let her eyes sweep over the rugged mountains in the distance. Then she slowly traced the lines of dozens of gullies and gulches as they groped their way toward the lake. The landscape here was much different than near the marina. Great pockmarked boulders were strewn over a gashed terrain that was a silent witness to climatic upheavals in the past. Wave after wave of pitted and swollen ridges climbed into the distance as though they had been beaten back by the blast of a giant blowtorch.

"You'd like to hike into that country, wouldn't you?" said a voice behind her.

She turned and saw her husband walking towards her.

"Could we?" she asked, holding her hand out to him. "We've just got to see what's up in those hills. Have you ever seen such country before?"

Dean smiled and gave his wife a quick kiss. "Let's take off as soon as we've eaten," he said. "Just you and I and all the canteens we can find."

The squeeze she gave his hand was all he needed to know she was pleased. Dean knew his wife well. She was an enthusiastic hiker who would always choose the challenge of venturing into a scorched desert over a dip in a cool lake.

After a quick lunch of tuna sandwiches and potato salad, Buddy saw his father sit down and begin to lace up his hiking boots. "Mom dragging you off through the burning desert?" he asked.

"You guessed it, son."

"We'll be thinking about you while we're sipping lemonade and taking dips in the coooool water. Send up some smoke signals if you need any help.

"Don't worry about us. There's probably an air-conditioned shopping mall just over the next ridge. Your mother has a feel for those kind of things."

"If there is, bring back a couple gallons of ice cream." With that, Buddy ran to the water where most of the others were already swimming.

When Dean and Linda arrived back at the boat three hours later, they found everyone stretched out on deck chairs in the shade of the houseboat's overhanging roof. John saw them approaching. "Great fishing around here," he said to them as he leaned over the railing and pulled a full stringer out of the water.

"The swimming is great, too, dad," said Tommy. "We found an overhanging rock that makes a super diving board. Can we stay here for the night?"

"That's all right with me if that's what everyone else wants."

"Fine with us," said Jim. "We don't want to get any farther from the marina anyway."

"Did you have a good time?" asked Carol as Dean and Linda made their way up the gangplank.

"It was fascinating," said Linda. "We discovered a desert wonderland, and we were led there by a beautiful little burro trail "

"Burros!" said Tommy. "Really? Did you see them. How big were they? Could we catch one? How many---"

"Hold on," said Dean. "One question at a time. No, we didn't see them, but their tracks were fresh. They're up there somewhere."

"And what were you saying about a desert wonderland?" asked Carol.

"It's almost too unusual and too beautiful to describe," said Linda. "We discovered a whole forest of petrified wood and hundreds of boulders balanced on pedestals of hardened mud and incredible views of the lake and---"

"That's enough," said Jim, "I'm convinced. Sounds like something worth seeing. How about taking us all up this magic trail tomorrow?"

Jim's suggestion was greeted with enthusiasm, and it was decided that bright and early the next morning, they would all hike up the burro trail. The rest of the afternoon was spent swimming and fishing.

Later, after the evening meal, Buddy and Eddie announced they'd planned a treasure hunt and invited everyone to meet on the shore to receive a list of clues. Linda, Barbara, and Carol stayed behind to clean up, saying they'd join the game later if the treasure still hadn't been found.

When the dishes were finished, the women fixed themselves glasses of iced tea and found a shady place on the deck to relax. From their vantage point they could catch glimpses of the treasure hunters scurrying around the areas, sometimes pausing to huddle together, and then disappearing into a gully or behind boulders from which only the excited squeals of the smaller children could be heard.

"How do they stand the heat?" said Barbara. "It must be close to a hundred degrees out there."

Carol nodded her head. "I'd say there are going to be several swimming breaks this evening."

Linda leaned back in her chair and slowly let her eyes shut. "Water and heat and hot rocks," she murmured. "This is better than a sauna." Another houseboat could be heard cruising into the channel in the distance.

"This has really been a great time," said Carol. "It's been like being in another world. And not just because Lake Powell is so beautiful. We've been talking about things that are so interesting and important, and what amazes me is that they are things I would normally not even think about. It's so easy to just kind of muddle through life without seriously thinking about what you're doing."

"Over here, daddy. Over here." Andy's excited voice piped in the distance. Carol saw John emerge from a clutter of boulders near the beach and disappear again behind a wave of slick rock.

"It's very easy to live lives with little meaningful content," said Linda. "We tend to think that if we were busy during the day, and we have something to show for it when it's over—even if it's nothing more than to have checked things off a list—then things are all right. But we're not used to asking ourselves if all the activity itself is meaningful."

"You mean we'd be better off if we cut out a lot of the rushing around we do."

"Not exactly. Running around isn't necessarily bad. It can also be meaningful. Meaningfulness is a matter of...well, I guess you have to say love—love for God and love for people around us. That's what makes anything meaningful in the deeper sense of the word. What John did for us this weekend is an example of what I mean."

"How's that?"

"When he was offered the houseboat, John could have just brought the family up here alone and enjoyed three days of fishing and swimming. It would have been a nice rest for the three of you, and that would have been the major meaning behind the trip. But John did some thinking about it and decided to make it a time not only of rest and relaxation, but also of learning, and not only for your family, but for ours as well. In other words, his thoughtfulness was the whole foundation for what has become much more than just a few days at the lake with the family. As I see it, those thoughts were mingled with his own desire to know the words of God better and his desire to let all of us in on his good fortune. That's why I think we'll all look back at this weekend and see it as a significant and meaningful time—even though there was quite a bit of 'running around' connected with it."

Barbara was gazing across the water.

"Thoughtfulness is an important part of what love is all about," Linda continued. "Love can't really be love without the right kind of thoughts behind it."

"I always thought love was more a matter of doing things for others," said Carol.

"That's not necessarily wrong," said Linda, "but all through the New Testament the topic of love is connected with the idea of truth. Love isn't just doing what we think is good for someone else; it's actually much more than that. It's doing what *God* thinks is good for someone else. That's why it's so important for us to know the teachings of Christ well. We can't really love—not our husbands or our children or our neighbors or anyone—unless we know God's thoughts about them and about the world we live in and about His way of doing things."

"I had never thought of love as being so complicated," said Carol. "I thought it was something that comes naturally—not easily, of course, but naturally—if you let it. I thought we had trouble loving because we chose not to love for some reason—anger or selfishness—not because we didn't have enough information."

Linda asked Barbara to hand her the New Testament on one of the deck chairs beside her. "Love and truth always belong together. If they go their separate ways then both become empty. A doctor, for example, cannot do what is best for a patient unless he's a master of the laws and principles of medicine, anatomy, and many other related areas of knowledge.

"Good intentions are certainly to be desired in a doctor, but it takes more than good intentions to perform a complicated operation. The key is adherence to reliable information. That's also what the Scriptures teach about love."

She found a passage in the fifth chapter of I John: *"This is how we know that we love the children of God: by loving God and carrying out His commands. This is love for God: to obey His commands.* Love is more than good intentions or busy hands. It's the task of carrying out the commands of God. That's why wisdom, insight, understanding, and obedience are also part and parcel of what love is all about. And that's why we need to know the Scriptures as precisely as possible. Who'd like to be operated on by a doctor who was not particularly concerned about being accurate, or a doctor who couldn't tell a liver from a stomach."

Barbara was becoming increasingly interested in the conversation.

"When it comes to performing operations of love, the need for reliable information is no different. Adherence to the instructions of God becomes the key. We can easily assume, for example, that we're loving our children, but if we don't know or understand God's thoughts accurately, we're actually not in a position to love them at all. Then it's as though we're performing operations without having ever been through medical school. We end up doing more harm than good, despite our good intentions.

"Hey!" Jim was hollering to the women from the shore in front of the boat. "The treasure is still out there somewhere. Want to help us look for it?"

"We're coming," said Carol. She turned to Linda and Barbara. "I'm finding out there are a *lot* of treasures to find on this lake."

Catfish and Motivation

Children's voices were echoing from the canyon walls when John opened his eyes the next morning. He could easily pick out Andy's high-pitched soprano. "I see them! I see them!" he was yelping.

"There must be a thousand of them," said another voice.

Then he heard Jim: "Holy mackerel! I've never seen anything like it. John, get down here. An old fisherman like you has got to see this."

John catapulted out of his sleeping bag and pulled on his cut-off jeans. Looking around, he saw he was alone on the roof. "What's all the commotion?" He hollered, peering over the railing.

"Daddy, daddy. Look at the fish! Look at the fish!" squealed Andy.

"What fish? I don't see anything."

"Look a yard or two out from the shore," said Jim. "Tell us if you can see anything just under the surface."

John let his gaze penetrate the clear water and then he saw them—swarms of black shapes, cruising in slow circles like miniature submarines.

"Catfish! They're everywhere!"

"What did I tell you," said Jim, looking around at the others. "They're catfish, just like I said."

"They're catfish, all right," said John, "but never in my life have I seen so many of them. They're having a convention right here beside our boat." As far as he could see along the canyon wall the water was thick with fish.

"Some of 'em must be two-and-a-half feet long," said Tommy. "Can we try to catch some, dad?"

"Go to it," said Dean. "Last one to catch his dinner is a dog-eared catfish."

Dean's word had the effect of a starter's gun going off. Within minutes most of the merry crew was armed with an assortment of spinners, worms, bobbers, colorful plastic night crawlers, and dozens of other shiny contraptions guaranteed to make a fish's mouth water. They were convinced the deck would soon be covered with catfish. After a half hour, however, not a single fish had shown even the slightest interest in anything that was being lowered into the water. High hopes were replaced by bewilderment.

"You'd think there'd be at least one hungry fish down there," lamented Eddie.

"I don't think they're fish at all," said Buddy. "I'll bet some mad inventor is playing a trick on us. We're surrounded by little mechanical U-boats."

To everyone's surprise, it was Barbara who caught the first fish. After watching the unsuccessful fishermen for a while, she had asked her husband for a length of line and a hook and disappeared into the kitchen. No one noticed when she came back and let the line with the baited hook slowly glide into the water. It was when she hauled a nice twenty-inch catfish over the railing that she raised a few eyebrows, including those of her husband.

"How did you do that?" he asked, scratching his head.

"With a hook and a line. Nothing to it."

"Did you use a worm?"

"Nope."

"No? Then what did you use?"

"Sausage," she said.

Jim's eyes widened. "Sausage! What made you try sausage?"

"It's an old trick I learned from my father. He used to take me fishing with him at a big reservoir in Texas when I was growing up. He always said that there was only one way to catch catfish if they weren't biting and that was with sausage. He said it's the only thing they can't resist."

"How about that," said John. "The Garveys have a bait expert in the family."

Amy and Jimmy were beaming at their mother and eyeing the dark-skinned fish still flip-flopping at the end of the line in her hand.

"Any more of that sausage around?" asked Eddie.

"Four pounds of it," said Barbara.

John and Eddie headed for the kitchen.

The only one who hadn't caught a fish in the next twenty minutes was Jim, who ended up taking the fish off the hooks and cleaning them.

When the excitement died down, Dean noticed that the sun was just beginning to show its fiery face above the distant cliffs, and he remembered they had planned to take a hike before it got hot. "I hate to pull you away from the catfish," he called out to the anglers, "but if we want to take our hike, we need to eat breakfast and get moving. It's going to heat up around here fast."

Carol and Barbara headed for the kitchen while the others stowed away the fishing gear.

After breakfast, they found the burro trail and started up a ravine. They proceeded at a slow pace, taking time to enjoy the unusual sights. The sun was still low in the sky, and a pleasant breeze picked up coolness from the lake and followed them up the trail.

Buddy and Eddie lingered behind. "I'm sure we can get you all the books you need," Buddy was saying. "And besides, even if we have to wait awhile, you can borrow any of mine that you need."

"That's great, but I don't really have a place to keep them. They might as well stay at your place. I could borrow one at a time."

"Yeah, that would be possible, but it would be better if you had enough room for a desk of your own. I talked to dad about it last week and he had an interesting suggestion."

"What do you mean?"

"Well, he happens to know someone with one of those campers."

"Huh?"

"You know, those things that fit inside the back of a pickup truck."

"And?"

"Well, the guy wants to get rid of it. Says it's old and just takes up room in his backyard. Dad saw it and says it's one of the bigger ones, the kind that has a bed compartment over the cab. It's pretty roomy inside. Big enough for a table and a little study area. How would you like to have it?"

"Are you kidding?"

"I'm serious. We could mount it on barrels or something right beside your house and run a cord inside for electricity. I'll bet your parents would think it's a good idea. Dad said he'd talk to them. It'd be like adding a little room to the house, and you'd have a nice, quiet place where you could get some work done. We could even get one of those little air conditioners to mount in a window. It wouldn't take much to cool off a cubbyhole like that."

"But won't that all cost a lot?"

"Nah. Like I said, the camper is free. The guy's glad to get rid of it. And a little air conditioner doesn't cost much. Two weekends of work and we'd have it paid for. Whaddya say?"

"It sounds great, if it's not too much trouble for your dad."

"Trouble? It'll be fun. Just think, you'll have your own apartment. Sixty square feet of pure luxury."

"Yeah. We'll invite all our friends over and have a big party in it to celebrate."

"Great idea. With or without a live band?"

Laughing, they quickened their pace to catch up to the others who had come to a place where a boulder as big as a house was stuck in the ravine like a cork in a bottle. The boulder was imbedded at such an angle in the steep walls that a man-sized tunnel was formed on one side. Filing through the tunnel, they were met with an amazing sight. The swirling action of water caused by the position of the boulder had sculpted out of rocks and clay a fairy land of unusual forms, the most prominent being the golf-ball-on-a-tee motif which was represented in dozens of variations. The sun had baked the entire display into an exquisite exhibit of desert fantasy.

"Wow," said John, "it really is a wonderland. How is it possible, though? How can a huge boulder get up on a small column of clay?"

"I've been trying to figure that out since yesterday," said Dean. "I can only guess that somehow the combination of water, weight, and heat harden and compact the clay directly under a boulder to such a degree that, as the earth around it is washed or blown away, the compacted clay resists the erosion and turns into a pedestal that in some cases perfectly balances the boulder."

"Sounds possible," said John. "You archaeologists are the dirt experts, so I guess you know what you're talking about."

They threaded their way through the maze of mud sculptures and continued up the wash until they came to a particularly steep and rugged stretch. Because the heat was rapidly increasing, Dean suggested they return to the boat.

As they carefully made their way down the wash, Jim waited for Dean who was at the tail end of the line of hikers. They walked together for several minutes before Jim broke the silence. "I've been thinking about a lot of things in the last few months. It's become clear to me I've worked myself into too many corners, and I'm not sure how I should back out of them. I was wondering if we could talk about it. Maybe you'd have some good suggestions for me."

"What kind of corners are you talking about?"

"There's probably more than I'd care to admit, but the main ones are at work, in the family, in the way I use my free time, and at church. I guess that covers the main problem areas."

"Let's see: work, family, free time, church. That doesn't leave too much: eating, sleeping and brushing your teeth, and that's about it."

"I'm good at those things, so I didn't mention them. But you're right; a few minor repairs will never do the job; it's looking like a total overhaul or nothing."

"I'm acquainted with your situation in the office. Tell me about the family. Aren't you satisfied with how things are going there?"

Jim slackened his pace as he thought. " Satisfied? In many ways our marriage has been very fulfilling, but there are also times when I feel like a stranger in my own home. It's not because Barbara and I have any serious disagreements. We don't. It's just that sometimes I feel like an onlooker. There are times when I wonder if our home has turned into a dormitory. I come and go. Barbara comes and goes. The kids come and go. We meet at the crossroads every now and then, but nothing much ever happens there. We tell each other where we were and where we're going next, but that's not much communication. I guess I'd say I feel locked into a pattern of just letting the wheels turn, and I can't seem to make important things important."

"Important things important?"

"Right. My children, for instance. I know they're supposed to be important, but I just can't seem to make them important so they really *are* important. Oh good grief, what a confused way to talk. Can you understand what I'm trying to get at?"

"Sure, I think I know what you're saying. And what about your free time?"

"I waste a lot of it. Period. There's no other way to say it. It's not that I lay around like an oaf; it's just that the things I do with my free time aren't very meaningful. It's pretty obvious I don't need someone to tell me what the problem is. I'm not even at a loss for answers. I'm just not doing what I know needs to be done."

"And at the church?"

"Yeah, the church. That's a little more difficult to explain. You see, it's like this: I'm kind of a... a superstar at the church."

"A superstar?"

"I know it sounds silly, and maybe I'm just imagining a lot of it, but what I mean is that at the church I'm kind of viewed as an all-American type. You know: tall, successful, with a nice home, a pretty wife, and I'm a committed Christian to boot. Almost too good to be true."

"Is this your problem or the problem of the people in the church?"

"Oh, it's mine all right. I've tended to promote my own image. You know me with my gift of gab; I can make myself sound pretty spiritual. Well, I've gotten myself into some positions of responsibility I really shouldn't be in. My own family isn't even in order. People have...no, I mean I've allowed people to set me up on a pedestal as though I were Moses. It's disgusting when you think about it." They had quit walking and were standing in the shade of a high wall of black rock. The others were out of sight. "Any words of wisdom for me?"

"It sounds like you're willing to stand up like a man and admit to some serious wrongdoing. That's the hard part, and it's probably the best start you could make. In fact, it's the only start that I think the Lord would recommend."

"And what do I do now?"

"If you're really serious about making a major overhaul, then my main suggestion would be that you be sure to start at the beginning."

"The beginning?"

"I know it doesn't sound very profound, but it's a summary of what Jesus meant when he said you have to be like a child to enter the kingdom of heaven. In other words, if you want God to be putting things in order in your life, then you've got to go back to being a child and begin again with Him."

"How does that look practically, though?"

"As I see it, you're beginning to take the Scriptures seriously, and that's certainly a good practical start. You can't take God seriously and learn to be His obedient child if you don't take His words seriously. Secondly, I can't think of a better and more practical place to begin the rest of the process than in your own family.

"Sometimes we grown men tend to think all the big important things in the world are out there in the worlds of business and science and politics and all the other showy places where money and power are so evident. It's good for us to remember, however, that God is interested in human hearts—all kinds of human hearts—and the great events of this world make little impression on Him. He wants us to be interested in hearts, too, and for us fathers that means beginning at home with the little people who are in our care.

"The needs of a small child are every bit as important, if not more so, than the demands of an important-looking businessman. Unfortunately though, we tend to jump to our feet if a man with a three-piece suit walks in the door, but pay little attention to the small voices of our own children. If we can learn to take them seriously and be good examples for them, then God will be pleased to make us responsible fathers in His great family. God wants us to be responsible fathers, because that's what He is. Loving and serving and leading our wives and children are the most important things we need to learn to do before we can be of any real use anywhere else.

"If I were to sum up the problems you shared with me, I'd choose the words *pride* and *priorities*, and it seems to me that becoming like a child is a good way to tackle both those problems."

"That hits the nail on the head all right."

"I'm sure you realize that a major overhaul of any kind requires a big investment of thought and effort to insure you do a thorough job of it. Don't forget how much planning and work you had to do when you reorganized your company; restructuring your life won't be any less of a task. Just be sure that you give God a big say with the planning part of it. If it's going to have His stamp of approval, then He's got to be the One giving the orders. For now, I'd recommend that you read the two letters Paul sent to Timothy. I think you'll find advice in those writings that will be of immediate help in regard to the things you've shared with me. What do you think?"

"I reckon I'll be having some questions, but you've given me plenty to think about for now."

The two men headed back down the wash. When they arrived back at the boat, everyone was in the water cooling off. John was treading water near the boat. "Ah, you made it," he said to them as they walked up the gangplank. "Glad you didn't get lost. We'll need to be shoving off soon. This evening we should try to camp close to the marina. Tomorrow morning is check-in time for the houseboat.
"Right you are, cap'n," said Jim. "We'll take a quick dip and get the crew back on board ready to work."

The sun was high in the sky when Eddie and Buddy lifted the gangplank to the front platform, pushed the big pontoons away from the shore, and scrambled on board. John started the engines and slowly backed the houseboat into deeper water. Soon they were headed upstream through the narrow channel leading back towards the marina.

Barbara and Carol prepared a huge fish dinner with all the trimmings that afternoon. Jim had the task of convincing the younger children that each of them was actually eating the fish he or she had caught that morning. Afterwards, John, Buddy, and Eddie washed the dishes while the others sat out on the deck and watched the sun turn the canyon walls a deep red.

Jim was sitting with his lanky legs up on the railing. "How about we get that session on motivation going?" he suggested.

"I'm for it," said Carol. "This is our last day on the lake. We'd better take advantage of the time while we have it."

"I'm ready when you are," said Dean. As they gathered in the dining area, they were delighted to find coffee and a chocolate cake waiting on the table. Barbara had been busy baking.

When the last piece of cake had disappeared, Dean opened the discussion. "The second topic we targeted for discussion, was *motivation*. I think we all know instinctively that without being highly motivated, no one is going to learn New Testament Greek. To get everyone warmed up and thinking, I want to begin by asking a few questions. The first is this: What are some things that sap our motivation and leave us with empty tanks?"

There was a moment of silence. "Come on, speak right up. Don't be bashful."

"How about *being bashful*," quipped Jim.

"A good start! Bashfulness can definitely put you on ice.

"What else?"

"Fear," said Carol.

"Right. The big brother of bashfulness. And?"

"Not having the right tools." It was John's voice.

"That's an interesting one. Can you explain that a bit?"

"It's always discouraging for me to tackle a job without the right tools. I know if I try it, the job will take longer and probably not end up right."

"That makes sense. In fact, it illustrates exactly what we were talking about yesterday: the importance of having the right books which are the tools we need to do a good, thorough job of learning Greek. Any other motivation killers?"

"Lack of interest," said Buddy.

"Lack of know-how."

"Feelings of inferiority." The answers were coming faster.

"Confusion."

"Danger."

"Too little time."

"Too little money."

"Exhaustion."

"Disappointment."

"Messiness."

"All right," said Dean, holding out his hand. "That's enough to give us a feeling for the kind of motivational mine fields waiting for us out there. Now let's shift our focus a bit: What is it that you think motivates people? What puts them into high gear?"

"Encouragement," said John.

"Friendship," said Eddie.

"The desire to be happy."

"Love."

"Meaningful goals."

"Hold up a moment," said Dean, "You're right, of course. All these things are great motivators. But you're being a bit heavy on the positive side. Are these the only kinds of things that motivate people to undertake something?"

"I run across people every day who are motivated by dollar signs," said Jim.

"Aha," said Dean. "Money is definitely one of the biggest motivators. What are others?"

"Prestige"

"Adventure."

"The desire for power and influence is also a big motivator," said Jim.

"Hate or anger also drive people to do some pretty extreme things," said Carol.

"Anyone care to make any observations about the motives we've thought of thus far?" asked Dean.

"There are good ones and bad ones," said Eddie.

"Does that tell us anything?"

"It tells us that not all motives are legitimate," said Jim, "that we can't just be concerned about being motivated to learn Greek, but about being motivated to do it for the right reason."

"OK. I think we're warmed up now. I just wanted us to be reminded that when we talk about motivation, we're not just touching on a side issue, but we're entering the whole thorny world of the human spirit and its struggle to submit to the Spirit of God. The struggle between love and hate, bitterness and forgiveness, fear and courage, and all the other motivational opposites are conflicts of cosmic proportions. Problems in these areas are not going to be solved with a few easy tips. No one less than the master motivator himself can give us the clues we need here.

"Jesus also faced the task of motivating a group of men who were a real mixed bag of motivations: his own disciples. His approach, as recorded in Matthew, is a gold mine of motivational principles."

Dean thumbed through a small notebook. "According to the record in the fifth chapter of Matthew, right after Jesus chose the disciples, he sat them down and had a heart to heart talk with them.

> *I want to begin by telling you what kind of men are the most fortunate men in the world. You're fortunate...*
>> *if you give your lives to others, because that means you're on God's team*
>> *if you refuse to forget the suffering of others, because that means you'll not be forgotten when you suffer."*

"Just a minute," Jim broke in, staring at a page in his Bible. "What translation are you using anyway?"

"It's a translation Buddy and I made for some of his friends once. I thought I'd try it out and see if it communicates to adults."

"It's communicating, all right," said Jim. "Sorry I interrupted. Read on."

"I'll start again.

> *I want to begin by telling you what kind of men are the most fortunate men in the world. You're fortunate...*
>> *if you give your lives to others, because that means you're on God's team*
>> *if you refuse to forget the suffering of others, because that means you'll not be forgotten when you suffer.*
>> *if you treat others as more important than yourselves, because that means you'll one day own the whole world.*
>> *if you do what's right regardless of the cost, because that means you'll be paid back in full.*
>> *if you don't look away when others need help, because that means you'll be helped when you need it.*
>> *if you have nothing to hide, because that means you'll be able to look God in the eye.*

> *if you help people come to God and begin loving their family and friends and neighbors, because that means you'll be known as a child of God.*
> *if you have to take a lot of punishment for doing what's right, because that means you're in the middle of God's plan.*
> *if you're hasseled and harassed and have lies told about you just because you're my friends, because that means God has a big reward for you just like He did for the prophets.*

"This is right at the beginning of Jesus' time with his disciples. What is he doing here to motivate them?"

"I don't know why," said Carol, "but it doesn't sound all that motivating to me. It strikes me as more sobering than anything else."

"It's not hard to have that first impression," said Dean. "Being hasseled and harassed and having lies told about you and having to take a lot of punishment for doing what's right are not exactly inviting descriptions of what discipleship will be like. A public relations man would probably tell the Lord his approach is all wrong, that he should ease his followers into his program with a pep talk and wait with the tough lessons until they've gotten their feet wet.

"Can anyone explain why Jesus chose not to do this?"

"I learned a number of years ago," said John, "that when I hire a new man, I shouldn't give him the wrong idea about what will be expected of him. There were a few times when I was so anxious to get help that I made the mistake of misrepresenting the job. You know, I dressed it up a bit to make it appear more attractive. Well, it ended up getting me into hot water, and those workers didn't stay very long. My experience has been that it's the men who really know what they're getting into who last longer."

"That's an excellent example of the motivating power of leveling with people right up front," said Dean. "Knowing what you're getting into is actually one good way of solving a lot of those barriers to motivation that we mentioned earlier. If they crop up like a surprise left hook, then they can put us out of the ring, but if we know certain kinds of punches are coming, we can put up a defense and take the pounding without losing the fight."

Dean noticed Eddie whispering something to Buddy. "Have you guys thought of something?" he asked.

"Eddie did."

"I don't know if it's very important," said Eddie.

"Tell us about it."

"Well, I was just thinking, the best teachers in school, the ones who get the most work out of us, seem to be the ones who demand a lot, and they usually pile it on right from the beginning. They're not always the best-liked teachers, but they're the ones who get us working."

"Our football coach is also a good motivator," said Buddy. "And he sure doesn't hide anything from anybody. When he gives his recruiting talk to the freshman boys, he makes football sound like the third world war. You'd think he was trying to discourage them from coming out for football. It usually has the opposite effect though."

"These are some interesting parallels to the principle Jesus was following," said Dean. "I think we could continue to pull a lot of good insights out of this passage in Matthew, particularly because learning Greek to understand the teachings of Christ better is intimately related to the process of discipleship—a task and a responsibility that has a high cost attached to it.

"Jesus wasn't out to get his men to jump on a bandwagon. He wanted to prepare them for a lifetime of being committed to his own trustworthiness, and that required an uncompromising commitment to the truth. His eye was on the long haul. He knew all their false expectations would one day be dashed, and when the time came he wanted them to know that he had always leveled with them, and that he could be trusted, because he told them the truth, and for no other reason than that.

"We, too, need to understand and accept the reality accompanying anything we undertake, and that includes learning New Testament Greek. Many of you are going to need many months and even years to learn Greek. And those years will not be easy ones if you're really serious about learning it. You'll find there's a price to be paid which will be different for each of you depending on your own strengths and weaknesses. Some will painstakingly need to learn discipline, others will have to cut out certain pleasurable but time-consuming activities, and still others will have to struggle with repeated failure, which will put pressure on you to throw in the towel.

"These are the things that need to be clear from the start. On the surface, it may seem self-defeating to paint a tough picture, but reality, if it's looked in the face, is an excellent, long-range motivator. It may daunt you, but it will not disappoint you. It's our own tendency to twist the truth, and our own propensity to sidestep problems that in the end frustrate and disappoint us."

"It almost seems from that passage," said Carol, "that Jesus was telling the disciples they would have *more* problems if they followed him."

"In a sense that's true," said Dean, "and it's logical. Knowledge of any kind usually puts additional responsibility on a person's shoulders. Doctors get burdened with other people's health problems; builders get burdened with construction problems; and a follower of Christ who is a skillful workman in the Scriptures is going to end up with responsibilities he would otherwise never have. Anyone who starts out to take the words of the Lord seriously has to ask himself if that's what he really wants, because learning the Scriptures is a preparation for service. But it's also a preparation for the future. Do you see where that's mentioned in the passage?"

"There are incredible promises following each of Christ's statements," said Linda. "They must be the reasons why Jesus uses the word *fortunate* to describe

Catfish and Motivation

people who are asked to do the difficult things he mentions. I doubt that anyone can be really motivated to do a task—particularly something unpleasant or dangerous—who doesn't believe there's a reason for doing it that can be expressed in terms of some kind of a desirable goal or reward.

"Ah, yes. *Goals* and *rewards*," said Dean. "They always play a big role in motivating people. How do you think your employees would respond, Jim, if you were to announce one day that they should keep coming to work, but you couldn't be sure what the company would be doing in the coming months, and there would be no more pay checks?"

"I know exactly how they'd respond: They'd never show up again."

"Jesus wanted men who would keep showing up and be faithful to the end, so he didn't leave them in doubt about what they could expect in the future and for all eternity. Reviewing the future benefits could also motivate us to keep showing up to work in our Greek New Testaments.

"The second principle of motivation Jesus mentions is what I call the spur of the spotlight. He said: *You are the salt of the earth...You are the light of the world... If people are going to get a taste of God and see what He's like, it's going to be through you, so don't spoil the taste or ruin the picture for others.*

"There were two times in my life when I experienced the motivating power of this principle at work. Once was during my student days in Germany when I had begun playing soccer for one of the local clubs. One day before a game when the coach was reading off the line-up, he said: 'McLain, from now on you're the middle forward. Let's see if we can't get some goals out of that position.

"Wham. That really brought me to attention, and talk about motivated! I was ready to run my legs off.

"The other time was not too many years after that. I was standing at the side of my wife as we shared one of life's greatest moments. I'll never forget the impression made on me by the attending doctor's words right after Buddy was born. He said, 'Congratulations, Mr. McLain, you're the father of a son.' The father of a son! In that moment I became a different person, and a new motivation for living entered my life.

"Can someone explain why the two experiences I just described were so motivating, and what they have to do with what Jesus told his disciples about being the salt of the earth and the light of the world?"

"In both instances," said Jim, "you had an important responsibility dropped in your lap, and they were both responsibilities in which other people would be depending on you. That's motivating, because it puts things on the line. No one wants to let someone down."

"Your change of identity also seemed to play a big part," said Carol. "Being a father was something you'd never been before, but it was probably a concept for you that carried with it a certain set of expectations, and therefore you were motivated to be something different than you were before."

"I think both of these observations," said Dean, "clue us in to the motivating power behind the spotlight principle.

"A new identity is often necessary for us before we have the confidence that we can do something. It's particularly important when it comes to learning New Testament Greek. Most people think that to learn something like Greek you'd have to be a linguist or a scholar before you had a chance. And quite frankly, many people in our society don't even think of themselves as being readers and writers, much less scholars.

"The disciples had the same problem. Most of them were uneducated, simple fishermen and the like. Jesus changed their identity by making them his own special representatives. Then he told them they were the salt of the earth and the light of the world, and those simple men became some of the most knowledgeable men of their day. Even the academic big-shots were amazed at what they knew.

"None of us will get far in learning New Testament Greek if we don't believe God can use the raw material we have to offer Him, regardless of how modest it may be. I'm convinced that God is still in the business of taking average Joes and Josephines and turning them into wise and knowledgeable representatives of Christ, and he still does it by telling them *You're the salt of the earth and the light of the world.* Anyone who can believe something like that is not going to have trouble believing he can learn New Testament Greek.

"Fathers and mothers should be particularly motivated by this principle. They're constantly in the spotlight at home. The mere fact that a father or mother invest time and effort in the learning of the Scriptures will not go unnoticed by the children. Parents who make that a top priority in their lives will never have to sit their kids down and lecture them to take the Scriptures seriously. The kids will have gotten the idea loud and clear."

"If the parents aren't doing it themselves," said John, "it probably wouldn't do much good to tell the kids anyway. It might even produce the opposite effect."

"You're right there," said Dean. "Kids have a real nose for sniffing out phonies. I have four excellent sniffers at home, and they've caught me more often that I'd like to mention."

Dean looked around the circle. "Is everyone still on board, or should we take a break?"

"Things are just getting interesting," said Jim. "If the gals keep the coffee coming and the cookie bowl full, I'm for plowing on. How's that for being motivated?"

"OK. Let's keep moving," said Dean. "The next principle I want to mention is an example of Jesus' teaching regarding pure motives. At the beginning of the sixth chapter of Matthew, we read: *Don't get in the habit of putting on a show in front of people or expecting a pat on the back whenever you do the things you know you're supposed to be doing... If you want to keep things on the up and up with God, then cut out the show and leave the applause to Him.*

"In this passage we get a good look at the two sides of the word *self*: its most honorable side which lives for the praise of God, and its most detestable side which lives for the praise of men.

"This principle is one of the reasons why I like to encourage people to become self-learners, because self-learning constantly forces a person into the situation where he is alone with God. There is no teacher to please, no grade to be given, no ranking to attain, no diploma to earn. Only God is there. The self-learner either begins to work for Him, to take His presence seriously, or he quits.

For those who begin to solo with God, however, it becomes extremely motivating, perhaps the greatest of all motivations: to live with Him and for Him, desiring only His approval, only His 'well done', not being dependent—enslaved is the word used in the Scriptures—on the approval of men."

"What about *encouragement?*" asked Carol. "Isn't that something we all need. How does that fit in with what you were saying about seeking someone's approval?"

"Encouragement is certainly something we'll always need. It's important, however, that we quickly learn to depend on the encouragement of the Lord and not that of men. It's through the example of men that we often learn the meaning of such words as forgiveness, kindness, encouragement, correction, sacrifice, patience, and many other spiritual skills. But as with all human or earthly sources, they will always remain merely a shadow or a taste of the eternal realities. A believer who is dependent on the encouragement or patience or forgiveness of his fellowmen will eventually be disappointed. It's a part of what it means to be mature in Christ to transfer our dependence to him. Only he is sufficient, and only he will never let us down.

"This is not to say we will never need the encouragement of a friend, but, in general, growing out of the need for human encouragement is an expected part of what it means to become spiritually mature. It's the sort of thing, for instance, that we expect as a natural result of children growing up. Take a child, for instance, who is expected to help mom wash the dishes. Initially he may only do it to avoid discipline from dad, but that same child ten years later will most likely no longer need dad's 'encouragement' to wash the dishes. He will most likely be motivated by his own commitment to the importance of cleanliness which he has grown to understand and be committed to over the years. In other words, he is motivated by a principle of truth and a strong inner voice that *encourages* him not to ignore the principle. And when he has his own children, he will become the *encourager* as his father was before him. For us this kind of behavior is a sign of maturity.

"If a forty-year-old father still needs the encouragement of his sixty-five-year-old father to make sure the dishes get done in his home, then that would strike us as grotesque and childish. A forty-year-old should no longer need that kind of encouragement."

"Do you think we run the risk of separating ourselves from other Christians if we become self-learners?" asked Jim. "This is something I've heard suggested a few times."

"If a person *wanted* to separate himself from others, then I guess self-learning would be as good a way as any," said Dean. "But with the right motives, becoming a self-learner is a giant step toward maturity, and leads to greater competence and opportunities for service among other believers. Can anyone think of any examples of self-learning you or others have been involved in, and the results at the group level. Was the self-learning beneficial or detrimental to the group?"

"All those hours I spent alone at the computer," said Jim, "obviously benefited the employees and customers in the company as a whole. Just the fact that we were able to cut out those miserable year-end inventories, for example, lifted the spirits of our whole staff."

"Buddy has taught himself to play several instruments," said Eddie, "and he's always being asked to lead singing at parties or at youth groups."

"Some of you have heard of Joe Maxwell," said Buddy. "He's about the best athlete at our school. One reason he's so good is because he does a lot of training on his own. You can see him running early in the morning down at the mall during the summer, for example. Every football and basketball team in Phoenix would like to have him."

"All of these examples," said Dean, "show that self-learning is by no means anti-social. It can be and should be exactly the opposite. All those lonely hours Joe has spent tanking up on muscles and conditioning benefit not only himself, but also the members of the teams he plays on. My experience has been that motivated self-learners are usually key people in their team situation.

"Obviously Jesus wanted all his disciples to be team players, and paradoxically though it may seem, that meant getting their eyes and expectations off each other. As we've already mentioned, the motives of the disciples were not always the best. Some had political motives, for example, hoping Jesus would deliver Israel from the Romans, and others were concerned about their place in the pecking order of the coming kingdom. In the Scriptural accounts it is not unusual to see pride, indignation, anger, jealousy, and other examples of motivational gangrene dogging the feet of the disciples. That's why Jesus was concerned that the disciples get their eyes off each other and onto him. If we want to be learning Greek for the right reasons, then we'll need to have our eyes on him, too."

"I have to be very honest about my own reasons for deciding to learn Greek," said Carol. "I began simply because John wanted to do it, and...well, that's not quite true, maybe also because Linda had made me curious about it, but I don't think my motives go very deep. I'm probably a good candidate to be a drop-out."

"You may be right," said Dean. "You could end up like the boy who went out for football just because his best friend did, and soon came to the conclusion that football's not cut out to be a fun outing with a friend.

"It doesn't have to be that way, however. Beginning something through the influence of a friend is not necessarily a bad motive. In fact, that may be how most people first come to Jesus Christ. Motives, like anything else, are initially often weak and shaky. With time, however, there's no reason why they can't grow and develop deep roots of personal conviction. That's exactly what Jesus is out to do with the disciples: shore up their motives and deepen their faith. Can anyone give us a personal example of how a weak desire grew into a solid commitment?"

"My wife can answer that herself," said John. "It took me quite a while to convince her to marry me. She wasn't wild about the idea at first."

"Well, well," said Dean, "a clear case of a change of heart. How did it come about, Carol?"

Carol blushed slightly, "It just kind of——"

"Developed?" asked Dean.

"I guess you could say that."

"We've surely all experienced a change of heart at one time or another, and it probably happened because someone or something managed to turn our skepticism into conviction. That could also happen with New Testament Greek. If you were to become convinced of it's value, you might find yourself motivated to learn it.

"And that brings us to our next principle, one which has to do with changing hearts. It's a powerful motivator and easily understood by people living in our age. Jesus mentions it right after the passage on having pure motives. He said *Don't be concerned about having a hefty portfolio invested in human corporations...Invest in God's corporation...Because wherever your investment is, that's where your heart is going to be.*

"This is one of the fastest and most practical ways to change the human heart that I know of. Look at that last statement again: *Wherever your investment is, that's where your heart is going to be.* Anyone needing a change of heart just has to make a change of investment. You can't get much more practical than that.

"I once had a musician friend who seldom missed an opportunity to moan about the condition of his Christian life. He had an almost macabre interest in getting down on himself. 'Pray for me' was his standard request. He was a fine fellow, but he had somehow gotten the idea that he'd never be much use until God stepped in and did a transplant job on his attitude. He had the investment principle backwards. He was telling God to change his heart, and then he'd begin investing in God's program. God's principle, however, was *make an investment, and I'll change your heart.*

"One day I finally said to him, 'Do you remember that school for the handicapped where we gave a concert once?'

"'Yeah,' he said, 'what about it?'

"I told him I just happened to know they needed a new van big enough to hold four people in wheel chairs. 'Why don't you just run down there and buy them one?' I said.

"'What? Me?' he said. 'That would cost a mint!'

"'Right,' I said, 'You might even have to sell your custom pick-up, but you need two vehicles like you need another hole in the head anyway.'

"Very frankly I was put out with him, and didn't really think my words would have much of an effect. It must have hit him hard though, because he did just that. He went out and bought a full-size van for the school.

"What is more interesting, however, is what happened afterwards. *He's* the one who ended up driving the van for the school on the weekends, and right now he's on the board, is involved in fund-raising projects, and regularly organizes musical presentations for the students there.

"Can anyone tell me what happened to this guy?"

"In the business world," said Jim, "we call it putting your money where your mouth is. It's not unusual for me to have a prospective customer ask me to work through some very detailed plans for a building project, giving the impression that our company is going to be one of the major suppliers. I've learned over the years, however, that everything is up in the air until the first sizable check is written. That signals the beginning of a commitment, and that's when the customer really gets interested in us."

"It's in our nature," said Dean, "to be deeply interested in anything that's of real value to us. Has anyone else experienced other examples of this principle?"

"My brothers spend a lot of money on their cars," said Eddie, "and that's about all they ever talk about."

"Once again we see how hearts and dollars have a reciprocal relationship," said Dean. "The one chases the other."

"Does this principle only work with money?" asked Carol.

"Not at all. It functions with any kind of investment. Time, effort, and thought are also valuable possessions that are part of a person's investment capital.

"Does anyone have any ideas how we could make this principle work for us in terms of learning New Testament Greek?"

"This morning," said John, "we talked about the books we're going to need if we really want to get into the Greek New Testament. Buying them would be a step in the right direction, even if we can't use them right away. If I say I want to be able to read the New Testament in Greek, then it's only logical that I get the books I need. After all, if I were to say I wanted to learn to ski, I'd no doubt invest in some skis."

"Right," said Jim, "but I'm afraid I'm going to have to do more than buy a pile of books. If my heart is really where my investments are, then I've already got my heart divided up and distributed into too many accounts. I'm going to have to cancel a few investments I've already made before I have anything substantial to invest elsewhere."

"Now you're talking about a restructuring of priorities," said Dean. "The investment principle gives us a great means of making sure such a restructuring is really carried out and doesn't merely turn into an exercise of wishful thinking. It's nothing less than a reallocation of the raw materials out of which our lives consist: *time, energy, and possessions.* Wherever we end up investing these things is going to determine the placement of our hearts.

"One of the next principles that Jesus mentions is just as practical and compelling as the *investment* principle. It contains good advice for overcoming a lot of the barriers to motivation that we mentioned earlier.

Toward the beginning of Matthew 7, Jesus put it to his men like this: *You're not going to get any answers if you don't ask questions; and don't expect to find what you're looking for, if you don't get out and beat the bushes; and how will you get any help, if you don't start knocking on some doors?*

"It's amazing that grown people have to be told such simple methods of problem solving. What could be more logical than asking about what you don't know, looking for what you don't have, and knocking on a closed door you'd like to see opened.

"Are there ever times when you need help at the office, Jim?"

"Plenty. The business world is just too big to know everything, even my little part of it."

"How do you get the help you need?"

"If I didn't have a telephone and a list of troubleshooters waiting for me on the other end, I'd be in big trouble."

"And how is it in construction, John? Do you ever need information you can't dig up yourself?"

"Sure, some kinds of jobs can get me into areas I don't know much about: zoning laws, geological unknowns, structural design. There's always something new waiting around the corner."

"What do you do to get the answers you need?"

"Get on the telephone, usually."

"You mean you always know whom to call?"

"Not really, but I can usually find someone who puts me on the right track."

"You mean you've got a few key people out there who kind of function like information sources, and through them you can get to the contacts you need?"

"Exactly."

"Could you tell us about one of these people?"

"Let's see. There's ol' Chuck who's sort of semi-retired. I got to know him through the first contractor I ever worked for. If I need to know how to find something, he's the man. He's lived and worked in Phoenix all his life, and is just one of those kinds of people who knows a little bit about everything—everything that needs fixing, at any rate."

"Does Chuck ever get mad at you for calling him?"

"Chuck? No, sir. He's the friendliest guy in the world. I always have trouble getting him off the phone."

"I think we can all learn a lot about the whole process of getting answers when we need them from what Jim and John have just told us.

"Over the years I've found that of the people who began to learn New Testament Greek, it was the ones who developed the habit of writing lists who were the ones who made by far the most progress."

"What do you mean by *writing lists?*" asked John.

"I mean the person who makes it a point to regularly write down his questions, his needs, and his plans; and who is not satisfied until he can check them off his list.

"There's a real difference, for example, between the person who struggles with learning Greek and tells me: 'I just don't seem to be able to figure it all out. I'll keep trying, but it sure is hard.' and the person who shows up and asks me to help him work through a detailed list of all the things he hasn't understood in the last few weeks. The first person is bogged down, and it's difficult to know how to help him. The second, however, is easy to help because he's recorded each problem, and it's just a matter of working them out one at a time.

"It's amazing, however, how difficult it is to get people to do simple things like jot down questions and call up for an appointment to go through them. Many would rather sit and stew in their frustration than risk asking a few questions. Getting over that hump, however, is almost a sure guarantee that someone will continue to make progress.

"I would encourage everyone here to become a list writer. As soon as you run into a problem you can't solve with reasonable effort yourself, just add the problem to your list, and when the list has some length to it, call and say it's time to clear up your list of questions."

"Isn't that a lot to ask," said Carol. "I mean if you have dozens of people all showing up with lists of questions, you'll go batty."

"Don't worry about that," laughed Dean. "First of all, going through lists goes very quickly, and secondly, I'm not the only one who can help you; there's other folks who can help and not just the others in my family. It's just a matter of finding the people who can help—you know, doing some creative knocking on doors. Don't forget ol' Chuck. Most people *like* to offer their help. Calling on them is a compliment. Remember, too, that your questions don't always have to be answered by an expert. In fact, you'll be surprised at how much you can help one another. Just make sure to carry your list of questions around, and don't give up until you get good answers. I've carried questions around for months.

"This principle can help convince even the most skeptical people that they, too, can learn Greek. It may be difficult for many people to imagine themselves learning Greek, but they can certainly imagine themselves asking questions, searching for something, or knocking on a door. These are no big, impossible tasks. Anyone can do them, and that's motivating.

"Finally, don't forget that these three methods of solving problems open the door to the One who should be the real source of our motivation. Jesus summed up the principle by saying, *All of you know that asking questions, searching, and knocking on doors works. It's standard operating procedure between fathers and sons, isn't it? Well, guess what. It also works with your heavenly Father. Whatever you do, don't forget to go to Him with your questions, your needs, and your plans.*

"That's a good word for all of us. We need to keep lists and take them regularly to God who's always ready to give us the motivational help we could get nowhere else."

"I don't think we're far from the marina," called Buddy from his place at the helm.

John looked out the window. "You're right. We're close enough now. All we need is a place to dock for the night."

"We've covered enough principles for now," said Dean. "Let's get out on the deck and see if we can sight a good parking place for our last night on the lake."

After the others had left the dining area, Jim sat down next to Dean as he was gathering his papers together. "Those principles hit hard. I thought they were written for me personally."

"The Scriptures probably hit everyone that way."

"Anyone who's willing to listen, that is. That hasn't always been the case with me. I hope for the sake of my family that I'm listening now."

"Sounds like you're glad you came."

"I sure am. This weekend at Lake Powell was worth every pothole we hit getting here."

PART V:

Their Next Twenty-Five Steps

Contents

26.	SW, ὁ-Words, σωτήρ	251
27.	SW, ὁ-Words, φύλαξ, Dictionary Forms	253
28.	SW, ἡ-Words, λαμπάς	255
29.	SW, ὁ-Words, αγών	258
30.	SW, τό-Words, γένος	260
31.	SW, ὁ-Words, βασιλεύς, πόλις	262
32.	AW, PARTs, Video Live/Active, Middle, Passive; Future Photo/Active	264
33.	AW, Future Photo/Middle and Passive	268
34.	CW, Current Photo	271
35.	CW, Previous Photo	274
36.	AW, Current Photo/Middle and Passive	275
37.	CW, Current Photo/Active, Current Photo/Small All-Around Word	277
38.	CW, Previous Photo/Active; AW, Current Photo	279
39.	AW, Normal Photo/Middle; CW Normal Photo/Middle	281
40.	CW, Normal Photo/Middle/Dim and Flashing Light	283
41.	CW, Normal Photo/Bright	285
42.	AW, Normal Photo/Active	287
43.	AW, Normal Photo/Passive/Bright Light; CW, Normal Photo/Passive	289
44.	CW, Normal Photo/Passive/Dim and Flashing Light; AW, Small All-round Word	291
45.	CW, Future Photo/Passive	293
46.	EW, Add-a-Thought Words, ὅς, ἥ, ὅ	295
47.	EW, Add-a-Thought words, ἵνα, γάρ, καί, εἰ	298
48.	CW, ποιέω, When Two Vowels Meet	300
49.	CW, τιμάω, When Two Vowels Meet	303
50.	CW, δουλόω, When Two Vowels Meet	306

Key to Abbreviations: SW=Something-Words, CW=Camera-Words, EW=Extra-Information Words, AW=All-Around Words

STEP 26

SOMETHING-WORDS		
ROLE	sing.	pl.
	ὁ σωτήρ-	
Necessary	-	-ες
General supporting	-ος	-ων
Directing	-ι	-σιν
Accomplishing	-α	-ας
See pages 65-67, Word Chart L-3		

What you need to know:
The something-words in STEPS 26-30 change their endings in very similar ways. If you closely examine the six words following σωτήρ (L-3) on the Word Chart, you'll notice the slight differences in the endings. These differences result because of the 'chemical reaction' that occurs when certain Greek letters run into each other. We have already seen examples of this 'reaction' with the extra-information words and camera-words in STEPS 17, 19, and 20.

Don't miss it:
A group of ὁ-words ending in -ρ, change their endings like σωτήρ (μάρτυς is an exception).

Give it a try:
What roles are the following words playing?
ἀέρ-ι, ἀρτέρ-ων, σωτήρ-α, χαρακτήρ-ος, ἀλέκτορ-ες, ῥήτορ-σιν, φωστήρ-ας, παντοκράτορι, Καίσαρα, ἀλέκτορες, κοσμοκράτορος, ἀστέρσιν, μάρτυσιν

Now you're the translator:
1. Ὁ κοσμοκράτωρ κελεύσει τοὺς ἡγεμόνας τῆς βασιλείας αὐτοῦ τῷ υἱῷ αὐτοῦ ἐν ὑπακοῇ δουλεύειν.   2. οἱ ἄνθρωποι θεῷ τῷ παντοκράτορι ἐν δικαιοσύνῃ δουλεύσουσιν.   3. ὁ θεὸς μάρτυς μού ἐστιν, ὅτι τὴν ἀλήθειαν λέγω.   4. οἱ ἀπόστολοι πιστοὶ κήρυκες τοῦ εὐαγγελίου τῆς σωτηρίας ἦσαν.   5. ὁ κύριος ἐν τῇ δεξιᾷ ἑπτὰ ἀστέρας ἔχει.   6. Χριστός ἐστιν ὁ σωτὴρ τοῦ κόσμου.   7. ἐγώ εἰμι τὸ ἄλφα καὶ τὸ ὦ, λέγει κύριος ὁ θεός, ὁ παντοκράτωρ.

8. ὁ Πέτρος ἐστὶν συμπρεσβύτερος καὶ μάρτυς τῶν τοῦ Χριστοῦ παθημάτων. 9. μόνῳ θεῷ σωτῆρι ἡμῶν διὰ ᾽Ιησοῦ Χριστοῦ τοῦ κυρίου ἡμῶν δόξα καὶ ἐξουσία. 10. ὁ δὲ ᾽Ιησοῦς εἶπεν αὐτοῖς· τὰ Καίσαρος ἀπόδοτε Καίσαρι καὶ τὰ τοῦ θεοῦ τῷ θεῷ.

Any questions?
Q: I'm having trouble keeping all the vocabulary in my head and when I forget a word, it takes a long time to look back through all the STEPS to find the word. How could I find words faster?
A: There is a complete list of all the vocabulary in the back of the book. It would be faster at this time to use that list to find words. In fact, why not just rip out the whole list and use it as a place marker. Then you'd always have the list handy.
Q: Rip it out?
A: Sure. The purpose of the book is to help you learn Greek. Why not get it in as handy a form as possible. If you don't like the idea of tearing out the vocabulary section, then you could photocopy it or tag it in some way, so you can turn to it quickly.

New words:

ἀήρ,ἀέρος, ὁ	air	κρίνω	judge
ἀλέκτωρ,ορος, ὁ	rooster	μάρτυς,υρος, ὁ	witness
ἀστήρ,έρος, ὁ	star	πάθημα,ματος, τό	suffering
δεξιός,ά,όν	right, right side	παντοκράτωρ, ορος, ὁ	almighty ruler
διαφέρω	differentiate	ῥήτωρ,ορος, ὁ	speaker
ἑπτά	seven	σελήνη, ἡ	moon
ἡγεμών,όνος, ὁ	prince, governor	σωτήρ,ῆρος, ὁ	savior
		φωστήρ,ῆρος, ὁ	star, radiance
Καῖσαρ,αρος, ὁ	Caesar	χαρακτήρ,ῆρος, ὁ	reproduction, trait
κοσμοκράτωρ, ορος, ὁ	world ruler		

STEP 27

SOMETHING-WORDS

ὁ φύλα-ξ

ROLE	sing.	pl.
Necessary	-ξ	-κες
General supporting	-κος	-κων
Directing	-κι	-ξιν
Accomplishing	-κα	-κας

Wordchart M-3

What you need to know:

In their dictionary forms (*necessary role/I* form), some ὁ- and ἡ-words end with ξ or ψ. In their other endings, however, ξ and ψ almost disappear. That happens because the actual stem of φύλαξ is φύλακ-. φύλακ- changes to φύλαξ because κ and ς come together. The resulting κς is the same sound as ξ (ksi), so ξ steps in and takes over. This happens again in the plural directing role when σιν is added to the stem. Once again κ and σ bump into each other and the result is ξ. The κ remains in the other endings.

This sort of thing happens all the time in Greek. Whenever κ or γ run into σ, ξ takes over, and whenever π, φ, or β run into σ, ψ takes over.

Don't forget!

The *general-supporting* form of a word gives you the major clue as to how a something-word changes its endings. That's why the ending of the general supporting role is always included after a something-word in a Greek dictionary.

φλόξ, for example, is listed like this: φλόξ, φλογός, ἡ.

φλόξ is the *necessary role/singular* form of the word, which is always the dictionary form. φλογός is the *general supporting/singular* form, which is your clue as to how φλόξ changes its endings, and ἡ tells you it's an ἡ-word.

Give it a try:

What role is each of the following words playing?

μάστιγι, νύκτα, φλογός, πτέρυξ, σαρκός, λαίλαπες, φύλαξι(ν), κήρυκας, σάλπιγγι, Φήλικα

How to Read New Testament Greek

Translate the following words:
θώρακα, κηρύκων, φύλαξι, νύκτας, Φῆλιξ, λαίλαψι, μάστιγος, φλογῶν, σαρκί, πτέρυξι, σάλπιγγες, ἀλέκτορσιν, σωτῆρα, μάρτυσιν, φωστῆρας, ἀέρος

Now you're the translator:
Οἱ στρατιῶταί εἰσιν φύλακες πρὸ τοῦ μνημείου. 2. τὰ πλοῖα ἐν τῇ λαίλαπι τῆς θαλάσσης ἦν. 3. ὁ κύριος τοὺς ἀγγέλους αὐτοῦ μετὰ σάλπιγγος ἀποστέλλει. 4. ὑμεῖς κατὰ τὴν σάρκα κρίνετε. 5. φανερὰ δέ ἐστιν τὰ ἔργα τῆς σαρκός. 6. οἱ μαθηταὶ κήρυκες τοῦ κυρίου ἐν τῇ σκοτίᾳ τοῦ κόσμου ἦσαν. 7. ἡ ἡμέρα τοῦ κυρίου ἔρχεται ὡς κλέπτης ἐν νυκτί. 8. ὁ ᾽Ιησοῦς ἐθεράπευεν ἀνθρώπους ἀπὸ τῶν νόσων καὶ τῶν μαστίγων. 9. οὐκ ἐσμεν τέκνα τῆς νυκτός, ἀλλὰ τῆς ἡμέρας· τῷ γὰρ κυρίῳ Χριστῷ δουλεύομεν. 10. ἔχουσιν θώρακας ὡς θώρακας σιδηροῦς καὶ ἡ φωνὴ τῶν πτερύγων αὐτῶν ὡς φωνὴ ἁρμάτων.

New words:

θώραξ, ακος, ὁ	armor	πτέρυξ,υγος, ἡ	wing
κῆρυξ,υκος, ὁ	proclaimer, announces	πῦρ,πυρός, τό	fire
		σάλπιγξ,ιγγος, ἡ	trumpet
λαῖλαψ, λαίλαπος, ἡ	storm	σάρξ,σαρκός, ἡ	flesh, body, human nature
μάστιξ,ιγος, ἡ	lashing, torment	φλόξ,φλογός, ἡ	flame
		φύλαξ,ακος, ὁ	guard
μνημεῖον, τό	grave	Φῆλιξ,ικος, ὁ	Felix
νύξ,νυκτός, ἡ	night	ὡς	as, like
περικεφαλαία, ἡ	helmet		

STEP 28

SOMETHING-WORDS		
ROLE	sing.	pl.
	ἡ λαμπά-ς	
Necessary	-ς	-δες
General supporting	-δος	-δων
Directing	-δι	-σιν
Accomplishing	-δα	-δας
Word Chart N-3		

What you need to know:
The stem of many ἡ- and τό-words ends in -δ or -τ. When δ or τ come together with σ, the σ simply swallows them. λαμπάδ + σ, for example, becomes λαμπάς. In the endings that follow (λαμπάδος, λαμπάδι, etc.), however, the δ reappears.

Strange but true:
These kinds of τό-words (τὸ γράμμα, for example) have no ending in the singular form of the necessary role. The τ or δ simply disappear, because in Greek a word cannot end in τ.

Give it a try:
What roles are the following words playing?
ἐλπίδι, λαμπάδα (looks like a τό-word ending, but it isn't), μυριάδες, πατρίς, βάπτισμα, γράμματα (τό-word!), κηρύγματος

Translate the following words:
πραΰτητι, σφραγῖδες, αἷμα, ῥήματος, λαμπάδων, πατρίς, μυριάσιν, πλήρωμα, βρώματα, ῥήμασιν, θελήματι, δικαιώματος, ἔριδι, ἁπλότητα, θέλημα, ὀνομάτων, στόματι, ὑποδήματα, γράμμασιν, κέρατι, ὁράματος, γόνατα

Now you're the translator:
1. Ἐνώπιον τοῦ θρόνου ἑπτὰ λαμπάδες πυρὸς ἦσαν. 2. οἱ δὲ ὀφθαλμοί αὐτοῦ ὡς φλὸξ πυρός, καὶ ἐπὶ τὴν κεφαλὴν αὐτοῦ στέφανον χρυσοῦν ἔχει. 3. οὐ γὰρ ἐστε ὑπὸ νόμον ἀλλὰ ὑπὸ χάριν. 4. οἱ ἄπιστοι οὐκ ἔχουσιν τὴν

How to Read New Testament Greek

σφραγῖδα τοῦ θεοῦ. 5. δουλεύετε ἐν ἁπλότητι τῆς καρδίας τῷ κυρίῳ. 6. ἔχετε τὸν πλοῦτον τῆς χάριτος αὐτοῦ ἐν χρηστότητι καὶ ἀγάπῃ. 7. Μαριάμ, ἔχεις τὴν ἀγαθὴν μερίδα· μακαρία εἶ. 8. ὁ Χριστὸς ἡ ἐλπίς τῆς δόξης ἐστίν. 9. καὶ ἤκουον φωνὴν ἀγγέλων, καὶ ἦν ὁ ἀριθμὸς αὐτῶν μυριάδες μυριάδων καὶ χιλιάδες χιλιάδων. 10. αἱ ἔριδες ἐν τῇ ἐκκλησίᾳ πονηρὸν μαρτύριον πρὸ τοῦ κόσμου εἰσίν. 11. πολιτεύεσθε ἐν πραΰτητι καὶ ἀγάπῃ. 12. Ὑμεῖς δὲ οὐκ ἐστε ἐν σαρκὶ ἀλλὰ ἐν πνεύματι. 13. ἡ ἐκκλησία τοῦ Χριστοῦ τὸ πλήρωμα τῶν χαρισμάτων ἔχει. 14. οἱ πιστοὶ ἀπέλουον τὰ ἱμάτια αὐτῶν ἐν τῷ αἵματι τοῦ ἀρνίου.

Any questions?
Q: We seem to run into so many exceptions to the rule. Doesn't that lead to a lot of misunderstandings?
A: All languages, including English, find ways of going against the normal flow of things. Think about how we form plurals in English: The general rule is *add an s*. But what about *children?* Or *mice?* Or *sheep?* Or *curricula?* Or *tomatoes?* Or *amphorae?*

Another general rule in English is that camera-words follow the pattern *talk, talked, talked (I talk, I talked, I have talked)*. But what about *I run, I ran, I have run?* *I sing, I sang, I have sung?* Or *I drive, I drove, I have driven?* Or *I hit, I hit, I have hit?* Sometimes, the exceptions seem to outnumber the well-behaved words that follow the rule!

Do these exceptions to the rule in English lead to misunderstandings? Do they cause children to get hopelessly confused? Do they lead to a lot of head-scratching and the need for pesky clarifications?

Not really. Each exception becomes, in a sense, a little rule unto itself; it's recognized as such, and takes its place as a member of the language in good standing.

The moral to all of this is *be patient*. Accept the exceptions and with time they will become as natural as *sing, sang, sung*.

New words:

ἀγαθωσύνη, ἡ	goodness, uprightness
αἷμα, αἵματος, τό	blood
ἁπλότης, ὁτητος, ἡ	simplicity, sincerity
βάπτισμα, ματος, τό	washing
βῆμα, βήματος, τό	judgement seat
βρῶμα, βρώματος, τό	food
γόνυ, γόνατος, τό	knee
γράμμα, ματος, τό	letter, writing
γυμνότης, ὁτητος, ἡ	nakedness, want
δικαίωμα, ώματος, τό	regulation
θέλημα, ματος, τό	will
ἐγκράτεια, ἡ	self-control
ἐλπίς, ίδος, ἡ	expectation
ἔρις, ἔριδος, ἡ τὴν ἔριν	quarrel
κέρας, κέρατος, τό	horn
κήρυγμα, ματος, τό	announcement
κρίμα, ματος, τό	judgement
λαμπάς, άδος, ἡ	lamp
μακάριος, ία, ιον	well off, fortunate

STEP 28

μακροθυμία, ἡ	patience	στόμα,ματος, τό	mouth
μερίς,ίδος, ἡ	part	σφραγίς,ίδος, ἡ	seal
μυριάς,άδος, ἡ	10,000 or large number	σῶμα,σώματος, τό	body
		ὑπόδημα,ματος, τό	sandals
ὄνομα,ματος, τό	name	χάρις,χάριτος, ἡ	grace
ὅραμα,ματος, τό	face, vision	τὴν χάριν	
πατρίς,ίδος, ἡ	fatherland	χάρισμα,ματος, τό	gift of (God's) grace
πλήρωμα,ματος, τό	fullness		
πορνεία, ἡ	evil	χιλιάς,άδος, ἡ	1000
πραΰτης,ΰτητος, ἡ	gentleness	χρηστότης,ότητος, ἡ	goodness
ῥῆμα,ῥήματος, τό	word	χρῖσμα,ματος, τό	anointing
σπέρμα,ματος, τό	seed		

STEP 29

SOMETHING-WORDS		
ROLE	sing.	pl.
	ὁ ἀγ-ών	
Necessary	-ών	-ῶνες
General supporting	-ῶνος	-ώνων
Directing	-ῶνι	-ῶσιν
Accomplishing	-ῶνα	-ῶνας
Word Chart K-5		

Strange but true!

Words like ἀγών, λεών, and ὁδούς have stems ending in -οντ. As you know from the last STEP, however, Greek words refuse to end in -τ.

ἀγών solved the problem by lengthening ο to ω and dropped the τ in *all* of its endings.

λεών followed suit by lengthening its ο to ω, but it kept the τ in its other endings.

ὁδούς took the most desperate measures: It added an -ς which resulted in -οντς. That caused three consonants to come together, however—another unacceptable situation. ὁδούς reacted by dropping the ντ and then lengthened the ο to ου. The result? ὁδούς, of course. What could be more logical than that!

Give it a try:

What roles are the following words playing?

μηνός, ποιμένες, αἰῶνα, λεόντων, ἀμπελῶσιν, ἡγεμόνα, ὁδούς, δράκοντας, κανῶνα, ἄρχουσιν, μήν, πυλῶνες, αἰών, μησίν, ποιμένων, δράκουσιν, πυλῶν

Now you're the translator:

1. Οἱ ἐργάται ἐν τῷ ἀμπελῶνι τοῦ πολίτου ἦσαν τὰς ἀμπέλους φυτεύειν. 2. ὁ δοῦλος ὑπὸ τοῦ πολίτου πρὸς τὸν ἡγεμόνα ἀποστέλλεται. 3. αἱ μάχαι αἱ ἐπίγειοι τύπος τῆς μάχης τῶν ἁγίων ἐπὶ τῆς ὁδοῦ πρὸς τὴν αἰώνιον δόξαν εἰσίν. 4. οἱ μαθηταὶ τοῦ Χριστοῦ ἀπαγγέλλουσιν τὴν χάριν τὴν σωτήριον τοῦ θεοῦ ἕως τῆς συντελείας τοῦ αἰῶνος. 5. ἦσαν ποιμένες ἐν τῇ χώρᾳ μετὰ τῶν προβάτων αὐτῶν. 6. ἡ ἐκκλησία τὸν αὐτὸν ἀγῶνα ἔχει

ὡς οἱ ἀπόστολοι τοῦ ᾽Ιησοῦ. 7. τὸ πνεῦμα τὸ ἅγιον τῆς ἐπαγγελίας ἀρραβὼν τῆς κληρονομίας ἐστίν. 8. Χριστός ἐστιν ἡ εἰκὼν τοῦ θεοῦ τοῦ κοσμοκράτορος. 9. προσεύχεσθε δὲ ἵνα μὴ γένηται ἡ φυγὴ ὑμῶν χειμῶνος μηδὲ σαββάτῳ. 10. ὁ θρόνος σου, ὁ θεός, εἰς τὸν αἰῶνα τοῦ αἰῶνος.

New words:

ἀγών,ῶνος, ὁ	contest, struggle	κανών,όνος, ὁ	standard
ἀμπελών,ῶνος, ὁ	vineyard	κληρονομία, ἡ	inheritance
αἰών,ῶνος, ὁ	age, eternity	λέων,λέοντος, ὁ	lion
ἀπαγγέλλω	report	μάχη, ἡ	fight
ἀποκαλύπτω	reveal	μήν,μηνός, ὁ	month
ἀρραβών,ῶνος, ὁ	deposit, pledge	ὀδούς,ὀδόντος, ὁ	tooth
ἄρχων,οντος, ὁ	ruler, prince	ποιμήν,ένος, ὁ	shepherd
δράκων,οντος, ὁ	dragon	προσεύχομαι	pray
εἰκών,όνος, ἡ	picture	πυλών,ῶνος, ὁ	gate
ἐνώπιον	in sight of, before	συντέλεια, ἡ	completion
		χειμών,ῶνος, ὁ	winter

STEP 30

SOMETHING-WORDS		
ROLE	sing.	pl.
	τὸ γέν-ος	
Necessary role	-ος	-η
General supporting role	-ους	-ῶν
Directing role	-ει	-εσιν
Accomplishing role	-ος	-η
Word Chart L-5		

What you need to know:
τό-words ending in -ος have endings that have little in common with the endings of any other Greek something-words. The results can be quite confusing: The singular endings of the accomplishing role (-ος), for example, look like the endings of the necessary role of words like λόγος or the singular endings of the general supporting role of words like σωτήρ (σωτέρος).

It would be much too involved to try to explain how these unusual endings came about. You just have to be aware of these individualistic τό-words, so they'll not baffle you when you run across them in a Greek text.

Give it a try:
What roles are the following words playing?
βάθος, βρέφει, κράτους, ἐθνῶν, ψεύδεσιν, ἔθους, ὄρη, σκεῦος, τέλους, μέλη, ἔτεσιν, σκότους

Add the correct form of *the* to the following words:
βάθει, βρέφους, γενῶν, ἔθνη, ἔθεσιν, ἔλεος, ἔτη, κράτει, μέλους, μέρη, ὀρῶν, πλήθους, σκεύη, σκότους, τέλει, ψεύδη

Now you're the translator:
1. Ὁ κύριος σὺν τοῖς μαθηταῖς αὐτοῦ ἐπὶ τὸ ὄρος τῶν ἐλαιῶν εἰσεπορεύετο. 2. ἐκ τοῦ βάθους τῆς φθορᾶς ὁ κύριος ἀπολύσει τὸ γένος τῶν ἁμαρτωλῶν. 3. τὰ ἔθνη τὸ εὐαγγέλιον τῆς βασιλείας ἀκουέτωσαν. 4. οἱ πιστοὶ μέλη τοῦ σώματος τοῦ Χριστοῦ καὶ ἅγια σκεύη τῆς δόξης εἰσίν. 5. τὸ πλῆθος ἐν τῷ σκότει τῆς ἁμαρτίας καὶ τοῦ ψεύδους ἦν. 6. οἱ

ἄνθρωποι κατὰ τὸ ἔθος τῆς χώρας εἰς τὸν ναὸν ἦλθον. 7. οἱ πιστοὶ βασιλεύσουσιν μετὰ Χριστοῦ χίλια ἔτη. 8. τὰ σώματα τῶν ἁγίων μέλη τοῦ Χριστοῦ ἐστιν. 9. τὸ πλῆθος τῶν ἐθνῶν τὸν λόγον τῆς ζωῆς ἤκουον. 10. ὑμεῖς δέ ἐστε σῶμα Χριστοῦ καὶ μέλη ἐκ μέρους.

New words:

βάθος,ους, τό	deep	κράτος,ους, τό	strength, power
βρέφος,ους, τό	small child	μέλος,ους, τό	member
γένος,ους, τό	generation	μέρος, ους	part
ἔθνος,ους, τό	people	οἴδατε	you know
ἔθος,ους, τό	custom	ὄρος,ους, τό	mountain
ἔτος,ους, τό	year	πλῆθος,πλήθους, τό	crowd
ἔλεος,έους, τό	compassion	σκεῦος,σκεύους, τό	dish, tool, object
εἷς, μία, ἕν	one	σκότος,ους, τό	darkness
ἔσται	he will, she will, it will	τέλος,ους, τό	goal
		χίλιοι,αι,α	thousand
καθώς	since, just as	ψεῦδος,ψεύδους, τό	lie

STEP 31

SOMETHING-WORDS						
ROLE	sing.	pl.	sing.	pl.	sing.	pl.
	ὁ ἰχθύ-ς		ὁ βασιλ-εύς		ἡ πόλ-ις	
Nec.	-ς	-ες	-εύς	-εῖς	-ις	-εις
Gen.supp.	-ος	-ων	-έως	-έων	-εως	-εων
Directing	-ι	-σιν	-εῖ	-εῦσιν	-ει	-εσιν
Accompl.	-ν	-ας	-έα	-εῖς	-ιν	-εις
	Word Chart M-5		Word Chart N-5		Word Chart O-5	

What you need to know:
A final group of something-words have stems that end with vowels.

Give it a try:
What is the *dictionary form* (*necessary role/1* form) of the following words?
ἰχθύς, ἰχθύων, ἰχθύν, ἰχθύας, ἰσχύος, ἰσχύν, ἰχθύες, μέλει, κρίσει, ἱερεῖ, ἀφέσεως, ἁλιέως, θλίψεων, ἱερέων, ἐτῶν, ψεύδεσιν, παρακλήσεσιν, γνώσεις, βασιλεῖς, βρῶσιν, καυχήσει

What roles are the following words playing?
βασιλεῖ, γραμματεύς, ἀρχιερέα, ἁλιέως, ἱερεῦσιν, ἰχθύν, γονεῦσιν, ἰσχύος, βασιλέως, ἰχθύας, διάβολος, ἔθνος, δοῦλον, ἱμάτιον, ποτήρια, σκοτία, ἐντολή, ὄρη, βρέφους, κυρίους, ἔτει, ἔχει, ἐλπίζεις, γονεῖς, χειμῶνα, σκάνδαλα

Now you're the translator:
1. Οἱ ἱερεῖς ἰσχύι τῆς καρδίας αὐτῶν τῷ θεῷ ἐν τῷ ναῷ τῷ ἁγίῳ δουλεύουσιν. 2. τὸν βασιλέα ἐν τῷ θρόνῳ τῆς δόξης βλέπετε. 3. οἱ γονεῖς τὰ τέκνα αὐτῶν ἐν τῇ ἀληθείᾳ τοῦ λόγου τοῦ θεοῦ παιδεύουσιν. 4. οἱ ἱερεῖς τῶν ἐθνῶν ἐν τῷ σκότει τῆς ἀσεβείας εἰσίν. 5. δουλεύεις τῷ θεῷ ἐξ ὅλης τῆς ἰσχύος σου. 6. οἱ ἀρχιερεῖς καὶ οἱ γραμματεῖς τῷ κηρύγματι τοῦ Ἰησοῦ οὐχ ὑπήκουον καὶ ἐκώλυον τοὺς Ἰουδαίους τῷ κυρίῳ τῆς ζωῆς δουλεύειν. 7. οἱ Ἰουδαῖοι κατὰ τὴν τάξιν αὐτῶν εἰς τὰς συναγωγὰς ἔρχονται. 8. ἡ ἐκκλησία ἐν τῇ θλίψει παράκλησιν ἐν τῷ κυρίῳ αὐτῆς ἔχει. 9. δουλεύετε ἐν πίστει καὶ σὺν ἀγαθῇ συνειδήσει τῷ κυρίῳ· ἐν αὐτῷ ἔχετε

STEP 31

τὴν ἀπολύτρωσιν, τὴν ἄφεσιν τῶν ἁμαρτιῶν ὑμῶν. 10. οἱ ἀπόστολοι μάρτυρες τῆς ἀναστάσεως Ἰησοῦ ἐκ τῶν νεκρῶν ἦσαν.

New words:

ἁλιεύς,έως, ὁ	fisherman	ἰχθύς,ύος, ὁ	fish
ἅλυσις,εως, ἡ	chain, imprisonment	καράκλησις,εως, ἡ	reminder, comfort
ἀνάστασις,εως, ἡ	resurrection	καύχησις,εως, ἡ	boasting
ἀποκάλυψις,εως, ἡ	revelation	κλῆσις,εως, ἡ	calling
ἀπολύτρωσις,εως, ἡ	liberation, redemption	κρίσις,εως, ἡ	judgement
		κτίσις,εως, ἡ	creation
ἀρχιερεύς,έως, ὁ	high priest	Μελχισέδεκ	Melchizedek
ἄφεσις,εως, ἡ	forgiveness	ὀπίσω	behind
βασιλεύς,έως, ὁ	king	ὄφις,εως, ὁ	snake
βρῶσις,εως, ἡ	eating, food	παράδοσις,εως, ἡ	tradition
γνῶσις,εως, ἡ	knowledge	παράπτωμα,ματος, τὸ	breaking rules; committing sin
γονεῖς,έων, οἱ	parents		
γραμματεύς,έως, ὁ	scribe	πέντε	five
δέησις,εως, ἡ	request	πίστις,εως, ἡ	faith
δεῦτε	come, come on	πόλις,εως, ἡ	city
δύναμις,εως, ἡ	power	πρόθεσις,εως, ἡ	intent, will
εἰ μή	if not, except	πρᾶξις,εως, ἡ	activity, action, deed
ἐπίγνωσις,εως, ἡ	knowledge		
θλῖψις,εως, ἡ	pressure, oppression	συνείδησις,εως, ἡ	conscience
		τάξις,εως, ἡ	order
ἱερεύς,έως, ὁ	priest	φύσις,εως, ἡ	nature
ἰσχύς,ύος, ἡ	power, might	ὧδε	so, here

STEP 32

ALL-ROUND WORDS			
PICTURE ⇒ ⇒ ⇒			VIDEO
ACTION	**R**OLE	**T**YPE	LIVE
A C T I V E	Nec. Gen.Supp. Dir. Accompl.	ὁ	παιδεύ-ων -ων -οντες -οντος -όντων -οντι -ουσιν -οντα -οντας
	Nec. Gen.Supp. Dir. Accompl.	ἡ	παιδεύ-ουσα -ουσα -ουσαι -ούσης -ουσῶν -ούσῃ -ούσαις -ουσαν -ούσας
	Nec. Gen.Supp. Dir. Accompl.	τό	παιδεύ-ον -ον -οντα -οντος -οντων -οντι -ουσιν -ον -οντα
			See pages 99, 101 Word Chart C-12,13,14
M I D D L E	Nec. Gen.Supp. Dir. Accompl.	ὁ	παιδευόμεν-ος -ος -οι -ου -ων -ῳ -οις -ον -ους

		παιδευόμεν-η	
Nec. Gen.Supp. Dir. Accompl.	ἡ	-η -ης -ῃ -ην	-αι -ων -αις -ας
		παιδευόμεν-ον	
Nec. Gen.Supp. Dir. Accompl.	τό	-ον -ου -ῳ -ον	-α -ων -οις -α

Word Chart L-15,16,17

Don't forget!
Thoughts are very much like videos or photos seen with the inner eyes of the mind. Three kinds of words make the pictures of thoughts possible:

1. *Something-words* play the roles: *Necessary, general supporting, directing, accomplishing.*

2. *Camera-words* take the picture according to a PLAN: *Picture, Light, Action, Necessary role.*

3. *Add-on words*, *add-on phrases,* and *add-on thoughts* add extra information.

What you need to know:
All-around words are so named, because they are able to function as a something-word, an add-on word, and—within the context of an add-on thought—as a camera-word.

As a *something-word,* an all-around word takes on the character of an ὀ-, ἡ-, or τό-word. It has three sets of endings to handle all the possible roles:

ὀ ἐρχόμενος - *the one who is coming* or *he who is coming,*
ἡ ἐρχομένη - *the one who is coming* or *she who is coming,*
τὸ ἐρχομένον* -*the one who is coming* or *that which is coming.*

How to Read New Testament Greek

Don't miss it!
A corresponding form of ὁ, ἡ, and τό almost always accompanies an all-around word when it functions as a something-word.

In English we have no words flexible enough to adequately translate a Greek all-around word alone. In the above translations of ἐρχόμενος, four kinds of English words are needed to express the meaning of one Greek all-around word: *The one* (something-word) *who* (add-a-thought word) *is* (camera-word) *coming* (all-around word).

Don't forget!
As an add-on word, an all-around word behaves just like a real add-on word (STEPS 13, 15, 17):

ὁ πιστεύων ἀδελφός - *the believing brother* or *the brother who believes*,
ἡ πιστεύουσα ἀδελφή - *the believing sister* or *the sister who believes*,
τό πιστεῦον τέκνον - *the believing child* or *the child who believes*.

Don't miss it!
An all-around word functions as a camera-word in add-on thoughts. Add-a-thought words (STEP 47) such as *while, because, since, when,* and *as* are best used to introduce the English translation.

κἀγὼ παιδεύων ὑμᾶς ἀδελφοί παιδεύω ὑμᾶς λόγοις μόνον
And **when I am training you**, brothers, I don't train you with words only.

Don't miss it!
The word *PART* helps you remember the information contained in an all-around word:

P = Picture (*live video, normal photo, future photo, current photo*)
A = Action (*active, middle, passive*)
R = Role (*necessary, general supporting, directing, accomplishing*)
T = Type (ὁ, ἡ, τό)

P and **A** (Picture and Action) are borrowed from the camera-words, **R** (Role) is borrowed from the something-words, and **T** (type) is borrowed from the extra-information words. The all-around word is truly an all-around performer.

Don't miss it:
The *future/active* form of the all-around word is formed by placing an σ between the root and the ending of the *live video/active form* of the all-around word: παιδεύων becomes παιδεύσων.

STEP 32

Give it a try:
What are the PARTs (**P**icture, **A**ction, **R**ole, **T**ype) of the following words (Example: παιδεύουσαν = *live video/active/acc.*/ ἡ-*word*): παιδεύοντι (2x), παιδευόντων (2x), παιδεύοντες, παιδεύοντα (3x), παιδεύων, παιδεῦον (2x), παιδευούσης, παιδεύουσαι, παιδευούσαις, παιδευούσῃ, παιδεύοντας, παιδεύουσαν, παιδεύουσιν (2x)

Don't miss it!
Because all-around words are part camera-word, they organize something-words into roles like any camera word. In sentence number 1 in the *Now you're the translator* section that follows, τὸν λόγον accomplishes the action of ἀκούω (not ἔκει) and τῷ θεῷ accomplishes the action of πιστεύων. The result is a unit of words that functions as one(!) something-word: ***The one who hears my word and believes my God*** has eternal life.

In the remaining sentences, there are more all-around words working together with something-words to form similar units of words.

Now you're the translator:
1. Ὁ τὸν λόγον μου ἀκούων καὶ πιστεύων τῷ θεῷ μου ἔχει τὴν αἰώνιον ζωήν. 2. βλέπομεν τὸν ἐρχόμενον ἐν ὀνόματι τοῦ κυρίου. 3. οἱ δουλεύοντες τῷ κυρίῳ μαρτυρία περὶ τοῦ κόσμου εἰσίν. 4. ὁ στρατευόμενος τὸν ἀγαθὸν ἀγῶνα δέχεται τὸν στέφανον τῆς αἰωνίου ζωῆς. 5. δουλεύετε τῷ καλῷ ποιμένι ἀπολύοντι ὑμᾶς διὰ τοῦ αἵματος αὐτοῦ ἐκ τῆς δουλείας τῆς φθορᾶς. 6. οἱ πρὸς τὸν κύριον ἐρχόμενοι τὸ πλήρωμα τῆς χάριτος δέχονται. 7. ὁ ἀκούσων τὸν λόγον τοῦ κυρίου καὶ πιστεύσων εἰς αὐτὸν τέκνον τοῦ θεοῦ ἔσται.

New words:

ἁγιότης,τητος, ἡ	holiness	περισσεύω	be abundant
ἀφθαρσία, ἡ	immortality	σαλεύω	shake
δωρεά, ἡ	present	στρατεύομαι	serve in army
θυσία, ἡ	sacrifice	ὑποτάσσω	submit, obey
κλῆμα,ματος, τό	branch, vine	φυλάσσω	guard
μορφή, ἡ	form		

STEP 33

ALL-AROUND WORDS

PICTURE ⇒⇒⇒			PHOTOGRAPH
ACTION	ROLE	TYPE	FUTURE
A C T I V E	Nec. Gen.Supp. Dir. Accompl.	ὁ	παιδεύ-σων -σων -σοντες -σοντος -σόντων -σοντι -σουσιν -σοντα -σοντας
	Nec. Gen.Supp. Dir. Accompl.	ἡ	παιδεύ-σουσα -σουσα -σουσαι -σούσης -σουσῶν -σούσῃ -σούσαις -σουσαν -σούσας
	Nec. Gen.Supp. Dir. Accompl.	τό	παιδεῦ-σον -σον -σοντα -σοντος -σοντων -σοντι -σουσιν -σον -σοντα
			Word Chart G-12,13,14
M I D D L E	Nec. Gen.Supp. Dir. Accompl.	ὁ	παιδευσόμεν-ος -ος -οι -ου -ων -ῳ -οις -ον -ους

STEP 33

		παιδευσομέν-η	
Nec. Gen.Supp. Dir. Accompl.	ἡ	-η -ης -ῃ -ην	-αι -ων -αις -ας
		παιδευσομέν-ον	
Nec. Gen.Supp. Dir. Accompl.	τό	-ον -ου -ῳ -ον	-α -ων -οις -α
		Word Chart G-15,16,17	

What you need to know:
The *future photo/middle and passive* form of the all-around word is formed by placing an σ between the root and the ending of the *live video/ middle and passive* form of the all-around word: παιδευ-όμενος = παιδευ-σ-όμενος

Give it a try:
What are the *PARTS* of the following all-around words and how would you translate them? (Example: ἐρχομένῳ = *live video/middle or passive/directing/ὁ- or τό-word*. Translation: *to/with the one who is coming*, or *to/with that which is coming*[1]):
ἐρχομένῳ (2x), ἐργαζόμεναι, ἀποκρινομένοις (2x), δεχομένης, ἀπολουομένων, πορευόμενα (2x), βουλευόμενον (3x), παυομένας, ἀποστελλόμενος, πολιτευομένοις (2x), διαφερομένου (2x), ἀποκαλυπτομένῃ, προσευχομέναις

Now you're the translator:
1. Ὁ ἐρχόμενος διὰ τῆς θύρας ποιμήν ἐστιν τῶν προβάτων. 2. ὁ ἔχων ὀφθαλμοὺς βλεπέτω. 3. ὁ ἀκούων ὑμῶν ἐμοῦ ἀκούει. 4. ὁ ἐν τούτῳ δουλεύων τῷ Χριστῷ ἄξιός ἐστιν τῆς ζωῆς τῆς αἰωνίου. 5. ἡ δόξα τῷ Χριστῷ τῷ λύοντι ἡμᾶς ἐκ τῶν ἁμαρτιῶν ἡμῶν ἐν τῷ αἵματι αὐτοῦ. 6. ἐγώ εἰμι ἡ ἄμπελος, ὑμεῖς τὰ κλήματα· ὁ μένων ἐν ἐμοὶ κἀγὼ ἐν αὐτῷ οὗτος φέρει καρπὸν πολύν.

[1] A reminder: Although ἐρχομενῳ is a middle form, it's one that has a 'departed' active form. Therefore, it is translated as though if were active.

How to Read New Testament Greek

Study tip!

How would you describe your general attitude toward Greek right now? Is it like a hobby? Is it a phase you're going through? Is it just another good thing to to be doing?

It's unlikely that any of these perspectives contain enough bedrock to support a Greek structure that will stand the test of time. Anyone who's serious about becoming proficient in Greek must develop a settled, long-range committment to the task.

It is best to approach Greek as one of the major projects of your life; comparable to getting married (forty to sixty years of relational learning), going to school (twelve to twenty years of academic learning), child raising (twenty to thirty years of pedagogical learning), or pursuing a career (thirty to fifty years of occupational learning).

If you understand this to be your commitment, then you will be content to gradually build your understanding of Greek: word by word, experience by experience, thought by thought, level by level, insight by insight—not in a hurry, but always involved in some way in the language, like a child growing up.

Viewing Greek as one of the major undertakings of your life will also motivate you to approach the language with greater thoroughness. Only then will you eventually feel 'at home' in the language and possess the confidence you will need to do responsible, accurate work in the Scriptures.

STEP 34

CAMERA-WORDS				
PICTURE ⇒ ⇒ ⇒				PHOTOGRAPH
LIGHT	ACTION	NEC. ROLE		CURRENT
B R I G H T	M I D D L E	I you he, she, it	we all of you they	πεπαιδευ-μαι I have trained myself -μαι -μεθα -σαι -σθε -ται -νται Word Chart H-3

What you need to know:

The current photo is a picture of a thought that has two sides to it. The first is an *action in the past*, and the second is a *current result*.

You may have looked at old photographs once and made the comment, *That was taken years ago; she doesn't look like that any more.* You were viewing a photo that was not up-to-date. It was not *current*.

A current photo, however, although taken in the past—most likely the very recent past—*still* depicts something or someone the way they are right now. That's the way it is with the current photo form of a Greek camera-word. It's a combination of both the past and the present.

Therefore, when translating a current photo camera-word into English, we are often forced to use two expressions to capture the full force of the Greek word: πεπαίδευμαι, *I have trained myself* (that's the past part) and *I am trained* (that's the current result part). You can sense a bit of this current idea in the English when you compare the difference between the helping words *did* and *has*. Consider, for example, the following two questions: *Did he come? Has he come?*

The first question can refer to something in the distant past: *Did he come to the party last year? Has he come?*, however, cannot be used in that context, because *has* is only for the very near past. Try it once: *Has he come last year?* See how strange that sounds. *Has he come?* just can't refer to something that far in the past. In fact, *Has he come?* is so near to the present that it can easily be exchanged with a present question such as *Is he here?* That's what the current photo does; it says *Has he come?* and *Is he here?* at the same time.

How to Read New Testament Greek

Don't miss it:
The *current photo* form of a camera-word, in addition to having a new set of endings, often *doubles* its beginning consonant: πεπαίδευμαι.
There are these exceptions to the rule:
1. If the first letter of a camera-word is φ, χ, or θ, it is "doubled" correspondingly with π, κ, and τ. φετεύω becomes πεφυτευ..., for example.
2. If the word begins with the consonants στ, ζ, ξ, or ψ, doubling does not take place. Only an ε is added: ψευδόμαι becomes εψευ...
3. If the first letter is a vowel, the vowel is lengthened: ἀκούω becomes ἤκου...
4. If a camera-word begins with an add-a-phrase word, then the doubled consonant is added *between* the add-a-phrase word and the camera-word: απολύω becomes απολέλυμαι.

Give it a try:
What's the PLAN (Picture, Light, Action, Necessary role) of the following words? How would you translate them?
Example: λέλουμαι = current photo, bright, mid/pass, I. Translation: *I have washed myself and am still washed (I'm clean!):*
πεπαίδευμαι, πεπαίδευσθε, πεπαιδεύμεθα, πεπαίδευσαι, λέλουμαι, βεβούλευσαι, κεκώλυνται, πεπορεύμεθα (departed form), λέλυται, πεπαύμεθα (departed form)

What's the PA (*Picture* and *Action*) of the following *small all-around* words? (Example: ἔχειν = live video/active):
ἠκοῦσθαι, δουλεύσειν, ἔχειν, πεπιστεῦσθαι, ἀπολελοῦσθαι, κελεύειν, ἀναπεπαῦσθαι, δέξεσθαι (from δεχ-σεσθαι) κωλύσειν, νηστεύειν

What's the PLAN of the following words?
ἤκουες, βλέπεται, πεπαίδευσαι, λέγουσιν, ἀπολέλυται, βασιλεύοντος, βουλεύσῃ, ᾐρηνεύετε, τεθεραπεύμεθα, ἐκυρίευεν, λατρεύσομεν, νήστευε, μνημονεύετε (2x), κεκώλυμαι, ὑπακούοντες, ἤλπιζον (2x), λαμβάνοντι, ἀπεστέλλετε, ἐργαζομένῃ, ἔρχονται, εἰσερχώμεθα, ἐπορεύοντο, ἀπεκρινόμην, δέχου, ἀπολέλουται, κελεύεις, βουλεύσεσθαι, πεφόνευνται, μοιχεύουσα, διεφέρετε, κρίνητε, ἀποκαλύπτων.

Now you're the translator:
1. Ἀναπέπαυται τὸ πνεῦμα αὐτοῦ ἀφ' ὑμῶν. 2. ἀδελφοί, ἐγὼ συνειδήσει ἀγαθῇ πεπολίτευμαι τῷ θεῷ ἄχρι ταύτης τῆς ἡμέρας. 3. γύναι, ἀπόλυσαι τῆς ἀσθενείας σου. 4. ἄνθρωποι ἀπὸ πνευμάτων πονηρῶν καὶ ἀσθενειῶν τεθεράπευνται ὑπὸ τοῦ Ἰησοῦ. 5. αἱ ἁμαρτίαι ἡμῶν οὐκ ἀπολέλουνται ἐν αἵματι τῶν μόσχων ἀλλ' ἐν αἵματι τοῦ Ἰησοῦ Χριστοῦ τοῦ υἱοῦ τοῦ θεοῦ. 6. οἱ πτωχοὶ διὰ τῆς πράξεως τῆς ἀγάπης ἀναπέπαυνται. 7. διὰ τῆς ἀναστάσεως Ἰησοῦ ἐκ τῆς δουλείας τῆς ἁμαρτίας καὶ ἐκ τῆς κρίσεως

ἀπολέλυσθε. 8. ἀπολελύμεθα ἀπὸ τῆς δουλείας τῆς ἐπιγείου ἀνομίας ὑπὸ τῆς ἐπουρανίου ἀληθείας.

New words:

ἄγω	lead, bring to	καθαρός,ά,όν	clean
ἄχρι	until	κάλαμος, ὁ	reed, writing instrument
βάλλω	throw		
ἔνδυμα,ματος, τό	clothing	κωφός	deaf
ἐνδύομαι	clothe oneself	μόσχος, ὁ	calf
ἐνδύω	dress	πνευματικός,ή,όν	spiritual
θυσιαστήριον, τό	altar	πράσσω	do

STEP 35

CAMERA-WORDS			
P ICTURE ⇒⇒⇒			PHOTOGRAPH
L IGHT	A CTION	N EC. ROLE	PREVIOUS
B R I G H T	M I D D L E	I we you all of you he, she, it they	ἐπεπαιδεύ-μην I had trained myself -μην -μεθα -σο -σθε -το -ντο Word Chart I-3

What you need to know:
The *previous photo* form of a camera-word depicts a thought that precedes another thought. Example: *We **had spoken** with one another, before the phone rang.* It expresses what happened *previous to* the ringing of the phone.

Don't miss it:
In addition to the double consonant (as with the *current photo*), an ε is also added to the front of the *previous photo* form of a camera-word. The only exceptions to this rule are words beginning with a vowel, in which case the vowel is simply lengthened (as with the *current photo*).

Give it a try:
What is the PLAN of the following words, and how would you translate them? (Example: ἐπεπαιδεύμεθα = *previous photo/bright/middle or passive/we*. Translation: *We had trained ourselves* [middle sense] or *We had been trained* [passive sense]): ἐπεπαίδευσο, ἐβεβούλευτο, ἐπεφύτευντο, ἐκεκωλύμεθα, ἀπελελούμην, εἰσεπεπόρευσθε.

Now you're the translator:
1. Οἱ ἄρχοντες ἐβεβούλευντο καὶ ἐστράτευντο κατὰ τῶν ἐχθρῶν. 2. διὰ τῆς παρακλήσεως τοῦ πρεσβυτέρου ἀνεπεπαύμεθα. 3. οἱ ἄνθρωποι ἀπὸ τῶν νόσων ὑπὸ Ἰησοῦ ἐτεθεράπευντο. 4. ἀπελέλυσθε ὑπὸ τοῦ βασιλέως ὑμῶν ἐκ τῆς ἀρχῆς τοῦ ἐχθροῦ.

STEP 36

ALL-AROUND WORDS

P I C T U R E ⇒ ⇒ ⇒			PHOTOGRAPH	
ACTION	**R**OLE	**T**YPE	CURRENT	
MIDLE & PASSIVE	Nec. Gen.Supp. Dir. Accompl.	ὁ	πεπαιδευμέν-ος -ος -ου -ῳ -ον	-οι -ων -οις -ους
	Nec. Gen.Supp. Dir. Accompl.	ἡ	πεπαιδευμέν-η -η -ης -ῃ -ην	-αι -ων -αις -ας
	Nec. Gen.Supp. Dir. Accompl.	τό	πεπαιδευμέν-ον -ον -ου -ῳ -ον	-α -ων -οις -α
Word Chart H-15,16,17				

What you need to know:

The *current photo/middle* and *passive* forms of the all-around word usually have the doubled consonant (with the exceptions as listed in STEP 34) and the very same endings as the *live video, middle/passive* form of the all-around word.

How to Read New Testament Greek

Give it a try:
What are the *PARTS* (**P**icture, **A**ction, **R**ole, **T**ype) of the following all-around words? (Example: δεχομένης = live video/medium or passive/gen. supp./ἡ-word): ἀκουσόμενοι, βλεπομένη, πεπιστευμένου (2x), ἀπολελυμέναις, βουλευομένῳ, τεθεραπευμένην, πεφυτευμένον, κωλυσόμεναι, λαμβανόμενα, πεπορευμένων (3x), δεχομένης, λελουμένοις (2x), λυσομένη, ἀναπεπαυμένους

Strange but true!
Sometimes the previous photo form of a camera-word is replaced by the current photo form of an all-around word and a form of εἰμί. (Example: λόγοι τῆς σωτηρίας ἐν τῇ χώρᾳ τῆς Γαλιλαίας ἡκουμένοι ἦσαν.)

Now you're the translator:
1. Καὶ ὁ βασιλεὺς ἔβλεπεν ἄνθρωπον οὐκ ἐνδεδυμένον ἔνδυμα γάμου. 2. λόγοι τῆς σωτηρίας ἐν τῇ χώρᾳ τῆς Γαλιλαίας ἡκουμένοι ἦσαν.

STEP 37

CAMERA-WORDS			
P ICTURE ⇒ ⇒ ⇒			PHOTOGRAPH
L IGHT	A CTION	N EC. ROLE	CURRENT
B R I G H T	A C T I V E	I we you all of you he, she, it they	πεπαίδευ-κα I have trained -κα -καμεν -κας -κατε -κεν -κασιν See page 77 Word Chart H-2

What you need to know:

The *active* form of a camera-word depicting a *current photo* has the doubled consonant as does the medium and passive form, and endings that are characterized by the addition of a κ.

The exceptions to the doubled consonants discussed in STEP 34 are also true of the active form.

The *current photo* form of the *small all-around word* (Word Chart H-21) also has a κ in the ending.

Don't miss it!

In addition to depicting a past act and its current result, current photo forms of a camera-word are also used to emphasize or strengthen the meaning of the camera-word.

Give it a try:

What is the PLAN of the following words and how would you translate them? (Example: ἤλπικεν = *current photo/bright/active/he, she, it.* Translation: *he has believed and still believes* or *he believes strongly.*): πεπαίδευκας, πεπιστεύκαμεν, δεδουλευκέναι, ἀπολελύκασιν, τεθεραπεύκατε, ἠρηνεύκασιν, λελατρευκέναι, κεκώλυκα, ἤλπικεν, λελουσκέναι.

How to Read New Testament Greek

What's the PLAN of these words? ἔβλεπον, γράφων, ἤκουσαι, λαμβανέτω, ἔχετε (2x), ἐλέγετο, πεπαιδευκέναι, φεῦγε, πεπιστεύκασιν, ἐλπίζομαι, ἀπέστελλες, ἤρχου, ἐπεπορεύμην, ἀποκρίνεσθαι, λούσοντες, δεχομένου, ἐβεβούλευντο, λύσῃ, μοιχεύωσιν.

Now you're the translator:
1. Δεδουλεύκαμεν τῷ κυρίῳ τῆς δόξης ἐν πίστει καὶ ἀγάπῃ. 2. οἱ ἄνθρωποι τῶν πόλεων καὶ τῶν κωμῶν τῷ ἀληθινῷ λόγῳ τῆς αἰωνίου ζωῆς πεπιστεύκασιν. 3. ὁ κύριος τοὺς κωφοὺς καὶ τοὺς τυφλοὺς τεθεράπευκεν. 4. ἀκηκόατε τοῦ ἀποστόλου περὶ τῆς εἰς τὸν Χριστὸν Ἰησοῦν πίστεως. 5. οἱ γονεῖς τὰ τέκνα αὐτῶν ἐν τῇ ἀληθείᾳ τῆς πίστεως πεπαιδεύκασιν.

Any questions?
Q: How should I know if a current photo form of a camera-word is emphasizing the meaning or not?
A: Unfortunately I can't give you an easy rule to follow. The context, however, plays the key role in determining which translation is preferred.
Q: What kind of context would be an example of emphasis?
A: Consider the following exchange:
"You mean you believe that?"
"I **certainly do believe** it."
That's an example of a context that calls for a translation emphasizing the camera-word.

New words:

ἀγγελία, ἡ	message	μήτηρ, ἡ	mother
ἀναγγέλλω	report	οὐδεμία	not one
γινώσκω	know, recognize	φῶς, τό	light
θυγάτηρ, ἡ	daughter		

STEP 38

CAMERA-WORDS			
P ICTURE ⇒⇒⇒			PHOTOGRAPH
LIGHT	ACTION	NEC. ROLE	PREVIOUS
B R I G H T	A C T I V E	I we you all of you he, she, it they	ἐπεπαιδεῖ-κειν I had trained -κειν -καιμεν -κεις -κειτε -κει -κεισαν See page 78 Word Chart I-2

What you need to know:
The *previous photo/bright/active* form of a camera-word adds an ε to the double consonant at the beginning of the word as is the case with the *medium and passive* form. The same exceptions concerning the added ε and the double consonant discussed in STEP 35 are also true of the active form.

Don't forget!
Previous photos depict an action *previous* to another action.

Give it a try:
What's the PLAN of the following words? ἐδεδουλεύκεις, ἐπεπιστεύκεισαν, ἀπελελύκειμεν, ἐτεθεραπεύκει, ἐπεφυτεύκειν

Don't miss it!
The *current photo/active* form of the all-around word (Word Chart H-12,13,14), also has the κ in the endings.

Now you're the translator:
1. Ὁ πατὴρ τὰ τέκνα αὐτοῦ ἐν εὐσεβείᾳ καὶ ὑπακοῇ ἐπεπαιδεύκει. 2. ὁ βασιλεὺς τοὺς ἄνδρας ἐκ τῶν χειρῶν τοῦ ἐχθροῦ ἀπελελύκει. 3. αἱ μητέρες τὰς θυγατέρας αὐτῶν ἐκεκελεύκεισαν τῷ λόγῳ τοῦ ἀληθινοῦ μάρτυρος πιστεύειν. 4. διὰ θλίψεως εἰσπεπόρευσθε εἰς τὴν βασιλείαν τοῦ θεοῦ· τῷ γὰρ κυρίῳ τῆς δόξης ἐδεδουλεύκειτε ἐν ἁπλότητι καὶ ἀγαθωσύνῃ. 5. τὸ

τέλος τῶν ὁδῶν τοῦ θεοῦ σὺν τοῖς πιστοῖς ἀπολελουκόσιν τὰς ἁμαρτίας αὐτῶν διὰ τοῦ αἵματος ᾽Ιησοῦ δόξα τῆς αἰωνίου ζωῆς ἐστιν. ὁ πεπιστευκὼς τῷ λόγῳ τοῦ κήρυκος ἐκ τοῦ φόβου ἀπολέλυται. 6. ἔλεγεν οὖν ὁ ᾽Ιησοῦς πρὸς τοὺς πεπιστευκότας αὐτῷ ᾽Ιουδαίους· ἐὰν ὑμεῖς μείνητε ἐν τῷ λόγῳ τῷ ἐμῷ, ἀληθῶς μαθηταί μού ἐστε. 7. ὁ πιστεύων εἰς αὐτὸν οὐ κρίνεται· ὁ μὴ πιστεύων ἤδη κέκριται, ὅτι μὴ πεπίστευκεν εἰς τὸ ὄνομα τοῦ μονογενοῦς υἱοῦ τοῦ θεοῦ.

Any questions?
Q: Could you give me some help with sentence 5?
A: It's probably confusing because of the general supporting words and the add-on phrases between τέλος and δόξα.

The basic thought is quite simple. Begin with the camera-word: ἐστιν = *it is*. Now, where is the word in the necessary role? There are two: τέλος and δόξα. This shouldn't surprise us because we know εἰμί is also completed with a word in the necessary role (STEP 8).

What is the thought then? τὸ τέλος ἐστιν δόξα, *The goal is glory.*

The fifteen words between τέλος and δόξα just support τέλος or add extra information to it: **The goal** *of the ways of God with those who have faithfully washed away their sins and are clean* (current photo meaning!) *through the blood of Jesus* **is the glory** *of eternal life.*

New Words:

αἰτία, ἡ	cause, guilt	πατήρ, ὁ	father
ἀνήρ, ὁ	man	χείρ, ἡ	hand
λειτουργία, ἡ	service (cultic)		

STEP 39

PICTURE ⇒⇒⇒			PHOTOGRAPH
ACTION	ROLE	TYPE	NORMAL
M I D D L E	Nec. Gen.Supp. Dir. Accompl.	ὁ	παιδευσάμεν-ος -ος -οι -ου -ων -ῳ -οις -ον -ους
	Nec. Gen.Supp. Dir. Accompl.	ἡ	παιδευσαμέν-η -η -αι -ης -ων -ῃ -αις -ην -ας
	Nec. Gen.Supp. Dir. Accompl.	τό	παιδευσάμεν-ον -ον -α -ου -ων -ῳ -οις -ον -α
Word Chart E-15,16,17			

What you need to know:

The *normal photo* form of a camera-word depicts a particular *aspect* of a thought. To illustrate what this means, let's say you've taken your camera to a track meet. First you take a picture of the *beginning* of a race. The photo shows eight runners coming out of the starting blocks. Next, you choose a wide-angle lens for a *panorama* shot of the whole track field. Then you fit the camera with a telephoto lens in time to capture a *close-up of the winner breaking the tape.*

Each picture is an *aspect* of the track meet. The *normal photo* form of a Greek camera-word depicts pictures of thoughts in a similar way: ἐπίστευσα, *I believed*

How to Read New Testament Greek

(the start in view), ἐπαίδευσα τὸν τέκνον, *I raised the child* (the whole panorama in view), ἀπέθανεν, *He died* (the end in view, obviously).

In other words, *normal photos* depict aspects of thoughts that are bundled together into *one* picture (I believed) as opposed to the video recording which depicts the continuous action of a moving picture (I was believing).

Don't miss it:

The *normal photo/middle* form of a camera-word (Word Chart E-3) has an ε on the front and a new set of endings.

The *normal photo* form of the all-around word and the small all-around word (Word Chart E-21) also depict the *normal-photo* aspects of a thought.

Give it a try:

What's the PLAN of the following camera-words and how would you translate them? ἠκούσατο, ἀπελυσάμην, ἐθεραπεύσασθε, ἐκωλυσάμεθα, ἐλούσαντο, ἐπαύσω, ἐβλέψατο (ψ from επ+σ), ἐβουλεύσω, ἀναπαύσασθαι, πολιτευσάμενος, ἀποκαλύψασθαι (ψ from πτ+σ), παιδευσαμέναις

What are the PARTs (Picture, Action, Role, Type) of the following all-around words? παιδευσαμένῳ, ἀπολυσάμενοι, θεραπευσαμένης, κωλύσαμένου

Translate the following camera-words, making sure to differentiate between the *video recording* forms and the *normal photo* forms: ἐβουλευσάμην πορεύεσθαι, ἐβουλευόμην τὸν φίλον, ἐκωλυσάμεθα λόγῳ, ἐκωλυόμεθα ἐν τῇ ὁδῷ, ἀπελούσατο ἀπὸ τῶν ἁμαρτιῶν, ἀπελούετο ἐν τῷ ποταμῷ

Now you're the translator:

1. ʹΕβουλεύσατο καὶ ἐστρατεύσατο ἐν τῇ νυκτὶ κατὰ τῶν ἐχθρῶν. 2. ἐπολιτευσάμεθα ἐν ἁπλότητι τῶν καρδιῶν ἡμῶν. 3. οὐ κατὰ σάρκα ἀλλὰ κατὰ λόγον τοῦ θεοῦ ἐστρατεύσω. 4. οἱ πρεσβύτεροι τῆς ἐκκλησίας ἐβουλεύσαντο ὑπὲρ τῆς ἀληθείας τοῦ λόγου στρατεύσασθαι. 5. δουλεύωμεν ἐν ἀληθείᾳ τῷ κυρίῳ ἐνδυσάμενοι θώρακα τῆς ἀγάπης καὶ περικεφαλαίαν ἐλπίδα σωτηρίας. 6. ἐπολιτεύσασθε κατὰ τὸν κανόνα τῆς ζωῆς. 7. ἐγεύσασθε ὅτι χρηστὸς ὁ κύριος. 8. ἐρρύσατο ἡμᾶς ἐκ τῆς ἐξουσίας τοῦ σκότους καὶ μετέστησεν εἰς τὴν βασιλείαν τοῦ υἱοῦ τῆς ἀγάπης αὐτοῦ, ἐν ᾧ ἔχομεν τὴν ἀπολύτρωσιν, τὴν ἄφεσιν τῶν ἁμαρτιῶν. 9. ὃς ἐκ τηλικούτου θανάτου ἐρρύσατο ἡμᾶς καὶ ῥύσεται. 10. καὶ χρόνῳ ἱκανῷ οὐκ ἐνεδύσατο ἱμάτιον, καὶ ἐν οἰκίᾳ οὐκ ἔμενεν.

New words:

ἀπεκδύομαι	undress, disarm	ῥύομαι	save
γεύομαι	taste	χρηστός,ή,όν	good
μνῆμα,ματος, τό	grave, tomb		

STEP 40

CAMERA-WORDS

PICTURE ⇒⇒⇒			PHOTOGRAPH
LIGHT	ACTION	NEC. ROLE	NORMAL
D I M	M I D D L E	I we you all of you he, she, it they	παιδεύ-σωμαι so I'd start training myself -σωμαι -σώμεθα -ση -σησθε -σηται -σωνται Word Chart E-6
F L A S H I N G	A C T I V E	you all of you he, she, it they	παίδευ-σον start training -σον -σατε -σάτω -σάτωσαν See page 79 Word Chart E-8
F L A S H I N G	M I D D L E	you all of you he, she, it they	παίδευ-σαι start training yourself -σαι -σασθε -σάσθω -σάσθωσαν Word Chart E-9

What you need to know:

When the normal photo is taken in *dim light* (possibility), it still depicts an *aspect* of the picture of a thought. The following example compares a *video live/*

How to Read New Testament Greek

dim light form of παιδεύω with a *normal photo/ dim light* form:

...ἵνα παιδεύῃ (video live) = *so you'd be training yourself,*
...ἵνα παιδεύσῃ (normal photo) = *so you'd train yourself.*

The same is true of the *flashing light* forms:
παιδεύου (video live/flashing) = *train yourself, you should be training yourself, keep on training yourself.*
παιδεύσαι (normal photo/ flashing) = *train yourself, start training yourself.*

Give it a try:
What's the PLAN of the following camera-words and how would you translate them? ἀκουσάσθω, δουλεύσασθε, βλεψάσθωσαν (ψ from π+σ), παίδευσαι, θεραπευσάσθωσαν, βούλευσαι, φυτεύσασθε, κωλυσάσθω, λούσηται, ἀναπαύσωμαι, ἀποκαλύψωνται (ψ from πτ+σ), φονεύσῃ (2x), λύσησθε, γραψώμεθα (ψ from φ+σ), ἀπολύσηται.

Now you're the translator:
1. Ὁ ἑκατοντάρχης τοῖς στρατιώταις ἔλεγεν, ἵνα ἀναπαύσωνται ἔτι χρόνον μικρόν. 2. ταῦτα ἐγράφομεν αὐτῷ, ἵνα τὸν ἀγαθὸν ἀγῶνα στρατεύσηται. 3. ἐνδυσώμεθα τὸν θώρακα τῆς δικαιοσύνης. 4. μὴ ἐνδύσησθε δύο χιτῶνας. 5. ἀναπαύσασθε ἀπὸ τῶν ἔργων ὑμῶν. 6. φύτευσαι τὰ δένδρα ἐν τοῖς ἀγροῖς. 7. ἀναπαύσασθε ὀλίγον. 8. πολιτεύσασθε κατὰ τὸ εὐαγγέλιον ἐν πραΰτητι καὶ ἀγάπῃ. 9. ἐνδύσασθε τὸν κύριον Ἰησοῦν Χριστόν. 10. οἵ τινες οὐ μὴ γεύσωνται θανάτου ἕως ἂν ἴδωσιν τὸν υἱὸν τοῦ ἀνθρώπου ἐρχόμενον ἐν τῇ βασιλείᾳ αὐτοῦ.

New words:

ἅμα	at the same time, together	λίαν	wholly, very much
διάνοια, ἡ	thought, understanding, plan	οὐ μή	not, by no means
		οὖν	therefore
δύο	two	παιδεία, ἡ	upbringing, training
κακός,ή,όν	evil, bad	χιτών,ῶνος, ὁ	tunic, shirt
κοινός,ή,όν	commonality	χωλός,ή,όν	lame

STEP 41

CAMERA-WORDS			
PICTURE ⇒⇒⇒			PHOTOGRAPH
LIGHT	**A**CTION	**N**EC. ROLE	NORMAL
B R I G H T	A C T I V E	I we you all of you he, she, it they	ἐπαίδευ-σα I trained -σα -σαμεν -σας -σατε -σεν -σαν See page 77 ; Word Chart E-2

Give it a try:
What's the PLAN of the following camera-words and how would you translate them? (Example: εθεράπευσαν = *normal photo/bright/active/they*. Translation: *They healed*...): ἐπίστευσας, ἠκούσαμεν, ἐβλέψατε (ψ from π+σ), ἐβασίλευσα, ἐβούλευσεν, ἐθεράπευσαν, ᾐρήνευσα, ἐκυρίευσαν, ἐλάτρευσεν, νηστευσάτω, φυτεῦσαι, μνημονεύσατε, κωλυσάτωσαν, ὑπάκουσον, λοῦσαι (2x, flashing + all-around), λῦσον (2x, flashing + all-around), ἔπαυσαν

Now you're the translator:
1. Ἀπὸ τῆς ἡμέρας ἐβουλεύσατο τὸν δοῦλον ἀπολῦσαι. 2. ἐκέλευσα ὑμᾶς ἐνδύσασθαι τὰ καινὰ ἱμάτια. 3. ὁ Φῆλιξ ἤκουσεν αὐτοῦ περὶ τοῦ Χριστοῦ (περὶ τῆς ὁδοῦ τῆς ζωῆς). 4. ἐδούλευσαν σὺν ἐμοὶ ἐν τῷ εὐαγγελίῳ. 5. ἦλθεν γὰρ Ἰωάννης πρὸς ὑμᾶς ἐν ὁδῷ δικαιοσύνης, καὶ οὐκ ἐπιστεύσατε. 6. δουλευσάτω μετὰ χαρᾶς τῷ υἱῷ τοῦ θεοῦ. 7. ὁ ἀμνὸς ἄξιός ἐστιν λῦσαι τὰς σφραγίδας. 8. ἐβασίλευσεν ὁ θάνατος ἀπὸ Ἀδὰμ μέχρι Μωϋσέως. 9. καὶ ἐνέδυσαν αὐτὸν τὰ ἱμάτια αὐτοῦ. 10. ἐξελθὼν ἔξω ἔκλαυσεν πικρῶς.

New words:
ἐγγύς	near	ἔξωθεν	from outside
ἐγγύτερον	nearer	ἔσωθεν	from inside
εἴτε...εἴτε	whether...or	κλαίω	weep, cry
ἔξεστιν	it is permitted, it is possible	(κλαι- /κλαυ-)	
		μέχρι	until
ἔξω	outside		

Μωϋσῆς, Μωϋσέως	Moses
νομικός, ή, όν	concerning the law
νομικός, ὁ	lawyer
ὅτε	when, while
οὕτως	so
πῶς	how

STEP 42

ALL-AROUND WORDS				
PICTURE ⇒⇒⇒			PHOTOGRAPH	
ACTION	**R**OLE	**T**YPE	NORMAL	
A C T I V E	Nec. Gen.Supp. Dir. Accompl.	ὁ	παιδεύ-σας -σας -σαντες -σαντος -σάντων -σαντι -σασιν -σαντα -σαντας	
	Nec. Gen.Supp. Dir. Accompl.	ἡ	παιδεύ-σασα -σασα -σασαι -σάσης -σασῶν -σάσῃ -σάσαις -σασαν -σάσας	
	Nec. Gen.Supp. Dir. Accompl.	τό	παιδεῦ-σαν -σαν -σαντα -σαντος -σάντων -σαντι -σασιν -σαν -σαντα	
			Word Chart E-12,13,14	

Give it a try:

What's the PLAN of the following camera-words and how would you translate them? (Example: θεραπεύσωσιν = *normal photo/dim/active/they.* Translation: *so they'd heal...*): σαλεύσῃς, θεραπεύσωσιν, μνημονεύσητε, νηστεύσῃ, βουλεύσωμεν, εἰρηνεύσω (2x)

What are the PARTs of the following all-around words and how would you translate them? (Example: πιστεύσασιν = *normal photo/active/directing/ἡ-word.* Translation: *to the one (her) who believed* or *with the one (her) who believed*):

How to Read New Testament Greek

Translation: *to the one (her) who believed* or *with the one (her) who believed*):
ἀκούσαντος, πιστεύσασιν, δουλεύσαντες, βλέψαντας, φονευσάντων, λατρεύσασα, κωλυσάσαις, ὑπακούσαντι, λούσαντες, λυσάσας

Now you're the translator:
1. Ταῦτα λέγομεν ὑμῖν, ἵνα πιστεύσητε ὅτι ᾽Ιησοῦς ὁ Χριστός ἐστιν. 2. αὕτη ἐστὶν ἡ ἐντολὴ αὐτοῦ, ἵνα πιστεύσωμεν τῷ ὀνόματι τοῦ υἱοῦ αὐτοῦ. 3. ὁ κύριος εἰς τὸν κόσμον ἦλθεν, ἵνα λύσῃ τὰ ἔργα τοῦ διαβόλου. 4. ἵνα ὥσπερ ἐβασίλευσεν ἡ ἁμαρτία ἐν τῷ θανάτῳ, οὕτως ἡ χάρις βασιλεύσῃ διὰ δικαιοσύνης εἰς ζωὴν αἰώνιον διὰ ᾽Ιησοῦ Χριστοῦ τοῦ κυρίου ἡμῶν. 5. ἐν ᾧ καὶ ὑμεῖς, ἀκούσαντες τὸν λόγον τῆς ἀληθείας, τὸ εὐαγγέλιον τῆς σωτηρίας ὑμῶν, ἐν ᾧ καὶ πιστεύσαντες ἐσφραγίσθητε τῷ πνεύματι τῆς ἐπαγγελίας τῷ ἁγίῳ. 6. τῷ ἀγαπῶντι ἡμᾶς καὶ λύσαντι ἡμᾶς ἐκ τῶν ἁμαρτιῶν ἡμῶν ἐν τῷ αἵματι αὐτοῦ, καὶ ἐποίησεν ἡμᾶς βασιλείαν, ἱερεῖς τῷ θεῷ καὶ πατρὶ αὐτοῦ, αὐτῷ ἡ δόξα καὶ τὸ κράτος εἰς τοὺς αἰῶνας τῶν αἰώνων· ἀμήν. 7. εὐχαριστοῦμεν τῳ θεῷ πατρὶ τοῦ κυρίου ἡμῶν ᾽Ιησοῦ Χριστοῦ πάντοτε περὶ ἡμῶν προσευχόμενοι ἀκούσαντες τὴν πίστιν ὑμῶν ἐν Χριστῷ ᾽Ιησοῦ καὶ τὴν ἀγάπην.

New words:
εἶπον	I said, they said	πλήν	nevertheless, but
εἶτα	then, next	σφραγίζω	seal
ἐκεῖ	there	τότε	then, at that time
ἐπειδή	when, after, since	χαίρω	be glad
ἤμην	I was	ὥσπερ	as
πάντοτε	always		

STEP 43

ALL-AROUND WORDS				
PICTURE ⇒⇒⇒			PHOTOGRAPH	
ACTION	**R**OLE	**T**YPE	NORMAL	
P A S S I V E	Nec. Gen.Supp. Dir. Accompl.	ὁ	παιδευ-θείς -θείς -θέντες -θέντος -θέντων -θέντι -θεῖσιν -θέντα -θέντας	
	Nec. Gen.Supp. Dir. Accompl.	ἡ	παιδευ-θεῖσα -θεῖσα -θεῖσαι -θείσης -θεισῶν -θείσῃ -θείσαις -θεῖσαν -θείσας	
	Nec. Gen.Supp. Dir. Accompl.	τό	παιδευ-θέν -θέν -θέντα -θέντος -θέντων -θέντι -θεῖσιν -θέν -θέντα	
			Word Chart E-18,19,20	

What you need to know:

The *normal photo* form of an all-around word has a *passive* form that is not identical with the *medium* form. It is easily recognizable by the θ in the ending.

The same is true of the *normal photo* form of the camera-word (Word Chart E-4).

How to Read New Testament Greek

Give it a try:
The following words are a mixture of camera-words and all-around words. What's the PLAN (**P**icture, **L**ight, **A**ction, **N**ecessary role) of the camera-words and what are the PARTs (**P**icture, **A**ction, **R**ole, **T**ype) of the all-around words? ἐπαιδεύθημεν, ἀπελύθη, ἐθεραπεύθησαν, ἐνεδύθην, κωλυθέντος, ἐσαλεύθην, λουθέντες, ἀνελύθη, παυθέν, ἀπολουθέντα, λυθείς, φονευθέντας, ἐβλέφθησαν (φ from π), ἠργάσθη (σ from ζ, ἀποκαλυφθέντων (φ from πτ).

Now you're the translator:
1. Οἱ πόδες καὶ αἱ χεῖρες μέλη τοῦ σώματός εἰσιν. 2. τοῦτο τὸ γένος ὦτα ἔχει ἀκούειν, καὶ οὐκ ἀκούει τοὺς λόγους τοῦ θεοῦ, καὶ ὀφθαλμοὺς ἔχει βλέπειν, καὶ οὐ βλέπει τὰ ἔργα τοῦ κυρίου. 3. βλέπετε τοὺς κύνας, βλέπετε τοὺς κακοὺς ἐργάτας. 4. ὁ κύριος καὶ ὁ σωτὴρ ἡμῶν τὰς κλεῖς τοῦ θανάτου ἔχει. 5. πολλοὶ ἄνθρωποι ἐν Γαλιλαίᾳ ὑπὸ ᾽Ιησοῦ ἐθεραπεύθησαν. 6. αἱ βίβλοι καὶ αἱ ἐπιστολαὶ τῆς ἐκκλησίας ὑπὸ τῶν ζηλωτῶν ἐν τῷ πυρὶ πρὸ τῆς πύλης ἐκαύθησαν. 7. ἐκεῖνο τὸ τέκνον τὸ μικρὸν ὑπὸ τῆς μητρὸς ἐν τῷ ὕδατι τοῦ ποταμοῦ ἐλούθη. 8. ὁ ἀνὴρ θεραπευθεὶς ὑπὸ ᾽Ιησου ἦλθεν εἰς τὴν ἐκκλησίαν. 9. οἱ πυλῶνες τῆς πόλεως διὰ τὸν ἐχθρὸν ἐκλείσθησαν. 10. καὶ αἱ φρόνιμοι εἰσῆλθον μετ᾽ αὐτοῦ εἰς γάμους, καὶ ἐκλείσθη ἡ θύρα.

New words:
δυνατός,ή,ό	strong, powerful	κύων, ὁ	dog
θύω	sacrifice	οὖς, τὸ	ear
καίω (και-/καυ-)	burn	πάσχα, τὸ	passover
κατακαίω	burn down	πούς, ὁ	foot
κλείς, ἡ	key	πύλη, ἡ	gate, door
κλείω	close	ὕδωρ, τὸ	water

STEP 44

CAMERA-WORDS			
PICTURE ⇒⇒⇒			PHOTOGRAPH
LIGHT	ACTION	NEC. ROLE	NORMAL
D I M	P A S S I V E	I we you all of you he, she, it they	παιδευ-θῶ (so) I'd be trained -θῶ -θῶμεν -θῇς -θῆτε -θῇ -θῶσιν Word Chart E-7
F L A S H I N G	P A S S I V E	you all of you he, she, it they	παιδεύ-θητι start being trained -θητι -θητε -θήτω -θήτωσαν Word Chart E-10

Don't forget!

Translate a *normal photo* so that the resulting thought-picture is really a photo and not a video. Remember that there's more than one way to do this. (There's always more than one way to take a photo of something). *Start being trained*, for example, or *Be trained*. The first translation zeroes in on the *beginning* of the process, whereas the second includes the beginning, the end, and everything in the middle.

Give it a try:

How would you translate the following words? παιδευθῶσιν, βλεφθῇς, ἀπολυθήτωσαν, φυτευθῇ, θεραπευθῶμεν, κωλύθητε, λούθητι, ἀναλυθῆναι, ἐπαύθην

How to Read New Testament Greek

Now you're the translator:
1. Τάδε λέγει ὁ υἱὸς τοῦ θεοῦ, ὁ ἔχων τοὺς ὀφθαλμούς ὡς φλόγα πυρός, καὶ οἱ πόδες αὐτοῦ ὅμοιοι χαλκολιβάνῳ. 2. καὶ ἦν Ἰωάννης ἐνδεδυμένος τρίχας καμήλου. 3. ἡ γυνὴ δὲ δόξα ἀνδρός ἐστιν. οὐ γάρ ἐστιν ἀνὴρ ἐκ γυναικός, ἀλλὰ γυνὴ ἐξ ἀνδρός. 4. ὧδε ἡ σοφία ἐστίν· ὁ ἔχων νοῦν ψηφισάτω τὸν ἀριθμὸν τοῦ θηρίου. 5. Οὐκ ἦλθεν ὁ υἱὸς ἀνθρώπου δουλευθῆναι ἀλλὰ δουλεῦσαι.

New words:
γυνή, ἡ	woman	νοῦς, ὁ	understanding, mind
θηρίον, τό	animal	οἴδαμεν	we know
θρίξ, ἡ	hair	σκηνή, ἡ	tent, dwelling
κάμηλος, ἡ	camel	σκῆνος, ους, τό	tent, dwelling
καταλύω	destroy		

STEP 45

CAMERA-WORDS			
P ICTURE ⇒⇒⇒			PHOTOGRAPH
LIGHT	ACTION	NEC. ROLE	FUTURE
B R I G H T	P A S S I V E	I we you all of you he, she, it they	παιδευ-θήσομαι I will be trained -θήσομαι -θησόμεθα -θήσῃ -θήσεσθε -θήσεται -θήσονται Word Chart G-4

What you need to know:
The future photo form of a camera-word also has a passive form that is not identical with the medium form. Like the normal photo, it is also characterized by a θ in the ending.

Give it a try:
The following words are a mixture of camera-words, all-around words, and small all-around words. Identify them and determine their PLAN (camera-words), PARTs (all-around words), or PAs (small all-around words): παιδευθήσεσθε, παιδευθήσεσθαι, παιδευθησόμενοι, ἀπεκδυθήσομαι, καταλυθησομένου, κλεισθήσεται, καυθήσεσθαι (from καίω), ἀκουσθήσῃ, ἀπολυθησομέναις, φυτευθήσονται

Do the same with the following words from previous STEPS:
παιδεύομαι, παιδευσόμεναι, ἐπαίδευον (2x), παιδεῦσαι (different than παίδευσαι), πεπαίδευσαι, ἐπεπαιδεύκειν, παιδεύωσιν, παιδευθήσεσθαι, ἐπαιδευσάμην, ἐπαιδεύοντο, πεπαιδευκυίᾳ, ἐπεπαίδευσο, παιδεύῃ (3x), παιδεύσεσθαι, παίδευε, παίδευσον, (different than παιδεῦσον), παιδεύσαντος, παιδεύσει

Now you're the translator:
1. Οἱ μάρτυρες τοῦ ἀληθινοῦ εὐαγγελίου ἐκωλύθησαν ὑπὸ τῶν ἐχθρῶν τοῦ θεοῦ· ἐν τῇ ἡμέρᾳ τῆς σωτηρίας αἰωνίῳ χαρᾷ ὑπὸ τοῦ κυρίου αὐτῶν

ἀναπαυθήσονται. 2. τὰ ἔργα τὰ πονηρὰ τῶν ἀνθρώπων ἐν τῷ πυρὶ τῆς αἰωνίου κρίσεως καυθήσεται. 3. ἰδοὺ μυστήριον ὑμῖν λέγω· πάντες οὐ κοιμηθησόμεθα, πάντες δὲ ἀλλαγησόμεθα, ἐν ἀτόμῳ, ἐν ῥιπῇ ὀφθαλμοῦ, ἐν τῇ ἐσχάτῃ σάλπιγγι. 4. καὶ οἱ νεκροὶ ἐγερθήσονται ἄφθαρτοι, καὶ ἡμεῖς ἀλλαγησόμεθα. 5. καὶ κηρυχθήσεται τοῦτο τὸ εὐαγγέλιον τῆς βασιλείας ἐν ὅλῃ τῇ οἰκουμένῃ εἰς μαρτύριον πᾶσιν τοῖς ἔθνεσιν, καὶ τότε ἥξει τὸ τέλος.

New words:

ἀλλάσσω	change	κηρύσσω	proclaim
ἄτομος,ον	indivisible	κοιμάομαι	sleep
ἄφθαρτος,ον	immortal	μακράν	far
ἐγείρω	wake up, rise	μακρόθεν	from far away, from a distance
ἔσονται	they will be		
ἔσχατος,η,ον	last	πᾶς, πᾶσα, πᾶν	each, all
ἥξει	the time will come	ῥιπή, ἡ	throw
ἰδού	see	σεισμός, ὁ	earthquake

STEP 46

EXTRA-INFORMATION WORDS

Role	Type	singular		plural
	ὁ		ὅς	
Nec.		-ός	who, which	-οί
Gen.Supp		-οῦ	whose	-ῶν
Dir.		-ῷ	to whom, to which	-οῖς
Accompl.		-όν	whom, which	-οῦς
	ἡ		ἡ	
Nec.		-ή	who, which	-αί
Gen.Supp		-ῆς	whose	-ῶν
Dir.		-ῇ	to whom, to which	-αῖς
Accompl.		-ήν	whom, which	-άς
	τό		ὅ	
Nec.		-ό	who, which	-ά
Gen.Supp		-οῦ	whose	-ῶν
Dir.		-ῷ	to whom, to which	-οῖς
Accompl.		-ό	whom, which	-ά

See pages 92-94; Word Chart K-18,19,20

Don't forget:
There are three kinds of extra-information words:
1. Add-on words: *the **big** man, he ran **quickly***
2. Add-on phrases: *the man **with a hat**, he ran **with agility***
3. Add-on thoughts: *the man **who walks with a limp***

What you need to know:
The clause *who walks with a limp* is an add-on *thought,* because it contains a camera-word. Only a camera-word is capable of taking a picture of a thought.

How to Read New Testament Greek

Add-on thoughts are introduced by *add-a-thought words*, the most common of which are ὅς, ἥ, and ὅ.

ὁ ἄνθρωπος ὅς - *the man who...*
ὁ ἄνθρωπος οὗ - *the man whose...*
ὁ ἄνθρωπος ᾧ - *the man to whom...*
ὁ ἄνθρωπος ὅν - *the man whom...*

ἡ γυνή ἥ - *the woman who...*
ἡ γυνή ἧς - *the woman whose...*
ἡ γυνή ᾗ - *the woman to whom...*
ἡ γυνή ἥν - *the woman whom...*

τὸ τέκνον ὅ - *the child who...*
τὸ τέκνον οὗ - *the child whose...*
τὸ τέκνον ᾧ - *the child to whom...*
τὸ τέκνον ὅ - *the child whom...*

Give it a try:
Which Greek add-a-thought word could be used to replace the underlined words? (Example: The man **whose** cat... = οὗ): The woman **whose** child..., The child **to whom** I gave..., The men **that** I saw..., The men **whose** children are..., The children **to whom** we gave...The women **who** went to...
What role are the following add-on-thought words playing and how would you translate them? ᾧ (2x), ἧς, ὧν (3x), οἵ, αἷς, ἡ, ἅ (2x), ὅς, ᾗ, ὅν (1x), ὅ (2x), οὕς, αἵ, οὗ (2x), ἥν, ἅς.

Now you're the translator:
1. Ὁ παράκλητος ὅν δεχόμεθα ἀπ' αὐτοῦ, τὸ πνεῦμα τὸ ἅγιον ἐστιν. 2. οἱ ἄνθρωποι οἵ οὐ πιστεύουσιν εἰς τὸν κύριον ὑπὸ τὴν ὀργὴν τοῦ θεοῦ μένουσιν. 3. ἀκούεις τοὺς λόγους τῶν ἀποστόλων οὕς ἐκεῖνοι πρὸ τοῦ πλήθους λέγουσιν. 4. καὶ ἄλλα πρόβατα ἔχω ἅ οὐκ ἔστιν ἐκ τῆς αὐλῆς ταύτης. 5. μάρτυς γάρ μού ἐστιν ὁ θεός ᾧ λατρεύω ἐν τῷ πνεύματί μου ἐν τῷ εὐαγγελίῳ τοῦ υἱοῦ αὐτοῦ. 6. ἡ ἐντολὴ ἡ παλαιά ἐστιν ὁ λόγος ὅν ἠκούσατε

New words:
ἀκολουθέω	follow	ἔμπροσθεν	in front, before
ἀμήν	truly, amen	ἐξομολογέω	promise
ἀναχωρέω	leave	ἐπιζητέω	look for, research
αὐλή, ἡ	courtyard	ἐπιτελέω	end, complete, fulfill
γέγονεν	he was, it happened		
διακονέω	serve	εὐλογέω	bless, praise
ἐλεέω	have compassion	εὐχαριστέω	give thanks

STEP 46

ζητέω	search
ζωοποιέω	make alive
ἦλθον	I came, they came
θεωρέω	see, observe
καλέω	call
κατανοέω	notice, observe, consider
κατοικέω	live in
κοσμέω	order, decorate
λαλέω	speak, say
μαρτυρέω	testify
μετανοέω	change one's mind, repent
νοέω	understand, recognize, be reasonable
ὁμολογέω	admit, confess
πενθέω	lament, be sad
περιπατέω	walk about
πλουτέω	be rich
ποιέω	do
προσκαρτερέω	be faithful, devoted
πρότερος,ἐρα,ον	earlier, before
πρῶτος,η,ον	first
συζητέω	discuss, dispute
τελέω	complete, finish
ὑστερέω	be late, miss
ὠφελέω	use, Pass: to be useful

STEP 47

EXTRA-INFORMATION WORDS

ADD-A-THOUGHT WORDS

ἀλλά- but   ὅπου- wherever
γάρ- because   ὅταν- when
ἐάν- if   ὅτι- that, because
ἵνα- in order that ὡς- as
καί- and   ὥστε- so that
μέχρι- until

See pages 93-94, Word Chart L-18,19

What you need to know:

Some *add-a-thought* words like ὅς *(who)* and ὅπου *(where)* add a thought to another word. *The man **who** likes me. The place **where** I live.* Others, however, add a thought to another thought. These are words like ἵνα *(so that)*, γάρ *(because)*, καί *(and)*, and ὥστε *(therefore, in order to)*.

Some, like καί, express *association*:
    *He went shopping **and** bought himself a shirt.*
Some, like ἵνα, express *purpose*:
    *He went shopping, **in order to** buy a shirt.*
Some, like γάρ, express *cause*:
    *He went shopping, **because** he had to buy a shirt.*
Some, like εἰ or ἐάν, express a *condition*:
    ***If** he goes shopping, he'll buy a shirt.*
Some, like ὥστε, express *result*:
    *He needed a shirt, **so** he went shopping.*
Some, like μήποτε, express a *warning* or *negative results:*
    He's going shopping for a shirt,
    ***otherwise** he'll have to wear an old one.*

Don't miss it!

Notice how each thought introduced by these add-a-thought words, adds information to the *entire* sentence and not just to a something-word or to a camera-word.

STEP 47

Now you're the translator:
1. πίστευον ἐπὶ τὸν κύριον Ἰησοῦν, καὶ σωθήσῃ σὺ καὶ ὁ οἶκός σου. 2. ἡμεῖς ἠκούσαμεν ἐκ τοῦ νόμου ὅτι ὁ Χριστὸς μένει εἰς τὸν αἰῶνα, καὶ πῶς λέγεις σὺ ὅτι δεῖ ὑψωθῆναι τὸν υἱὸν τοῦ ἀνθρώπου; 3. ὡς ἐπαύσατο, εἶπέν τις τῶν μαθητῶν αὐτοῦ πρὸς αὐτόν· κύριε, δίδαξον ἡμᾶς προσεύχεσθαι. 4. μὴ εἰσενέγκῃς ἡμᾶς εἰς πειρασμόν, ἀλλὰ ῥῦσαι ἡμᾶς ἀπὸ τοῦ πονηροῦ. 5. ἐὰν ὑμεῖς μείνητε ἐν τῷ λόγῳ τῷ ἐμῷ, ἀληθῶς μαθηταί μού ἐστε. 6. ταῦτα λέγομεν ὑμῖν, ἵνα πιστεύσητε ὅτι Ἰησοῦς ὁ Χριστός ἐστιν. 7. ἐν Χριστῷ ἤδη τὸν πλοῦτον τοῦ οὐρανοῦ ἔχομεν· τῷ γὰρ λόγῳ τοῦ θεοῦ πιστεύομεν.

New words:

ἀλλά	but, rather, nevertheless,	εἴτε	then	ὅτε	when
γάρ	because, for	ἤ	or, than	ὅτι	because, that
δέ	and, but	ἵνα	in order that	οὖν	therefore, then
διό	therefore	καί	and, also, even	τέ	and
ἐάν	if			ὡς	as
εἰ μή	if not	μήποτε	lest, otherwise	ὥστε	so that
		ὅταν	whenever		

STEP 48

WHEN TWO VOWELS MEET: ε-

LIGHT	ACTION	LIVE VIDEO	
B R I G H T	ACTIVE	ποιέ+ω = ποι-ῶ	
		-ῶ	-οῦμεν
		-εῖς	-εῖτε
		-εῖ	-οῦσιν
	MEDIUM and PASSIVE	ποιέ+ομαι = ποι-ούμαι	
		-οῦμαι	-ούμεθα
		-ῇ	-εῖσθε
		-εῖται	-οῦνται
D I M	ACTIVE	ποιέ+ω = ποι-ῶ	
		-ω	-ῶμεν
		-ῃς	-ῆτε
		-ῃ	-ῶσιν
	MEDIUM and PASSIVE	ποιέ+ωμαι = ποι-ῶμαι	
		-ωμαι	-ώμεθα
		-ῃ	-ῆσθε
		-ηται	-ῶνται
F L A S H I N G	ACTIVE	ποίε+ε = ποί-ει	
		-ει	-εῖτε
		-είτω	-είτωσαν
	MEDIUM and PASSIVE	ποιέ+ου = ποι-οῦ	
		-οῦ	-εῖσθε
		-είσθω	-είσθωσαν

What you need to know:

Some camera-words have stems that end with a vowel. When the various endings are added to these words, two vowels often come together. You have already learned (STEPS 17, 19) what happens when two Greek vowels bump into each other. Here's an overview of the changes that occur when a stem ending in ε comes together with other vowels.

ε + ε = ει   ε + ει = ει
ε + η = η   ε + ῃ = ῃ
ε + ο = ου   ε + ου = ου
ε + ω = ω   ε + οι = οι

Give it a try:
What's the PLAN of the following words? ποιεῖς, ἐποίεις, ποιῶ (2x), ποιοῦμεν, ἐποίησας, ποιεῖν, ποιήσουσιν, ποίει, ποιήσαντι, ποιεῖτε (2x), πεποιήκαμεν, ἐποίουν (2x), ἐπεποιήκειν, ποιοῦσιν (2x; 1x all-around), ποιείτωσαν, πεποιηκόσιν, ἐποιεῖτε, ποιῇς, ποιῶσιν, ποιήσω (2x),ποιείτω

Now you're the translator:
1. Ἐν ἀρχῇ ἐποίησεν ὁ θεὸς τὸν οὐρανὸν καὶ τὴν γήν. 2. εὐχαριστῶ τῷ θεῷ μου διὰ Ἰησοῦ Χριστοῦ περὶ πάντων ὑμῶν. 3. ὁ ποιῶν τοὺς ἀγγέλους αὐτοῦ πνεύματα καὶ τοὺς λειτουργοὺς αὐτοῦ πυρὸς φλόγα. 4. ἀμὴν ἀμὴν λέγω ὑμῖν, ὁ πιστεύων εἰς ἐμὲ τὰ ἔργα, ἃ ἐγὼ ποιῶ, κἀκεῖνος ποιήσει, καὶ μείζονα τούτων ποιήσει, ὅτι ἐγὼ πρὸς τὸν πατέρα πορεύομαι. 5. Ἰωάννης μαρτυρεῖ περὶ αὐτοῦ λέγων· οὗτος ἦν, ὃν εἶπον· ὁ ὀπίσω μου ἐρχόμενος ἔμπροσθέν μου γέγονεν, ὅτι πρῶτός μου ἦν. 6. ἀκούσας τὴν καθ᾽ ὑμᾶς πίστιν ἐν τῷ κυρίῳ Ἰησοῦ καὶ τὴν ἀγάπην τὴν εἰς πάντας τοὺς ἁγίους, οὐ παύομαι εὐχαριστῶν ὑπὲρ ὑμῶν μνείαν ποιούμενος ἐπὶ τῶν προσευχῶν μου. 7. ἔλεγεν δὲ πρὸς τοὺς κεκλημένους παραβολήν. 8. ὁ υἱὸς τοῦ ἀνθρώπου οὐκ ἦλθεν διακονηθῆναι, ἀλλὰ διακονῆσαι καὶ δοῦναι τὴν ψυχὴν αὐτοῦ λύτρον ἀντὶ πολλῶν. 9. ἐστὲ ἐπιστολὴ Χριστοῦ διακονηθεῖσα ὑφ᾽ ἡμῶν. 10. ἐκλήθη δὲ καὶ ὁ Ἰησοῦς καὶ οἱ μαθηταὶ αὐτοῦ εἰς τὸν γάμον.

New words:

ἀκολουθέω	follow	εὐχαριστέω	give thanks
ἀμήν	truly, amen	ζητέω	search
ἀναχωρέω	leave	ζωοποιέω	make alive
αὐλή, ἡ	courtyard	ἦλθον	I came, they came
γέγονεν	he was, it happened	θεωρέω	see, observe
διακονέω	serve	καλέω	call
ἐλεέω	have compassion	κατανοέω	notice, observe, consider
ἔμπροσθεν	in front, before		
ἐξομολογέω	promise	κατοικέω	live in
ἐπιζητέω	look for, research	κοσμέω	order, decorate
ἐπιτελέω	end, complete, fulfill	λαλέω	speak, say
εὐλογέω	bless, praise	μαρτυρέω	testify

μετανοέω	change one's mind, repent
νοέω	understand, recognize, be reasonable
ὁμολογέω	admit, confess
πενθέω	lament, be sad
περιπατέω	walk about
πλουτέω	be rich
ποιέω	do
προσκαρτερέω	be faithful, devoted
πρότερος,έρα,ον	earlier, before
πρῶτος,η,ον	first
συζητέω	discuss, dispute
τελέω	complete, finish
ὑστερέω	be late, miss
ὠφελέω	use, Pass: to be useful

STEP 49

WHEN TWO VOWELS MEET: α-			
LIGHT	ACTION	LIVE VIDEO	
B R I G H T	ACTIVE	τιμά+ω = τιμ-ῶ -ῶ -ῶμεν -ᾷς -ᾶτε -ᾷ -ῶσιν	
	MIDDLE and PASSIVE	τιμά+ομαι = τιμ-ῶμαι -ῶμαι -ώμεθα -ᾷ -ᾶσθε -ᾶται -ῶνται	
D I M	ACTIVE	τιμά+ω = τιμ-ῶ -ῶ -ῶμεν -ᾷς -ᾶτε -ᾷ -ῶσιν	
	MIDDLE and PASSIVE	τιμά+ωμαι = τιμ-ῶμαι -ῶμαι -ώμεθα -ᾷ -ᾶσθε -ᾶται -ῶνται	
F L A S H I N G	ACTIVE	τίμα+ε = τίμ-α -α -ᾶτε -άτω -άτωσαν	
	MIDDLE and PASSIVE	τιμά+ου = τιμ-ῶ -ῶ -ᾶσθε -άσθω -άσθωσαν	

What you need to know:
   Here's an overview of the changes that occur when a stem ending in α comes together with other vowels.

How to Read New Testament Greek

α + ε = α   α + ει = ᾳ
α + η = α   α + ῃ = ᾳ
α + ο = ω   α + ου = ω
α + ω = ω   α + οι = ῳ

Give it a try:
What's the PLAN, PARTs, or PA of the following words and how would you translate them? (Example: νικῶσαι = all-around word = *video live/active/ necessary role/ἡ-word*. Translation: *the ones who are winning*): νικᾶτε (2x), νικῶ (3x), ἐνικώμην, νικᾶσθε (2x), νικᾷ (3x), νικᾷς (2x), νικάτω, νικώμεθα (2x), νικάσθω, ἐνίκων, νικᾶν, νικωμένων, νικῶσιν (2x), νικᾶσθαι, νικᾶται (2x), ἐνίκων (2x), νικῶντα, νικῶσαι, νικῶνται, ἐνίκα

Now you're the translator:
1. Καὶ ἀγαπήσεις κύριον τὸν θεόν σου ἐξ ὅλης τῆς καρδίας σου καὶ ἐξ ὅλης τῆς ψυχῆς σου καὶ ἐξ ὅλης τῆς ἰσχύος σου. 2. πολλαῖς τιμαῖς ἐτίμησαν ἡμᾶς. 3. καὶ πολλοὶ ψευδοπροφῆται πλανήσουσιν πολλούς. 4. ὁ μὴ ἀγαπῶν μένει ἐν τῷ θανάτῳ. 5. ἀγαπήσας τοὺς ἰδίους τοὺς ἐν τῷ κόσμῳ, εἰς τέλος ἠγάπησεν αὐτούς. 6. καὶ ἐβόησεν ὁ ᾽Ιησοῦς φωνῇ μεγάλῃ. 7. ἐσίγησεν δὲ πᾶν τὸ πλῆθος. 8. ἐν γὰρ Χριστῷ ᾽Ιησοῦ διὰ τοῦ εὐαγγελίου ἐγὼ ὑμᾶς ἐγέννησα. 9. ἐπιστάτα, δι᾽ ὅλης νυκτὸς κοπιάσαντες οὐδὲν ἐλάβομεν ἐπὶ δὲ τῷ ῥήματί σου χαλάσω τὰ δίκτυα. 10. ὁ οὖν ἀρχιερεὺς ἠρώτησεν τὸν ᾽Ιησοῦν περὶ τῶν μαθητῶν αὐτοῦ καὶ περὶ τῆς διδαχῆς αὐτοῦ.

New words:

ἀγαλλιάω	rejoice	κλάω	break (bread), begin meal
ἀγαπάω	love		
βοάω	holler, call	κοπιάω	work hard, become weary
γελάω	laugh		
γεννάω	conceive, bear	κἀγώ	and I
ἐάω	let, allow	νικάω	win
ἐπερωτάω	ask, request	οὐχί	not (emphasized οὐ)
ἐπιστάτης,ου, ὁ	master	πεινάω	be hungry
ἐπιτιμάω	rebuke, have a serious talk with	πλανάομαι	deceive oneself
		πλανάω	deceive
		πλούσιος,ία,ιον	rich
ἐρωτάω	ask, request	προσδοκάω	expect
ζάω	live	προσέχω	pay attention to, concern oneself with
θεάομαι	see, observe		
ἰάομαι	heal, restore	σιγάω	be silent
ἴδιος,ία,ιον	own	σιωπάω	be silent, still
κατανάω	come to, arrive	ταπεινός,ή,ον	humble
καυχάομαι	boast	ταπείνωσις, ἡ	humility

STEP 49

τελευτάω	die
τιμάω	honor
τολμάω	dare
ὑπαντάω	come towards, meet
χαλάω	let down
χράομαι	use

STEP 50

WHEN TWO VOWELS MEET: ο-

LIGHT	ACTION	VIDEO-LIVE	
B R I G H T	ACTIVE	δουλό+ω = δουλ-ῶ	
		-ῶ	-οῦμεν
		-οῖς	-οῦτε
		-οῖ	-οῦσιν
	MIDDLE and PASSIVE	δουλό+ομαι = δουλ-οῦμαι	
		-οῦμαι	-ούμεθα
		-οῖ	-οῦσθε
		-οῦται	-οῦνται
D I M	ACTIVE	δουλό+ω = δουλ-ῶ	
		-ῶ	-ῶμεν
		-οῖς	-ῶτε
		-οῖ	-ῶσιν
	MIDDLE and PASSIVE	δουλό+ωμαι = δουλ-ῶμαι	
		-ῶμαι	-ώμεθα
		-οῖ	-ῶσθε
		-ῶται	-ῶνται
F L A S H I N G	ACTIVE	δούλο+ε = δούλ-ου	
		-ου	-οῦτε
		-ούτω	-ούτωσαν
	MIDDLE and PASSIVE	δουλό+ου = δουλ-οῦ	
		-οῦ	-οῦσθε
		-ούσθω	-ούσθωσαν

STEP 50

What you need to know:
Here's an overview of the changes that occur when a stem ending in o comes together with other vowels.

o + ε = ου   o + ει = οι
o + η = ω   o + ῃ = οι
o + ο = ου   o + ου = ου
o + ω = ω   o + οι = οι

Give it a try:
What's the plan of the following camera-words? ζηλῶ (2x), ζηλοῦνται, ζηλοῦν, ζηλῶν, ἐζήλουν (2x), ζηλοῦται, ζηλῶμεν, ζηλοῦτε (2x), ἐζηλοῦ, ζηλοῖς (2x), ζηλοῦσθε (2x), ζηλώμεθα, ἐζήλου, ζηλοῖ (4x).

Now you're the translator:
1. Ζηλοῦτε δὲ τὰ χαρίσματα τὰ μείζονα. 2. ἦν δὲ ὥρα τρίτη καὶ ἐσταύρωσαν αὐτόν. καὶ ἦν ἡ ἐπιγραφὴ τῆς αἰτίας αὐτοῦ ἐπιγεγραμμένη· Ο ΒΑΣΙΛΕΥΣ ΤΩΝ ΙΟΥΔΑΙΩΝ. 3. καὶ γνώσεσθε τὴν ἀλήθειαν, καὶ ἡ ἀλήθεια ἐλευθερώσει ὑμᾶς. 4. τίνι δὲ ὁμοιώσω τὴν γενεὰν ταύτην. 5. ἀλλ᾽ ὅτι ταῦτα λελάληκα ὑμῖν, ἡ λύπη πεπλήρωκεν ὑμῶν τὴν καρδίαν.

New words:

γενεά, ἡ	generation	ὁμοιόω	make the same
γνώσεσθε	you will recognize	οὔπω	not yet
δέδωκας	you gave	πάρεστιν	he (it) is present
ἐλευθερόω	free	πληρόω	fulfill
ἐπιγραφή, ἡ	inscription	σταυρόω	crucify
ἕτοιμος	ready	τρίτος	third
ζηλόω	strive		
νομίζω	mean, assume, believe		

307

PART VI:

What They're Thinking after a Year

The Interview

"Harmon! Glad to have you back in the valley. And you brought Louise along, too. Wonderful that both of you could come. And...would you look who's coming up the walk: Liz, home from a summer in Europe. Welcome back!"

Dean was manning the front door. In full cry he was directing guests into the living room. It had been over five months since the Greek learners had last met together. In the meantime, the scalding Arizona summer had moved in, forcing those who could to flee to the mountains or to cooler regions of the North. Although temperatures hadn't noticeably subsided, the opening of school doors signaled the return of most travelers.

"Linda, quick, come here, you won't believe who just drove up."

Linda broke off a conversation and made her way to the front door just as Marian Lawson stepped in.

"Marian! What a surprise." They hugged each other. "We thought you'd be in Wyoming for at least another month."

"Oh, it was one of those spur-of-the-moment things, you know. The Hansens decided to come down early, so I hitched a ride with them." A wide smile on her face, Marian made her way around the room, jovially greeting one after the other.

There was so much news to be shared, that it was a good half hour before Dean took advantage of a slight drop in the intensity of the chatter to start the meeting. "Almost exactly a year ago," he said, "we began the process of learning Greek, and throughout the year, Linda and I tried to stay in close contact with each of you. As we shared your struggles and watched your efforts to solve many different kinds of problems, we saw each of you learning valuable lessons—so valuable, in fact, that we felt they were well worth sharing with the others. That explains why I sent each of you a letter asking you to prepare answers to a number of specific questions which we would then use in an interview this evening.

"I'd like to begin with Jim. In his letter I asked him to share how he's approached the whole matter of how to use *time*, a topic that should get us into the nitty-gritty real quick. That okay with you, Jim?"

"Mr. Nitty-Gritty at your service."

"We all know you've got many demands on your time, Jim, so it will interest us to know how well you've managed to wedge learning Greek into a tight schedule."

"I'd better start by setting the books straight. I know it may look like my time is pretty tied up, but I think the major thing I've learned in this past year is that my problem with time was more myth than reality. Meeting men like you, Harmon and John got me to looking at the way I use my time in a much different way. All of you had jobs and you didn't let those jobs keep you from doing a lot of meaningful things with your time. It didn't take a lot of soul-searching to convince myself that my problems didn't come from a lack of time, but from a screwy set of priorities."

"Would you tell us exactly what you mean by *soul-searching, Jim*? Did you go for long walks in the desert? How did you come to the conclusion your priorities were wrong?"

"I actually used a bit of advice you gave me once: I decided to determine how I was using my time by keeping exact records over a period of several months. During each day of those months, I jotted down exactly what I did during every fifteen minutes of every day. Then I put the data on a spreadsheet and worked up a time profile."

"That must have taken a lot of time itself," said John.

"It did, but it turned out to be a good investment. The result was rather sobering. I'd always thought of myself as being quite well-organized, but the facts showed I was slopping a lot of time down the drain. Basically my profile showed a man who got time-conscious as soon as he went to work, but who turned into a time-shredder everywhere else. Considering how much organizational effort I pumped into those hours at the office and how little I invested in the other areas of my life, the result was rather logical. I was forced to ask myself why I had let things go so badly at home, and why I had no meaningful concept for my free time. I concluded that deep inside, I believed that if I put in a lot of hours at the office, then I'd earned myself the right to sort of let myself go for the rest of the day—take it easy and pamper myself a bit, if you know what I mean."

"Can't imagine it," said John, shaking his head.

"Sure," Jim grinned, "I know it's a pretty typical thing, and I suppose that's why I never thought it too strange. The point is, however, that I never thought of it as killing time. It was like time I thought I had coming to me; if I felt like wasting it, then that was my business. After all, I'd paid for it with the sweat of my brow. I would probably never have said anything like that to anyone, but basically, that was my attitude."

"But I don't think you're saying you wasted *all* of your free time," said Dean, "You've always been real involved in your church, for example, and done a lot with the youth there."

"But my survey showed I spent more time with magazines and newspapers than with the kids. The amount of quality time I actually spent with them was pretty meager. I did just enough to make sure Jim Garvey had a decent paint job."

"How did you approach the whole matter of making changes in your use of time?"

"If you don't mind my using computer language, *delete* and *insert* are the two words that come to mind. It was obvious to me that if I wanted to insert more meaningful things into my schedule, I had to make room for them by deleting the unnecessary things."

"Can you give us an example?"

"An example? Well, I decided to cut back on the amount of time I spend on the job, and surprisingly, it turned out to be a fairly easy decision to implement. It was just a matter of delegating some of the work at the office, and letting a few other people have bigger pieces of the pie. The major difficulty I had to overcome was one of perspective. The problem, as I see it now, is that I've always associated real work with the kind of work that makes money. Nothing else ever qualified as work for me. I've had to learn that some of the most important kinds of work we can do will never result in a paycheck—at least not the kind we can deposit in a bank. There never was anything wrong about my putting in ten-, twelve-, or even fourteen-hour work days. It's the *way* I was spending those hours that was the problem. I never got around to working at the really important things like raising my kids or learning the Scriptures or helping my neighbors. Those big jobs were treated more like games."

"Would you be willing to reveal any of the other items on your 'delete' list?"

"Sure, there's no secrets. It's just embarrassing that the list is so long and still growing. There's the time I spend doing work on the house, for example, and the time I spend *thinking* about the work I would like to do on the house. Not half of it is really necessary. I've just spent too many years trying to be the Jones that everyone else is supposed to keep up with, and I'm having trouble getting it out of my system. There's also all the meetings and social engagements I have. There's more show than substance behind a lot of it.

"Then there's my sport life which is supposed to keep me healthy and fit, but sometimes I think I spend more time driving to the tennis club than actually playing tennis. And speaking of driving, that's another item on the list. The way we use the car is...well, *childish*. We're in the habit of driving distances that just aren't necessary. We'll put on thirty miles just to go to a fast food place. It's insane when you think about it."

"Could I break in and make a comment?" Marian asked. "Listening to Jim, I just have to say something about the whole matter of time wasting."

"Sure. We'd like to hear what you have to say."

"You all know it's a favorite pastime of us old folks to point a finger at the younger generation, often complaining about the way young people use their time. But when it comes to using time, some of us old fogies don't set much of an example. We busy ourselves with this, occupy our time with that, and are often tickled pink if we manage to fill up our day, even if it's with the silliest things. And I can talk about it, because I've always been a champ at that sort of thing. My problem is that I'm a *putterer*. If I don't watch it, I just putter my life away. I hate to think of the many hours my husband and I used to spend just puttering. He had his workshop, and I had my kitchen and sewing room and all my collections. There were always hundreds of little tasks and projects to do.

"It wasn't all bad, of course, but mercy, when I think I poured so much of my lifeblood into shuffling around my own four walls doing the little things I did, it makes me want to explode. And if I don't watch it, I go right back to it or worse. It's just too easy to switch on the TV or thumb through magazines or start another knitting project or dust the bookshelves for the fifth time in a week."

"From the looks on a few faces," said Dean, "including my own, we must have a few more addicted putterers in the crowd."

"Well, I think it's marvelous what Jim has been sharing. He said something about setting the record straight when he started to talk, and I just wanted to set a few records straight, too."

How about Barbara and the kids, Jim? What do they think about your restructuring of time?"

"They're seeing dad around the house a lot more and don't seem to mind it. But to be truthful, I've found it's been a lot easier to find time than it has been to use it in a meaningful way. For too many years, I took better care of my employees than I did of my own kids. I'm still working on getting my job description of being a *father* straightened around."

"Thanks for your words, Jim. I know you've done some hard-hitting evaluating in the last year, and it's obvious that you've had the courage to confront some touchy problems.

"In my letter to Eddie I asked him if learning New Testament Greek has been of any practical value to a young man like him. It's pretty obvious that it's not the sort of thing most eighteen-year-olds are out doing on the weekends. What do you think, Eddie?"

"I think that learning Greek has made me *think* about things a lot differently than I used to. It's made me think about how there are so many languages in the world and so many different kinds of people and so many different ways of thinking; and how it's so difficult to understand someone the way they should be understood. Do you know what I mean?"

"I think we do, Eddie. Did thinking about all that help you understand your family and other people any better?"

"Yeah. It sort of explained a lot of things to me. There are so many different cultures and all that. Buddy and I talked about how even Jesus was different in that way. He was God and came to earth and became a man, and he had to give up a lot to do it. And he always had to work hard to make people understand him, and even then most people didn't really understand."

The room had grown silent.

"I don't know. I guess it kind of helped to know that. It made me feel I wasn't so different."

"That's a lot to have learned. Anything else?"

"Learning Greek has also made me see Jesus in a different way. Before, whenever I thought of him, I always thought of pictures and statues I'd seen in the church. He didn't seem like a real person. Now I think of what he said and who he said it to and it seems like he's a person, not a picture or someone in a story."

"Thanks, Eddie, I think you learned some principles that are important for all of us to keep in mind. And you said it better than I could have.

"When I wrote John and Carol, I asked them to tell us about *how* they had gone about learning Greek, and to let us know what's worked and what hasn't worked. You two got any juicy tidbits for us?"

"I'd say the most important thing I've done," said John, "has been more of a habit than a particular method of learning Greek."

"What's that?"

"Every evening I always make sure I've gotten my Greek materials organized and all set up to be used the next day."

"What do you mean when you say *all set up*?"

"Nothing fancy, just that everything is where I know I can find it, and that it's ready for immediate use. The main thing is that I don't have to waste time getting started or trying to figure out where I am."

"What made you think this would be important?"

"On the job, I clean the tools every day and make sure they're ready to go for the next day's work. If I didn't, I'd end up wasting time and money. Tools left laying around not only get lost, but also get dirty and wear out faster. I figured it would be the same way with the tools I use to learn Greek, and I'd say it's paid off. Besides, you once told us that it's not as important to have a great method to learn Greek as it is to make sure that whatever we do, that we do it *regularly*. I've tried to take that principle to heart and set things up so that no days go by without at least a few minutes of Greek."

"Can you give us a few examples of what you've done?"

"When we first started, I figured I'd forget trying to do anything on the job. Things are just too hectic. But then I noticed that I spend anywhere from one to three hours a day in my pickup, which means I spend a lot of time sitting at stop lights. I noticed a lot of time was being wasted at those lights, so I started keeping a pack of review cards on the dash. It's amazing how much I use them. And if someone happens to be with me, which is often the case, my little packet of cards sometimes leads to an interesting conversation."

"How about at home, Carol, have you found anything that works there?"

"Oh, John's the creative one. He's always thinking of something."

"Like what?"

"Well, a few months ago he started putting review cards all over the place—in the car, the van, pasted around the house, stuck in flower pots and a lot of things like that. He even teaches Andy words, and they play games with them. Andy knows some words better than I do."

"So it's really become a family project."

"That's right."

"But it's also had an effect on other relationships," said John. "Like Eddie was saying, the whole idea that people think differently in different cultures has made me look at people differently, too. I don't assume anymore that I understand them or that they understand me."

"What do you mean exactly?"

"Some of the men who work for me are from Mexico, like Eddie's mom and dad. I've tried to show some interest in their language and culture. I get them to teach me a little Spanish every now and then, and it's amazing what that does. It removes some of the boss-man image."

"Our conversation around the house has changed, too," said Carol. "It's amazing how often we talk about a particular word and what it means. That may not seem like much, but I've noticed how it gets our minds going in a good direction."

"It's interesting you'd mention that," said Dean. "I've seen the same thing happen over the years around our house. When Linda or one of the kids began to learn Greek, it opened the doors to hours of great conversations.

"Speaking of cultural barriers, it's time we heard something from Liz. She spent the summer with her family in Germany. How did things go, Liz? Were you able to keep up your Greek learning?"

"Some, but not as much as I would have liked to. We were on the go too much."

"Thanks for sending so many cards," said Linda. "It sounds like you met plenty of people."

"I sure did. I went to a conference for Christian college students in Berlin that was particularly interesting. Students from all over Europe were there, even some from Eastern Europe."

"What were your impressions?"

"That's a long story. As you know only too well, it's a different world over there—a very intellectual kind of a world, especially among students. I guess that's why I was surprised that a lot of the ones I talked to didn't seem to know much about the New Testament."

"How did you come to that conclusion?" Jim asked.

"In my conversations, I used some of those questions about sources we've often talked about, and there weren't that many who seemed concerned about tracking down source level information. Most of them felt at least in theory that the documents in the New Testament were the most important sources we have, but they still seemed to play a minor role in their thinking. Philosophies and ideologies and some pretty entrenched religious traditions played bigger roles in my opinion."

"What I've learned in the last year helped me see through a lot of the intellectual veneer that you run into in Europe. I think in the past I let it threaten me too much. On this trip I had better conversations and was able to zero in on essential topics much better.

"How was it with your family?" asked Linda.

"I had a good time with them. I hope you can meet them sometime. My father was fascinated by my Greek New Testament. I showed him the introduction and all the information about the manuscripts, and I showed him how the notes record text deviants and how scholars approach resolving them. He was quite impressed. He had never realized the amount of work people had put into the basic documents of the New Testament. It was definitely a step in the right direction."

"That's good to hear, and now you're back on campus?"

"Yes, and there have been a couple of good developments. A few of the girls in the sorority have decided to get together every week for a Bible study, and two of the leaders in our college group told me they were interested in learning Greek and asked if I had any suggestions. I put them in contact with Professor Smith. I think he's been helping them get started."

"Well, it sounds like Liz is back in the thick of things, and Harmon, too," said Dean. "How are things going over at Phoenix College, Harmon? A new school year just began for you. Has everything gone well?"

"Great. No place I'd rather be than in the classroom."

"As most of you know, Harmon has more or less thrown himself into learning Greek and is quite a ways down the road. If I'm not wrong, he just completed his first time through the whole New Testament. I've asked him to share with us if he's begun to find that Greek is a useful tool."

"It's definitely opened new doors for me. For many years—too many years—I sort of hovered over the text of the Scriptures not knowing how to land my interpretational helicopter."

"His what?" Marian blurted out, loosing a peel of laughter in the room.

A big smile creased Harmon's face. "I mean to say," he began again, "I just didn't do a good job of getting into the Scriptures *themselves*—not at a factual level at any rate. For many years I was quite satisfied to stay above the text. Fortunately it began to bother me. Greek is a tool that is putting me into the text itself. I'm not completely there yet, but it's nice to know I'm not hovering anymore and am getting some solid ground under my feet."

"Has all this made any practical differences in your life?"

"It's certainly thrust me into a new relationship with other Christians. Down at the college, for example, there are several believers on the staff who come from a number of different churches and traditions. When we get into discussions I find it a lot easier to steer questions to basic issues by simply raising the question of information sources, which makes it possible to relate to them on a factual basis rather than an emotional one."

"Information sources?" asked Marian. "Liz said something like that, too. I think I know what you mean, but maybe you could explain it a bit more."

"Sure. If some controversial matter comes up, instead of my shooting off an opinion of some kind, I'm finding it better to say something like: 'Where would we expect to find a comprehensive answer to this question in the Scriptures?' or 'How do you think the first readers of the Scriptures understood that concept?' or 'Where did a New Testament author directly address this matter?' Those kind of questions point back to the source. They're not the kind of questions people are used to asking, but they're the crucial questions. I've found that such questions are helpful, because they cause people to question their own thoughts, and avoid a polarizing of opinions by getting us into content rather than conflict."

"And do you know all the answers to those questions?" Marian asked, a touch of awe in her voice.

"No, of course not. And that's the whole point. The source questions don't focus on my view of things, but on the Scriptures' view of things, and that gets a conversation moving in the right direction. And it's interesting to me to hear how people react to these kinds of questions. It may be that Liz's comment about entrenched traditions is not only true in Europe. At any rate, I've found that emphasizing sources has given me a much better basis for communicating with people who are flying many different theological flags. And I feel much better about the kind of conversations that result. Too often in the past, instead of propagating the teachings of Christ, I was out propagating *my understanding* of them. I made it too much of a personal matter, as though they were *my* words I was defending. It's much better to be concerned about the understanding of the men who originally wrote those documents."

"Thank you, Harmon. I know you've already gotten some of your colleagues interested in the Scriptures. It would be interesting to hear more about that, but we need to conduct our last interview now.

"When I wrote to Marian, I asked her to tell us if learning Greek had done anything for her personally. Marian, we're delighted you were able to make it to our get-together. I hope my request won't be putting you on the spot."

"Oh, not at all. It's no wonder you think it could, though. The way I talk sometimes, you'd think that learning Greek was the worst thing that could ever happen to an old lady. But don't pay any attention to all that nonsense. I'm pleased as punch about how this last year has gone.

"When I look back at it, I can't help but think about the first and second graders who came to school all those years I taught. At the beginning of the year they were so fresh and exuberant and a little scared. They were all wondering if they'd make any friends, if the teacher would be nice to them, and if they'd be able to keep up with the others in their class. Well, I've kind of felt like that this year: new and fresh in a way, and yet also unsure and scared—just like going back to school.

"In fact, the more I think about it, the more it seems that getting old is like becoming a child again: you begin to feel weaker, more dependent, less sure of yourself, threatened by all the new developments in the big world out there, and you tend to want to go back to playing games...and to puttering around. Mothers and fathers, however, know they can't just let their children stay around home and play games, so they take them—sometimes kicking and screaming—to school where toys are replaced by books and where even small children have to start thinking about preparing themselves for the future.

"That's exactly what some of you have done for me, you've gently told me to put down my knitting needles, and you've shoved a very important book into my hands, telling me it's time to think about the future again. In a nutshell, that's what learning Greek has done for me: It's put the future back in my life. It's made me believe I'm getting myself prepared for some important tasks.

"I'd begun to think the important things of life were already over. There was nothing left for me to do but take a few bows, have a few last flings, and dress up my curtain call with a few good works. The fact is, however, that I really do have a future, and the best way to look at it is like a child going back to school. I once thought it was a quaint little saying when Jesus said to *become like a little child*. But it's quite a difficult and scary thing to do, especially if you think of all the hard challenges a child faces—like having to learn to read and write for the first time."

"And what's it been like going back to school?"

"Not easy, I can tell you that. But I haven't missed a day, I know my letters, I can sound them all out, and I know a whole list of words and even a few sentences. Unfortunately I still can't read worth a hoot so I don't know if they'll let me into the second grade."

"Has it been worth it?"

"It's all been worth it, even if I can't read Greek yet. The past year I've learned how important words are—all words—and that's made me take more notice of what people are saying, and made me pay closer attention to the words in my English Bible. I don't read it like I used to, as though it were just a nice thing to do every now and then. Now I read it to try and *understand* it. I'm actually treating my New Testament like I used to treat my cookbook and my sewing magazines. That may not sound very high up the ladder, but anyone who knows me, knows it's *way* up there."

"You know, Marian," said Dean, "I think we're all wishing right now that we could have had you as our teacher when we were in the first grade. I think we could sit here and listen to you all day. Thank you for making the effort to be with us tonight, and thank you for your willingness to go 'back to school' and show us all how important that is.

"That completes the interviews and I want to thank all of you for putting so much thought into the questions I sent to you. You've all done an excellent job getting involved in self-learning, and I think you'll agree, based on what you heard this evening, that there's much encouragement and many good practical suggestions to be had from one another. I've often observed how people who are at about the same place in a learning process can be great teachers for one another. Experts don't necessarily have to be around for effective teaching and learning to take place.

"Do we have any particular plans for this year?" asked John. "I'm all for self-learning, but I wouldn't mind a session or two to shorten up my list of questions."

"If I'm not mistaken, each of you just may be receiving an invitation in the mail in a few weeks. I've heard rumors that Universal Greek Pictures will soon be conducting the second part of its tour[1].

"You may remember that the first tour only took you through the departments of word-pictures and thought-pictures. You still haven't seen the department of literature-pictures or the department of translating. If I were you, I'd keep my eyes and ears open and not forget to read my mail. I have a feeling we'll be seeing each other at Universal Greek Pictures soon."

---

[1] See the second volume in the *With People Just Like You* series entitled *Learning How to Use New Testament Reference Books*.

PART VII:

Their Final Twenty-Five Steps

Contents

51.	SW, τίς, τις	323
52.	EW, ἐμός, σός, ἡμέτερος, ὑμέτερος	325
53.	SW, ἐμαυτοῦ, σεαυτοῦ, ἑαυτοῦ	327
54.	EW, Add-On Words, ἀληθής	329
55.	New Testament Reference Books	332
56.	Traditional Grammatical Terms	335
57.	CW, Major Forms, δοξάζω	344
58.	CW, ἄγω	348
59.	CW, βλέπω	350
60.	CW, αἴρω	352
61.	CW, Normal Photo 2, Miniphoto	354
62.	AW, Add-on Words, Comparisons	358
63.	AW, Numbers	360
64.	CW, τίθημι	362
65.	CW, δίδωμι	364
66.	CW, ἵστημι	366
67.	CW, πίμπλημι	368
68.	CW, δείκνυμι, κεῖμαι, Optative	370
69.	CW, Irregular Camera-words	373
70.	CW, οἶδα	375
71.	CW, εἰμί	377
72.	Evaluation	379
73.	Review and Preparation	381
74.	The Goal	382
75.	The Source	383

Key to Abbreviations: **SW**=*Something-Words*, **CW**=*Camera-Words*,
EW=*Extra-Information Words*, **AW**=*All-Around Words*

STEP 51

SOMETHING-WORDS

ROLE	singular	plural	singular	plural
	τίς		τί	
Nec.	τίς who?	τίνες who?	τί which?	τίνα which?
Gen.supp	τίνος whose?	τίνων whose?	τίνος which one's?	τίνων which ones'?
Directing	τίνι to whom?	τίσίν to whom?	τίνι to which one?	τίσίν to which ones?
Accompl.	τίνα whom?	τίνάς whom?	τί which one?	τίνά which ones?
	τις		τι	
Nec.	τις someone	τινές certain ones	τι something	τινά certain things
Gen.supp	τινός someone's	τινῶν certain ones'	τινός something's	τινῶν certain things'
Directing	τινί to someone	τισίν to certain ones	τινί to something	τισίν to cert. things
Accompl.	τινά someone	τινάς certain ones	τι something	τινά certain things

Word Chart K,L,M,N-8

Strange but true:

τίς and τις are both used over 500 times in the New Testament, and the only difference in the spelling is the placement of an accent mark.

τίς is a *question-word*. Used alone and in combination with other words, it asks Who? Which? Whose? Whom? With whom? What for? Why? What kind? So what?, etc.

τις, however, is a word that refers to something *indefinite: someone, something, anyone, somebody, some, certain ones, any, several,* etc.

Don't miss it:

There are no ἡ-word forms for τίς or τις. ὁ-word forms are used in their places.

τί ποιῶμεν; *What shall we do?*

τίς ἐστιν οὗτος; *Who is this?*

γράφω τι τῳ ἀνθρωπῳ. *I'm writing something to the man.*

τινες ἐξ αὐτῶν ἔρχονται. *Some of them are coming.*
τίνος υἱός ἐστιν; *Whose son is he?*
σὺ τίς εἶ; *Who are you?*
τίς σοφὸς ἐν ἡμῖν; *Who is wise among you?*

Any questions?

Q: How will I ever recognize the difference between τίς and τις if the only difference between them is a tiny accent mark?

A: It's not as difficult as you might think. The context solves the problem. You only have to remember that there are two basic meanings for τις—the *question* meaning and the *indefinite* meaning—whether it has an accent mark or not. You'll automatically know which one is meant.

Q: Automatically?

A: Sure. It's something you've been doing with words all your life, because almost all words have more than one meaning. A word like *buck*, for example, can mean *a male deer, a dollar,* or the *straight-up jump* of a wild horse. You know automatically which is meant when you hear the word in a sentence. The other words in the sentence actually determine the meaning for you. The same will be true of texts in which you find τις and τίς.

STEP 52

EXTRA-INFORMATION WORDS

ROLE	ἐμός, ἐμή, ἐμόν - mine					
	ἐμός		ἐμή		ἐμόν	
Nec.	-ός	-οί	-ή	-αί	-όν	-ά
Gen.supp.	-οῦ	-ῶν	-ῆς	-ῶν	-οῦ	-ῶν
Directing	-ῷ	-οίς	-ῇ	-αίς	-ῷ	-οίς
Accompl.	-όν	-ούς	-ήν	-άς	-όν	-ά

ROLE	σός, σή, σόν - yours					
	σός		σή		σόν	
Nec.	-ός	-οί	-ή	-αί	-όν	-ά
Gen.supp.	-οῦ	-ῶν	-ῆς	-ῶν	-οῦ	-ῶν
Directing	-ῷ	-οίς	-ῇ	-αίς	-ῷ	-οίς
Accompl.	-όν	-ούς	-ήν	-άς	-όν	-ά

ROLE	ἡμέτερος, ἡμέτερα, ἡμέτερον - ours					
	ἡμέτερος		ἡμέτερα		ἡμέτερον	
Nec.	-ος	-οι	-α	-αι	-ον	-α
Gen.supp.	-ου	-ων	-ας	-ων	-ου	-ων
Directing	-ω	-οις	-α	-αις	-ω	-οις
Accompl.	-ον	-ους	-αν	-ας	-ον	-α

ROLE	ὑμέτερος, ὑμέτερα, ὑμέτερον - yours					
	ὑμέτερος		ὑμέτερα		ὑμέτερον	
Nec.	-ος	-οι	-α	-αι	-ον	-α
Gen.supp.	-ου	-ων	-ας	-ων	-ου	-ων
Directing	-ω	-οις	-α	-αις	-ω	-οις
Accompl.	-ον	-ους	-αν	-ας	-ον	-α

Strange but true:

The *owner* or *possessor* of something is usually indicated in Greek by a something-word in the *general supporting* role: ὁ οἶκος ἡμῶν *(our house)* and ὁ οἶκος ἐμοῦ *(my house)*.

ἐμός, σός, ἡμέτερος, and ὑμέτερος, however, are also words that indicate possession, but they function like add-on words. Therefore, they have all the ὁ-, ἡ-, and τό-word endings.

ὁ οἶκος ἡμέτερος *(our house)*
ὁ οἶκος ὁ ἐμός *(my house)*

Now you're the translator:
1. ῾Η βασιλεία ἡ ἐμὴ οὐκ ἔστιν ἐκ τοῦ κόσμου. 2. ὁ λόγος ὁ σὸς ἀλήθειά ἐστιν. 3. ὑμετέρα ἐστὶν ἡ βασιλεία τοῦ θεοῦ. 4. καὶ αὐτὸς ἱλασμός ἐστιν περὶ τῶν ἁμαρτιῶν ἡμῶν, οὐ περὶ τῶν ἡμετέρων δὲ μόνον ἀλλὰ καὶ περὶ ὅλου τοῦ κόσμου. 5. λέγει οὖν αὐτοῖς ὁ ᾿Ιησοῦς· ὁ καιρὸς ὁ ἐμὸς οὔπω πάρεστιν, ὁ δὲ καιρὸς ὁ ὑμέτερος πάντοτέ ἐστιν ἕτοιμος. 6. ἐγὼ περὶ αὐτῶν ἐρωτῶ· οὐ περὶ τοῦ κόσμου ἐρωτῶ, ἀλλὰ περὶ ὧν δέδωκάς μοι, ὅτι σοί εἰσιν, καὶ τὰ ἐμὰ πάντα σά ἐστιν καὶ τὰ σὰ ἐμά.

Any questions?
A: You don't even have to ask. I can guess the question: *Why are there various ways of saying 'my' and 'your' and 'our'?*

ἐμός, σός, ἡμέτερος, and ὑμέτερος were commonly used during the classical period of the Greek language (before 300 B.C.). They began to disappear after that.

The same kind of thing happened to the English words like *thee* and *thou.* Years ago they gradually disappeared and were replaced by *you* and *your.* Since they didn't disappear over night, however, there was a time when *thee* and *thou* and *you* and *your* were all used together. (In some circles, you can still hear a *thee* or a *thou* being used even today.) That's the way it was in the first century with ἐμός, σός, ἡμέτερος, and ὑμέτερος. They were on their way out but still hadn't taken their final bow.

In some cases the use of ἐμός, σός, ἡμέτερος, and ὑμέτερος *emphasizes* the possession: *my house, not yours.* Other words, however, such as ἴδιος *(one's own)* and τὰ ὑπάρχοντα *(possessions)* are usually used for this purpose.

STEP 53

SOMETHING-WORDS

ROLE	ὁ-words	ἡ-words	ὁ-words	ἡ-words
Gen.supp	ἐμαυτοῦ myself	ἐμαυτῆς myself	σεαυτοῦ yourself	σεαυτῆς yourself
Directing	ἐμαυτῷ to myself	ἐμαυτῇ to myself	σεαυτῷ to yourself	σεαυτῇ to yourself
Accompl.	ἐμαυτόν myself	ἐμαυτήν myself	σεαυτόν yourself	σεαυτήν yourself
Gen.supp	ἑαυτοῦ himself	ἑαυτῆς herself	ἑαυτῶν themselves	ἑαυτῶν themselves
Directing	ἑαυτῷ to himself	ἑαυτῇ to herself	ἑαυτοῖς to themselves	ἑαυταῖς to themselves
Accompl.	ἑαυτόν himself	ἑαυτήν herself	ἑαυτούς themselves	ἑαυτάς themselves

Word Chart K,L,M,N-10

Don't miss it:

Myself (ἐμαυτοῦ), *yourself* (σεαυτοῦ), and *himself* (ἑαυτοῦ) play only three roles. There is no "self" word that plays the necessary role, because *myself, yourself, himself,* and *herself* are repeats of the word in the necessary role (*I myself, you yourself, etc.*).

Strange but true:

ὅστις is a combination of ὅς and τις and means *each one who...* or *everyone who...*(plural). When ὅστις changes endings, in some cases *both* of the combined words change:

ὁ-words = ὅστις, οὗτινος, ᾧτινι, etc.
ἡ-words = ἥτις, ἥτινος, ᾗτινι, etc.
τό-words = ὅτι, ὅτινος, ᾧτινι, etc.

Now you're the translator:

1. Οὐκ ἔρχῃ ἀπὸ σεαυτοῦ. 2. βλέπετε (ἐπὶ) ὑμᾶς αὐτούς. 3. καὶ οὐκ ἔχουσιν ῥίζαν ἐν ἑαυτοῖς ἀλλὰ πρόσκαιροί εἰσιν. 4. οὐκ ἀπαγγέλλομεν ἡμᾶς αὐτούς, ἀλλὰ Χριστὸν τὸν κύριον, ἡμᾶς αὐτούς δὲ δούλους διὰ τὸν κύριον. 5. διὸ οὐδὲ ἐμαυτὸν ἠξίωσα πρὸς σέ ἐλθεῖν· ἀλλὰ εἰπὲ λόγῳ, καὶ ἰαθήτω ὁ παῖς μου. 6. πᾶς οὖν ὅστις ἀκούει μου τοὺς λόγους τούτους καὶ ποιεῖ αὐτούς, ὁμοιωθήσεται ἀνδρὶ φρονίμῳ, ὅστις ᾠκοδόμησεν αὐτοῦ τὴν οἰκίαν ἐπὶ τὴν πέτραν. 7. ὅστις δὲ ὑψώσει ἑαυτὸν ταπεινωθήσεται, καὶ ὅστις ταπεινώσει ἑαυτὸν ὑψωθήσεται.

New words:

ἀλλήλων,οις,ους	one another	λυτρόω	redeem, set free
ἀξιόω	make worthy, consider worthy	ὁμοθυμαδόν	unanimous
δίδωμι	give	ὅπως	as, so that
δικαιόω	justify, make just	οὐδέ	and not, not yet
		παῖς,παιδός, ὁ	boy, servant boy, son
δουλόω	enslave	πρόσκαιρος	temporary
ἐλθεῖν	come	στεφανόω	crown
ἐσχήκαμεν	we have had	ταπεινόω	humble, humiliate
θανατόω	kill		
καθαρίζω	cleanse	τελειόω	complete
κοινόω	make common, impure	ὑψόω	raise up
		φανερόω	reveal
λυτρόομαι	set free		

STEP 54

ROLE	TYPE	singular	plural
EXTRA-INFORMATION WORDS			
Nec. Gen.Supp. Dir. Accompl.	ὁ	ἀληθ-ής -ής -οῦς -εῖ -ή	-εῖς -ῶν -έσιν -εῖς
Nec. Gen.Supp. Dir. Accompl.	ἡ	ἀληθ-ής -ής -οῦς -εῖ -ή	-εῖς -ῶν -έσιν -εῖς
Nec. Gen.Supp. Dir. Accompl.	τό	ἀληθ-ές -ές -οῦς -εῖ -ές	-ή -ῶν -έσιν -ή
Word Chart N-12,13,14			

What you need to know:

1. Add-on words ending in -ης have no ἡ-word endings. When they add their extra information to an ἡ-word, they use their ὁ-word endings.

2. Add-on words ending in -υς (Word Chart O-12,13,14) have endings that are somewhat similar to ἀληθής. Notice, however, that they do have their own ἡ-word endings.

Give it a try:

What roles do the following endings indicate? ἀσθεν-ές, -ῶν, -έσιν, -ής, -οῦς,-εῖ, -εῖς (2x), -ή (3x); βαθ-ύς, -εῖ, εῖς (2x),-ύ (2x), -είας, -έα (2x), -είαις, -ύν, -έσιν, -ειῶν, -έος, -έων, -εία; μελαίν-ῃ

How To Read New Testament Greek

Now you're the translator:
1. Στέφανος δὲ πλήρης χάριτος καὶ δυνάμεως ἐποίει τέρατα καὶ σημεῖα μεγάλα ἐν τῷ λαῷ. 2. διδάσκαλε, οἴδαμεν ὅτι ἀληθὴς εἶ καὶ τὴν ὁδὸν τοῦ θεοῦ ἐν ἀληθείᾳ διδάσκεις. 3. ἐντολὴν καινὴν γράφω ὑμῖν, ὅ ἐστιν ἀληθὲς ἐν αὐτῷ καὶ ἐν ὑμῖν, ὅτι ἡ σκοτία παράγεται καὶ τὸ φῶς τὸ ἀληθινὸν ἤδη φαίνει. 4. αἱ ἐντολαὶ αὐτοῦ βαρεῖαι οὐκ εἰσίν. 5. ἡ γὰρ καρδία σου οὐκ ἔστιν εὐθεῖα ἔναντι τοῦ θεοῦ. 6. ἀπῆλθεν ὁ ἄνθρωπος καὶ εἶπεν τοῖς Ἰουδαίοις ὅτι Ἰησοῦς ἐστιν ὁ ποιήσας αὐτὸν ὑγιῆ. 7. καὶ θεραπεύετε τοὺς ἐν αὐτῇ ἀσθενεῖς, καὶ λέγετε αὐτοῖς· ἤγγικεν ἐφ' ὑμᾶς ἡ βασιλεία τοῦ θεοῦ. 8. τὴν ἐλπίδα ὡς ἄγκυραν ἔχομεν τῆς ψυχῆς ἀσφαλῆ τε καὶ βεβαίαν. 9. καὶ ἐθεασάμεθα τὴν δόξαν αὐτοῦ, δόξαν ὡς μονογενοῦς παρὰ πατρός, πλήρης χάριτος καὶ ἀληθείας. 10. καὶ ἔλεγεν αὐτοῖς ὁ Ἰησοῦς ὅτι οὐκ ἔστιν προφήτης ἄτιμος εἰ μὴ ἐν τῇ πατρίδι αὐτοῦ καὶ ἐν τοῖς συγγενεῦσιν αὐτοῦ καὶ ἐν τῇ οἰκίᾳ αὐτοῦ.

Any questions?
Q: How do I keep the vocabulary from piling up on me. For every ten new words I learn, I seem to forget ten old ones.
A: This is to be expected. Due to the fact that you're beginning to understand the basic framework of Greek better and better, you're naturally upping your tempo through the STEPS. That, in turn, causes your vocabulary circuits to overload.

If you've done your best to develop a good system of review (see pages 144 and 154) and used some creativity in developing memory helps (see page 125), then you're probably doing all you can. You'll just have to keep looking up the words you forget. Remember, however, that *looking up words is a constant necessity for anyone who wants to be proficient in New Testament Greek*. There will most likely *never* be a time when you will be able to totally avoid it.

Rest assured that a core of words you know well will begin to grow over the years. If you think of this as a process that will continue for your lifetime, then you'll be content to build on this core as a way of life.

Does that seem discouraging? It shouldn't be. You'll find as time passes that your mind will warm up to the task and understanding will come more quickly. Linguistically our minds grow like plants: The first shoot supports two more shoots, each of those two support two more, each of those four support two more, and so on. The amount of growth in the third or fourth year is a surprising *multiple* of that in the first year.

This is the miracle of growth. To make the miracle possible, all you have to do is continue to plant as best you know how, waiting patiently, and the One who makes all harvests possible will also produce in you the fruit of remembrance and understanding.

STEP 54

New words:

ἀληθής,ές	true
ἀσεβής,ές	godless
ἀσθενής,ές	weak
ἀσφαλής,ές	sure
ἄτιμος, ἄτιμον	dishonorable
βαθύς,εῖα,ύ	deep
βαρύς,εῖα,ύ	heavy
βραχύς,εῖα,ύ	short
διδάσκω	teach
ἐγένετο	it happened
ἔναντι	before
εὐθύς,εῖα,ύ	straight
μέλας, μέλαινα,μέλαν	black
μονογενής	only conceived
ὀξύς, εῖα, ύ	sharp
πλήρης, πλῆρες	full
σάκκος, ὁ	sack
συγγενής,ές	related
ταχύς,εῖα,ύ	fast
τέ	and (often untranslated)
τρίχινος,η,ον	hairy
τέρας,τέρατος,τὸ	wonder, omen
ὑγιής	healthy

STEP 55

THE GREEK TEXT

Aland, K. and M. Black, C. Martini, B. Metzger, A. Wikren (Eds). 1983. *The Greek New Testament.* Third corrected edition. Stuttgart: United Bible Societies.

Aland, K. and B. Aland. 1982. *The Text of the New Testament.* Stuttgart: The German Bible Society.

Metzger, B. 1971. *A Textual Commentary on the Greek New Testament.* London and New York: United Bible Societies.

Metzger, B. 1964. *Text of the New Testament: Its Transmission, Corruption, and Restoration.* Oxford: The Clarendon Press.

THE LINGUISTIC CONTEXT

Bauer, W. and W. Arndt, F. Gingrich, F. Danker. 1979. *A Greek-English Lexicon of the New Testament.* Chicago and London: The University of Chicago Press.

Blass, F. and A. Debrunner. 1961. *A Greek Grammar of the New Testament and Other Early Christian Literature.* Chicago: University of Chicago Press.

Dana H. E. and J. R. Mantey. 1949. *A Manual Grammar of the Greek New Testament.* New York: The Macmillan Company.

Friberg, B. and T. Friberg (Eds). 1981. *Analytical Greek New Testament.* Grand Rapids: Baker Book House.

Han, N. 1971. *A Parsing Guide to the Greek New Testament.* Scottsdale, PA and Kitchener, ONT: Herald Press.

Louw, J. and E. Nida (Eds). 1989. *Greek-English Lexicon of the New Testament Based on Semantic Domains.* New York: United Bible Societies.

Moull C. F. D. 1960. *An Idiom Book of New Testament Greek.* 2nd Edition. Cambridge: Cambridge University Press.

Moulton and Geden. 1978. *A Concordance to the Greek New Testament.* 5th Edition. Edinburgh: T & T Clark.

Wigram, G. 1970. *The Englishman's Greek Concordance of the New Testament.* Grand Rapids: Zondervan Publishing House.

THE CULTURAL CONTEXT

Aharoni, Y. and A. Michael. 1977. *The Macmillan Bible Atlas.* New York: The Macmillan Publishing Company.

Barrett C. K. 1989. *The New Testament Background: Selected Documents.* Revised Edition. San Francisco: Harper and Row.

Bruce, F. 1980. *New Testament History.* Doubleday-Galilee Edition. New York: Doubleday and Company, Inc.

STEP 55

Coleman W. L. 1984. *Today's Handbook of Bible Times and Customs.* Minneapolis: Bethany House Publications.

Josephus, F. 1960. *The Complete Works of Josephus.* Grand Rapids: Kregal Publications.

TRANSLATING

Black D. A. 1988. *Linguistics for Students of New Testament Greek.* Grand Rapids: Baker Book House.

de Waard, J. and E. Nida. 1986. *From One Language to Another.* Nashville, Camden, and New York: Thomas Nelson Publishers.

Nida E. and C. R. Taber. 1969. *The Theory and Practice of Translation.* Leiden: E. J. Brill for the United Bible Societies.

What you need to know:

The STEPS were designed to be your first guides on the road to proficiency in New Testament Greek. Although you've not yet completed all of them, it's now time for you to make practical preparations for the phase of learning following the STEPS.

Your guides along the second stretch of the road are an armful of remarkable reference books that will lead you into the intricacies of the Greek mind as it expressed itself in the first century. When you've finished the STEPS, learning how to use these books will be your next goal.

Since locating and obtaining these books may require considerable time, it would be advisable to begin now, so the books are available when you need them.

How do you best go about it?

You can order a book by writing directly to the company that publishes it, or you can go to a Christian bookstore and ask for help in ordering the books. There are also some discount distributors whose catalogues include several of the recommended reference books.

For further tips, updates, or assistance, write to the address on page 129.

Don't miss it!

Learning How to Use New Testament Reference Books with People Just Like You, the companion book to *Learning How to Read New Testament Greek with People Just Like You,* continues the story of the McLains, the Garveys, the Freys, and all the others. In a tour through the department of literature-pictures and the department of translating at Universal Greek Pictures, Dean McLain introduces you to each of the reference books on the above list and gives you creative suggestions as to how to best use them. *Learning How to Use New Testament Greek Reference Books* is due to be published in 1993.

The newsletter, *Universal Greek Pictures Update*, supplements the 'With-People-Just Like You' books with additional information under the familiar headings: *Don't miss it!, Study Tips, Strange but true, What you need to know,* and *Any questions?* Ask for it from the folks at *Context Scripture Translating*.

STEP 56

What you need to know:

The STEPS are designed to take you to the first plateau in your quest to reach the summits of New Testament Greek. The New Testament reference books mentioned in the last STEP then accompany you into the high mountains of the Greek language. To use the reference books effectively, however, it is going to be necessary for you to learn the traditional grammatical terms for all the inner workings of New Testament Greek.

Pause. I hear you asking yourself: *Is this really necessary?*

Yes, I'll say it again. It's necessary to learn the traditional terms. It is the dictionaries, lexicons, concordances, grammars, and other New Testament reference books that pave the way to the heart and soul of the Greek mind, *and they all use the traditional grammatical terms.* To use these remarkable books you will have to understand the vocabulary they employ.

It is understandable that the thought of plunging into dependent clauses and adverbial participles is enough to freeze the blood of anyone who ever endured the ordeal of a typical grammar class, but there is no need to fear replays of past failures. You will find that the plain English words you have learned to describe the functions of New Testament Greek words will be effective bridges into the vocabulary of traditional grammar. In fact, without your knowing it, a lot of the traditional terms have been smuggled into the fabric of what you have already learned.

Do you remember, for example, the PARTs of an all-around word? Have you guessed by now that the traditional term for an all-around word is *participle?* The letters *PART* should make it easy for you to remember that *participle* is the traditional label for an all-around word, as well as remind you of the information contained in a participle: **P**icture, **A**ction, **R**ole, and **T**ype.

Or what about the *roles* played by something-words? Let's line them up beside their traditional counterparts:

      Necessary........................Nominative
      General supporting.............Genitive
      Directing.........................Dative
      Accomplishing..................Accusative

They are so similar that it will not be difficult to relate the traditional terms to their more understandable counterpart.

Now, look at that list again. Perhaps you're understanding for the first time what those words really mean. *Nominative* means nothing more than the necessary role, *genitive* is simply the general supporting role, and so on. Not all of the traditional terms will be as easy to learn as the ones just mentioned, but the task is manageable and could even prove interesting; after all, you're finally going to find out what all those words really mean.

How to Read New Testament Greek

Don't miss it!

There are three basic reasons why the traditional grammatical terms have probably given you trouble in the past:

1. Many of them are like foreign words that have no meaning for us. Words like *dative* and *predicate* and *adverbial participle* just aren't the kind of words we use around the house.

2. Some of the terms are actually misleading. The *imperfect tense* in Greek, for example, is nothing more than our familiar *recorded video*. What is *imperfect* or *tense* about a video recording?

3. Many of the terms do not overlap cleanly. What we call a *participle* in the English language, for example, is similar to, but not the same as what the traditional grammar calls a participle in Greek. The traditional grammars *do* try to solve this problem by redefining the terms, but using one word as the label for words which have different functions continues to be a factor of confusion.

This is why we've chosen to call words like ἐρχόμενος and παιδεύων *all-around words*. *All-around* is a good description of their function in Greek. Calling a Greek all-around word a participle easily leads a person to think the Greek all-around word is like an English participle.

English participles and Greek all-around words have some similarities, but, as you have learned, no English word is as flexible as a Greek all-around word. Trying to press a Greek all-around word into the mold of an English participle is like trying to outfit a sportscar with horseshoes. (Well, not exactly, but you get the point.)

Made-to-order terms such as those used in the STEPS will help you more naturally understand the traditional grammatical terms of Greek grammar. By transferring from the traditional terms back to those that better fit Greek, you'll avoid the three main causes for confusion: *unfamiliar* terminology, *misleading* terminology, and *overlapping* terminology.

Give it a try:

Let's begin learning the traditional terms by determining how many of them you already know. Two lists of words follow on the next two pages: On the left is a list of terms used in the STEPS, and on the right is a list of matching traditional terms, but in jumbled order. Fill in the blank beside each word on the left with the letter of the word on the right that you think corresponds to it. Use a pencil and write lightly so you can erase the letters and use the list again. **Don't make guesses.** Just write in the letters of the words you think you know. The purpose of this exercise is not to get the best possible score, but to determine what you know and what you need to learn.

STEP 56

GRAMMAR CHECK

1.__ Camera-word　　　　　A. person
2.__ Picture　　　　　　　　B. imperative
3.__ Light　　　　　　　　　C. middle
4.__ Action　　　　　　　　 D. perfect
5.__ Necessary role　　　　 E. passive
　　　(as part of camera-word)
6.__ Necessary role　　　　 F. complete sentence
7.__ Departed　　　　　　　G. mood
8.__ Live video　　　　　　 H. aorist
9.__ Recorded video　　　　 I. tense
10.__ Normal photo　　　　 J. subjunctive
11.__ Future photo　　　　　K. verb
12.__ Current photo　　　　 L. number (sing./pl.)
13.__ Previous photo　　　　M. present
14.__ I, you, he, she, it　　　 N. action
　　　we, all of you, they
15.__ Complete thought　　　O. future
16.__ Bright　　　　　　　　P. indicative
17.__ Dim　　　　　　　　　Q. pluperfect
18.__ Flashing　　　　　　　R. deponent
19.__ Active　　　　　　　　S. imperfect
20.__ Middle　　　　　　　　T. nominative
21.__ Passive　　　　　　　　U. active

Now turn to page 384 and check your answers.

How did it go?

If you got up to ten right, then you got the obvious ones. But don't let that deject you. Ten right answers means you're almost fifty percent of the way there. If 11 to 14 were correct, then you're retaining a residue from those grammar classes you had years ago.

If 15 to 20 were correct, then you've probably already given Greek a try at some time. If you correctly answered more than 20, you're in great shape. But before you get too confident, turn to the next page and let's see how well you do on the next list of grammatical terms.

How to Read New Testament Greek

GRAMMAR CHECK #2

1. __ All-around word
2. __ Small all-around word
3. __ Role
4. __ Type
5. __ ὁ-word
6. __ ἡ-word
7. __ τό-word
8. __ Matching endings
9. __ General supp. role
10. __ Directing role
11. __ Accomplishing role
12. __ Something-word
  (two answers)
13. __ Add-on word
  (add to a camera-word)
14. __ this, that
15. __ Add-on word
  (add to a something word)
16. __ Add-a-thought word
  (add to another thought)
17. __ Add-on phrase
18. __ Add-a-phrase word
19. __ Add-a-thought word
20. __ Add-on thought
  (add to a word)

A. adverb
B. relative pronoun
C. noun
D. conjunction
E. adjective
F. neuter
G. preposition
H. substantive
I. demonstrative pronoun
J. prepositional phrase
K. dependent clause
L. feminine

M. gender

N. genitive
O. case

P. dative

Q. congruence
R. accusative
S. participle
T. infinitive
U. masculine

Turn to page 384 to check your answers.

How did you do this time? If you got about 8 right, you're still getting the obvious ones. If 9 to 12 were correct, your grammatical past is still alive. If you answered 13 to 16 correctly, you *have* had some Greek. If you hit pay dirt with 17 to 20, you really *are* sitting pretty.

Now, what if you weren't part of the last group? How do you best learn the traditional terms? First of all, this little exercise should have convinced you that there really aren't as many terms to learn as you may have thought. There are more than those included on the list, of course, but not that many more. That should be encouraging. Besides, even if you only knew the obvious ones, no more than sixty percent of the total remain to be learned.

STEP 56

Study tips!

1. Jot traditional terms that you don't know well onto your Word Chart next to the terms that corresponding them. For example, just above or below the word *Picture* write in *tense*. This will help you visually place the terms in your mind. The adaptation chart on pages 342-343 will help you make the right matches.

2. Apply the principles you learned in STEP 4 and STEP 11 to learn the traditional terms. Review them every now and then until you've finished the STEPS and are ready to start learning how to use the reference books. Any remaining terms that still give you problems can be put on a card and kept handy for easy reference.

3. The lists on the next four pages will help you orient yourself to the traditional grammatical terminology. The first is an alphabetical listing of the terms you learned at *Universal Greek Pictures* with the corresponding traditional terms in parenthesis. The second list is an alphabetical listing of the traditional terms with the *UGP* terms in parenthesis. The third list is arranged topically along the lines of the Universal Greek Pictures Word Chart with the UGP terms in **bold** letters and the traditional terms in *italics*.

The first list can be used to look up the traditional terms when you're working in the STEPS. The second list can be used to look up the UGP terms when working in the reference books. The third list can be used as a topical overview to quickly locate both sets of terms.

Study tip!

The first two lists—*Universal Greek Pictures Grammatical Terms* and *Traditional Grammatical Terms*—have each been printed to fit on one side of pages 340 and 341 so they can be removed from the book or copied and used as a convenient reference.

Give it a try:

Use the *UGP Grammatical Terms* list to answer the following questions: What are the traditional terms for *current photo? roles? flashing light? double vowels?*

Use the *Traditional Grammatical Terms* list to answer the following questions: What the Universal Greek Pictures terms for *aorist tense? gender? subjunctive mood?*

UNIVERSAL GREEK PICTURES GRAMMATICAL TERMS

A (Indefinite article)
Accents (Accents)
Accomplishing role
  (Accusative case)
Action (Voice)
Active (Active)
Add-a-phrase words (Prepositions)
Add-a-thought words
  (Relative pronouns,
  Conjunctions)
Add-on thoughts (Clauses,
  Dependent sentences)
Add-on words (Adjectives, Adverbs)
All-around word (Participle)
Breathing marks (Spiritus)
  rough (Spiritus asper)
  smooth (Spiritus lenis)
Bright light (Indicative mood)
Camera-words (Verbs)
Combined words (Compound words)
Current photo (Perfect tense)
Departed form (Deponent form)
Determining the PLAN (Parsing)
Dim light (Subjunctive mood)
Directing role (Dative case)
Double vowel (Diphthong)
Extra-information word
  (Adjective,
  Adverb,
  Preposition,
  Relative pronoun,
  Conjunction)
ἡ-word (Feminine word)
Flashing light (Imperative mood)
Form change of a word (Inflection)
Future photo (Future tense)
General supporting role
  (Genitive case)

Himself, herself, itself, themselves
  (Reflexive pronouns)
I, you, he, she, it, we, you, they
  (Personal pronouns)
Light (Mood)
Live video (Present tense)
Matching forms (Congruence)
Middle (Middle)
Necessary role (Nominative case)
Normal photo (Aorist tense)
Numbers (Numerals)
ὁ-word (Masculine word)
Passive (Passive)
Picture (Tense)
Plural (Plural)
Previous photo (Pluperfect tense)
Punctuation (Punctuation)
Recorded video (Imperfect tense)
Role (Case)
Singular (Singular)
Small all-around word (Infinitive)
Something-word (Noun, Gerund)
τό-word (Neuter word)
The (Definite article)
This, that (Demonstrative pronouns)
Type (Gender)
Vowel (Vowel)
Vowel change (Contraction)
Who, which, that
  (Relative pronouns)
*Who? Why? Where? When?
What? How?*
  (Interrogative pronouns)

TRADITIONAL GRAMMATICAL TERMS

Accent (Accent)
Accusative case
　(Accomplishing role)
Active (Active)
Adjective (Add-on word)
Adverb (Add-on word)
Aorist tense (Normal photo)
Case (Role)
Compound word (Combined word)
Congruence (Matching forms)
Conjunction (Add-a-thought word)
Contraction (Vowel change)
Dative case (Directing role)
Definite article (*The*)
Demonstrative pronouns (*This, that*)
Dependent clause
　(Add-on thought)
Deponent form (Departed form)
Diphthong (Double vowel)
Feminine word (ἡ-word)
Future tense (Future photo)
Gender (Type)
Genitive case
　(General supporting role)
Imperative mood (Flashing light)
Imperfect tense (Recorded video)
Indefinite article (*A*)
Indicative mood (Bright light)
Infinitive (Small all-around word)
Inflection (Changing the form
　of a word)
Interrogative pronouns
　(*Who? Why? Where? When?
　What?*)
Masculine word (ὁ-word)

Middle (Middle)
Mood (Light)
Neuter word (τό-word)
Nominative case (Necessary role)
Noun (Something-word)
Numerals (Numbers)
Parsing (Determine the PLAN)
Participle (All-around word)
Passive (Passive)
Perfect tense (Current photo)
Personal pronouns
　(*I, you, he, she, it,
　we, you, they*)
Pluperfect tense (Previous photo)
Plural (Plural)
Preposition (Add-a-phrase word)
Present tense (Live video)
Pronoun (Something-word)
Punctuation (Punctuation)
Reflexive pronouns
　(*Himself, herself,
　itself, themselves*)
Relative pronoun
　(Add-a-thought word)
Relative pronouns
　(*Who, which, that*)
Singular (Singular)
Spiritus asper (Rough breathing)
Spiritus (Breathing mark)
Spiritus lenis (Smooth breathing)
Subjunctive mood (Dim light)
Substantive (Something-word)
Tense (Picture)
Verb (Camera-word)
Voice (Action)
Vowel (Vowel)

UNIVERSAL GREEK PICTURES GRAMMATICAL TERMS
AND
TRADITIONAL GRAMMATICAL TERMS
ARRANGED TOPICALLY

CAMERA-WORDS *VERBS*				
Picture *Tense*			**Video** *Progressive*	**Photograph** *aspect*
Light *Mood*	**Action** *Voice*	**Necessary Role** *Person*		
		Sing. Pl. *Number*		
Bright *Indicative*	**Active** *Active*	I we 1st sing. 1st pl.	**Live** *Present*	**Normal** *Aorist*
Dim *Subjunctive*	**Middle** *Middle*	you all of you 2nd sing. 2nd pl.	**Recorded** *Imperfect*	**Future** *Future*
Flashing *Imperative*	**Passive** *Passive*	he, she, they it 3rd sing. 3rd pl.		**Current** *Perfect*
				Previous *Pluperfect*

SOMETHING-WORDS		
NOUNS, PRONOUNS		
Role *Case*	**Type** *Gender*	
Necessary *Nominative*	ὁ-**word** *Masculine*	**The** *the* *The definite article*
General supporting *Genitive*	ἡ-**word** *Feminine*	**The** *a* *The indefinite article*
Directing *Dative*	τό-**word** *Neuter*	
Accomplishing *Accusative*		

EXTRA-INFORMATION WORDS	
MODIFIERS	
Add-on words *Adjectives, Adverbs*	
Add-a-phrase words *Prepositions*	**Add-on phrases** *Prepositional phrases*
Add-a-thought words *Relative pronouns* *Conjunctions*	**Add-on thoughts** *Dependent clauses* *Adjectival clauses* *Adverbial clauses*
ALL-AROUND WORDS	
PARTICIPLES	
Small all-around words	
Infinitives	

STEP 57

What you need to know:

Not all camera-words change their endings exactly like παιδεύω. In Steps 48-50 you learned how the endings of words like ποιέω and γεννάω are affected when the vowel in their stems bumps into a vowel in their endings.

Endings are also altered when the stem of a camera-word ends with the consonants δ, τ, θ, γ, κ, χ, β, π, and λ. It would take hundreds of pages to reproduce complete charts of even a small sampling of all the forms of Greek camera-words that differ because of these kinds of form changes.

Fortunately, complete charts are not necessary to know what the endings of a particular camera-word are. If you've been a very attentive observer of the changes the camera-words make to achieve their various PLANs, then you've noticed that they often use the same sets of endings. Even the ε on the beginning is typical of several different forms. The real distinguishing features between PLANs is usually a change of another kind: The endings of *live video* and *future photo* words are the same, for example. It's the σ in the middle that is the *major* change (παιδεύω = *live video*, παιδεύσω = *future photo*). That's a change on the *root* of the word.

In general, not counting the endings and the ε that often appears at the beginning of a camera-word, there are six or seven *major* changes that can occur in the structure of a camera-word. The remaining forms take their cues, so to speak, from one of these *major forms* and merely add their endings to them. (The *live video/active* form of a camera-word, for example, provides enough information to figure out all the other *live video and recorded video* forms). Therefore, if we know these *major forms*, then we can also figure out all of the other forms. It is helpful to know these major forms, particularly for those camera-words that change in ways that are irregular or unusual.

Don't miss it!

In this STEP and STEPS 58-60 and 64-69—all of which introduce you to new forms of camera-words—examples of these forms will be listed with their *major forms*: those forms from which other forms take their clues.

The following chart shows the PLANs of the *major forms* of δοξάζω, ἁγιάζω, and γνωρίζω:

STEP 57

VIDEO	PHOTO		
LIVE	NORMAL	FUTURE	CURRENT
δοξάζω	ἐδόξασα	δοξάσω	δεδόξακα
	ἐδοξάσθην p	δοξασθήσομαι p	δεδόξασμαι m/p
ἁγιάζω	ἡγίασα	ἁγιάζω	ἡγίακα
	ἡγιάσθην p	ἁγιασθήσομαι p	ἡγίασμαι m/p
γνωρίζω	ἐγνώρισα	γνοριῶ	ἐγνώρικα
	ἐγνώρισα p	γνωρίσω p	ἐγνώρικα m/p

Don't miss it!
You notice that the *major forms* are *live video/active, normal photo/active, normal photo/passive, future photo/active, future photo/passive, current photo/active, current photo/middle and passive*. When you know these forms of a camera word, you can figure out all the other forms.

These forms of δοξάζω, ἁγιάζω, and γνωρίζω, for example, give you enough clues to fill in the missing forms. Just check the endings of παιδεύω on the Word Chart and add the missing endings to the correct major form. This is easier said than done, of course, but you'll find, with time, that many of the endings will become second nature to you. You'll automatically recognize them without having to look them up. That may sound impossible now, but the day will come.

The letters *p* and *m/p* are included after the words in the second row to remind you that for these forms either the *passive (p)* form or the *middle and passive (m/p)* form are meant. Don't forget that the normal photo and future photo forms have *both* middle forms and passive forms.

Give it a try:
What is the PLAN of the following camera-words?
ἠγωνισάμην, κεχάρισται, ἥσπασμαι, ἐψεύσω, ἐγγεῖν, ἀφορίσθητε, ἤργαστο, ἐβασάνιζεν, εὐαγγελίσαι, δαιμονισθείς, σωζομένους, διελογίζεσθε, ἔχρισεν, διαμεμερισμένοι, δοξασθῶσιν, ἐμφανίσω, ἡτοίμασται, κατεσκευασμένων, θαυμάσῃς, κομιεῖσθε, κατηρτισμένα, ξενισθῶμεν, κτισθέντες, πιάσαι, λογιζέσθω, σχίσωμεν, πέπεισμαι, κεχωρισμένος, πειρασθῆναι, ἐσπλαγχνίσθη, σκανδαλισθήσονται

How to Read New Testament Greek

Now you're the translator:
1. Καὶ ἐγνώρισα αὐτοῖς τὸ ὄνομά σου καὶ γνωρίσω,ἵνα ἡ ἀγάπη, ἣν ἠγάπησάς με ἐν αὐτοῖς ᾖ, κἀγὼ ἐν αὐτοῖς. 2. καὶ τῷ ὀνόματι αὐτοῦ ἔθνη ἐλπιοῦσιν. 3. ἐν ᾧ καὶ πιστεύσαντες ἐσφραγίσθητε τῷ πνεύματι τῆς ἐπαγγελίας. 4. οὗτοι ἠγοράσθησαν ἀπὸ τῶν ἀνθρώπων ἀπαρχὴ τῷ θεῷ καὶ τῷ ἀρνίῳ. 5. ἀγωνίζου τὸν καλὸν ἀγῶνα τῆς πίστεως, ἐπιλαβοῦ τῆς αἰωνίου ζωῆς. 6. ἡ πίστις σου σέσωκέν σε. καὶ ἐσώθη ἡ γυνή. 7. Ἔχρισέν με εὐαγγελίσασθαι πτωχοῖς. 8. τοῦτο δέ ἐστιν τὸ ῥῆμα τὸ εὐαγγελισθὲν εἰς ὑμᾶς. 9. καὶ ὑπὲρ αὐτῶν ἁγιάζω ἐμαυτόν, ἵνα ὦσιν καὶ αὐτοὶ ἡγιασμένοι ἐν ἀληθείᾳ. 10. καὶ οὐχ ἁρπάσει τις αὐτὰ ἐκ τῆς χειρός μου.....καὶ οὐδεὶς δύναται ἁρπάζειν ἐκ τῆς χειρὸς τοῦ πατρός.

Any questions?
Q: Is it necessary to learn *all* the major forms for *all* the camera-words?
A. No. Some camera-words like παιδεύω are fairly easy to recognize in their various forms. It's those words that change radically or in unusual ways from form to form that are sometimes difficult to recognize. That's why it's important to be aware of the major ways that Greek camera-words change from form to form.

Naturally, you can't be expected to remember all these changes. Nor is it necessary. When you begin to use a Greek-English Dictionary and other New Testament reference works, they will do most of the work for you. For now, it is simply necessary for you to get used to the kind of changes that are typical for camera-words, so you will know how to use the information in the reference books.

Q: Why doesn't ἐλπίζω have all the major parts.
A: Some words are only represented in the New Testament with a limited number of forms.

New words:

ἁγιάζω	make holy	γέ	at least, even
ἀγοράζω	buy	γνωρίζω	make known
ἀγωνίζομαι	fight	δαιμονίζομαι	be possessed by a demon
ἀπαρχή, ἡ	first fruit		
ἀπειθέω	be disobedient	διαλογίζομαι	consider, discuss
ἁρπάζω	steal	διαμερίζω	share, distribute
ἀφορίζω	set aside, choose	δοκιμάζω	test
ἀσπάζομαι	greet	δοξάζω	glorify, honor
βαπτίζω	dip oneself, wash	ἐγγίζω	come near
βασανίζω	torture, force	ἐμφανίζω	reveal, explain

346

STEP 57

ἐπιλαμβάνω	take, receive	πιάζω	hold, grab, arrest
ἑτοιμάζω	make ready, equip	σαλπίζω	trumpet
		σκανδαλίζω	cause to sin, give offense to
εὐαγγελίζομαι	proclaim the good news	σπλαγχνίζομαι	have compassion
εὐαγγελίζω	proclaim the good news	σπουδάζω	hasten, make every effort
θαυμάζω	wonder, be amazed	σχίζω	divide
κατάπαυσις, ἡ	rest	σώζω, σῴζω	save, help
καταρτίζω	repair, make right	τις	someone
κατασκευάζω	restore	φείδομαι	spare someone trouble
κομίζω	bring, carry off, receive	χαρίζομαι	give freely, forgive
κτίζω	create	χρίω	anoint
λογίζομαι	mean, figure, consider	χωρίζω	separate, Pass: leave
ξενίζω	be hospitable	ψεύδομαι	lie
πείθομαι	obey		
πείθω	convince		
πειράζω	tempt, test		

STEP 58

VIDEO	PHOTO		
LIVE	NORMAL	FUTURE	CURRENT
ἄγω	ἤγαγον normal photo 2	ἄξω	ἦχα
	ἤχθην p	ἀχθήσομαι p	ἦγμαι m/p
δέχομαι	ἐδεξάμην	δέξομαι	δέδεγμαι
	ἐδέχθην p	δεχθήσομαι p	
κηρύσσω	ἐκήρυξα	κηρύξω	
	ἐκηρύχθην p	κηρυχθήσομαι p	

What you need to know:

The camera-words in this STEP have stems that end in γ, κ, or χ. Notice, however, how γ, κ, or χ often disappear from the word to be replaced by σ, σσ, ζ, or ξ.

Give it a try:

What's the dictionary form of the following words?

ἀχθήσεσθε   ἐστήρικται
ἀναχθέντες   τέτακται
τεταραγμένοι   τίκτουσα
ἀρξάμενος   ἐπιτάξῃ
διώξετε   φευγέτωσαν
ἀνοίξαντες   φύλαξον
ἔκραξαν   πατάξω
παρῆγεν   ἐσφαγμένον
ἐμπαῖξαι   ἀνέξονται
πράσσουσιν   προσεδέξασθε

STEP 58

Now you're the translator:
1. Οἶδα τὰ ἔργα σου καὶ τὸν κόπον καὶ τὴν ὑπομονήν σου, καὶ ὅτι οὐ δύνῃ βαστάσαι κακούς, καὶ ἐπείρασας τοὺς λέγοντας ἑαυτοὺς ἀποστόλους. 2. πᾶς γὰρ ὁ φαῦλα πράσσων μισεῖ τὸ φῶς καὶ οὐκ ἔρχεται πρὸς τὸ φῶς. 3. καὶ ἤγετο ἐν τῷ πνεύματι ἐν τῇ ἐρήμῳ ἡμέρας τεσσεράκοντα πειραζόμενος ὑπὸ τοῦ διαβόλου. 4. μακάριοι οἱ δεδιωγμένοι ἕνεκεν δικαιοσύνης, ὅτι αὐτῶν ἐστιν ἡ βασιλεία τῶν οὐρανῶν. 5. καὶ εἰς πάντα τὰ ἔθνη πρῶτον δεῖ κηρυχθῆναι τὸ εὐαγγέλιον. 6. Ἰωάννης μαρτυρεῖ περὶ αὐτοῦ καὶ κέκραγεν λέγων· οὗτος ἦν, ὃν εἶπον· ὁ ὀπίσω μου ἐρχόμενος ἔμπροσθέν μου γέγονεν, ὅτι πρῶτός μου ἦν. 7. μὴ ταρασσέσθω ὑμῶν ἡ καρδία· πιστεύετε εἰς τὸν θεόν, καὶ εἰς ἐμὲ πιστεύετε. 8. καὶ ἡ γυνὴ ἔφυγεν εἰς τὴν ἔρημον, ὅπου ἔχει ἐκεῖ τόπον ἡτοιμασμένον ἀπὸ τοῦ θεοῦ. 9. μακάριοι οἱ ἀκούοντες τὸν λόγον τοῦ θεοῦ καὶ φυλάσσοντες. 10. καὶ λέγει αὐτοῖς ὁ Ἰησοῦς· κατὰ τὴν πίστιν ὑμῶν γενηθήτω ὑμῖν. καὶ ἠνεῴχθησαν αὐτῶν οἱ ὀφθαλμοί.

New words:

ἀνάγω	lead up	μέλει	concerns someone
ἀνέχομαι	endure, put up with	μέλλω	be about to
		ὅπου	where
ἀνοίγω	open	ὅταν	then, if
ἀπάγω	lead away, Pass: be missed	παράγω	bring in, introduce
		παρέρχομαι	pass by, pass away
ἄρσην	manly	πατάσσω	heat, beat
ἄρχομαι	begin	ποιμαίνω	shepherd
βαστάζω	lift up, carry	προσδέχομαι	receive, welcome, expect
γίνομαι	become, happen		
διατάσσω	order	στηρίζω	strengthen
διώκω	persecute	συνάγω	lead together
ἐμπαίζω	ridicule, trick	σφάζω	butcher
ἕνεκεν	because	ταράσσω	confuse, disturb
ἐξάγω	lead out, free	τάσσω	put in charge of
ἐπιτάσσω	command	τίκτω	give birth
ἔρχομαι	come	φαῦλος, φαύλη, φαῦλον	evil, bad
κατέρχομαι	come down from		
κράζω	cry out		

STEP 59

VIDEO	PHOTO		
LIVE	NORMAL	FUTURE	CURRENT
βλέπω	ἔβλεψα	βλέψω	βέβλεφα
γράφω	ἔγραψα	γράψω	γέγραφα
	ἐγράφην p	γραφήσομαι p	γέγραμμαι mp
κρύπτω	ἔκρυψα	κρύψω	κέκρυφα
	ἐκρύβην p		κέκρυμμαι mp

What you need to know:
The camera-words in this STEP have stems that end in β, π, and φ. Notice how often ψ results from β, π, and φ bumping into σ.

Give it a try:
What's the dictionary form of the following words?
ἀποκαλυφθήσεται, βλέπων, γέγραπται, λείπει, ἐπέτρεψεν, ἐπέμφθη, ἀπεκάλυψας, γεγραμμένην, κέκρυπται, κλέψεις, ἀποκαλυφθῶσιν, βλέψον

Now you're the translator:
1. Καὶ ἀπ᾽ ἐμαυτοῦ οὐκ ἐλήλυθα, ἀλλ᾽ ἔστιν ἀληθινός, ὁ πέμψας με. 2. δικαιοσύνη γὰρ θεοῦ ἐν αὐτῷ ἀποκαλύπτεται ἐκ πίστεως εἰς πίστιν, καθὼς γέγραπται· ὁ δὲ δίκαιος ἐκ πίστεως ζήσεται. 3. ἡμᾶς δεῖ ἐργάζεσθαι τὰ ἔργα τοῦ πέμψαντός με ἕως ἡμέρα ἐστίν· ἔρχεται νὺξ ὅτε οὐδεὶς δύναται ἐργάζεσθαι. 4. μετανοήσατε οὖν καὶ ἐπιστρέψατε πρὸς τὸ ἐξαλειφθῆναι ὑμῶν τὰς ἁμαρτίας... 5. καὶ ἐν τῷ νόμῳ δὲ τῷ ὑμετέρῳ γέγραπται, ὅτι δύο ἀνθρώπων ἡ μαρτυρία ἀληθής ἐστιν. 6. ἐλπίζω γὰρ χρόνον τινὰ ἐπιμεῖναι πρὸς ὑμᾶς, ἐὰν ὁ κύριος ἐπιτρέψῃ. 7. μνημόνευε οὖν πόθεν πέπτωκας, καὶ μετανόησον καὶ τὰ πρῶτα ἔργα ποίησον. 8. ἦτε γὰρ ὡς πρόβατα πλανώμενοι, ἀλλὰ ἐπεστράφητε νῦν ἐπὶ τὸν ποιμένα καὶ ἐπίσκοπον τῶν ψυχῶν ὑμῶν. 9. Καὶ οἶδα, ὅτι ἡ ἐντολὴ αὐτοῦ ζωὴ αἰώνιός ἐστιν. ἃ οὖν ἐγὼ λαλῶ, καθὼς εἴρηκέν μοι ὁ πατήρ, οὕτως λαλῶ. 10. ὑμᾶς δὲ εἴρηκα φίλους, ὅτι πάντα, ἃ ἤκουσα παρὰ τοῦ πατρός μου, ἐγνώρισα ὑμῖν.

New words:

ἀναβλέπω	look upwards	θάπτω	bury
ἀναπίπτω	lay down, lean back	θλίβω	pressure, oppress, limit
ἀναστρέφω	upset, turn back and forth	καταλείπω	leave, abandon
ἀπέχω	receive and receipt, mid: keep distant	κλέπτω	steal
ἀπολείπω	leave behind	κρύπτω	hide
ἅπτω	light, kindle, mid: touch	λέγω (εἴπω)	say
		λείπω	leave behind
γι(γ)νώσκω	recognize	νίπτω	wash
διαλέγομαι	discuss, speak	παρέχω	offer, grant, bring about
δύναμαι	be able	πέμπω	send
ἐγκαταλείπω	abandon, turn over	πίπτω	fall
ἐκκόπτω	cut off	πόθεν	from where
ἐμβλέπω	look at, observe, give attention to	σέβομαι	honor
		στρέφω	turn
ἐπιπίπτω	fall out, lose, fail	συνέχω	hold together, pass: dispute
ἐπιστρέφω	turn around, return	τοσοῦτος	so large, so much
ἐπιτρέπω	allow	τύπτω	hit
ἔχω	have		

STEP 60

VIDEO	PHOTO		
LIVE	NORMAL	FUTURE	CURRENT
αἴρω	ἦρα (ἆραι: small all-around word)	ἀρῶ	ἦρκα
	ἤρθην p	ἀρθήσομαι p	ἦρμαι mp
ἀπαγγέλλω	ἀπήγγειλα	ἀπαγγελῶ	ἀπήγγελκα
	ἀπηγγέλην p normal photo 2	ἀπαγγελή-σομαι p	ἀπήγγελμαι mp
βάλλω	ἔβαλον	βαλῶ	βέβληκα
	ἐβλήθην p	βληθήσομαι p	βέβλημαι mp

What you need to know:
The camera-words in this STEP have stems that end in λ, ν, or ρ. Notice in the future/active forms and the normal photo/active and passive forms how the σ disappears.

Give it a try:
What's the dictionary form of the following words?
ἀγγέλλουσα, ἀπέστειλον, βάλλεται, ἔδειραν, διακρινέτωσαν, ἀπαγγελεῖ, ἀπεκρίνατο, ἀποστείλῃ, βάλλοντες, ἔσπειρας, φαίνεσθε, ἀπαγγέλλει, ἀποκρίθητε, ἀπέστειλεν, βληθήσῃ, φαίνοντι, δείραντες, ἀπέσταλκεν, φαίνωσιν, ἀπήγγελλον, δέροντες, ἀποστεῖλαι, σπείρουσιν, ἀπαγγείλατε.

Now you're the translator:
1. Μὴ στενάζετε, ἀδελφοί, κατ' ἀλλήλων, ἵνα μὴ κριθῆτε. 2. ὁ πιστεύσας καὶ βαπτισθεὶς σωθήσεται, ὁ δὲ ἀπιστήσας κατακριθήσεται. 3. καὶ ταχὺ πορευθεῖσαι εἴπατε τοῖς μαθηταῖς αὐτοῦ, ὅτι ἠγέρθη ἀπὸ τῶν νεκρῶν, καὶ ἰδοὺ προάγει ὑμᾶς εἰς τὴν Γαλιλαίαν, ἐκεῖ αὐτὸν ὄψεσθε. ἰδοὺ εἶπον ὑμῖν. 4. εἰ γὰρ ἐξ ἡμῶν ἦσαν, μεμενήκεισαν ἂν μεθ' ἡμῶν. 5. καὶ ἀποκριθεὶς ὁ Ἰησοῦς εἶπεν αὐτοῖς· πορευθέντες ἀπαγγείλατε Ἰωάννῃ, ἃ ἀκούετε καὶ

STEP 60

βλέπετε. 6. ἰδοὺ ἐξῆλθεν ὁ σπείρων τοῦ σπείρειν. καὶ ἐν τῷ σπείρειν αὐτὸν ἃ μὲν ἔπεσεν παρὰ τὴν ὁδόν. 7. ἔχοντες δὲ τὸ αὐτὸ πνεῦμα τῆς πίστεως, κατὰ τὸ γεγραμμένον· ἐπίστευσα, διὸ ἐλάλησα, καὶ ἡμεῖς πιστεύομεν, διὸ καὶ λαλοῦμεν, εἰδότες, ὅτι ὁ ἐγείρας τὸν κύριον Ἰησοῦν καὶ ἡμᾶς σὺν Ἰησοῦ ἐγερεῖ καὶ παραστήσει σὺν ὑμῖν. 8. καθὼς ἠγάπησέν με ὁ πατήρ, κἀγὼ ὑμᾶς ἠγάπησα· μείνατε ἐν τῇ ἀγάπῃ τῇ ἐμῇ. 9. ὁ δεχόμενος προφήτην εἰς ὄνομα προφήτου μισθὸν προφήτου λήμψεται, καὶ ὁ δεχόμενος δίκαιον εἰς ὄνομα δικαίου μισθὸν δικαίου λήμψεται. 10. πάντοτε γὰρ τοὺς πτωχοὺς ἔχετε μεθ᾽ ἑαυτῶν, καὶ ὅταν θέλητε, δύνασθε αὐτοῖς εὖ ποιῆσαι, ἐμὲ δὲ οὐ πάντοτε ἔχετε.

New words:

ἀνακρίνω	ask, question	καταγγέλλω	proclaim
ἀναλαμβάνω	accept, take along	καταισχύνω	dishonor, put to shame
γέμω	be full		
δέρω	beat someone	κατακρίνω	sentence
διακρίνω	examine	καταλαμβάνω	seize, win
διαμαρτύρομαι	swear, urge, witness to	λαμβάνω	take
		ὁράω	see
ἐκτείνω	stretch out, relax	παραγγέλλω	instruct
ἐντέλλομαι	command, give orders	περιβάλλω	throw something around, put on
ἐξαποστέλλω	send out, send away	προάγω	lead, go before
ἐπαγγέλλομαι	report, promise	προσλαμβάνομαι	take in, take along
ἐπαισχύνομαι	be ashamed	σπείρω	sow
ἐπιβάλλω	throw something on, put on	συλλαμβάνω	seize, catch, support, help
ἐπιμένω	remain, continue	ὑγιαίνω	be healthy
εὐφραίνω	cheer someone, Pass: be glad	φαίνομαι	appear
		φαίνω	shine
θέλω and εθέλλω	want		

STEP 61

CAMERA-WORDS			
P ICTURE ⇒⇒⇒			PHOTOGRAPH
LIGHT	ACTION	NEC. ROLE	NORMAL 2
B R I G H T	ACTIVE	I — we you — all of you he, she, it — they	ἔλαβ-ον -ον -ομεν -ες -ετε -εν -ον
B R I G H T	MIDDLE	I — we you — all of you he, she, it — they	ἐλαβ-όμην -όμην -όμεθα -ου -εσθε -ετο -οντο
D I M	ACTIVE	I — we you — all of you he, she, it — they	λάβ-ω -ω -ωμεν -ῃς -ητε -ῃ -ωσιν
D I M	MIDDLE	I — we you — all of you he, she, it — they	λάβ-ωμαι -ωμαι -ώμεθα -ῃ -ησθε -ηται -ωνται
F L A S H I N G	ACTIVE	you — all of you he, she, it — they	λάβ-ε -ε -ετε -έτω -έτωσαν
F L A S H I N G	MIDDLE	you — all of you he, she, it — they Word Chart	λαβ-οῦ -οῦ -εσθε -έσθω -έσθωσαν F-2,3,5,6,8,9

STEP 61

CAMERA-WORDS			
P I C T U R E ⇒ ⇒ ⇒			PHOTOGRAPH
LIGHT	ACTION	NEC. ROLE	MINI-NORMAL 2
BRIGHT	ACTIVE	I we you all of you he, she, it they	ἔγνω-ν -ν -μεν -ς -τε - -σαν
DIM	ACTIVE	I we you all of you he, she, it they	γνῶ γνῶ γνῶμεν γνῷς γνῶτε γνῷ γνῶσι(ν)
FLASH-ING	ACTIVE	you all of you he, she, it they	γνῶ-θι -θι -τε -τω -τωσαν

Strange but true:

There are two kinds of camera-words whose *photo* forms are different than those of παιδεύω (ἐπαίδευσα, ἐπαίδευσας, etc.):

1. *The normal photo 2:* This camera-word has *video* endings (recorded video endings when in *bright* light and live video endings when in *dim* light). And how do we tell it's a photo and not a recording if the endings are the same? Very simple: The word changes its *stem*.

λαμβάνω's *recorded video* form is ἐλάμβανον, for example, whereas its *normal photo 2* form is ἔλαβον; its *live video/dim* form is λαμβάνῃς, whereas its *normal photo 2/dim* form is λάβῃς.

You see that the endings stay the same, but the stem changes.

2. *The mini normal photo*: This camera-word is similar to the *normal photo 2* with the exception that when it changes its stem, it's whittled down to its very root. γινώσκω trims down to γνω as seen in the graph above. You can understand why we call it the mini-photo. These forms tend to be very short.

How to Read New Testament Greek

Give it a try:
What are the PLANs, PARTs, or PAs of the following words?
βαλέτω, βαλλόμενα, βάλωσιν, βεβληκότος, ἐβλήθη, φύγητε, φυγεῖν, ἔφυγον (2x), φεῦγε, φεύξονται, φευγέτωσαν, λιπών, βάλλεται, βληθήσῃ, βάλε, βληθῇ, βάληται, βάλλουσιν, βαλεῖν, βάλλοντες, ἔβαλον, λαβεῖν, ἐλάβετε, ἥμαρτον, ἁμαρτήσῃ, ἥμαρτεν, ἁμάρτανε, ἥμαρτες, ἁμαρτάνοντες

What are the PLANs, PARTs, or PAs of the following camera-words which have miniphoto forms? ἀνέβη, ἀναβαίνει, ἀναβαινόντων, ἀνέβησαν, ἀναβέβηκεν, ἀναβαίνοντα, ἀνάβητε, ἀνέβαινον, ἀναβήσεται, ἀνάβα, καταβαῖνον, καταβήσῃ, καταβάτω, καταβάς, καταβαίνουσα, ἐμβάς, μεταβήσεται, χαῖρε, χαίρειν, ἐχάρησαν, χαίρετε, χαίρῃ, ἐχάρητε, χαρήσεται, χαίροντες, χαρῆναι, χαίρω, χαρῆτε, χαίρωμεν, χαρήσομαι, γνώτω, ἔγνων, γινωσκέτω, γνωσθήσεται, ἐγνώκειτε, γνούς, γινώσκεται, γνῶναι, ἔγνωσαν, γινώσκετε, γνώσεσθε, ἔγνω, γνόντες, ἐγίνωσκεν, γνώσομαι, ἔγνως, ἐγνώσθη, γινώσκεις, ἔγνωκα, γνῶτε, γνώσεται, ἐγνώκαμεν, ἀνέγνωτε

Now you're the translator:
1. Καὶ εἶπεν αὐτῷ· ἀκολούθει μοι. καὶ καταλιπὼν πάντα ἀναστάς ἠκολούθει αὐτῷ. 2. τίς ὁ κατακρινῶν; Χριστὸς Ἰησοῦς ὁ ἀποθανών, μᾶλλον δὲ ἐγερθείς, ὅς ἐστιν ἐν δεξιᾷ τοῦ θεοῦ ὃς καὶ ἐντυγχάνει ὑπὲρ ἡμῶν. 3. ἃ καὶ ἐμάθετε καὶ παρελάβετε καὶ ἠκούσατε καὶ εἴδετε ἐν ἐμοί, ταῦτα πράσσετε. 4. πορεύσομαι πρὸς τὸν πατέρα μου καὶ ἐρῶ αὐτῷ· πάτερ, ἥμαρτον εἰς τὸν οὐρανὸν καὶ ἐνώπιόν σου, οὐκέτι εἰμὶ ἄξιος κληθῆναι υἱός σου. 5. ἔπρεπεν γὰρ αὐτῷ δι' ὃν τὰ πάντα καὶ δι' οὗ τὰ πάντα, πολλοὺς υἱοὺς εἰς δόξαν ἀγαγόντα τὸν ἀρχηγὸν τῆς σωτηρίας αὐτῶν διὰ παθημάτων τελειῶσαι. 6. καίπερ ὢν υἱός, ἔμαθεν ἀφ' ὧν ἔπαθεν τὴν ὑπακοήν. 7. καὶ εὐθέως ἐπελάθετο ὁποῖος ἦν. 8. οὐ γὰρ ἄδικος ὁ θεὸς ἐπιλαθέσθαι τοῦ ἔργου ἡμῶν καὶ τῆς ἀγάπης ἧς ἐνεδείξασθε εἰς τὸ ὄνομα αὐτοῦ. 9. παντὸς ἀκούοντος τὸν λόγον τῆς βασιλείας καὶ μὴ συνιέντος ἔρχεται ὁ πονηρὸς καὶ ἁρπάζει τὸ ἐσπαρμένον ἐν τῇ καρδίᾳ αὐτοῦ. 10. οὐ δύναται πόλις κρυβῆναι ἐπάνω ὄρους κειμένη.

New words:

αἴρω	lift, carry, remove	ἐπάνω	more, over and above
ἁμαρτάνω	sin	ἐπιλανθάνομαι	forget
ἀναβαίνω	go up, ascend	εὑρίσκω	find
ἀναγινώσκω	read	καταβαίνω	go down, descend
ἀποθνῄσκω	die	κερδαίνω	gain something
ἀρχηγός, ὁ	leader	μανθάνω	learn
ἐμβαίνω	enter	μεταβαίνω	go somewhere else, go over,
ἐπαίρω	lift up, rise up against, put on airs	ὅσος,η,ον	as great, how great, as much, how much

STEP 61

παραλαμβάνω	take over, receive, take along
πάσχω	suffer
περιτέμνω	circumcise, Pass: be circumcised
πολέω	sell
προγράφω	write beforehand, display
σφόδρα	very (much)

STEP 62

ADD-ON WORDS MAKE COMPARISONS
(in necessary role)

TYPE	COMPARATIVE	SUPERLATIVE
ὁ ἀγαθός	κρείσσων	κράτιστος
ἡ ἀγαθή	κρείσσων	κρατίστη
τό ἀγαθόν	κρεῖσσον	κράτιστον
good	better	best
ὁ ἅγιος	ἁγιώτερος	ἁγιώτατος
ἡ ἁγία	ἁγιώτερα	ἁγιωτάτη
τό ἅγιον	ἁγιώτερον	ἁγιώτατον
holy	holier	holiest
ὁ καλός	καλλίων	κάλλιστος
ἡ καλή	καλλίων	καλλίστη
τό καλόν	κάλλιον	κάλλιστον
beautiful	more beautiful	most beautiful
ὁ μέγας	μείζων	μέγιστος
ἡ μεγάλη	μείζων	μεγίστη
τό μέγα	μεῖζον	μέγιστον
large	larger	largest
ὁ πολύς	πλείων	πλεῖστος
ἡ πολλή	πλείων	πλείστη
τό πολύ	πλεῖον	πλεῖστον
many	more	most

What you need to know:

Add-on words sometimes need to make comparisons: They don't just want to say something is *big*, for example, but that it's *bigger* or *greater* than something else; or even that it's the *biggest* or the *greatest*.

In English we just add an *-er* or an *-est* to an add-on word and we get the *biggers*, *betters,* and *greatests* that we need. If that doesn't work, then we always have made-to-order words like *worse* and *worst* to help us out.

Greek comparisons are achieved in much the same way. Sometimes -τερος, or -τατος are added to the stem of an add-on word which is the same as adding an *-er* or an *-est* to an English add-on word (ἰσχυρός *[strong]*, ἰσχυρότερος

STEP 62

[stronger], ἰσχυρότατος *[strongest]*). Sometimes irregular forms are used, such as ὀλίγος *(few)*, ἐλάσσων *(fewer)*, ἐλάχιστος *(fewest)*.

Strange but true!
It often happens that there is no third form in Greek. In that case, the second form is used in its place, and the context determines the intended meaning.

Don't miss it!
Add-on words can also add information to camera-words. To do this, add-on words often take their *plural/general-supporting* form—καλῶν *(beautiful)*, for example—and replace the ν with an ς. The result is καλῶς, *(beautifully, well)*.

Other examples are ἀκριβῶς *(accurately)*, ἁπρῶς *(simply)*, βαρέως *(heavily)*, and εὐσχημόνως *(decently)*.

New words:

ἄνωθεν	from above
ἐνεργής,ές	effective
ἐπιφαίνω	appear, become visible
εὐγενής,ές	weil-born, noble-minded
εὐσεβής,ές	godly
καθεύδω	sleep
κοσμικός,ή	earthly, worldly
μήποτε	so that...not, lest

STEP 63

NUMBERS	ADD-ON NUMBERS	
1 εἷς, μία, ἕν	πρῶτος,η,ον *first*	ἅπαξ *once*
2 δύο	δεύτερος,ερα,ον *second*	δίς *twice*
3 τρεῖς, τρία	τρίτος,η,ον *third*	τρίς *three times*
4 τέσσαρες, τέσσαρα	τέταρτος,η,ον *etc.*	τετράκις *etc.*
5 πέντε	πέμπτος,η,ον	πεντάκις
6 ἕξ	ἕκτος,η,ον	ἑξάκις
7 ἑπτά	ἕβδομος,η,ον	ἑπτάκις
8 ὀκτώ	ὄγδοος,η,ον	ὀκτάκις
9 ἐννέα	ἔνατος,η,ον	ἐνάκις
10 δέκα	δέκατος,η,ον	δεκάκις
20 εἴκοσι	εἰκοστός	εἰκοσάκις
90 ἐνενήκοντα	ἐνενηκοστός	
100 ἑκατόν	ἑκατοστός	
200 διακόσιοι	διακοσιοστός etc.	
300 τριακόσιοι		
400 τετρακόσιοι		
500 πεντακόσιοι		
600 ἑξακόσιοι		
700 ἑξακόσιοι		
800 ὀκτακόσιοι		
900 ἐνακόσιοι		
1000 χίλιοι	χιλιοστός	χιλιάκις
2000 δισ-χίλιοι	δισ-χιλιοστός	etc.
3000 τρισ-χίλιοι	τρισ-χιλιοστός	
10000 μύριοι,αι,α	μυριοστός	μυριάκις

Word Chart K,L-15

What you need to know:
Only the first four numbers (and the hundreds) change their endings.

Give it a try:
What roles are the following words playing and how would you translate them?
ἕξ, ἕν, δεκάτῳ, τέσσαρσιν, τριακοσίαις, ἑβδομηκοστοῦ, εἴκοσι, ἑκατόν, χιλίους, ἐννέα, δυσίν, τριῶν, πεμπτοί, διακοσίους, ὀγδόη, τρεῖς, δεκατέσσαρα, μιᾶς, ἕνδεκα, ἑξακοστά, ὀκτακοσιοστῆς

STEP 63

Now you're the translator:
1. Οἱ δὲ λέγουσιν αὐτῷ· οὐκ ἔχομεν ὧδε εἰ μὴ πέντε ἄρτους καὶ δύο ἰχθύας. 2. ἔπειτα μετὰ τρία ἔτη ἀνῆλθον εἰς Ἱεροσόλυμα ἱστορῆσαι Κηφᾶν. 3. λέγω ὑμῖν, ταύτῃ τῇ νυκτὶ ἔσονται δύο ἐπὶ κλίνης μιᾶς, ὁ εἷς παραλημφθήσεται καὶ ὁ ἕτερος ἀφεθήσεται. 4. εἷς κύριος, μία πίστις, ἓν βάπτισμα· εἷς θεὸς καὶ πατὴρ πάντων, ὁ ἐπὶ πάντων καὶ διὰ πάντων καὶ ἐν πᾶσιν. 5. ἔπειτα ὤφθη ἐπάνω πεντακοσίοις ἀδελφοῖς ἐφάπαξ, ἐξ ὧν οἱ πλείονες μένουσιν ἕως ἄρτι. 6. καὶ εἶπαν αὐτῷ· κύριε, ἔχει δέκα μνᾶς. 7. καὶ μεθ᾽ ἡμέρας ὀκτὼ πάλιν ἦσαν ἔσω οἱ μαθηταὶ αὐτοῦ, καὶ Θωμᾶς μετ᾽ αὐτῶν. 8. ἀνέβη Σίμων Πέτρος καὶ εἵλκυσεν τὸ δίκτυον εἰς τὴν γῆν μεστὸν ἰχθύων μεγάλων ἑκατὸν πεντήκοντα τριῶν. 9. οὐ καταλείπει τὰ ἐνενήκοντα ἐννέα ἐν τῇ ἐρήμῳ καὶ πορεύεται ἐπὶ τὸ ἀπολωλὸς ἕως εὕρῃ αὐτό; 10. καὶ ὅτι ἐγήγερται τῇ ἡμέρᾳ τῇ τρίτῃ κατὰ τὰς γραφάς.

New words:

ἄρτι	now
αὔριον	tomorrow, soon
δέκατος,η,ον	tenth
ἕκτος,η,ον	sixth
ἔνατος,η,ον	ninth
ἑνδέκατος,η,ον	eleventh
ἐπαύριον	tomorrow
ἔπειτα	so that, then
ἐσθίω	eat
ἔσω	into, inwardly
ἐφάπαξ	at once
μνᾶ,ᾶς,ᾷ,ᾶν, ἡ	coin, mina (monetary unit)
πολλάκις	often
ποῦ	where
πρίν	earlier
πρωΐ	early in the morning
ὡσαύτως	in the same way, also

STEP 64

VIDEO		PHOTO	
LIVE	NORMAL	FUTURE	CURRENT
τίθημι	ἔθηκα	θήσω	τέθεικα
	ἐτέθην p	τεθήσομαι p	τέθειμαι mp

Word Chart G-6

What you need to know:

Up to now you've only been introduced to camera-words that end in -ω (-ομαι in the case of departed forms) in their dictionary forms. Some Greek camera-words change their endings according to a much different system than παιδεύω. We call them the μι camera-words, because their dictionary form (*live video/ bright/active/I* form) ends with -μι.

A complete chart of the endings of τίθημι is included on the Word Chart in the lower right-hand corner of the camera-word section. The μι words do not have exactly the same endings in all the forms as does τίθημι (due to vowels running into each other), but τίθημι serves well as a general pattern for the endings of the μι words.

The seven principle forms of the μι camera-words follow the general pattern of τίθημι.

Don't miss it!

The *live-video* and *normal-photo* forms of τίθημι's all-around word are also on the Word Chart: D-12 through 20, and I-12 through 20.

Give it a try:

What is the PLAN of the following forms of τίθημι?
τίθεσαι, τίθεσθαι, θέσθαι, τίθεσο, ἐτίθεσο, τίθενται, τέθειται, ἐτίθεντο, ἐτίθετο, θέσθωσαν, τιθεμένης, θοῦ, τιθῆσθε, τιθέσθω, τιθέσθωσαν, ἔθου, τίθημι, τιθῇς, τιθέναι, ἐτίθεις, ἔθηκεν, τέθηκεν, τιθεῖσα, θεῖσα, τεθηκώς, τίθησιν, τιθέτω, θεῖναι, θέν, ἔθεσαν, ἐτίθεμεν, τιθῶσιν, τιθέτωσαν, ἐτίθην

Now you're the translator:

1. Καὶ φωνήσας φωνῇ μεγάλῃ ὁ ᾿Ιησοῦς εἶπεν· πάτερ, εἰς χεῖράς σου παρατίθεμαι τὸ πνεῦμά μου. 2. ταύτην τὴν παραγγελίαν παρατίθεμαί σοι, τέκνον Τιμόθεε, κατὰ τὰς προαγούσας ἐπὶ σὲ προφητείας, ἵνα στρατεύῃ ἐν αὐταῖς τὴν καλὴν στρατείαν. 3. οὐκ ἔθετο ἡμᾶς ὁ θεὸς εἰς ὀργὴν ἀλλὰ εἰς περιποίησιν σωτηρίας διὰ τοῦ κυρίου ἡμῶν ᾿Ιησοῦ Χριστοῦ. 4. χάριν ἔχω τῷ ἐνδυναμώσαντί με Χριστῷ ᾿Ιησοῦ τῷ κυρίῳ ἡμῶν, ὅτι πιστόν με

ἡγήσατο θέμενος εἰς διακονίαν. 5. προσέχετε ἑαυτοῖς καὶ παντὶ τῷ ποιμνίῳ, ἐν ᾧ ὑμᾶς τὸ πνεῦμα τὸ ἅγιον ἔθετο ἐπισκόπους, ποιμαίνειν τὴν ἐκκλησίαν τοῦ θεοῦ. 6. ἐγείρεται ἐκ τοῦ δείπνου καὶ τίθησιν τὰ ἱμάτια, καὶ λαβὼν λέντιον διέζωσεν ἑαυτόν. 7. καὶ λέγει αὐτῷ· πᾶς ἄνθρωπος πρῶτον τὸν καλὸν οἶνον τίθησιν. 8. κατὰ μίαν σαββάτου ἕκαστος ὑμῶν παρ' ἑαυτῷ τιθέτω θησαυρίζων ὅ τι ἐὰν εὐοδῶται. 9. ὁ δὲ ἑνὶ ἑκάστῳ αὐτῶν τὰς χεῖρας ἐπιτιθεὶς ἐθεράπευεν αὐτούς. 10. οὐχ ὑμεῖς με ἐξελέξασθε, ἀλλ᾽ ἐγὼ ἐξελεξάμην ὑμᾶς, καὶ ἔθηκα ὑμᾶς ἵνα ὑμεῖς ὑπάγητε καὶ καρπὸν φέρητε καὶ ὁ καρπὸς ὑμῶν μένῃ.

New words:

ἀγνός, ή, όν	holy, pure
ἀλλότριος, α, ον	not one's own, strange
ἀποτίθεμαι	take off, undress
διατίθεμαι	decree, assign
διότι	therefore, because
ἐκλέγομαι	choose
ἐνδυναμόω	strengthen
ἐπιτίθημι	lay on, put on
ἡγέομαι	lead, be of the opinion
θεμέλιον, τό	foundation
θερίζω	harvest
θησαυρίζω	collect, save
κακόω	do evil
καταλλαγή, ἡ	reconciliation
καταλλάσσω	reconcile
ὅπλα, τά	weapons
παρατίθημι	lay before, entrust to
πίνω	drink
προστίθημι	add to
τίθεμαι	set, place, lay
τίθημι	set, place, lay
φέρω	carry, bear, bring along
ὑπάγω	go away

STEP 65

VIDEO	PHOTO		
LIVE	NORMAL	FUTURE	CURRENT
δίδωμι	ἔδωκα	δώσω	δέδωκα
	ἐδόθην p	δοθήσομαι p	δέδομαι mp

What you need to know:
The endings of δίδωμι are similar to those of τίθημι, but because the stem of δίδωμι ends in -o, o's and ω's replace the ε's and η's.

Give it a try:
What's the PLAN of the following forms of δίδωμι?
δίδοσαι, δέδοται, διδόμενον, δεδομένον, ἔδου, δῷ, διδῷ, δίδοσο, ἐδίδοσθε, δοῦ, δίδοσθαι, δόσθαι, δεδόσθαι, δώσω, δίδωμι, δός, δίδου, δίδοτε, δοθήσεται, δώσουσιν, δῶτε, διδόναι, δώσει, δότε, δοθῇ, δοῦναι, ἐδόθη, δέδωκεν, ἔδωκεν, δέδωκας, δίδωσιν, δῷ

Now you're the translator:
Οἴδατε ὅτι μετὰ δύο ἡμέρας τὸ πάσχα γίνεται καὶ ὁ υἱὸς τοῦ ἀνθρώπου παραδίδοται εἰς τὸ σταυρωθῆναι. 2. συστρεφομένων δὲ αὐτῶν ἐν τῇ Γαλιλαίᾳ εἶπεν αὐτοῖς ὁ Ἰησοῦς· μέλλει ὁ υἱὸς τοῦ ἀνθρώπου παραδίδοσθαι εἰς χεῖρας ἀνθρώπων, καὶ ἀποκτενοῦσιν αὐτόν, καὶ τῇ τρίτῃ ἡμέρᾳ ἐγερθήσεται. 3. πᾶν ὃ δίδωσίν μοι ὁ πατὴρ πρὸς ἐμὲ ἥξει, καὶ τὸν ἐρχόμενον πρός με οὐ μὴ ἐκβάλω ἔξω. 4. εἰρήνην τὴν ἐμὴν δίδωμι ὑμῖν· οὐ καθὼς ὁ κόσμος δίδωσιν ἐγὼ δίδωμι ὑμῖν. 5. παντὶ αἰτοῦντί σε δίδου, καὶ ἀπὸ τοῦ αἴροντος τὰ σὰ μὴ ἀπαίτει. 6. μηδενὶ κακὸν ἀντὶ κακοῦ ἀποδιδόντες· προνοούμενοι καλὰ ἐνώπιον πάντων ἀνθρώπων.

Don't miss it!
In sentence 2, you see two words together in the general-supporting role. One of the words is an all-around word. This is a special *general-support/add-on thought*. It is a special way the Greek language has of adding an extra thought to the main thought. It is characterized by both an all-around word and a something-word together in the general-supporting role.

If the *live-video* form of the all-around word is used, then the translation is usually begun with *when...* or *as....* If a normal- or current-photo form is used, then the translation is usually begun with *after....*

STEP 65

Strange but true:
αὐτῶν in this case is actually playing the *necessary role* although it has a general-supporting role ending and, therefore, συστρεφομένον αὐτῶν means *as <u>they</u> were coming together*.

Give it a try:
How would you translate the following *general-supporting/add-on thoughts*?
δύνοντος δὲ τοῦ ἡλίου (δύνω = going down), καθημένου (καθῆσθαι = sit down) δὲ αὐτοῦ ἐπὶ τοῦ ὄρους τῶν ἐλαίων προσῆλθον αὐτῷ οἱ μαθηταί, ταῦτα αὐτοῦ λαλοῦντος αὐτοῖς, ἰδοὺ ἄρχων προσεκύνει αὐτῷ σοῦ ποιοῦντος ἐλεημοσύνην μὴ γνώτω ἡ ἀριστερά σου.

New words:

αἰτέω	ask, demand	κρούω	knock
ἀντίλυτρον, τό	ransom	κἀκεῖθεν	from there
ἀεί	always	μεσίτης, ὁ	go between
ἀπαιτέω	ask for, demand back	μεταδίδωμι	impart, share
		ὅθεν	from where
ἀποδίδωμι	give away, return, reward	παραδίδωμι	hand over, deliver
		παραιτέομαι	ask for, decline, reject
ἀποκτείνω	kill		
δηνάριον, τό	denarius	πιπράσκω	sell
δίδωμι	give	συστρέφω	gather up, come together
ἐκβάλλω	throw out, release		
ἐπιδίδωμι	hand over, give up	χρεία, ἡ	need, deficiency
ἐποικοδομέω	build up	χωρίον, τό	field
ἥκω	come, be present		
θνητός,ή,όν	mortal		
κατακλίνω	settle in, Med: sit down to dinner		

STEP 66

VIDEO	PHOTO	
LIVE	NORMAL	FUTURE
ἵστημι	ἔστησα	στήσω
	ἐστάθην p	σταθήσομαι p

What you need to know:
The endings of ἵστημι are similar to those of τίθημι, but because the stem ends with -α, α's replace the ε's. The *current-photo* form of ἵστημι means *I stand*. The *previous-photo* form is εἱστήκειν which means *I stood*.

Strange but true!
The *normal-photo medium* form of ἵστημι means *I place (something) for myself* and not *I placed myself* as you would normally expect. This is because ἵστημι has a special *miniphoto* (STEP 59) form (ἔστην) that means *I place myself*. ἔστην changes its endings as do the *miniphoto* camera-words.

Strange but true!
The *current-photo* form of ἔστηκα has the *future-photo* form: ἐστηζω,*I will stand*. Plus, the plural current-photo forms are short (ἔσταμεν instead of ἐστήκαμεν), the small all-around word is short (ἑστάναι instead of ἐστηκέναι), and the all-around word is short (ἑστώς, ἑστῶτος, etc.).

Give it a try:
What is the PLAN of the following forms of ἵστημι?
ἐστάθη, ἑστώτων, στῆτε, ἀφίστατο, ἀναστῇ, συνέστηκεν, καθίσταται, παρεστηκότων, σταθήσεται, στῆναι, ἀναστάς, ἐξίσταντο, ἀντίστητε, ἐπίστηθι, συνίστασθαι, σταθῇ, ἑστώς, ἀναστάντες, ἀποστήτω, ἐπιστάς, ἀνθίστατο, ἔστησεν, καθίστησιν, στήσαντες, συνιστάνειν, στήσει, ἐξιστάνων, ἔστησαν, στήσητε, καθιστάνοντες, ἀναστήσω, συνίστημι, παρεστήσατε, συνιστάνω, στῆσαι, ἀναστήσας, συνιστάνομεν

Now you're the translator:
1. Καὶ οὗτοι ῥίζαν οὐκ ἔχουσιν, οἳ πρὸς καιρὸν πιστεύουσιν καὶ ἐν καιρῷ πειρασμοῦ ἀφίστανται. 2. ὃς ἐὰν οὖν βουληθῇ φίλος εἶναι τοῦ κόσμου, ἐχθρὸς τοῦ θεοῦ καθίσταται. 3. καὶ αὐτὴ χήρα ἕως ἐτῶν ὀγδοήκοντα

τεσσάρων, ἣ οὐκ ἀφίστατο τοῦ ἱεροῦ νηστείαις καὶ δεήσεσιν λατρεύουσα νύκτα καὶ ἡμέραν. 4. ἐξίσταντο δὲ πάντες οἱ ἀκούοντες αὐτοῦ ἐπὶ τῇ συνέσει καὶ ταῖς ἀποκρίσεσιν αὐτοῦ. 5. καὶ ἐξίσταντο πάντες οἱ ὄχλοι καὶ ἔλεγον· μήτι οὗτός ἐστιν ὁ υἱὸς Δαυίδ. 6. συνίστημι δὲ ὑμῖν Φοίβην τὴν ἀδελφὴν ἡμῶν, ... ἵνα αὐτὴν προσδέξησθε ἐν κυρίῳ ἀξίως τῶν ἁγίων, καὶ παραστῆτε αὐτῇ ἐν ᾧ ἂν ὑμῶν χρῄζῃ πράγματι. 7. ἐπισκέψασθε δέ, ἀδελφοί, ἄνδρας ἐξ ὑμῶν μαρτυρουμένους ἑπτὰ πλήρεις πνεύματος καὶ σοφίας, οὓς καταστήσομεν ἐπὶ τῆς χρείας ταύτης. 8. ἢ δοκεῖς ὅτι οὐ δύναμαι παρακαλέσαι τὸν πατέρα μου, καὶ παραστήσει μοι ἄρτι πλείω δώδεκα λεγιῶνας ἀγγέλων; 9. ἀγαγόντες δὲ αὐτοὺς ἔστησαν ἐν τῷ συνεδρίῳ.

New words:

ἀνίσταμαι	stand up, rise, arise	μήτι	it can't be that... (assumes negative answer)
ἀνίστημι	raise up		
ἀνθίσταμαι	oppose	νουθετέω	rebuke, remind, warn
ἀποκαθίστημι	restore	παρίσταμαι	approach, come to aid of
ἀρκέω	be enough, Pass: be satisfied with		
ἀτενίζω	look intently at something	παρίστημι	place beside, make available, present
ἀφίσταμαι	go away, fall away	προΐσταμαι	be in charge of, care for
ἀφίστημι	cause to revolt		
βούλομαι	want, wish	πρᾶγμα,ατος, τό	deed, event, undertaking
ἐνίσταμαι	be present, have come	συνέδριον, τό	Sanhedrin, high council of priests and scribes
ἐξίσταμαι	drive one out of one's senses, confuse		
ἐξίστημι	lose one's mind	συνίσταμαι	stand with, consist of
ἐπισκέπτομαι	examine, visit	συνίστημι	bring together, recommend
εὐνοῦχος, ὁ	eunich		
εὐώνυμος,ον	left	χρῄζω	have need of (question)
ἐφίσταμαι	stand by, approach	ὑπάρχω	be available
ἵστημι	place	ὡσεί	as, approximately
καθίστημι	bring to		
καθίσταμαι	bring, appoint, cause		
κἄν	and if, (καὶ + εαν)		
μερίζω	divide		

STEP 67

VIDEO	PHOTO		
LIVE	NORMAL	FUTURE	CURRENT
δύναμαι		δυνήσομαι	
	ἐδυνήθην p		δεδύνημαι mp
πίμπλημι	ἔπλησα	πλήσω	πέπληκα
	ἐπλήσθην p	πλησθήσομαι	πέπλησμαι mp

What you need to know:
πίμπλημι, δύναμαι, and ἐπίσταμαι have no live video forms in the New Testament. πίμπλημι is only found in the normal photo form in the New Testament (one future/passive form is the exception). δύναμαι and ἐπίσταμαι have only middle forms and change endings as does the medium form of ἵστημι.

ἵημι is only used in combined words in the New Testament. ἀφίημι, for example, is a combination of ἀπό + ἵημι and means *to send away*.

Give it a try:
What's the PLAN of the following words?
ἐπλήσθη, πλήσας, πλησθήσεται, ἐπλήσθησαν, πλησθῇς, ἔπλησαν, πλησθῆναι, δύναται, δυνάμενος, δύνασαι, δύνασθαι, ἐδύνασθε, δύνανται, ἀφίησιν, συνήκατε, ἀφεθήσεται, ἀφίενται, συνιείς, ἀφίετε, ἀφέντες, καθῆκαν, ἀφεθῇ, ἀφεῖναι, ἀφίεται, συνιᾶσιν, ἀφήσει, συνίων, παρεῖναι

Now you're the translator:
1. Καὶ μὴ δόξητε λέγειν ἐν ἑαυτοῖς· πατέρα ἔχομεν τὸν Ἀβραάμ· λέγω γὰρ ὑμῖν ὅτι δύναται ὁ θεὸς ἐκ τῶν λίθων τούτων ἐγεῖραι τέκνα τῷ Ἀβραάμ. 2. καὶ ἐὰν βασιλεία ἐφ' ἑαυτὴν μερισθῇ, οὐ δύναται σταθῆναι ἡ βασιλεία ἐκείνη· καὶ ἐὰν οἰκία ἐφ' ἑαυτὴν μερισθῇ, οὐ δυνήσεται ἡ οἰκία ἐκείνη στῆναι. 3. σὺ τίς εἶ ὁ κρίνων ἀλλότριον οἰκέτην; τῷ ἰδίῳ κυρίῳ στήκει ἢ πίπτει· σταθήσεται δέ, δυνατεῖ γὰρ ὁ κύριος στῆσαι αὐτόν. 4. καὶ ἰδὼν ὁ Ἰησοῦς τὴν πίστιν αὐτῶν εἶπεν τῷ παραλυτικῷ· θάρσει, τέκνον, ἀφίενταί σου αἱ ἁμαρτίαι. 5. διὰ τοῦτο λέγω ὑμῖν, πᾶσα ἁμαρτία καὶ βλασφημία ἀφεθήσεται τοῖς ἀνθρώποις, ἡ δὲ τοῦ πνεύματος βλασφημία οὐκ ἀφεθήσεται. 6. οὗ χάριν λέγω σοι, ἀφέωνται αἱ ἁμαρτίαι αὐτῆς αἱ πολλαί, ὅτι ἠγάπησεν πολύ· ᾧ δὲ ὀλίγον ἀφίεται, ὀλίγον ἀγαπᾷ. εἶπεν δὲ αὐτῇ·

ἀφέωνταί σου αἱ ἁμαρτίαι.

New words:

ἀμφότεροι,αι,α	both, all together (when more than 2)
ἀνίημι	let go, leave, give up
ἀρχαῖος,α,ον	ancient, old
ἀφίημι	let (someone) go, send away, forgive
ἄφρων,ον	foolish
ἐκεῖθεν	from there
ἐπίσταμαι	know, understand
θαρρέω and θαρσέω	be confident, courageous
ἵημι	send
καθίημι	let down from
κατεργάζομαι	accomplish, produce, subdue
κοιλία, ἡ	stomach
ναί	yes
οἰκέτης, ὁ	member of household, slave
ὀφείλω	be guilty, responsible
οὔτε	and not
παραλυτικός, ὁ	cripple
παρίημι	neglect
περιτίθημι	put or place around
πίμπλημι	fill up, fulfill
ποτίζω	give to drink, water (animals)
συνίημι	understand
χάριν	(in combination with οὗ) therefore
ὥστε	therefore, so that

STEP 68

VIDEO		PHOTO	
LIVE	NORMAL	FUTURE	CURRENT
δείκνυμι	ἔδειξα	δείξω	δέδειχα
	ἐδείχθην p	δειχθήσομαι p	δέδειγμαι mp

What you need to know:
 1. Camera-words ending with -νυμι change their endings much like camera-words ending with -μι (υ's often show up, however, in place of ε's, ο's, and ει's).
 2. κεῖμαι, κάθημαι, and φημί are only found in very few forms in the New Testament.

Strange but true:
 Sometimes endings similar to those of παιδεύω creep into the endings of words like δείκνυμι as though it were actually δεικνύω. This explains *live video/bright/active* forms like δεικνύεις and δεικνύει.

Give it a try:
 What's the PLAN of these words? δείκνυσιν, δεῖξον, δεικνύειν, δείξει, δείξατε, ἔδειξεν, δεικνύεις, ἔδειξα, δείκνυμι, δείξω, δειχθέντα, δειξάτω, δεικνύοντος, δεῖξαι; ἐνδείξωμαι, κεῖται, καθήμενος, καίμενα, κάθου, κεῖμαι, κάθηται, φασίν, κειμένη, ἐκάθητο, κείμεθα, καθήσεσθε, φησίν, καθημένῳ, ἔκειτο, φημί, κείμενον

Now you're the translator:
 1. Ὅσοι γὰρ ἀνόμως ἥμαρτον, ἀνόμως καὶ ἀπολοῦνται. 2. πορεύεσθε δὲ μᾶλλον πρὸς τὰ πρόβατα τὰ ἀπολωλότα οἴκου Ἰσραήλ. 3. οὐδεὶς ἐξ αὐτῶν ἀπώλετο εἰ μὴ ὁ υἱὸς τῆς ἀπωλείας, ἵνα ἡ γραφὴ πληρωθῇ. 4. μηδὲ γογγύζετε, καθάπερ τινὲς αὐτῶν ἐγόγγυσαν, καὶ ἀπώλοντο ὑπὸ τοῦ ὀλεθρευτοῦ. 5. (ὁ κύριος) μακροθυμεῖ εἰς ὑμᾶς, μὴ βουλόμενός τινας ἀπολέσθαι ἀλλὰ πάντας εἰς μετάνοιαν χωρῆσαι. 6. ἤδη δὲ ἡ ἀξίνη πρὸς τὴν ῥίζαν τῶν δένδρων κεῖται. 7. οὐ δύναται πόλις κρυβῆναι ἐπάνω ὄρους κειμένη. 8. αὐτοὶ γὰρ οἴδατε ὅτι εἰς τοῦτο κείμεθα. 9. καὶ εὐλόγησεν αὐτοὺς Συμεὼν καὶ εἶπεν πρὸς Μαριὰμ τὴν μητέρα αὐτοῦ ἰδοὺ οὗτος κεῖται εἰς πτῶσιν καὶ ἀνάστασιν πολλῶν ἐν τῷ Ἰσραὴλ καὶ εἰς σημεῖον ἀντιλεγόμενον. 10. (Ἰησοῦς) οὐκ ἔστιν ὧδε· ἠγέρθη γὰρ καθὼς εἶπεν· δεῦτε ἴδετε τὸν τόπον ὅπου ἔκειτο.

Seldom but noteworthy:
There is a fourth kind of *light* in New Testament Greek besides *bright, dim*, and *flashing*. Traditionally it has been called the *optative mood*, and it was often used to express a *wish* or a *desire* in classical Greek. Because its meaning is a close relative of the meanings expressed by *dim* light forms; the *dim* light forms gradually replaced the optative forms.

Some of the optative forms, however, continued to be used in the first century when the books and letters of the New Testament were written. Although there are less than seventy occurrences of the optative mood in the New Testament, it's enough so you should know what it is when it shows up.

Since the optative is only used in a very few forms, it is not necessary to reproduce complete charts of all its possible forms. Following are examples of the optative forms most often found in the New Testament:

Often:
    γένοιτο = *he, she, it* form of γίνομαι and is always used with μή: *May it never be!*
    εἴη = *he, she, it* form of εἰμί

Seldom in *live video*:
    πάσχοιτε = *all of you* form of πάσχω
    θέλοι = *he, she, it* form of θέλω
    ἔχοι = *he, she, it* form of ἔχω
    ἔχοιεν = *they* form of ἔχω

Seldom in *normal photo:*
    ἁγιάσαι = *you* form of ἁγιάζω
    καταρτίσαι = *he, she, it* form of καταρτίζω
    εὐαίμην = *he, she, it* form of εὔχομαι
    ψηλαφήσειαν = *they* form of ψηλαφάω
    φάγοι = *he, she, it* form of ἐσθίω
    εὔροιεν = *they* form of εὑρίσκω
    λάβοι = *he, she, it* form of λαμβάνω

Seldom with -μι camera-words:
    ὀναίμην = *I* form of ὀνίναμαι
    δύναιντο = *they* form of δύναμαι

New words:

ἀθετέω	give up, abandon
ἄκανθα, ἡ	thorn plant
ἀνάκειμαι	lie, be stored
ἀνατέλλω	cause to rise, rise up
ἀπ-όλλυμι	ruin, destroy, lose
ἀπ-όλλυμαι	be ruined, destroyed, lost
ἀσκός, ὁ	leather bag, wineskin
βέλος, τὸ	arrow
δείκνυμι	point out, prove
ἐκχέω	pour out, spill
ἐνδείκνυμαι	demonstrate
ἐξουθενέω	despise
ἐσθής, ῆτος, ἡ	clothing
ῥήγνυμι	tear, break (to pieces)
καθάπερ	just as
κάθημαι	sit
κεῖμαι	lie, recline, destined for something
κληρονομέω	inherit
λαμπρός, ά, όν	bright, shining
μακροθυμέω	have patience
ὄμνυμι	swear
πλησίον, ὁ	neighbor, one who is near
προσκυνέω	fall on knees, worship
σβέννυμι	eliminate, suppress
σκιά, ἡ	shadow
στέγη, ἡ	roof
φημί	say, claim
χωρέω	go away, make progress, contain
χωρίς	without

STEP 69

VIDEO	PHOTO		
LIVE	NORMAL	FUTURE	CURRENT
ἁμαρτάνω	ἡμάρτησα	ἁμαρτήσω	ἡμάρτηκα
	ἡμαρτήθην	ἁμαρτηθήσομαι	ἡμάρτημαι
αὐξάνω	ηὔξησα	αὐξήσω	ηὔξηκα
	ηὐξήθην	αὐξηθήσομαι	ηὔξημαι
γί(γ)νομαι	ἐγενόμην	γενήσομαι	γέγονα
	ἐγενήθην		γεγένημαι
διδάσκω	ἐδίδαξα	διδάξω	δεδίδαχα
	ἐδιδάχθην		δεδίδαγμαι
ἔρχομαι	ἦλθον	ἐλεύσομαι	ἐλήλυθα
λαμβάνω	ἔλαβον	λήμψομαι	εἴληφα
	ἐλήμφθην	λημφθήσομαι	εἴλημμαι
λέγω	εἶπον, εἶπα	ἐρῶ	εἴρηκα
	ἐρρέθην		εἴρημαι
ὁράω	εἶδον, ἴδον	ὄψομαι	ἑώρακα
	ὤφθην	ὀφθήσομαι	ἑώραμαι
τρέχω	ἔδραμον	δραμοῦμαι	δεδράμηκα
φέρω	ἤνεγκον	οἴσω	ἐνήνοχα
	ἠνέχθην		ἐνήνεγμαι

How to Read New Testament Greek

What you need to know:
There are a number of camera-words which are "irregular" in various ways. The very common word λέγω *(I say)*, for example, has the normal-photo form εἶπον, the future-photo form ἐρῶ, and the current-photo forms εἶπα or εἴρηκα. There are obviously three different stems: λεγ, ἐρ, and ἐπ.

This probably happened because originally there were three different words that meant *to say* (much like *say, speak,* and *talk* in English) and through general usage each became identified with one picture of a thought.

Now you're the translator:
1. Καὶ ἐγένετο ὅτε ἐτέλεσεν ὁ ᾽Ιησοῦς τοὺς λόγους τούτους, ἐξεπλήσσοντο οἱ ὄχλοι ἐπὶ τῇ διδαχῇ αὐτοῦ. 2. τότε ἰδὼν ὁ ἀνθύπατος τὸ γεγονὸς ἐπίστευσεν, ἐκπλησσόμενος ἐπὶ τῇ διδαχῇ τοῦ κυρίου. 3. ἀλλὰ ἔπεσεν εἰς τὴν γῆν τὴν καλὴν καὶ ἐδίδου καρπὸν ἀναβαίνοντα καὶ αὐξανόμενα καὶ ἔφερεν εἰς τριάκοντα καὶ ἐν ἑξήκοντα καὶ ἐν ἑκατόν. 4. οὐδὲ τὸν πατέρα τις ἐπιγινώσκει εἰ μὴ ὁ υἱὸς καὶ ᾧ ἐὰν βούληται ὁ υἱὸς ἀποκαλύψαι. 5. πάντα δὲ ταῦτα ἐνεργεῖ τὸ ἓν καὶ τὸ αὐτὸ πνεῦμα, διαιροῦν ἰδίᾳ ἑκάστῳ καθὼς βούλεται.

New words:

ἀναιρέω	take away, destroy	λαγχάνω	receive, obtain, be chosen by lots, cast lots
ἀρέσκω	try to please someone, be pleasing		
αὐξάνω	make grow, Pass: grow	λῃστής, ὁ	robber
		μεριμνάω	worry, be concerned
ἀφαιρέω	take away, cut off, Pass: be taken away	μιμνῄσκομαι	remember, care for
		ξηραίνω	make dry, Pass: dry out
γαμέω	marry		
διψάω	have thirst	πληθύνω	multiply, increase
δοκέω	be of the opinion, think, decide	προσφέρω	bring to, offer
		πυνθάνομαι	inquire
ἐκπλήσσομαι	be amazed, shocked	σαπρός, ά, όν	decayed, rotten, unwholesome
ἐλέγχω	expose, convince, correct		
		τρέφω	feed, take care of
ἐπέχω	hold fast	τρέχω	run, race
κατέχω	hold back, restrain, keep, occupy	τυγχάνω	meet, attain, happen
καύχημα, τό	source of pride		

STEP 70

CAMERA WORDS	οἶδα *know* Active	
P<small>ICTURE</small> ⇒ ⇒	PHOTOGRAPH	
	Current	Previous
BRIGHT	οἶδα οἴδαμεν οἶσθα οἴδατε οἶδεν οἴδασιν	ᾔδειν ᾔδειμεν ᾔδεις ᾔειτε ᾔδει ᾔδεισαν
DIM	εἰδῶ εἰδῶμεν εἰδῇς εἰδῆτε εἰδῇ εἰδῶσιν	
FLASHING	ἴσθι ἴστε ἴστω ἴστωσαν	
ALL-AROUND WORDS	εἰδώς, εἰδυῖα, εἰδός	
ὁ	εἰδώς εἰδότες εἰδότος εἰδότων εἰδότι εἰδόσι εἰδότα εἰδότας	
ἡ	εἰδυῖα εἰδυῖαι εἰδυίας εἰδυιῶν εἰδυίᾳ εἰδυίαις εἰδυῖαν εἰδυίας	
τό	εἰδός εἰδότα εἰδότος εἰδότων εἰδότι εἰδόσι εἰδός εἰδότα	
Small all-around words	εἰδέναι	

How to Read New Testament Greek

What you need to know:
οἶδα *(know)* is the *current-photo* form of a word that no longer has *live-video, recorded-video,* or *normal-photo* forms.
The previous-photo form of οἶδα is ᾔδειν *(knew).*

Give it a try:
Translate the following forms of οἶδα: οἶδεν, οἴδασιν, οἴδατε, εἰδώς, εἰδότα, εἰδῶ, εἰδῆτε, οἴδαμεν, εἰδόσιν, εἰδότες, ᾔδει, εἰδότας

Now you're the translator:
1. Οἶδεν γὰρ (ὁ θεός) ὁ πατὴρ ὑμῶν ὧν χρείαν ἔχετε πρὸ τοῦ ὑμᾶς αἰτῆσαι αὐτόν. 2. ἵνα δὲ εἰδῆτε ὅτι ἐξουσίαν ἔχει ὁ υἱὸς τοῦ ἀνθρώπου ἐπὶ τῆς γῆς ἀφιέναι ἁμαρτίας. 3. τότε λέγει τῷ παραλυτικῷ ἔγειρε, ἆρόν σου τὴν κλίνην καὶ ὕπαγε εἰς τὸν οἶκόν σου.

New words:

ἄπειμι	be absent, go away	πάρειμι	be present
δαιμονιώδης,ες	demonical	πέραν	on the other side
δόμα,ματος, τό	gift	πόσος,η,ον	how large?, how many?
εἰδέναι	know, understand	ποῖος,α,ον	of what kind,
εἶναι	be		which, what
καθαίρεσις, ἡ	destruction	τοιοῦτος,	so, of such a kind
κλίνη, ἡ	bed	τοιαύτη,	
λυχνός, ὁ	light, lamp	τοιοῦτον	
μάννα, τό	manna	φωτίζω	shine, reveal
νήπιος	infant, minor		
οὔ	no		
οἷος,α,ον	as		

STEP 71

CAMERA WORDS	εἰμί *I am* Active		
Picture ⇒ ⇒	VIDEO		PHOTO
	Live	Recorded	Future
BRIGHT	εἰμί ἐσμέν εἶ ἐστέ ἐστίν εἰσιν	ἤμην ἦμεν ἦς ἦτε ἦν ἦσαν	ἔσομαι ἐσόμεθα ἔσῃ ἔσεσθε ἔσται ἔσονται
DIM	ὦ ὦμεν ᾖς ἦτε ᾖ ὦσιν		
FLASHING	ἴσθι ἔσθε ἔστω ἔστωσαν		
ALL-AROUND WORDS	ὤν, οὖσα, ὄν		
ὁ	ὤν ὄντες ὄντος ὄντων ὄντι οὖσι(ν) ὄντα ὄντας		
ἡ	οὖσα οὖσαι οὔσης οὐσῶν οὔσῃ οὔσαις οὖσαν οὔσας		
τό	ὄν ὄντα ὄντος ὄντων ὄντι οὖσι(ν) ὄν ὄντα		
Small all-around words	εἶναι Active		ἔσεσθαι Middle

How to Read New Testament Greek

What you need to know:
In STEP 8 you were introduced to εἰμί, *I am*. In *dim light,* the forms of εἰμί are identical to the *dim light/ active* endings of παιδεύω.

The forms of εἰμί's all-around word (ὤν, οὖσα, ὄν) are also identical to the endings of the *live video/ active* all-around word of παιδεύω (παιδεύων, -ουσα, -ον (see Word Chart C-12,13,14).

The form of εἰμί's *small all-around word* is εἶναι, and the *flashing light* forms are ἴσθι, ἔστω, and ἔστε.

Give it a try:
Translate the following forms of εἰμί: ἦτε (2x), εἴ, ὦ, ἔσῃ, ἔστε, ἦν, οὖσα, ἔσεσθαι, εἰσίν, ἴστε, ὦσιν, ἔσεσθε, ἦμεν

Now you're the translator:
1. Καὶ νὺξ οὐκ ἔσται ἔτι, καὶ οὐκ ἔχουσιν χρείαν φωτός λύχνου καὶ φωτός ἡλίου, ὅτι κύριος ὁ θεὸς φωτίσει ἐπ᾽ αὐτούς. 2. καὶ οὕτως πάντοτε σὺν κυρίῳ ἐσόμεθα. 3. καὶ προσῆλθεν αὐτῷ μία παιδίσκη λέγουσα· καὶ σὺ ἦσθα μετὰ Ἰησοῦ τοῦ Γαλιλαίου. 4. οὐ περὶ τούτων δὲ ἐρωτῶ μόνον, ἀλλὰ καὶ περὶ τῶν πιστευόντων διὰ τοῦ λόγου αὐτῶν εἰς ἐμέ, ἵνα πάντες ἓν ὦσιν. 5. ὅτε ἤμην νήπιος, ἐλάλουν ὡς νήπιος.

STEP 72

TO EVALUATE:	THEN	NOW
Understanding of *_____		
Attitude toward *_____		
Work habits		
Life style		
Relationship with *_____		
Organization		
Goals		
Ability to recognize		
Ability to analyze		
Interest in *_____		
Patience towards *_____		
Use of time		
Place to study		
Motivation		
* = Fill in the blanks with the people and topics you think are important.		

Don't miss it!

This STEP is reserved for your evaluation of your own progress. It's designed to help you determine how far you've come and where you want to go from here?

379

How to Read New Testament Greek

Give it a try!

Use the above chart to get yourself thinking. Write your actual evaluation on another sheet of paper. Think of the topics on the chart in terms of where you were when you *began* learning Greek and where you are *now*.

Then try to identify your areas of strength and weakness. Ask yourself, *Where would I like to see improvement? What should I be doing that I'm not doing now?*

What you need to know:

The last four STEPS raise questions that are crucial to your further progress. You have ventured a good ways into the foothills of the Greek language, but the toughest trails and the steepest slopes still lie ahead. Now is the time to test your resolve and prepare yourself physically, mentally, and spiritually for the road ahead.

Don't miss it!

Have you ever noticed how people learn at different paces? Take toddlers who are learning to walk, for instance. A few are go-getters who take off at nine or ten months of age. The great majority get moving sometime between eleven and fourteen months. A final little group of slowpokes needs up to two years to find it's legs.

Sometimes the parents of the slowpokes get a little nervous about their kids' development (or lack of it). But by the time the first grade rolls around, you can't tell the go-getters from the late starters. All worries are long forgotten.

Could it be that you're a little nervous about the pace of your development in the Greek language? Is it possible you're questioning your ability to learn Greek because of some language go-getter out there who seems to soak up language like a sponge?

Don't let thoughts like that get under your skin. Keep plodding along and enjoy the skinned-knee phase of your Greek childhood. You'll grow out of it and find out after a few years that not even the go-getters are that much better than you are.

STEP 73

What you need to know:
Reviewing and preparing are to language learning, what watering and cultivating are to gardening. It's reviewing the work of the past that keeps language fresh and healthy, and it's preparing for the tasks ahead that promotes linguistic growth and assures a future harvest of understanding.

Don't miss it!
A good system of review doesn't have to be complicated or time-consuming, but it does need to be regular. Even thirty minutes of review every other day is enough to retain everything you've learned. Don't make the mistake of thinking that because you've finished the book, you can now set it aside. I've not yet set it aside myself, and I wrote it!

Don't miss it!
Now is the time to begin preparing for your next stage of learning New Testament Greek. Remember that *Learning How to Read New Testament Greek with People Just Like You* is only an introduction. It's like a small tool that helped you plant your garden of Greek. The reference books mentioned on pages 220 and 332 are the heavy-duty tools you will need in the coming days to cultivate your garden and bring in the harvest. The book following this one, *Learning How to Use New Testament Reference Books with People Just Like You,* can help you learn how to use these tools; after that you will be on your own.

Like any serious student, you must have a good library at your disposal. No worker can do a thorough job without the necessary tools. If you do not have the books you need, do what is necessary to get them—even if you have to sell your television, your stereo, your golf clubs, and your mountain bike to do it. Without the right tools, you'll not be able to get the work done. Now is the time to get equipped for the challenging task ahead.

STEP 74

What you need to know:

Take up your cross and follow me. Words like these from Jesus confronted his disciples with the reality of the life awaiting them. He knew that on the path he was taking, unrealistic expectations could waylay the hardiest of men.

The same is true of learning how to read the New Testament in Greek. Anyone who gets serious with the Scriptures is venturing onto the discipleship trail.

Don't miss it!

Many have set out to learn New Testament Greek, but few have continued the journey. Some quit because they'd not realized the complexity of the task, others underestimated the discipline that was required, and still others shied away from the sacrifices that were necessary.

Shouldering a cross does not sound pleasant, but it is the posture of a disciple, and it's the posture of anyone who is serious about learning to read the New Testament in Greek.

I'll not hide it from you. If you continue on, learning the Greek Scriptures will at times be painful; painful, because you will have to invest much time and energy before you'll be able to skillfully use the Greek New Testament, and painful, because you will find yourself going further down the road of discipleship. It's a marvelous road to travel, but it can only be traveled with a cross. It's good to know that from the very beginning.

Give it a try!

Read through Matthew in the New Testament and test your expectations. Are they realistic? Are they prepared for some adversity? Are they looking forward to the lessons to be learned from the underside of a cross?

STEP 75

Don't miss it!

I don't have a prayer of a chance. These are words that at one time or another run through the minds of even the most diligent people who are struggling to learn New Testament Greek. It is a task that can easily seem insurmountable.

What you need to know:

You *do* have a chance, particularly if you pray. So pray and plunge on, looking to the One who once said:

>Αἰτεῖτε καὶ δοθήσεται ὑμῖν
>ζητεῖτε καὶ εὑρήσετε
>κρούετε καὶ ἀνοιγήσεται ὑμῖν
>πᾶς γὰρ ὁ αἰτῶν λαμβάνει
>καὶ ὁ ζητῶν εὑρίσκει
>καὶ τῷ κρούοντι ἀνοιγήσεται
>
>Matt. 7:7-8

(Aren't you amazed you can actually understand some of that?)

Now you're the translator:

Διὸ αἰτεῖτε. ζητεῖτε. κρούετε.

The answers to the quizzes on pages 337 & 338

GRAMMAR CHECK #1

1. **K**   Camera-word
2. **I**   Picture
3. **G**   Light
4. **N**   Action
5. **A**   Necessary role
6. **T**   Necessary role
7. **R**   Departed
8. **M**   Live video
9. **S**   Recorded video
10. **H**   Normal photo
11. **O**   Future photo
12. **D**   Current photo
13. **Q**   Previous photo
14. **L**   I, you, he, she, it we, all of you, they
15. **F**   Complete thought
16. **P**   Bright
17. **J**   Dim
18. **B**   Flashing
19. **U**   Active
20. **C**   Middle
21. **E**   Passive

GRAMMAR CHECK #2

1. **S**   All-around word
2. **T**   Small all-around word
3. **O**   Role
4. **M**   Type
5. **U**   ὁ-word
6. **L**   ἡ-word
7. **F**   τό-word
8. **Q**   Matching endings
9. **N**   General supp. role
10. **P**   Directing role
11. **R**   Accomplishing role
12. **C,H**   Something-word
13. **A**   Add-on word
14. **I**   This, that
15. **E**   Add-on word
16. **D**   Add-a-thought word
17. **J**   Add-on phrase
18. **G**   Add-a-phrase word
19. **B**   Add-a-thought word
20. **K**   Add-on thought

Vocabulary

Αα

ἄβυσσος, ἡ	abyss, underworld
ἀγαθός, ή, όν	good
ἀγαθωσύνη, ἡ	goodness, uprightness
ἀγαλλιάω	rejoice
ἀγαπάω	love
ἀγάπη, ἡ	love
ἀγαπητός, ή, όν	beloved
ἀγγελία, ἡ	message
ἄγγελος, ὁ	messenger
ἁγιάζω	make holy
ἁγιασμός, ὁ	holiness
ἅγιος, ία, ον	holy
ἁγιότης, ητος, ἡ	holiness
ἁγιωσύνη, ἡ	holiness
ἄγκυρα, ἡ	anchor
ἁγνός, ή, όν	holy, pure
ἀγορά, ἡ	market place
ἀγοράζω	buy
ἀγρός, ὁ	field
ἄγω	lead, bring to
ἀγών, ῶνος, ὁ	contest, struggle
ἀγωνίζομαι	fight
Ἀδάμ	Adam
ἀδελφή, ἡ	sister
ἀδελφός, ὁ	brother
ᾅδης, ὁ	underworld
ἀδικία, ἡ	injustice
ἀδύνατος, ον	weak
ἀεί	always
ἀήρ, ἀέρος, ὁ	air
ἀθετέω	give up, abandon
Αἴγυπτος, ἡ	Egypt
αἷμα, ατος, τό	blood
αἴρω	lift, carry, remove
αἰσχύνη, ἡ	shame
αἰτέω	ask, demand
αἰτία, ἡ	cause, guilt
αἰών, ῶνος, ὁ	age, eternity
αἰώνιος, ον	eternal
ἀκαθαρσία, ἡ	impurity
ἀκάθαρτος, ον	impure
ἄκανθα, ἡ	thorn plant
ἀκοή, ἡ	hearing, report
ἀκολουθέω	follow
ἀκούω	hear
ἀκροβυστία, ἡ	uncircumcision
ἁλιεύς, έως, ὁ	fisherman
ἀλέκτωρ, ορος, ὁ	rooster
ἀλήθεια, ἡ	truth
ἀληθής, ές	true
ἀληθινός, ή, όν	true
ἀλλά	but, rather
ἀλλάσσω	change
ἀλλήλων, οις, ους	one another
ἄλλος, η, ο	other
ἀλλότριος, α, ον	not one's own, strange
ἅλυσις, εως, ἡ	chain, imprisonment
ἅμα	at the same time, together
ἁμαρτάνω	sin
ἁμαρτία, ἡ	sin
ἁμαρτωλός, ὁ	sinner
ἀμήν	truly, amen
ἀμνός, ὁ	lamb
ἄμπελος, ἡ	grapevine
ἀμπελών, ῶνος, ὁ	vineyard
ἀμφότεροι, αι, α	both, all together

ἄν	if	ἀνοίγω	open
ἀνά	acc: among, between	ἀνομία, ἡ	lawlessness
		ἀντί (ἀντ'/ἀνθ')	gen: in place of
ἀναβαίνω	go up, ascend	ἀντίλυτρον, τό	ransom
ἀναβλέπω	look upwards	ἄνω	above
ἀναγγέλλω	report	ἄνωθεν	from above
ἀναγινώσκω	read	ἄξιος, α, ον	worthy
ἀνάγκη, ἡ	necessity	ἀξιόω	consider worthy
ἀνάγω	lead up		make worthy
ἀναιρέω	take away, destroy, slay	ἀπαγγέλλω	report
		ἀπάγω	lead away,
ἀνάκειμαι	lie, recline		Pass: be missed
ἀνακρίνω	ask, question	ἀπαιτέω	ask for,
ἀναλαμβάνω	accept, take along		demand back
		ἀπαρνέομαι	deny, refuse,
ἀναλύω	depart, untie	ἀπαρχή, ἡ	first fruit
ἀναπαύομαι	rest, be refreshed	ἀπειθέω	be disobedient
		ἄπειμι	be absent,
ἀναπαύω	let rest		go away
ἀναπίπτω	lay down, camp, come upon	ἀπεκδύομαι	undress, disarm
		ἀπέρχομαι	leave
ἀνάστασις,εως, ἡ	resurrection	ἀπέχω	receive and
ἀναστρέφω	turn over, turn back and forth		receipt, Med: keep
ἀναστροφή, ἡ	conduct		away
ἀνατέλλω	cause to rise, rise up	ἀπιστία, ἡ	unbelief
		ἄπιστος, ον	unfaithful
ἀνατολή, ἡ	east, sunrise	ἁπλότης, ητος, ἡ	simplicity,
ἀναχωρέω	leave		sincerity
ἄνεμος, ὁ	wind	ἀπό (ἀπ'/ἀφ')	gen: from,
ἀνέχομαι	endure, put up with		away from
		ἀποδίδωμι	give away,
ἀνήρ, ὁ	man		return, reward
ἀνθίσταμι	oppose	ἀποθήκη, ἡ	barn
ἄνθρωπος, ὁ	man	ἀποθνῄσκω	die
ἀνίημι	let go, release, give up	ἀποκαθίστημι	restore
		ἀποκαλύπτω	reveal
		ἀποκάλυψις,εως, ἡ	revelation
ἀνίσταμαι	stand up, rise, arise	ἀποκρίνομαι	answer
		ἀποκτείνω	kill
ἀνίστημι	raise up	ἀπολείπω	leave behind

Greek-English Vocabulary

ἀπόλλυμαι	be ruined, destroyed, lost	ἀσεβής, ές	godless
ἀπόλλυμι	ruin, destroy, lose	ἀσέλγεια, ἡ	indecent conduct
ἀπολογέομαι	defend oneself	ἀσθένεια, ἡ	weakness, sickness
ἀπολούομαι	clean oneself up	ἀσθενής, ές	weak
ἀπολούω	wash up	ἀσκός, ὁ	leather bag, wineskin
ἀπολύτρωσις,εως,ἡ	liberation, redemption	ἀσπάζομαι	greet
		ἀσπασμός, ὁ	greeting
ἀπολύω	set free	ἀστήρ, έρος, ὁ	star
ἀποστέλλω	send	ἀσφαλής, ές	sure
ἀπόστολος, ὁ	envoy	ἀτενίζω	look intently
ἀποτίθεμαι	take off, undress	ἄτιμος, ἄτιμον	dishonorable
		ἄτομος, ον	indivisible
ἄπτω	light, kindle, Med: touch	αὐλή, ἡ	courtyard
		αὔριον	tomorrow, soon
ἀπώλεια, ἡ	waste, destruction	αὐξάνω	make grow, Pass: grow
ἄρα	therefore		
ἀργύριον, τό	silver, money	αὐτός, ή, ό	he, she, it
ἀργυροῦς,ᾶ οὖν	silver	ἀφαιρέω	take away, cut off, Pass: be taken away
ἀρέσκω	please, be pleasing		
ἀριθμός, ὁ	number		
ἀρκέω	be enough Pass: be satisfied with	ἄφεσις, εως, ἡ	forgiveness
		ἀφθαρσία, ἡ	immortality
		ἄφθαρτος, ον	immortal
ἀρνέομαι	refuse, deny	ἀφίημι	let go, forgive send away
ἀρνίον, τό	lamb		
ἁρπάζω	steal	ἀφίσταμαι	go away, fall away
ἀρραβών, ῶνος, ὁ	deposit, pledge	ἀφίστημι	cause to revolt
ἄρσην	manly		
ἄρτι	now	ἀφορίζω	set aside, choose
ἄρτος, ὁ	bread		
ἀρχαῖος, α, ον	ancient, old	ἄφρων, ον	foolish
ἀρχή, ἡ	beginning	ἄχρι	until
ἀρχηγός, ὁ	leader		
ἀρχιερεύς,έως, ὁ	high priest		
ἄρχομαι	begin		
ἄρχων,οντος, ὁ	ruler, prince		
ἀσέβεια, ἡ	ungodliness		

387

Β β

βάθος, ους, τό	depth
βαθύς, βαθεῖα	deep
βάλλω	throw
βαπτίζω	dip oneself, wash
βάπτισμα, ατος, τό	washing
βαπτιστής, ὁ	baptizer
βαρύς, εῖα, ύ	heavy
βασανίζω	torture, force
βασιλεία, ἡ	kingdom
βασιλεύς, έως, ὁ	king
βασιλεύω	rule
βαστάζω	lift up, carry
βέβαιος, α, ον	reliable
βέλος, τό	arrow
βῆμα, βήματος, τό	judgement seat
βιβλίον, τό	book
βίβλος, ἡ	book
βλασφημέω	blaspheme
βλασφημία, ἡ	blasphemy
βλέπω	see
βοάω	holler, call
βουλεύομαι	deliberate, resolve
βουλεύω	advise
βουλή, ἡ	advice, decision
βούλομαι	want, wish
βραχύς, εῖα, ύ	short
βρέφος, ους, τό	small child
βροντή, ἡ	thunder
βρῶμα, ατος, τό	food
βρῶσις, εως, ἡ	eating, food

Γ γ

Γαλιλαία, ἡ	Galilee
γαμέω	marry
γάμος, ὁ	wedding
γάρ	because
γέ	at least, even
γέεννα, ἡ	hell
γελάω	laugh
γέμω	be full
γενεά, ἡ	generation
γεννάω	conceive, bear
γένος, ους, τό	generation
γεύομαι	taste
γεωργός, ὁ	farmer
γῆ, ἡ	earth
γι(γ)νώσκω	recognize, know,
γίνομαι	become
γλῶσσα, ἡ	tongue, language
γνώμη, ἡ	opinion, decision
γνωρίζω	make known
γνῶσις, εως, ἡ	knowledge
γνωστός, ή, όν	known
γονεῖς, έων, οἱ	parents
γόνυ, ατος, τό	knee
γράμμα, ατος, τό	letter, writing
γραμματεύς, έως, ὁ	scribe
γραφή, ἡ	writing
γράφω	write
γρηγορέω	be watchful, keep eyes open
γυμνός, ή, όν	naked
γυμνότης, ητος, ἡ	nakedness, want
γυνή, ἡ	woman

Δ δ

δαιμονίζομαι	be demon-possessed
δαιμόνιον, τό	demon
δαιμονιώδης, ες	demonical
δάκρυον, τὸ	tears, weeping
δέ	but, and

Greek-English Vocabulary

δέησις, εως, ἡ	request
δεῖ	it is necessary, one must
δείκνυμι	point out, prove
δεῖπνον, τό	meal
δέκα	ten
δέκατος, η, ον	tenth
δένδρον, τό	tree
δεξιός, ά, όν	right, right side
δέομαι	ask
δέρω	beat someone
δέσμιος, ὁ	prisoner
δεσμός, ὁ	chains
δεσπότης, ὁ	master, owner
δεῦτε	come, come on
δέχομαι	receive
δέω	bind
δηνάριον, τό	denarius
διά (δι')	gen: through acc: because of
διάβολος, ὁ	devil
διαθήκη, ἡ	testament
διακονέω	serve
διακονία, ἡ	service
διάκονος, ὁ	servant
διακρίνω	examine
διαλέγομαι	discuss
διαλογίζομαι	consider, discuss
διαλογισμός, ὁ	thought, consideration
διαμαρτύρομαι	swear, urge, witness to
διαμερίζω	share, divide distribute
διάνοια, ἡ	thought, plan, understanding
διατάσσω	order
διατίθεμαι	decree, assign
διαφέρω	differentiate
διδασκαλία, ἡ	teaching
διδάσκαλος, ὁ	teacher
διδάσκω	teach
διδαχή, ἡ	teaching
δίδομαι	give
δίδωμι	give
διέρχομαι	go through
δικαιος, α, ον	just
δικαιοσύνη, ἡ	justice
δικαιόω	justify, make just
δικαίωμα, ατος, τό	regulation
δίκτυον, τό	net
διό	therefore
διότι	therefore, because
διψάω	have thirst
διωγμός, ὁ	persecution
διώκω	persecute
δοκέω	be of the opinion, think, decide
δοκιμάζω	test
δοκιμή, ἡ	approval, character, test
δόλος, ὁ	treachery
δόμα, ατος, τό	gift
δόξα, ἡ	glory, honor
δοξάζω	glorify, honor
δουλεία, ἡ	slavery
δουλεύω	serve
δοῦλος, ὁ	slave
δουλόω	enslave
δράκων, οντος, ὁ	dragon
δύναμαι	be able
δύναμις, εως, ἡ	power
δυνατός, ή, ό	strong, powerful
δύο	two
δωρεά, ἡ	present
δῶρον, τό	gift

Εε

ἐάν	if, in case that	ἐκκόπτω	cut off
ἐάω	let, allow	ἐκλέγομαι	choose
ἐγγίζω	come near	ἐκλεκτός, ή, όν	chosen
ἐγγύς	near	ἐκλογή, ἡ	selection, election
ἐγγύτερον	nearer	ἐκπλήσσομαι	be amazed, shocked
ἐγείρω	abandon, turn over	ἐκπορεύομαι	go away
ἐγκαταλείπω	abandon, turn over	ἐκτείνω	stretch out, relax
ἐγκράτεια, ἡ	self control	ἕκτος, η, ον	sixth
ἐγώ	I	ἐκχέω	pour out, spill
ἔθνος, ους, τό	people	ἐλαία, ἡ	olive tree
ἔθος, ους, τό	custom	ἔλαιον, τό	oil
εἰδέναι	know, understand	ἐλέγχω	expose, convince, correct
εἴδωλον, τό	idol		
εἰκών, όνος, ἡ	picture	ἐλεέω	have compassion
εἰ μή	if not, except		
εἶναι	be	ἐλεημοσύνη, ἡ	good deed, alms
εἶπεν	he said		
εἶπον	I said, they said	ἔλεος, έους, τό	compassion
		ἐλευθερία, ἡ	freedom
εἰρηνεύω	make peace	ἐλευθερόω	free
εἰρήνη, ἡ	peace	ἐλθεῖν	come
εἷς, μία, ἕν	one	ἐλπίζω	expect
εἰς	acc: in, into	ἐλπίς, ίδος, ἡ	expectation
εἰσέρχομαι	enter	ἐμβαίνω	enter
εἰσπορεύομαι	go in	ἐμβλέπω	look at, observe, give attention to
εἶτα	then, next		
εἴτε...εἴτε	whether...or		
ἐκ (ἐξ)	gen: out of		
ἕκαστος, η, ον	each one	ἐμπαίζω	ridicule, trick
ἑκατοντάρχης, ὁ	centurion	ἔμπροσθεν	in front, before
ἐκβάλλω	throw out, release	ἐμφανίζω	reveal, explain
ἐκεῖ	there		
ἐκεῖθεν	from there	ἐν	dir: in
ἐκεῖνος, η, ο	that	ἔναντι	before
ἐκκλησία, ἡ	family of believers, gathering of believers	ἔνατος, η, ον	ninth
		ἐνδείκνυμαι	demonstrate
		ἑνδέκατος, η, ον	eleventh
		ἔνδυμα, ατος, τό	clothing

Greek-English Vocabulary

ἐνδυναμόω	strengthen
ἐνδύομαι	clothe oneself
ἐνδύω	dress
ἕνεκεν	because
ἐνέργεια, ἡ	power
ἐνεργέω	work, be effective
ἐνεργής, ές	effective
ἐνιαυτός, ὁ	year
ἐνίσταμαι	be present, have come
ἔνοχος, ον	guilty
ἐντέλλομαι	command, give orders
ἐντολή, ἡ	command
ἐνώπιον	in sight of, before
ἐξάγω	lead out, free
ἐξαποστέλλω	send out, send away
ἐξέρχομαι	go out
ἔξεστιν	it is permitted, it is possible
ἐξίσταμαι	drive out of one's senses, confuse
ἐξίστημι	lose one's mind
ἐξομολογέω	promise
ἐξουθενέω	despise
ἐξουσία, ἡ	authority
ἔξω	outside
ἔξωθεν	from outside
ἑορτή, ἡ	festival
ἐπαγγελία, ἡ	promise
ἐπαγγέλλομαι	report, promise
ἔπαινος, ὁ	praise
ἐπαίρω	lift up, rise up against, put on airs
ἐπαισχύνομαι	be ashamed
ἐπάνω	more, over and above
ἐπαύριον	tomorrow
ἐπειδή	when, after, since
ἔπειτα	so that, then
ἐπερωτάω	ask, request
ἐπέχω	hold fast
ἐπί	gen: on, at, with dir: on, because of acc: on, over, up to
ἐπιβάλλω	put on, lay on,
ἐπίγειος, ον	earthly
ἐπίγνωσις, εως, ἡ	knowledge
ἐπιγραφή, ἡ	inscription
ἐπιδίδωμι	hand over, give
ἐπιζητέω	look for, research
ἐπιθυμία, ἡ	desire
ἐπιλαμβάνω	take, receive
ἐπιλανθάνομαι	forget
ἐπιμένω	remain, continue
ἐπιπίπτω	fall out, lose, fail
ἐπισκέπτομαι	examine, visit
ἐπίσκοπος, ὁ	overseer
ἐπίσταμαι	know, understand
ἐπιστάτης, ου, ὁ	master
ἐπιστολή, ἡ	letter
ἐπιστρέφω	turn around, return
ἐπιτάσσω	command
ἐπιτελέω	end, fulfill complete
ἐπιτίθημι	lay on, put on

How to Read New Testament Greek

ἐπιτιμάω	rebuke, talk earnestly with	εὐσεβής, ές	godly
ἐπιτρέπω	allow	εὐφραίνω	cheer someone, Pass: be glad
ἐπιφαίνω	appear, become visible	εὐχαριστέω	give thanks
ἐποικοδομέω	build up	εὐχαριστία, ἡ	thanksgiving
ἐπουράνιος, ον	heavenly	εὐώνυμος, ον	left
ἑπτά	seven	ἐφάπαξ	at once
ἐργάζομαι	work	ἐφίσταμαι	stand by, approach
ἐργάτης, ὁ	worker		
ἔργον, τό	work	ἐχθρός, ὁ	enemy
ἔρημος, ἡ	desert	ἔχω	have
ἔρημος, ον	alone, desolate	ἕως	until
ἔρις, ἔριδος, ἡ	quarrel		
ἔρχομαι	come	**Ζζ**	
ἐρωτάω	ask, request	ζάω	live
ἐσθής, ῆτος, ἡ	clothing	ζῇ	he lives
ἐσθίω	eat	ζῆλος, ὁ	zealot
ἔσονται	they will be	ζηλόω	strive
ἔσχατος, η, ον	last	ζηλωτής, ὁ	zealot
ἔσω	into, inwardly	ζητέω	search
ἔσωθεν	from inside	ζύμη, ἡ	yeast
ἕτερος, α, ον	another	ζωή, ἡ	life
ἔτι	yet	ζωοποιέω	make alive
ἑτοιμάζω	make ready, equip	ζῷον, τό	animal
ἕτοιμος	ready		
ἔτος, ους, τό	year	**Ηη**	
εὐαγγελίζομαι	proclaim the good news	ἤ	or
		ἡγεμών, όνος, ὁ	prince, governor
εὐαγγελίζω	proclaim the good news	ἡγέομαι	lead; be of the opinion
εὐαγγέλιον, τό	good news		
εὐαγγελιστής, ὁ	evangelist	ἤδη	already
εὐγενής, ές	well-born, noble-minded	ἥκω	have come, be present
εὐθύς, εῖα, ύ	straight	ἦλθον	I came, they came
εὐθύς, εὐθέως	immediately		
εὐλογέω	bless, praise	ἥλιος, ὁ	sun
εὐλογία, ἡ	blessing	ἡμέρα, ἡ	day
εὐνοῦχος, ὁ	eunuch		
εὑρίσκω	find		
εὐσέβεια, ἡ	godliness		

Greek-English Vocabulary

Θθ

θάλασσα, ἡ	sea
θάνατος, ὁ	death
θανατόω	kill
θάπτω	bury
θαρρέω; θαρσέω	be confident, courageous
θαυμάζω	wonder, be amazed
θεάομαι	see, observe
θέλημα,ατος, τό	will
θέλω; εθέλλω	want
θεμέλιον, τὸ	foundation
θεμέλιος, ὁ	cornerstone
θεός, ὁ	God
θεραπεύω	heal
θερίζω	harvest
θερισμός, ὁ	harvest
θεωρέω	see, observe
θηρίον, τὸ	animal
θησαυρός, ὁ	treasure
θησαυρίζω	collect, save
θλίβω	pressure, oppress, limit
θλῖψις,εως, ἡ	pressure, oppression
θνητός, ἡ, όν	mortal
θρίξ, ἡ	hair
θρόνος, ὁ	throne
θυγάτηρ, ἡ	daughter
θυμός, ὁ	anger
θύρα, ἡ	door
θυσία, ἡ	sacrifice
θυσιαστήριον, τό	altar
θύω	sacrifice
θώραξ,ακος, ὁ	armor

Ιι

ἰάομαι	heal, restore
ἴδιος, ἴα, ιον	own
ἰδού	see
ἱερεύς, έως, ὁ	priest
ἱερόν, τό	sanctuary
ἵημι	send
Ἰησοῦς	Jesus
ἱκανός, ἡ, όν	sufficient, appropriate
ἱλασμός	reconciliation
ἱμάτιον, τό	garment, cloak
ἵνα	in order that
Ἰορδάνης, ὁ	Jordan
Ἰουδαῖος, ὁ	Jew
ἵππος, ὁ	horse
ἴσος, η, ον	same
Ἰσραηλίτης, ὁ	Israelite
ἵστημι	place
ἰσχυρός, ά, όν	strong
ἰσχύς, ύος, ἡ	power, might
ἰσχύω	be strong, healthy
ἰχθύς, ύος, ὁ	fish
Ἰωάννης, ὁ	John

Κκ

κἀγώ	and I
καθαίρεσις, ἡ	destruction
καθάπερ	just as
καθαρίζω	cleanse
καθαρός, ά, όν	clean
καθεύδω	sleep
κάθημαι	sit
καθίημι	let down from
καθίσταμαι	bring, cause, appoint,
καθίστημι	bring to
καθώς	since, just as
καί	and, also
καινός, ἡ, όν	new
καιρός, ὁ	time
Καῖσαρ,αρος, ὁ	Caesar
καίω	burn
κἀκεῖθεν	from there
κακία, ἡ	badness

393

κακός, ή, όν	evil, bad	καταργέω	abolish, make ineffective
κακόω	do evil		
κάλαμος, ὁ	reed, writing instrument	καταρτίζω	repair, make right
καλέω	call	κατασκευάζω	construct
καλός, ή, όν	beautiful, good	κατεργάζομαι	accomplish, produce, subdue
κάμηλος, ἡ	camel		
κἄν	and if (καί+εαν)	κατέρχομαι	come down from
κανών, όνος, ὁ	standard	κατέχω	hold back, restrain, keep, occupy
καπνός, ὁ	smoke		
καρδία, ἡ	heart		
καρπός, ὁ	fruit	κατηγορέω	accuse
κατά (κατ'/καθ')	gen: down from, against acc: along, according to	κατοικέω	live in
		κάτω	under
		καυχάομαι	boast
		καύχημα, τό	source of pride
καταβαίνω	go down, descend		
		καύχησις, εως, ἡ	boasting
καταβολή, ἡ	founding, beginning	κεῖμαι	lie, recline, destined for something
καταγγέλλω	proclaim		
καταισχύνω	dishonor, put to shame	κελεύω	call, order
		κενός, ή, όν	empty, worthless
κατακαίω	burn down		
κατακλίνω	settle in, Mcd: sit down to dinner	κέρας, ατος, τό	horn
		κερδαίνω	gain something
κατακρίνω	sentence	κεφαλή, ἡ	head
καταλαμβάνω	seize, win	κήρυγμα, ατος, τό	announcement
καταλείπω	leave, abandon	κῆρυξ, υκος, ὁ	proclaimer, announcer
καταλλαγή, ἡ	reconciliation	κηρύσσω	proclaim
καταλλάσσω	reconcile	κλάδος, ὁ	branch
καταλύω	destroy	κλαίω	weep, cry
κατανοέω	notice, observe, consider	κλάω	break (bread), begin meal
		κλείς, ἡ	key
κατανταω	come to, arrive	κλείω	close
		κλέπτης, ὁ	thief
κατάπαυσις, ἡ	rest	κλέπτω	steal

Greek-English Vocabulary

κλῆμα, ματος, τό	branch, vine	κώμη, ἡ	village
κληρονομέω	inherit	κωφός, ή, όν	deaf and dumb
κληρονομία, ἡ	inheritance		
κληρονόμος, ὁ	heir		
κλῆρος, ὁ	lot, share	**Λλ**	
κλῆσις, εως, ἡ	calling	λαγχάνω	receive, obtain, be chosen by lots, cast lots
κλίνη, ἡ	bed		
κοιλία, ἡ	stomach		
κοιμάομαι	sleep		
κοινός, ή, όν	commonality	λαῖλαψ, απος, ἡ	storm
κοινόω	make common, impure	λαλέω	speak, say
		λαμβάνω	take, receive
κοινωνία, ἡ	commonality	λαμπάς, άδος, ἡ	lamp
κοινωνός, ὁ	partner	λαμπρός, ά, όν	bright, shining
κομίζω	bring, carry off, receive		
		λαός, ὁ	people
κοπιάω	work hard, become weary	λατρεία, ἡ	service, worship (of God)
κόπος, ὁ	trouble, toil		
κοσμέω	order, decorate	λατρεύω	serve
		λέγω (εἴπω)	say
κοσμικός, ή, όν	earthly, worldly	λείπω	leave behind
		λειτουργέω	serve (as Priest), do a service
κοσμοκράτωρ, ορος, ὁ	world ruler		
κόσμος, ὁ	world		
κράβαττος, ὁ	bed	λειτουργία, ἡ	service (cultic)
κράζω	cry out		
κρατέω	grab, hold	λευκός, ή, όν	white
κράτος, ους, τό	strength, power	λέων, λέοντος, ὁ	lion
		λῃστής, ὁ	robber
κρίμα, ματος, τό	judgement	λίαν	wholly, very much
κρίνω	judge		
κρίσις, εως, ἡ	judgement	λίθος, ὁ	stone
κριτής, ὁ	judge	λίμνη, ἡ	lake, pool
κρούω	knock	λιμός, ὁ	hunger
κρυπτός, ή, όν	hidden	λογίζομαι	mean, figure, consider
κρύπτω	hide		
κτίζω	create	λόγος, ὁ	word
κτίσις, εως, ἡ	creation	λοιπός, ή, όν	remaining, from now on
κυριεύω	lord (over)		
κύριος, ὁ	lord	λούομαι	wash oneself
κύων, ὁ	dog	λούω	wash
κωλύω	hinder	λύπη, ἡ	grief, sorrow

λύτρον, τό	ransom	μετά (μετ'/μεθ')	gen: with
λυτρόομαι	set free		acc: after
λυτρόω	redeem, set free	μεταβαίνω	go somewhere else, go over
λυχνός, ὁ	light, lamp	μεταδίδωμι	impart, share
λύω	free, let loose	μετανοέω	change one's mind, repent
		μετάνοια, ἡ	repentance
Μμ		μεταξύ	between
μαθητής, ὁ	student	μετρέω	measure
μακάριος, ία, ιον	well off, fortunate	μέτρον, τό	measure
		μέχρι	until
μακράν	far	μήν, μηνός, ὁ	month
μακρόθεν	from a distance	μήποτε	so that...not, lest
μακροθυμέω	be patient	μήτηρ, ἡ	mother
μακροθυμία, ἡ	patience	μήτι	it can't be that (assumes negative answer)
μανθάνω	learn		
μάννα, τό	manna		
μαρτυρέω	testify	μικρός, ά, όν	small
μαρτυρία, ἡ	testimony	μιμνῄσκομαι	remember, care for
μαρτύριον, τό	witness		
μάρτυς, υρος, ὁ	witness	μισέω	hate
μάστιξ, ιγος, ἡ	lashing, torment	μισθός, ὁ	salary
		μνᾶ, ᾶς, ἡ	coin, mina (monetary unit)
μάχαιρα, ἡ	sword		
μάχη, ἡ	fight		
μέγας, άλη, α	large	μνεία, ἡ	remembrance, mention
μέλας, αινα, αν	black		
μέλει	it concerns someone	μνῆμα, ατος, τό	grave, tomb
		μνημεῖον, τό	grave
μέλλω	be about to	μνημονεύω	remember
μέλος, ους, τό	member	μοιχεύω	commit adultery
Μελχισέδεκ	Melchizedek		
μένω	stay	μονογενής, ές	only conceived
μερίζω	divide		
μέριμνα, ἡ	worry	μόνος, η, ον	only, alone
μεριμνάω	worry, be concerned	μορφή, ἡ	form
		μόσχος, ὁ	calf
μέρος, ους, τό	part	μυριάς, άδος, ἡ	10,000 or a large number
μεσίτης, ὁ	go between		
μέσος, η, ον	in middle of	μύρον, τό	ointment

Greek-English Vocabulary

μυστήριον, τό	secret		ξηραίνω	make dry, Pass: dry out
μωρός, ά, όν	foolish		ξύλον, τό	wood
Μωϋσῆς, Μωϋσέως	Moses			

Νν

ναί	yes		**Οο**	
ναός, ὁ	temple		ὅδε, ἥδε, τόδε	this
νεανίας, ὁ	young man		ὁδός, ἡ	way
νεανίσκος, ὁ	young man		ὀδούς, όντος, ὁ	tooth
νεκρός, ά, όν	dead		ὅθεν	from where
νέος, νέα, νέον	new		οἰκέτης, ὁ	member of household, slave
νεφέλη, ἡ	cloud			
νήπιος	infant, minor		οἰκία, ἡ	house
νῆσος, ἡ	island		οἰκοδεσπότης, ὁ	master of the house
νηστεύω	fast			
νικάω	win		οἰκοδομέω	build
νίκη, ἡ	victory		οἰκοδομή, ἡ	building
νίπτω	wash		οἰκονόμος, ὁ	house manager
νοέω	understand, recognize, be reasonable		οἶκος, ὁ	house
			οἰκουμένη, ἡ	construction, building
νομίζω	mean, assume, believe		οἶνος, ὁ	wine
			οἷος, α, ον	as
νομικός, ὁ	lawyer		ὀλίγος, η, ον	few
νομικός, ή, όν	concerning the law		ὅλος, η, ον	whole, all
			ὄμνυμι	swear
νόμος, ὁ	law		ὁμοθυμαδόν	unanimous
νόσος, ἡ	disease		ὅμοιος, α, ον	similar, same
νουθετέω	rebuke, warn remind,		ὁμοιόω	make the same
			ὁμολογέω	admit, confess
νοῦς, ὁ	understanding mind		ὄνομα, ατος, τό	name
			ὀξύς, εῖα, ύ	sharp
νύμφη, ἡ	bride		ὀπίσω	behind
νυμφίος, ὁ	groom		ὅπλα, τά	weapons
νῦν	now		ὅπου	where
νύξ, νυκτός, ἡ	night		ὅπως	as, so that
			ὅραμα, ματος, τό	face, vision
			ὁράω	see
Ξξ			ὀργή, ἡ	anger
			ὅριον, τό	border
ξενίζω	be hospitable		ὅρκος, ὁ	oath
ξένος, ὁ	stranger		ὅρος, ους, τό	mountain

ὅσος, η, ον	as great, how great, as much, how much	παλαιός, ά, όν	old
		πάλιν	again, return, furthermore
ὅταν	then, if	παντοκράτωρ,ορος,ὁ	almighty ruler
ὅτε	when, while	πάντοτε	always
ὅτι	because, that	παρά	gen: from
οὔ	no		dir: by, next to
οὐ/οὐκ/οὐχ	not		acc: along, past
οὐαί	woe! alas!		
οὐδέ	and not, not yet	παραβολή, ἡ	parable
		παραγγέλλω	instruct
οὐδεμία	not one	παραδίδωμι	hand over, deliver
οὐκέτι	no longer		
οὐ μή	not, by no means	παράδοσις,εως, ἡ	tradition
		παραιτέομαι	ask for, decline, reject
οὖν	therefore		
οὔπω	not yet	παράκλησις,εως, ἡ	reminder, comfort
οὐρανός, ὁ	heaven		
οὖς, τό	ear	παράκλητος, ὁ	lawyer, helper
οὔτε	and not	παραλαμβάνω	take over, receive, take along
οὗτος,αὕτη,τοῦτο	this		
οὕτως	so		
οὐχί	not	παραλυτικός, ὁ	cripple
		παράπτωμα,ατος, τό	false step, sin
ὀφείλω	be guilty, responsible for	παρατίθημι	lay before, entrust
ὀφθαλμός, ὁ	eye	πάρειμι	be present
ὄφις,εως, ὁ	snake	παρεμβολή, ἡ	military camp
ὄχλος, ὁ	crowd	παρέρχομαι	pass by, pass away
ὀψία, ἡ	evening	παρέχω	offer, grant, bring about
Ππ		παρθένος, ἡ	virgin
πάθημα,ατος, τό	suffering	παρίημι	neglect
παιδεία, ἡ	upbringing, training	παρίσταμαι	approach, come to aid of
παιδεύω	train	παρίστημι	place beside, be present, make available
παιδίσκη, ἡ	maid, servant-girl		
παῖς, παιδός, ὁ	boy, son, servant-boy	παρουσία, ἡ	coming, presence

Greek-English Vocabulary

παρρησία, ἡ	confidence
πᾶς, πᾶσα, πᾶν	each, all
πάσχα, τό	passover
πάσχω	suffer
πατάσσω	hit, beat
πατήρ, ὁ	father
πατρίς, ίδος, ἡ	fatherland
Παῦλος	Paul
παύομαι	cease
παύω	cause to stop
πείθομαι	obey
πείθω	convince
πεινάω	be hungry
πειράζω	to tempt, test
πειρασμός, ὁ	temptation
πέμπω	send
πενθέω	lament, be sad
πέντε	five
πέραν	on the other side
περί	gen: about, concerning acc: around
περιβάλλω	put around, put on
περικεφαλαία, ἡ	helmet
περιπατέω	walk around
περισσεύω	be abundant
περισσός, ή, όν	remarkable, abundant
περιστερά, ἡ	dove
περιτέμνω	circumcise, Pass: be circumcised
περιτίθημι	put or place around
περιτομή, ἡ	circumcision
πετεινόν, τό	bird
πέτρα, ἡ	rock
πηγή, ἡ	source, spring
πιάζω	hold, grab
πίμπλημι	fill up, fulfill
πίνω	drink
πιπράσκω	sell
πίπτω	fall
πιστεύω	believe
πίστις, εως, ἡ	faith
πιστός, ή, όν	faithful
πλανάομαι	deceive oneself
πλανάω	deceive
πλάνη, ἡ	error, deception
πλεονεξία, ἡ	greed
πληγή, ἡ	wound, a blow
πλῆθος, τό	crowd
πληθύνω	multiply, increase
πλήν	nevertheless, but
πλήρης, πλῆρες	full
πληρόω	fulfill
πλήρωμα, ατος, τό	fullness
πλησίον, ὁ	neighbor, one who is near
πλοῖον, τό	ship
πλούσιος, α, ιον	rich
πλουτέω	be rich
πλοῦτος, ὁ	plenty
πνεῦμα, τό	spirit
πνευματικός, ή, όν	spiritual
πόθεν	from where
ποιέω	do
ποικίλος, η, ον	various kinds
ποιμαίνω	shepherd
ποιμήν, ένος, ὁ	shepherd
ποῖος, α, ον	of what kind, which, what
πόλεμος, ὁ	conflict, quarrel
πόλις, εως, ἡ	city
πολιτεύομαι	live as a citizen (of a country)

How to Read New Testament Greek

πολίτης, ὁ	citizen
πολλάκις	often
πολύς,πολλή,πολύ	many, much
πονηρός, ά, όν	evil
πορεύομαι	walk, travel
πορνεία, ἡ	evil
πόρνη, ἡ	prostitute
πόσος, η, ον	how large? how many?
ποταμός, ὁ	river
ποτήριον, τό	cup
ποτίζω	give to drink, water (animals)
ποῦ	where?
πούς, ὁ	foot
πρᾶγμα, ατος, τό	deed, event, undertaking
πρᾶξις, εως, ἡ	activity, action, deed
πράσσω	do
πραΰτης,ὐτητος, ἡ	gentleness
πρεσβύτερος, ὁ	older man
πρίν	earlier
πρό	gen: before
προάγω	lead, go before
πρόβατον	sheep
προγράφω	write beforehand, display
πρόθεσις, εως, ἡ	intent, will
πρωΐ	early in the morning
προΐσταμαι	care for, be in charge of
πρός	gen: near, at acc: toward, to
προσδέχομαι	receive, welcome, expect
προσδοκάω	expect
προσευχή, ἡ	prayer
προσεύχομαι	pray
προσέχω	pay attention to, be concerned with
πρόσκαιρος	temporary
προσκαρτερέω	be faithful, devoted
προσκυνέω	fall on knees, worship
προσλαμβάνομαι	take in, take along
προστίθημι	add to
προσφέρω	bring to, offer
πρόσωπον, τό	face
πρότερος, έρα, ον	earlier, before
προφητεία, ἡ	prophecy
προφήτης, ὁ	prophet
πρῶτος, η, ον	first
πτέρυξ, υγος, ἡ	wing
πτωχός, ή, όν	poor
πύλη, ἡ	gate, door
πυλών, ῶνος, ὁ	gate
πυνθάνομαι	inquire
πῦρ, πυρός, τό	fire
πωλέω	sell
πῶλος, ὁ	horse
πῶς	how?

Ρρ

ῥάβδος, ἡ	staff
ῥήγνυμι	tear, break
ῥῆμα, ματος, τό	word
ῥήτωρ, ορος, ὁ	speaker
ῥίζα, ἡ	root
ῥιπή, ἡ	throw
ῥύομαι	save
Ῥωμαῖος, ὁ	Roman

Σσ

σάββατον, τό	sabbath
Σαδδουκαῖοι, οἱ	Sadducees

Greek-English Vocabulary

σάκκος, ὁ	sack
σαλεύω	shake
σάλπιγξ, ιγγος, ἡ	trumpet
σαλπίζω	trumpet
σαπρός, ά, όν	decayed, rotten, unwholesome
σάρξ, σαρκός, ἡ	flesh, body, human nature
σβέννυμι	eliminate, suppress
σέβομαι	honor
σεισμός, ὁ	earthquake
σελήνη, ἡ	moon
σημεῖον, τό	sign
σιγάω	be silent
σιδηροῦς, ᾶ, οῦν	iron
σῖτος, ὁ	grain
σιωπάω	be silent, still
σκανδαλίζω	cause to sin, give offense to
σκάνδαλον, τό	trap
σκεῦος, σκεύους, τό	dish, tool, object
σκηνή, ἡ	tent, dwelling
σκῆνος, ους, τό	tent, dwelling
σκιά, ἡ	shadow
σκοτία, ἡ	darkness
σκότος, ους, τό	darkness
σοφία, ἡ	wisdom
σοφός, ή, όν	wise
σπείρω	sow
σπέρμα, ατος, τό	seed
σπλάγχνα τά	intestines (heart: compassion)
σπλαγχνίζομαι	have compassion
σπουδάζω	hasten, make every effort
σπουδή, ἡ	haste, diligence
σταυρός	cross
σταυρόω	crucify
στέγη, ἡ	roof
στέφανος, ὁ	wreath, crown
στεφανόω	crown
στηρίζω	strengthen
στόμα, ατος, τό	mouth
στρατεύομαι	serve in army
στρατηγός, ὁ	chief, magistrate
στρατιώτης, ὁ	soldier
στρέφω	turn
σύ	you
συγγενής, ές	related
συζητέω	discuss, dispute
συκῆ, ἡ	fig tree
συλλαμβάνω	seize, catch, support, help
σύν	dir: with
συνάγω	lead together
συναγωγή, ἡ	assembly place
σύνδουλος, ὁ	fellow slave
συνέδριον, τό	Sanhedrin, high council of priest and scribes
συνείδησις, εως, ἡ	conscience
συνεργός, ὁ	fellow worker
συνέχω	hold together, Pass: dispute
συνίημι	understand
συνίσταμαι	stand with, consist of
συνίστημι	bring together, recommend
συντέλεια, ἡ	completion
συστρέφω	gather up, come together
σφάζω	butcher
σφόδρα	very (much)
σφραγίζω	seal

σφραγίς, ίδος, ἡ	seal	τίς	someone
σχίζω	divide	τοιοῦτος	of such a kind
σώζω, σῴζω	save, help	τολμάω	dare
σῶμα, σώματος, τό	body	τόπος, ὁ	place
σωτήρ, ῆρος, ὁ	savior	τοσοῦτος	so large, so much
σωτηρία, ἡ	salvation		
σωτήριος, ον	saving	τότε	then, at that time
		τράπεζα, ἡ	table

Ττ

		τρέφω	feed, take care of
τάλαντον, τό	a talent (60 to 80 lb.)	τρέχω	run, race
τάξις, εως, ἡ	order	τρίτος	third
ταπεινός, ή, όν	humble	τρίχινος, η, ον	hairy
ταπεινοφροσύνη, ἡ	humility	τρόπος, ὁ	way, means
ταπεινόω	humble, humiliate	τροφή, ἡ	food
		τυγχάνω	meet, attain, happen
ταπείνωσις, ἡ	humility		
ταράσσω	confuse, disturb	τύπος, ὁ	picture, model
		τύπτω	hit
τάσσω	put someone in charge of something	τυφλός, ή, όν	blind

Υυ

ταχύς, εῖα, ύ	fast	ὑγιαίνω	be healthy
τέ	and (often untranslated)	ὑγιής, ές	healthy
		ὕδωρ, τό	water
τέκνον, τό	child	ὑπάγω	go away
τελειόω	complete	ὑπακοή, ἡ	obedience
τελευτάω	die	ὑπακούω	listen to, obey
τελέω	complete, finish	ὑπαντάω	come toward, meet
τέλος, ους, τό	goal		
τελώνης, ὁ	tax-collector	ὑπάρχω	be available
τέρας, ατος, τό	wonder, omen	ὑπέρ	gen: for, on behalf of acc: above, more than
τεσσαράκοντα	forty		
τηρέω	keep guard		
τίθεμαι	set, place, lay		
τίθημι	set, place, lay	ὑπηρέτης, ὁ	helper
τίκτω	give birth	ὑπό	gen: from acc: under
τιμάω	honor		
τιμή, ἡ	honor	ὑπόδημα, ατος, τό	sandals
τίμιος, α, ον	valuable, honorable	ὑποκάτω	under
		ὑποκριτής, ὁ	hypocrite

Greek-English Vocabulary

ὑπομονή, ἡ	patience
ὑποτάσσω	submit, obey
ὑστερέω	be late, miss
ὕστερος, έρα, ερον	last
ὑψηλός, ἡ, όν	high, proud
ὕψιστος, η, ον	highest
ὑψόω	raise up

Φφ

φαίνομαι	appear
φαίνω	shine
φανερός, ά, όν	visible, obvious
φανερόω	reveal
Φαρισαῖος, οἱ	Pharisees
φαῦλος	evil, bad
φείδομαι	spare someone trouble
φέρω	carry, bear, bring along
φεύγω	flee
Φῆλιξ, ικος, ὁ	Felix
φημί	say, claim
φθορά, ἡ	destruction
φιάλη, ἡ	bowl
φιλαδελφία, ἡ	brotherly love
φιλέω	love, like
φίλος, ὁ	friend
φίλος, η, ον	devoted
φλόξ, φλογός, ἡ	flame
φοβέομαι	fear
φόβος, ὁ	fear
φονεύω	murder, kill
φορέω	carry
φρόνιμος, ον	reasonable
φύλαξ, ακος, ὁ	guard
φυλάσσω	guard
φύσις, εως, ἡ	nature
φυτεύω	plant
φωνέω	call
φωνή, ἡ	sound, voice
φῶς, τό	light
φωστήρ, ῆρος, ὁ	star, radiance
φωτίζω	shine, reveal

Χχ

χαίρω	be glad
χαλάω	let down
χαλκοῦς, ῆ, οῦν	copper
χαρά, ἡ	joy
χαρακτήρ, ῆρος, ὁ	reproduction, trait
χαρίζομαι	give freely, forgive
χάριν	therefore (in combination with οὗ)
χάρις, ιτος, ἡ	grace
χάρισμα, ατος, τό	gift of (God's) grace
χειμών, ῶνος, ὁ	winter
χείρ, ἡ	hand
χήρα, ἡ	widow
χιλίαρχος, ὁ	leader of 1000 men
χιλιάς, άδος, ἡ	thousand
χίλιοι, αι, α	thousandth
χιτών, ῶνος, ὁ	tunic, shirt
χοῖρος, ὁ	pig
χόρτος, ὁ	grass
χράομαι	use
χρεία, ἡ	need, deficiency
χρῄζω	have need of
χρηστός, ή, όν	good
χρηστότης, ητος, ἡ	goodness
χρῖσμα, ματος, τό	anointing
Χριστιανός, ὁ	Christian
Χριστός, ὁ	Christ, anointed one
χρίω	anoint
χρόνος, ὁ	time
χρυσίον, τό	gold
χρυσοῦς, ῆ, οῦν	golden

χωλός, ή, όν	lame
χώρα, ἡ	region, land
χωρέω	go away, make progress, contain
χωρίζω	separate, Pass: leave
χωρίον, τό	field
χωρίς	without

Ψψ

ψεύδομαι	lie
ψευδοπροφήτης, ὁ	false prophet
ψεῦδος, ψεύδους, τό	lie
ψυχή, ἡ	life

Ωω

ὧδε	so, here
ὥρα, ἡ	hour
ὡς	as, like
ὡσαύτως	in the same way, also
ὡσεί	as, approximately
ὥσπερ	as
ὥστε	therefore, so that
ὠφελέω	use, Pass: to be useful
ὠφέλιμος, ον	useful

Small Words

ἅπαξ	once	ἕως	gen: until
ἄρα	then	ἤ	or
ἀεί	always	ἤδη	already
ἀλλά	but, rather	κἀγώ	and I
ἀντί	gen: in place of	καθάπερ	just as
ἄνω	above	καί	and, also
ἀπό	gen: from, away from	καίπερ	although
		κἀκεῖθεν	from there
ἄρτι	now	κἄν	and if
ἄρχι	gen: until	κατά	gen: down from, against
γάρ	because		acc: according to, along
δεῖ	it is necessary		
δεῦτε	come!		
διά	gen: through acc: because of	κάτω	under
		ὁ μέν - ὁ δέ	the one, the other
διό	therefore	ὁ δέ	but whoever
ἐάν	if, in case that	μετά	gen: with acc: after
εἰ μή	except, if not		
εἰς	acc: in, into	μεταξύ	gen: between
εἴτε...εἴτε	whether...or	μέχρι	gen: until
ἐκ (ἐξ)	gen: out of	μήποτε	lest
ἐκεῖ	there	μήτι	it can't be that
ἐκεῖθεν	from there	νῦν	now
ἐν	dir: in	ὅθεν	from where
ἔναντι	gen: before	οἷος, α, ον	as
ἕνεκεν	gen: because	ὀπίσω	gen: behind
ἐνώποιν	gen: before	ὅπου	where
ἔξω	outside	ὅπως	as, so that
ἐπάνω	more, over and above	ὅσος, η, ον	as great, how great; as much, how much
ἔπειτα	so that, then		
ἐπί	dir: on		
ἔσω	into, inwardly	ὅταν	then, if
ἔτι	yet	ὅτε	when, while
ἐφάπαξ	at once	ὅτι	because, that

οὐ, οὐκ, οὐχ	not	χωρίς	without
οὐδέ	and not, not yet	ὧδε	here, so
οὐδέπω	not yet	ὡς	as
οὐκετι	no longer	ὡσεί	as, approximately
οὐ μή	not at all	ὥσπερ	as
οὖν	therefore	ὥστε	so that
οὔπω	not yet		
οὔτε	and not		
οὕτως	so		
οὐχί	not		
παντότε	always		
παρά	gen: from		
	dir: by, next to		
	acc: along, past		
πέραν	on the other side		
περί	gen: concerning		
	acc: around		
πόθεν	from where		
ποῖος, α, ον	of what kind, which		
πόσος, η, ον	how many, how large		
ποῦ	where		
πρό	gen: before		
πρός	dir: near, at		
πῶς	how?		
σύν	dir: with		
σφόδρα	very (much)		
τοιοῦτος	so, of such a kind		
τοσοῦτος	so large, so much		
τότε	then, at that time		
ὑπέρ	gen: for, in behalf of		
	acc: above		
ὑπό	gen: from		
	acc: under		

Index

A (Indefinite article), 115 *(STEP 2)*
Accents, 139 *(STEP 10)*
Accomplishing role (Accusative case), 63, 41 *(STEP 1)*
Accusative case (Accomplishing role), 63, 41 *(STEP 1)*
Action (Voice), 81, 160 *(STEP 18)*
Active, 81, 160 *(STEP 18)*
Add-a-phrase words (Prepositions), 90ff., 119 *(STEPS 3,4)*, 133 *(STEP 7)*
Add-a-thought words (Relative pronouns, Conjunctions), 91ff., 295 *(STEP 46)*
Add-on words (Adjectives, Adverbs), 88ff., *STEPS 13,54,62* (148, 329, 358)
Add-on thoughts (Dependent Clauses), 91ff., 295 *(STEPS 46,47)*
Adjectives (Add-on word), 91ff., *STEPS 13,54* (148, 329)
Adverbs (Add-on word), 90, 358 *(STEP 62)*
All-around words (Participle), 95, 264 *(STEP 32)*
Aorist tense (Normal photo), 77, 281 *(STEPS 39-44)*

Breathing marks (Spiritus) 139 *(STEP 10)*
Bright light (Indicative mood), 78, 168 *(STEP 21)*

Camera-words (Verbs), 70ff., 107 *(STEP Introduction)*
Case (Role), 59-65, 107 *(STEP Introduction)*
Combined words (Compound words), 166 *(STEP 20)*
Compound words (Combined words), 166 *(STEP 20)*
Congruence (Matching forms), 88 ff., 131
Conjunctions (Add-a-thought words), 91ff., 298 *(STEP 47)*
Contraction (Vowel changes), *STEPS 17,19,48-50* (158, 163, 300)
Current photo (Perfect tense), 77ff., 271 *(STEP 34)*

Dative case (Directing role), 63, 111 *(STEP)1*
Definite article (*The*), 58-59, *STEPS 1,5,6* (111, 127, 130)
Demonstrative pronouns (*This, that*), 156 *(STEP 16)*
Departed forms (Deponent forms), *STEPS 18,23* (160, 173)
Dependent clauses (Add-on thoughts), 91ff., 295 *(STEPS 46,47)*

How to Read New Testament Greek

Deponent forms (Departed forms), *STEPS 18,23* (160, 173)
Dictionary forms, *STEPS 18,27* (160, 253)
Dim light (Subjunctive mood) 78ff., 168 *(STEP 21)*
Diphthongs (Double vowels), 42
Directing role (Dative case), 63, *STEPS 1,3* (111, 119)
Double vowels (Diphthongs), 42

Evaluation, 311, 379 *(STEPS 72-75)*
Exceptions to Rule, *STEPS 28,33* (255, 268)
Expectations, 107 *(STEP Introduction)*
Extra-information words (Adjectives, Adverbs, Prepositions, Conjunctions, Relative pronouns), 86ff.

Feminine words (ἡ-words), 127
Finding answers, *STEPS 5,21* (127, 168)
Flashing light (Imperative mood), 79, 171 *(STEP 22)*
Future photo (Future tense), 77, 175 *(STEP 24)*
Future tense (Future photo), 77, 175 *(STEP 24)*

Gender (Type), 59
General supporting role (Genitive case), 62, 111 *(STEP 1)*
Genitive absolute (General Supporting/Add-On Thought), 364 *(STEP 65)*
Genitive case (General supporting role), 62, 111 *(STEP 1)*
Grammar, 335 *(STEP 56)*
Grammar overview, 107 *(STEP Introduction)*

Habitual or regular action (Customary usage), 163 *(STEP 19)*
Himself, herself, itself, themselves (Reflexive pronouns), 327 *(STEP 53)*

ἡ-words (Feminine words), *STEP 5, 9-11* (127, 137)

I, you, he, she, it, we, all of you, they (Personal pronouns), 81
Imperative mood (Flashing light), 79, 171 *(STEP 22)*
Imperfect tense (Recorded video), 76ff., 163 *(STEP 19)*
Indefinite article (A), 115 *(STEP 2)*
Indicative mood (Bright light), 78, 168 *(STEP 21)*
Infinitives (Small all-round words)
Interrogative pronouns (*Who? Why? Where? When? What?*)

Index

Iota subscript (Iota subscript), 132
Irregular verbs, 373 *(STEP 69)*

Light (Mood), 78, 168 *(STEP 21)*
Live video (Present tense), 76, 115 *(STEP 2)*

Major parts (Principle parts), 344 *(STEP 57)*
Masculine words (ò-words), 112
Matching forms (Congruence), 88ff., 131
Memory helps, *STEPS 4, 9, 11, 15, 19* (123, 137, 143, 153, 163)
Middle (Middle), 82, 160 *(STEP 18)*
Mini-photo (Root aorist), 354 *(STEP 61)*
Mood (Light), 78, 168 *(STEP 21)*
Motivation, 229,382 *(STEP 74)*

Necessary role (Nominative case), 61, 80, 111 *(STEP 1)*
Neuter words (τό-words), 130
Nominative case (Necessary role), 61, 80, 111 *(STEP 1)*
Normal photo (Aorist tense), 77, 281 *(STEPS 39-44)*
Normal photo 2 (Second Aorist), 354 *(STEP 61)*
Nouns, pronouns, gerunds (Something-words), 57, 65ff., 360 *(STEP 63)*
Numerals (Numbers), 363 *(STEP 63)*

Optative, 370 *(STEP 68)*
Ò-words (Masculine words), 111 *(STEP 1)*

Parsing (Determining the PLAN), 71, 76ff., 115 *(STEP 2)*
Participle (All-round word), 95ff., 264 *(STEP 32)*
PARTs, 264 *(STEP 32)*
Passive, 82, 160 *(STEP 18)*
Perfect tense (Current photo), 271 *(STEP 34)*
Personal pronouns (*I, you, he, she, it, we, you, they*), 81,
    STEPS 1,2,15 (111, 115, 153)
Photo, 175 *(STEP 24)*
Picture (Tense), 50, 107 *(STEP Introduction)*
PLAN, determining (Parsing), 71, 76ff., 115 *(STEP 2)*
Pluperfect tense (Previous photo), 78, *STEPS 35,38* (274, 279)
Possessives, 325 *(STEP 52)*

409

Preparation, 381 *(STEP 73)*
Prepositions (Add-a-phrase words),90ff., *STEPS 3,4,7* (119, 123, 133)
Present tense (Live video), 76
Previous photo (Pluperfect tense), 78, *STEPS 35,38* (274, 279)
Principle parts (Major parts), 344 *(STEP 57)*
Punctuation, 111, *(STEP 1)*

Recorded video (Imperfect tense), 76ff., 163 *(STEP 19)*
Reference books, *STEPS 19,55* (163, 332)
Reflexive pronouns (*Himself, herself*), 327 *(STEP 53)*
Relative pronouns (Add-a-thoug words), 91ff., 295 *(STEP 46)*
Reviewing, *STEPS 2,73* (115, 381)
Roles (Cases), 59-65, 111 *(STEP 1)*
Root Aorist (Mini-photo), 354 *(STEP 61)*

Second Aorist (Normal photo 2), 354 *(STEP 61)*
Sentence, 91ff.
Small all-around words (Infinitives), 177 *(STEP 25)*
Something-words (Nouns, Pronouns, Gerunds), 57, 65ff., 111 *(STEP 1)*
Spiritus asper (Rough breathing) 139
Spiritus lenis (Smooth breathing) 139
Spiritus (Breathing mark) 139
Subjunctive mood (Dim light), 78ff.

Tense (Picture), 50ff.
Terminology, 335 *(STEP 56)*
The (Definite article), 58-59, *STEPS 1,5,6* (111, 127, 130)
This, that (Demonstrative pronouns), 156 *(STEP 16)*
τό-words (Neuter words), 130 *(STEP 6)*
Translating, 119 *(STEP 3)*
Translations 188
Type (Gender), 59

Verbs (Camera-words), 70, 107 *(STEP Introduction)*
Video, 174 *(STEP 24)*
Vocative, 139 *(STEP 10)*
Voice (Action), 81, 160 *(STEP 18)*
Vowel changes (Contraction), *STEPS 17,19,48-50* (158, 163, 300)

Who, which, that (Relative pronouns), 92
Who? Why? Where? When? What? How? (Interrogative pronouns), 323
Word order, *STEPS 1,13,25* (111, 148, 177)

Study Tip!
Have you ever personalized the index of a book? It's a great idea, because an index seldom includes all the words and topics that interest you. Let's say, for example, that the conversation between Jim and Dean about priorities on page 233 includes some ideas you'd like to locate again. Just add the word *priorities* to the above index followed by the page number.

Indexing is one of the best ways to store and retrieve information. Give it a try.

About the Author

Randall D. McGirr describes himself as the husband and father of his four best friends. He is also the Director of Translating and resident writer at Context Scripture Translating, a young organization training members of linguistic subgroups to be translators of the New Testament Scriptures.